MORAL DEVELOPMENT

A Compendium

Series Editor
BILL PUKA
Rensselaer Institute

A GARLAND SERIES

SERIES CONTENTS

VOLUME

3

KOHLBERG'S ORIGINAL STUDY OF MORAL DEVELOPMENT

Edited with introductions by

BILL PUKA

GARLAND PUBLISHING, Inc.
New York & London
1994

Library of Congress Cataloging-in-Publication Data

Moral development : a compendium / edited with introductions by Bill
Puka.
    p.   cm.
    Includes bibliographical references.
    Contents: v. 1. Defining perspectives in moral development — v.
2. Fundamental research in moral development — v. 3. Kohlberg's
original study of moral development — v. 4. The great justice
debate — v. 5. New research in moral development — v. 6. Caring
voices and women's moral frames — v. 7. Reaching out.
    ISBN 0–8153–1550–3 (v. 3 : alk. paper).
    1. Moral development.   I. Puka, Bill.
BF723.M54M66 1994
155.2'5—dc20   94–462
                                           CIP

Printed on acid-free, 250-year-life paper
Manufactured in the United States of America

CONTENTS

SERIES INTRODUCTION

Moral development is an interdisciplinary field that researches moral common sense and interpersonal know-how. It investigates how children evolve a sense of right and wrong, good and bad, and how adults hone their abilities to handle ethical issues in daily life. This includes resolving value conflicts, fermenting trusting, cooperative, and tolerant relationships, and setting ethical goals. It focuses most on how we think about these ethical issues (using our cognitive competences) and how we act as a result.

These seven volumes are designed to function as a standard, comprehensive sourcebook. They focus on central concerns and controversies in moral development, such as the relation between moral socialization and development, moral judgment and action, and the effects of culture, class, or gender on moral orientation. They also focus on central research programs in the field, such as the enduring Kohlberg research on moral stages, Gilligan research on ethical caring and women's development, and related prosocial research on altruism.

The studies contained here were compiled from the "wish lists" of researchers and educators in the field. These are the publications cited as most important (and, often, least available) for effective teaching and research training and for conveying the field to others. Unfortunately, the most crucial studies and essays in moral development are widely scattered across hard-to-find (sometimes out-of-print) volumes. Compiling them for a course is difficult and costly. This compendium eases these problems by gathering needed sources in one place, for a single charge. Regrettably, rising reprint fees frustrated plans to include *all* needed resources here, halving the original contents of these volumes and requiring torturous excising decisions. Even so, compared to other collections, this series approaches a true "handbook" of moral development, providing key sources on central issues rather than "further essays" on specialized topics.

A major aim of this series is to represent moral development accurately to related fields. Controversies in moral development have sparked lively interest in the disciplines of philosophy, education, sociology and anthropology, literary criticism, political science, gender and cultural studies, critical legal studies, criminology and corrections, and peace studies. Unfortunately, members of these fields were often introduced to moral development through the highly theoretical musings of Lawrence Kohlberg, Carol Gilligan, or Jean Piaget—or by highly theoretical commentaries on them. Jumping into the fray over gender or culture bias in stage theory, theorists in the humanities show virtually no familiarity with the empirical research that gave rise to it. Indeed, many commentators seem unaware that these controversies arise in a distinct research field and are context-dependent.

This compendium displays moral development as a social science, generating research findings in cognitive developmental, and social psychology. (Students are invited to recognize and approach the field as such.) Theory is heavily involved in this research—helping define the fundamental notions of "moral" and "development," for example. But even when philosophically or ethically cast, it remains psychological or social scientific theory. It utilizes but does not engage in moral philosophy per se. Otherwise, it is not moral development theory, but meta-theory. (Several extensively criticized Kohlberg articles on justice are meta-theory.) The confusion of these types and levels of theory has been a source of pervasive confusion in the field. The mistaken assessment of psychological theory by moral-philosophical standards has generated extremely damaging and misguided controversy in moral development. Other types of theory (moral, social, interpretive, anthropological) should be directed at moral development science, focusing on empirical research methods and their empirical interpretation. It should be theory of data, that is, not meta-theoretical reflection on the "amateur" philosophizing and hermeneutics interpolations of psychological researchers. (Likewise, social scientific research should not focus on the empirical generalizations of philosophers when trying to probe social reality or seek guidance in doing so from this theoretical discipline.) The bulk of entries in this compendium present the proper, empirically raw material for such "outside" theoretical enterprise.

To researchers, theorists, and students in related fields, this series extends an invitation to share our interest in the fascinating phenomena of moral development, and to share our findings thus far. Your help is welcomed also in refining our treacherously qualitative research methods and theories. In my dual disciplines of psychology and philosophy, I have found no more inspiring area of study. Alongside its somewhat dispassionate research orientation, this field carries on the ancient "cause" of its pre-scientific past. This is to show that human nature is naturally good—that the human psyche spontaneously unfolds in good will, cleaving toward fair-mindedness, compassion, and cooperative concern.

The first volume, *Defining Perspectives*, presents the major approaches to moral development and socialization in the words of chief proponents: Kohlberg, Bandura, Aronfreed, Mischel, Eysenck, and Perry. (Piaget is discussed in detail.) This first volume is required reading for those needing to orient to this field or regain orientation. It is crucial for clarifying the relations and differences between moral development and socialization that define research.

The second volume, *Fundamental Research*, compiles the classic research studies on moral levels and stages of development. These studies expose the crucial relation of role-taking and social perspective to moral judgment and of moral judgment to action. They also divine the important role of moral self-identity (viewing oneself as morally interested) in moral motivation.

The third volume contains *Kohlberg's Original Study*, his massive doctoral research project. The study, which has never before been published, sets the parameters for moral development research, theory, and controversy. (Major critical alternatives to Kohlberg's approach share far more in common with it than they diverge.) Here the reader sees "how it all started," glimpsing the sweep of Kohlberg's aspiration: to uncover the chief adaptation of humankind, the evolving systems of reasoning and meaning-making that, even in children, guide effective choice and action. Most major Kohlberg critiques fault features of this original study, especially in the all-male, all-white, all-American cast of his research sample. (Why look here for traits that characterize all humans in all cultures through all time?) It is worth checking these criticisms against the text, in context, as depictions of unpublished work often blur into hearsay. It is also worth viewing this study through the massive reanalysis of its data (Colby, Kohlberg, et al.) and the full mass of Kohlberg research that shaped stage theory. Both are liberally sampled in Volume Five.

The Great Justice Debate, the fourth volume, gathers the broad range of criticisms leveled at moral stage theory. It takes up the range of "bias charges" in developmental research—bias by gender, social class, culture, political ideology, and partisan intellectual persuasion. Chief among these reputed biases is the equation of moral competence and development with justice and rights. Here key features of compassion and benevolence seem overlooked or underrated. Here a seemingly male standard of ethical preference downplays women's sensibilities and skills. Responses to these charges appear here as well.

Volume Five, *New Research*, focuses on cross-cultural research in moral development. Studies in India, Turkey, Israel, Korea, Poland, and China are included. While interesting in itself, such research also supports the generalizability of moral stages, challenged above. Indeed, Volume Five attempts to reconceive or re-start the central research program of moral development from the inception of its matured research methods and statistically well-validated findings. From this point research is more data-based than theory-driven. It can address criticism with hard evidence. Regarding controversy in moral development, Volumes Four and Five go together as challenge and retort.

Volume Six, *Caring Voices*, is devoted to the popular "different voice" hypothesis. This hypothesis posits a distinct ethical orientation of caring relationship, naturally preferred by women, that complements justice. Compiled here is the main record of Gilligan's (and colleagues') research, including recent experiments with "narrative" research method. The significant critical literature on care is well-represented as well, with responses. While Gilligan's empirical research program is more formative than Kohlberg's, her interpretive observations have influenced several fields, especially in feminist studies. Few research sources have more common-sense significance and "consciousness-raising" potential. The student reader may find Gilligan's approach the most personally relevant and useful in moral development.

Reaching Out, the final volume, extends moral development concerns to "prosocial" research on altruism. Altruistic helping behavior bears close relation to caring and to certain ideals of liberal justice. This volume emphasizes the role of emotions in helping (and not helping), focusing on empathic distress, forgiveness, and guilt. It also looks at early friendship and family influences. Moral emotions are related to ethical virtues here, which are considered alongside the "vices" of apathy and learned helplessness. Leading researchers are included such as Hoffman, Eisenberg, Batson, and Staub.

INTRODUCTION

This volume examines the empirical and theoretical foundation of moral development's chief paradigm. Kohlberg's original study of moral judgment is arguably the founding document of modern moral development. More than Piaget's *The Moral Judgment of the Child*, this study conceives moral development as a distinct field of research. It sets the field's distinct research methods and parameters and provides its theoretical framework. (Here moral philosophy, social theory, and the components of cognitive psychology—logical, social, moral—are uniquely linked.) This study also outlines moral development's first full theory, still dominant today.

(Kohlberg's approach includes, but far transcends, Piaget's structural psychology and use of moral philosophy. Distancing himself from Piaget's biological emphasis, Kohlberg embraces Durkheim, Baldwin, and Dewey's social theories and Meade's conception of social self. Kohlberg also argues, as Piaget did not, for true moral stages and a true stage progression in moral development.)

The most enduring value of Kohlberg's original study, however, may be as a model for breaking new ground in research. It self-consciously poses the problem of how to carve out a field of inquiry, distinguishing its empirical and theoretical components and carefully relating them. It devises research strategies fit to differences and complementarities in these relations, and devises a research program working at several empirical and theoretical levels at once.

Contained in this study are detailed accounts of how the original "moral judgment interview" was evolved as a research instrument and also why an "ideal typology" of moral "stages" was chosen to interpret responses. Explanations are offered for ordering different types of moral judgment in a conceptual hierarchy and singular sequence. This study also provides revealing samples of original interview responses on which Kohlberg's stage descriptions were based.

Kohlberg sets these innovations in an historical survey of moral development, covering utilitarian philosophers, "instinct" theorists such as Freud and Nietzsche, and the social theorists mentioned.

He also traces the relation of moral judgment to value preference, IQ, emotion, and action.

Kohlberg's approach to moral development takes "morality" and "development" more seriously than do his commentators. It figures moral theory into the design of empirical research hypotheses and the interpretation of results. It even tries to enhance the observational ground on which normative ethics stands. (This latter contribution bests the armchair generalizations of moral philosophers regarding moral "common sense.") Kohlberg not only furnishes conceptual criteria for distinguishing moral progress from moral change, but true development from learning or socialization.

By nature, Kohlberg argues, development is inherent to a person or thing, not simply something added on from outside and internalized. Our moral development is integral to the type of being we are and the systemic abilities we possess, partly expressing them and defining us. In his original study, Kohlberg looks beneath the common survey of value preferences and socially approved conventions to uncover these stabler more self-determined depths of character. He looks to something organic enough—something internally complex and self-cohering enough—to support its own evolution, yet retain its identity throughout radical transformations. This developmental phenomenon is the holistically structured schema or functionally unified system of moral cognition.

Many critics of Kohlberg "bias" have failed to heed the conscious limits set on his inquiry at the outset and the rationale he provides for them. As a result, moral development has been faulted for not being something else. Kohlberg's approach would be far more liable to bias were its tailored methods applied to broader-ranging phenomena such as moral motivation or attitudinal orientation. Yet even with its circumscribed concerns, one wonders how a study of several boys from Chicago suburbs could reveal a single, invariant sequence of moral reasoning that develops spontaneously in all individuals and cultures. Retracing Kohlberg's steps in this study helps confirm one's sense of how revolutionary or preposterous this "revelation" is.

THE UNIVERSITY OF CHICAGO

THE DEVELOPMENT OF MODES OF MORAL THINKING

AND CHOICE IN THE YEARS 10 TO 16

A DISSERTATION SUBMITTED TO

THE FACULTY OF THE DIVISION OF THE SOCIAL SCIENCES

IN CANDIDACY FOR THE DEGREE OF

DOCTOR OF PHILOSOPHY

DEPARTMENT OF PSYCHOLOGY

BY

LAWRENCE KOHLBERG

CHICAGO, ILLINOIS

DECEMBER   1958

1

ACKNOWLEDGMENTS

This study was partially financed by a Grant Foundation Fellowship at the Family Study Center. I wish to acknowledge the help and stimulation from the staff of the Center during this period. I am especially grateful for the support and guidance of its Director, Mr. Nelson Foote.

The subjects were made available through the following schools: the Whittier and Greenwood Elementary Schools, the Junior High School and the High School of Blue Island, Illinois; the Palos Park Elementary School, Palos Park, Illinois; and the Hinsdale Junior High amd the High Schools, Hinsdale, Illinois.

I am indebted to the superintendents, principals and teachers of these schools for their patience and cooperation. I am also grateful to the Park View Home of South Bend, Indiana, and its Director, Mr. Walter Risler, for making it possible to interview a group of delinquent boys. In addition, I wish to thank the staff of the Sociology Department of the Institute for Juvenile Research for allowing me to interview a group of boys with whom they were working in the Chicago Area Project. A special acknowledgment is owed to all the boys themselves for the enjoyment and learning that has come from interviewing them.

I wish to express my deep appreciation for the stimulation and help I have received over the years from Mr. William Stephenson, originally a member of my thesis committee.

Mr. John Butler has given much helpful advice on the methodology

ii

of the study. Mr. Leo Goodman also has been of valuable assistance on several methodological problems.

I owe much to the understanding and stimulation I have received from Mr. Anselm Strauss. Among the many forms this has taken, I may mention the unusual help he gave in going over the raw data with me in a remarkably insightful way and suggestive way.

Above all, I wish to express my appreciation for the wisdom, understanding, and continued interest which Miss Helen Koch has displayed throughout the many phases of the study. Perhaps only her other students will understand the gratitude aroused by her devotion as a teacher and scientist.

TABLE OF CONTENTS

iv

LIST OF TABLES

CHAPTER I

A PRELIMINARY CONCEPT OF MORALITY AND
THE PURPOSE OF THE RESEARCH

The present research deals with the interrelated development of
basic moral concepts and attitudes in the years ten to sixteen, concepts
and attitudes suggested by words such as good, rights, duties, authority,
group norms, ideal self, punishment, justice, law, contract, etc. It is
an attempt to study them as they are embodied in verbal reactions to
problems of moral choice and conflict.

In a sense, the purposes and concepts of such an investigation
would seem to lie within the fields of moral philosophy since it has always been a task of moral philosophy to explicate what people do mean by
value terms as well as what they should mean by them. However, from another perspective this study is related to the classical or traditional
problem of social psychology, a problem which may be stated as, "How does
the impulse and sensation bound infant (or savage) become moral?"

While the influence of the social psychological theories of such
men as Hume, Adam Smith, Mill, Durkheim, Wundt, Dewey, G. H. Mead, Bergson, Nietzsche, J. M. Baldwin, Hobhouse, Freud, and Piaget, continues to
be felt today, central problems which these theories were designed to
explain have tended to be neglected. Thus today, instead of phrasing the
central problem of developmental social psychology as, "How does man become moral?," we tend to consider the problem to be, "How does the child

1

9

learn his culture?," and to believe the first question will be answered
automatically as we study the second. It is hoped in the present thesis
to clarify and show the importance of the former question and perhaps to
make a few steps forward in elaborating and evaluating the very general
theories which have endeavored to answer it.

A. A General Conceptualization of Morality as a Developmental Attribute of the Individual

Our task requires some consideration of the meaning of the term
"moral," and of the empirical attributes which we believe such a term
should have.

1. Morality as Conformity to Cultural Rule

In an attempt to arrive at a concept of the moral which is empirically observable and independent of the observer's values, most modern
social scientists have ended up defining individual morality as behavioral
conformity to the more common rules of the individual's culture. This has
been true both for those interested in moral development unrelated to
whether it is good or bad to be moral, e.g., for such researchers as
Whiting (67) and Sears (50), and for those who are more directly interested in increasing individual morality as a social good, such as Hartshorne
and May (22), or Havighurst and Taba (23).

However, such a conception of individual morality necessarily
eliminates any special theoretical significance which could be assigned
to the question of how moral attitudes develop. Morality can no longer be
viewed as a higher stage of development to be accounted for, as something
which differentiates social man from social animal and the social adult
from the social infant. For the dog and infant may "conform" to many

rules of the culture, yet we do not view them as moral beings. When a view of the moral as simple behavioral conformity has been used in empirical studies of children by workers such as Turner (64) and Hartshorne and May (22), no age increase in such moral traits as honesty and altruism has been found. Perhaps an even more serious objection to the "conformity traits" conception of morality is the failure of its advocates to find general functional unities corresponding to such moral traits.

In addition this view eliminates any but a very minimal "moral" or social value from morality. Whatever be the reasons for which we admire and desire to encourage man's morality, that admiration and desire are not elicited by simple conformity to cultural rules. Even the thoughtful though "culture bound" layman, as well as the philosopher prizes conformity to rules only in terms of the aspects of morality he is apt to define as "having moral principles." Such aspects include selection and ordering of the rules, intelligent interpretation of them, and inner conformity to them in difficult situations rather than outer conformity in routine situations.

Even if we add the concept of guilt to the concept of behavioral conformity, our conception of morality will not allow us to define morality as it has been conceived by most social thinkers. Tendencies toward self punishment or selective inattentions associated with "instinctual" acts probably do not increase after the seventh or eighth year; they do not define a full developmental dimension. They obviously can be considered a social good even less than behavioral conformity. Equation of the concept of the "superego" or of "unconscious guilt" with ordinary language and philosophic meanings of the terms "conscience" or "morality" may be an obstacles to serious consideration of either set of concepts.

Many of the characteristics of an attitude which we think of when we call
it "moral" are not represented by a concept of some primitive guilt associated with the attitude. Whatever the reasons for feeling "unrealistic"
anxiety or self punitive tendencies about the performance of tabooed acts,
as long as this anxiety is felt only as an alien force to be avoided, we
cannot invest such anxiety with the traditional characteristics of conscience, nor even the usual concept of "guilt." The concepts of "universal guilt" and "the superego" have been frequently postulated a priori
and then used uncritically to explain or describe embarrassment, fear,
shame, social anxiety and fantasies of destruction, rather than to denote
"conscientious" self-blame and atonement tendencies related to the violation of a standard. With regard to the prevalence of the latter, there
is little evidence but it should be noted, that competent observers such
as D. Riesman and H. S. Sullivan question whether the phenomenon of
"true" guilt really occurs with much frequence in our culture (48, 60).
But regardless of the prevalence of guilt, it is clear that its measurement would bear a very uncertain relation to morality or the guidance
and judgment of action by standards of conduct.

These limitations of the conformity trait approach to morality
have been apparent to many of the users of the approach. A dissatisfac-
tion with the measurement of conformity traits as representing morality
is expressed throughout Havighurst and Taba's work (23). These authors,
like others in the field, are driven to setting up two opposed kinds of
morality, a conformist morality and a principled, rational autonomous
morality (which they find notably absent in their adolescents).

We shall not try to discuss the many reasons why such a dichotomy
between conformist morality and rational morality is fatal for the study

of both. However, it is fairly apparent that the dichotomy has not been
based on empirical fact but on a priori conceptions of morality. If the
basic concept of morality is conformity, then all the more subtle elements of morality not denoted by conformity must be put in a vague and
honorific wastebasket called rationality, autonomy, creativity, etc.[1]

2. Morality as Action Based on Moral Judgment

An alternative approach to the observation and assessment of
morality might be based on the characteristics of moral judgment, as
these have been considered by philosophers.

The endeavors of moral philosophers in this direction may be seen
as a clarification of the concept of the moral as it has been used generally by thoughtful men. The educated layman in Western cultures believes
that a man is moral if he acts in accordance with his conscience—that is,
if he acts in accordance with a previous judgment that such-and-such is
right to do in this situation. An action, regardless of its consequences
or its classification by the culture, is neither good nor bad unless it
has been preceded by a judgment of right or wrong.

If we infer that no such judgment took place before an act, we
say the actor did not know what he was doing and we make no moral evaluation of his act; if we infer that action was in accordance with such a
judgment, we feel we must so far approve the character of the actor regardless of our own evaluation of the consequences or the class of the
act.

---

[1]Frequently an effort is then made to define this wastebasket
behavioristically. In such cases, the autonomy category tends to become
simply the opposite of the moral one, it becomes resistance to social
pressure and rule just as morality was conformity to it.

The judgment of a person as morally good or bad is quite different from the judgment of an object or animal as good or bad. We tend to say that objects and animals are not moral agents because they do not have "free will," or because they do not "know right from wrong." We can state the meaning of this usage less metaphysically by saying that no object can be judged morally or can be said to be a moral agent unless its conduct can be itself guided or determined by its capacity for making moral judgments. We may not say with Kant that the only thing intrinsically and unequivocally good in the world is a good will, but we do tend to accept a moral will as intrinsically good if anything is.

We demand, however, that the judgment on which action is "based" fulfill certain conditions before we will consider it to be a moral judgment. If we can explicate a set of criteria which correspond to enlightened ordinary language usage of the concept of a moral judgment we may be in a position to begin psychological study of the moral in both a descriptive and normative sense. Working criteria do exist which many of us use every day in appraising our own judgments and those of others as moral. Succinct discussion of some of these criteria of the moral which we shall now present may be found in the work of Sidgewick, J. M. Baldwin, and in some recent works by logical analysts and phenomenologists (52, 5, 14, 19, 34).

The classical philosophers considered these criteria in analyzing the nature of morality, usually endeavoring to show that the essential characteristics of morality were "rational." The recent philosophers cited have left the question of rationality aside as a matter of belief content. They have rather asked whether there are common formal characteristics of moral judgments or orientations, regardless of the content which they assert.

The philosopher has not considered these criteria as forming a basis for saying one person is more moral than another, the primary interest of the social scientists previously mentioned. Nevertheless it seems possible by using such criteria, not only to discover what given individuals are moral about, but to say that one person is moral about more situations than another.

It immediately appears that such a quantitative concept of morality is dubious from a normative view. It would appear that an individual can be too moral in his judgments, in which case we call him "moralistic." We believe, however, that the kind of value judgment termed moralistic does not in fact meet the criteria for being a moral judgment.[1]

Our approach is essentially a qualitative and developmental one in which we see successive stages of development in value judgment increasingly approximating to the characteristics of a moral judgment. We are more interested in assessing the degree to which any of an individual's judgments approximate the criteria of a moral judgment than in assessing how many of them he makes or acts upon.

3. Formal Attributes of Moral Judgment

To present the criteria, we shall contrast two acts of our own, both trivial, one of which may be said to be "pre-moral" and one moral.

Example A

When I was a small boy I did not like to brush my teeth and I

---

[1]We shall offer some evidence to show that "moralism" is an expression of a partly developed or partly moral stage of moral judgment, in which moral judgments are not sufficiently differentiated from other types of value judgment. The confusion of other modes of valuing with moral judgment is as unfortunate for morality as it is for the other modes of valuing.

had to be constantly nagged and scolded to do it, since I was generally
sloppy and quite stubborn. This continued for many years until I finally reached a stage where I had "internalized" the tooth-brushing habit
or norm and external sanctions were no longer necessary. External sanctions of scolding were replaced by an inner need—my mouth felt uncomfortable if I didn't brush my teeth.

The cause of this might be attributed to secondary drive learning, to identification with the aggressor, or perhaps to my finally
coming to believe my parents' preaching that I wouldn't have to go to
the dentist so often if I brushed my teeth. In any case I brush my
teeth regularly in the morning and at night without external sanctions
or without much consideration of the utility of the act. The act would
be termed by the psychoanalyst, Ferenczi, "sphincter morality."

Example B

Some months ago my nephew visited me and I told him that I would
get him a book about magic for Christmas. In the meantime I decided not
to buy Christmas presents in order to meet a deadline. However, I went
downtown and hunted around to find a magic book for him.

Now we would say that brushing my teeth is an act not based on a
moral orientation, while the purchase of the book was based on such an
orientation, whatever the "rational" value of the two acts. From a simple
observation of the behavioral performance of the two acts, one could not
distinguish one from the other as being more moral. However, if someone
were to interview me about the two acts, several criteria would emerge
by which one could differentiate the two acts—one as moral and the other
as non-moral. The two acts are different with regard to the following
"motivational" characteristics of a moral orientation:

a) Moral action is oriented to or preceded by a value judgment.—
In act B, I said to myself, "I should buy the present" and more or less
felt it would be "wrong" not to. In acts of type A, I made no such judgments before performing the act. While I may be able to make value judgments about type A acts, performance of the act is not preceded by or
oriented to such a judgment.

This distinction does not mean that moral action is motivated by pure reason as Kant thought, but the need to see moral action as determined by reason seems to spring from the experience of moral judgments as motivating.

b) Moral judgments are viewed by the judge as taking priority over other value judgments.—Moral action involves a willingness to overcome opposition or disinclination to perform an act, and usually involves some conflict.

In case B, judgments that magic books were too expensive, were ugly and poorly written, were not appropriate gifts, etc., would be overridden by the judgment that I should keep my word in this case. In case A, judgments that tooth brushes were too expensive, were ugly, etc., might take precedence over any judgment of the advisability of brushing teeth. In case B, I experienced a definite disinclination or opposition to performing the act but strove to ignore those feelings and perform the act anyway. If I experienced any such disinclination to brushing my teeth I might not do it no matter how "strong" or frequently performed the tooth-brushing habit was. While the extent to which an act should be independent of inclination before it is considered a moral act is a matter of philosophic debate; nobody questions that some degree of experience of disinclination, and consistency in the face of it, is a necessary part of the moral act.

c) Moral actions and judgments are associated with judgments of the self as good or bad.—If I had not performed act B, I would have made a judgment that I had done something "wrong" and that I was "bad," though these judgments would not necessarily be accompanied by any overpowering emotion of sorrow and pain. If I did not perform act A, I might feel some mild anxiety; I might even dream that my teeth were decaying, but I would make no self-judgment. Thus, if guilt is taken simply to mean some vague diffuse anxiety or fear of punishment and various modes of warding off such anxiety, it is not necessarily an indicator of a moral orientation. Neither would a feeling or self-judgment of failure after not achieving a desired goal be such an indicator. Rather a process of painful self-reproach is such an indicator, a judgment that the self should not achieve pleasurable goals, should not be judged good.

d) Moral judgments tend to be justified or based on reasons or which are not limited to consequences of that particular act in that situation.—The interests, values, or purposes to which appeal is made in thought or argument about the moral attitude are more or less of an ideal nature.

If asked why I performed act A, I would answer that I felt a need to, or felt uncomfortable if I did not. Or I might answer that I thought I might get cavities if I did not and that then I would have an uncomfortable, time-consuming experience at the dentist's as a consequence. With regard to act B, I would reply in terms of the welfare of my nephew, the general importance of trust, contract and the like.

Usually moral judgments are relatable to legitimate claims or expectancies of other moral agents, i.e., to some concepts of rights and duties. The aspects of other persons, or norms, which are viewed as creating obligations are aspects which exist independently of their actual present or future value in terms of self's interests.

If a child tells me he should conform to a parental request because his parents have done so much for him in the past, this is an indicator of an "unselfish" sense of moral obligation; if he tells me that he should conform to his parents because his parents will be nice to him if he is nice to his parents, that is a "selfish" reason, and is an indicator of a non-moral though conforming orientation to his parents. The criterion that an interest be "ideal" is not the same as that it be "unselfish." Should someone be convinced that only selfish interests are "rational," and that some selfish interests in a given situation should be preferred to others, regardless of habitual tendencies or impulses, then he would be referring to an "ideal" selfish interest. An ideal interest or disposition is then not one which simply does exist in the self or the group but one which should exist.

Moral judgments can also be described in terms of the following "cognitive" criteria:

e) Moral judgments tend toward a high degree of generality, universality, consistency and inclusiveness.—If I were aware of a case similar to B in which I or someone else did not keep his word I would tend to judge the actor as wrong. That is, the judgment made had a universal nature, regardless of the particular persons, etc., involved. It applies to all acts of a given type regardless of the particular occurrence of the act, that is the judgment is general.

Generality need not be expressed in a belief that, "It is always wrong for anyone to break his word." It may be expressed, rather, in a belief that an actor should not break his word except through considering a limited number of other general rules or obligations which take primacy over it.

Thus the generality of a given moral judgment is related to the consistency of a number of moral judgments. If a discrepancy between my moral judgment of an act and my judgment of another similar act is disclosed, I would feel some pressure to change one or the other judgment to attain consistency between the judgments or the generality of one of them. While this may be true of non-moral judgments, there is usually a greater degree of striving for consistency or generality in moral judgments. Consistency and generality, in turn, imply _inclusiveness_ in the attributes of the act judged. Thus if we say, "He is a good man," or, "That act was right," these tend to be moral judgments, while if we say, "He is a good jockey," or, "He rode the horse right," these tend to be non-moral value judgments. The moral judgment tends to include all aspects of the man or act judged and to involve some criteria applicable to any man or act to a greater extent than other value judgments.

f) _Moral judgments tend to be considered as objective by their makers, i.e., to be agreed to independently of differences of personality and interest._—Someone who makes a moral judgment tends to expect other people believed capable of making moral judgments to agree with him. Where disagreement exists, the individual believes that discussion based on other shared beliefs or values will tend to lead to agreement.

Reverting to our example, if someone disagreed with me as to whether one should keep his word, I would attempt to convince him that it should be kept, if the situation permitted such discussion. If someone disagreed with me as to how often I should brush my teeth, I would have little tendency to argue the point regardless of how strongly I felt about the possibility of never brushing my teeth again. If we failed to come to agreement about keeping my word, I would not change my behavior in order to please the other discussant. If I did feel that obeying or conforming to the request of the other was itself prescribed by another moral judgment, I might obey, but I would continue to judge that the act should be done.

4. The Relation of Moral Judgments to
Principles Viewed as Rational

While honorific, these criteria are not claimed to be indicators
of rationality or correctness of moral orientation. However, a philosophical conception of rational moral action pre-supposes that the act be
moral in the preceding sense. The history of ethics may be viewed very
largely as the effort to find some content, some principle, some line of
argumentation whi h would logically justify, or show to be cognitively
correct, acts which are moral in the preceding sense.[1] Ethical thought
usually casts itself in terms of examining the rationality of action under
the assumption that the demonstration of the rationality of an action is a
sufficient reason for performing the action. For such an assumption to
make sense at all, it presupposes discourse with a man with moral attitudes.
A typical ethical treatise tells us "the good or the right means this,"
and to make sense presupposes a reader who wants to do whatever is good
and right.

This, in turn, seems to presuppose that basically the good or the
right can be traced back to some entelechy, some thing which is good in
itself, some principle which is right in itself. Regardless of the logical
possibility of finding such an entelechy, or of grounding all moral choices
on it, the moral attitude is responsible for the quest.

Genuinely moral orientations tend to be linked to moral principles
and it is moral principles which give rise to concepts of moral rational-

---

[1]It may be useful to make an oversimplified distinction between the
moral and the ethical. Ethical judgments are philosophical judgments defining the logical status of moral judgments in general, justifying moral
judgments in general, etc. In popular parlance, a person's morals seem to
mean his sex behavior and his ethics seem to mean his honesty within some
professional code.

ity.[1] We may note that our concept of the moral, with its criteria of
generality and objectivity, is linked to a concept of "acting on principle," if we do not give principle too narrow a meaning as some verbal
definite formula adhered to in all situations.

5. The Relations of Moral Judgment to Justice

The moral attitudes which tend to most easily or clearly take the
form of principles are called "a sense of justice."

The concept of justice is a rather vague collection of elements
which it is hard to summarize under any more definite formula, than "giving each man his due," or to differentiate from conformity to moral rules
in general.

The duties of justice comprise the strongest duties in the sense
that they are those which are demanded or that ought to be enforced, i.e.,
they can be demanded by a particular person in a particular situation.
The most important non-religious prohibitions may be brought under the
concept of injustice, e.g., physical injury, stealing, lying, cheating,
breaking promises, family neglect, or neglect of delegated tasks.

Following J. S. Mill (38) and others, we may indicate definite
constituent elements implied in judgment of an act as "just" or "unjust."

First, to characterize an act as unjust implies that the act violates the legal or moral rights of some individual. A sense of justice
implies some concept of rights and some definite localization of the wrong
in terms of injury to a concrete other person in a concrete situation,
where injury includes deprivation of something to which the other is
entitled.

---

[1]Our conception of a moral principle is developed in Chapter VII,
Section D-3.

The concept of a right implies a legitimate expectancy, a claim which I may expect others to agree I have and which they may help me in enforcing. There seem to be two basic general grounds for a right or legitimate claim, beyond sheer custom or law. The first is that of equality—that I should not be treated differently from another. The second is that of contract and various aspects of merit which may be based on contract. Contract usually implies agreement or prior expectancy plus some notion of exchange such that I give up or sacrifice something of value in terms of which I claim something else of value.

Thus the dominant demands of the society upon the individual may be seen in terms of justice. The sense of justice also refers to the dominant demands which an individual makes upon society, upon institutions and authorities. These are primarily those of distributive and retributive justice, as the way in which authorities or the system doles out rewards and punishment. The principles usually invoked in this field are again distributive equality or a quasi-contractual equal exchange of bad for bad or of good for good. On a vaguer level, which may be termed equity, justice may be seen in terms of the expression of attitudes of impartiality and respect for individual personality rather than in terms of concrete equalities.

The concept of justice then helps concretize the concept of the moral by delimiting situations and attitudes to which our criteria of the moral may be applicable. It also helps to delimit the concept of a "moral principle," as something more than a fixed verbal formula. Action o.. principle implies generality and self-consistency integrated with full consideration and analysis of the individual situation calling for action. We hope to offer evidence that such an integration is achieved through the "sense of justice," through a realization like Aristotle's that "the whole content of that which it is incumbent on us to do is described as arising from the nature of the situation, i.e., from the rights of the various persons affected" (3).

B. Implementation of a Formal Conception of Morality in the Present Research

In spite of the obviousness and philosophical currency of such formal criteria of morality as have been listed, a search through twenty-one published tests of moral judgment and fifty-nine empirical studies of individual morality published since 1890 in English and French failed to locate any systematic general observation of moral behavior, attitudes, or concepts in terms of some such set of formal criteria of morality although there have been several valuable studies of justice.

1. Focus of Observation

Perhaps the neglect of this approach in the empirical observation of morality is due to the impossibility of reducing it to simple paper and pencil tests, global ratings by acquaintances, performance tests and the like favored by most of the researches reviewed. Another reason is, perhaps, that such a type of observation cross-cuts the usual neat distinctions between moral knowledge or beliefs on the one hand and moral behavior or motivation on the other, since a moral act or attitude cannot be defined either by purely "cognitive" or by purely "motivational" criteria.

Such observation does not directly serve the purpose of prediction of moral behavior and so does not have obvious practical value. The focus of our study is not on behavioral prediction, but on analysis of children's thinking and attitudes about verbal conflict situations of clear moral import.

It is not within the scope of the present work to argue the importance of conscious moral thinking in the affairs of men. While we shall attempt to show some relations between our verbal materials and behavior, it is not for the purpose of showing the predictive power of these materials but rather because a rating of moral attitudes which was unrelated to behavior would indeed be questionable. The relations between moral thought and moral action are surely too complex and interesting to be considered primarily in terms of ability to predict choice in action from choice in thought.

2. Increased Morality as a Developmental Trend

At their face value, criteria such as those mentioned seem to require a fairly high degree of social and intellectual development. We wish to provide evidence not only that such is the case, but that morality is a genuine and fundamental trend in social development, as postulated by the writers first mentioned. The establishment of such a trend requires not only evidence of age differences in various formal attributes of moral thinking, but some evidence that these attributes cluster in a fairly unitary fashion.

However, evidence of clustering of such traits does not rule out the hypothesis that the increase with age is simply the product of increased exposure to particular contents of fixed conventional norms, or labels, or cliches about the types of situation presented. Age changes may be simply due to increased exposure to the cultural content involved and to increased general verbal intelligence in the manipulation of such verbal content.

Age differences in a dimensional or dichotomous trait in which the lower pole is naive amorality while the higher pole seems to be close to conventional thinking in the culture would not allow us to infer anything beyond increased cultural sophistication.

Evidence to support the view that increased morality is a developmental trend of greater depth rests primarily on a sequential analysis of such development. If a single or multiple sequence of stages intervening between amorality and full morality can be isolated, each stage showing its own more or less qualitative forms of continued naivete together with new advances toward a higher stage, then we may have some confidence in morality as a genuine developmental trend.

Another form of evidence will be derived from comparison of delinquent, sociometric and status groups hypothesized to be differentially favored in their rate or potential for moral development. Such comparisons would indicate the importance of social factors beyond age and intelligence in moral development, while at the same time showing that these social factors operate in the same direction as age and intelligence.

These comparisons will also offer us some chance to determine the degree to which our observations of moral development are subculturally relative. The dominant trend in sociological thought is to assume that types of thought and action which appear to indicate a "low" level of morality to the educated middle-class citizen reflect in actuality not less moral development, but simply a different set of morals or values which the middle-class man views from an ethnocentric perspective.

Again, a delinquent is not viewed as someone who does not conform to moral values, but as someone who conforms to a "delinquent" subculture or group with a different set of moral values. We hoped to determine

whether there are formal characteristics which distinguish moral conformity apart from the conventionality of content to which the individual
adheres, and which differentiates delinquents from others of their class
background.

C. Moral Development as a Field of Study with Special Problems Unanswered by General Theories of Behavior

The most general purpose of our research is to offer evidence for
considering the moral as we "formally" define it as a fairly basic and
general dimension of social development. We wish also to give a detailed
description of this development in terms of form and content of thinking
and belief. Such a task we believe to have theoretical and explanatory
value, though it may be difficult to understand this value if theory and
explanation is identified with general theories of behavior or with general laws.

1. The Problems Are Not Definable in Terms of Learning Theory

Our explanatory effects and problems differ sharply from those of
the general psychologist approaching social development. His interests
would be primarily in showing that morality develops in the same way
everything else does, according to his favorite general laws of behavior.
From his point of view, questions as to the nature of the moral attitude
and its relation to specific pre-moral cognitive content and attitudes
would be simply descriptive problems. They are preliminary tasks to be
performed so that an explanatory psychology of general laws can be fruit-
fully applied, ecological problems in isolating the stimulus and the
response.

From the point of view of the person interested in the classical problems of moral development, however, it is these tasks which are crucial. Only when we know what a moral attitude is and out of what experience it develops, does a statement by a psychologist about the lawful, mathematical relations between such experience and the moral attitude become possible. Such a formulation of laws adds little but elegance to already arrived at solutions of these problems.[1]

In the preceding section we saw that important defining characteristics of the moral attitude could be defined in terms which at first glance seem analogous to learning-theory discussions of internalization of customs or of habits through secondary reinforcement and of universalization or generalization of habits occurring through increased habit-strength raising the level of a habit generalization gradient. However, a learning-theory conceptualization of these criteria does not give us a basis for differentiating what we called a "pre-moral" orientation from a "moral orientation." In our example, the toothbrushing habit is already internalized and generalized, in learning-theory terms, and yet it is not internalized and generalized in a "moral sense," and it is difficult to think of the difference as merely one of differential strength of the habit.

---

[1]Prior to this, a general psychologist's set toward isolating responses and antecedent environmental events is perhaps more likely to be misleading than helpful. His approach to isolation of functional unities in behavior is usually one of common sense concreteness. Responses tend to be classified in terms of similarities in content, of a rather concrete sort and related to environmental events which might have some obvious repetitive spatio-temporal proximity to the event in question. Such a set tends to limit the study of children's morality to routine conformity in relation to routines of punishment and reward by parents.

2. Natural Connections between the Form and Content of Morality

We may summarize our doubts about the fruitfulness of general theories of psychology for our "descriptive" problems by noting that, to be general, such theories must make a complete division between form and content in a response. A general theory of behavior tends to consider only those formal qualities of a response which it shares with any other response, whether these formal qualities be the quantitative ones of learning theory—e.g., drive or habit strength—or the qualitative ones of gestalt—e.g., rigidity, differentiation, etc. The content characteristics of the response are of no theoretical interest to the general psychologist, so that the definition of such characteristics is merely a matter of convenience in the specific situation in which he is working.

The general psychologist's dichotomy between form and content is one which he tends to share with the sociologist. However, where the psychologist tends to treat all social content as identical and focus on variations in the formal properties of the response, the sociologist tends to focus on variations in content assuming that all content has the same form as "culture," "values," etc. From the time of Durkheim, he has tended to see all shared patterns of belief and action as having the formal characteristics of the moral.

Contemporary social scientific thinking about morality tends to make an a priori divorce of attitudinal form from cognitive content and then claims that the formal characteristics of the moral attitude are the same as those of some more general non-moral attitude to which it reduces it. Thus it denies any "natural," i.e., intrinsic or lawful, connection of moral form or attitude to particular concepts or beliefs.

As opposed to such reductions, we have endeavored to define formal properties which are more or less unique to the moral attitude and which define it. We believe there is a wide but not unbounded range of cognitive content to which such an attitude may be attached. Developmental variation in moral beliefs should be related to developmental variations in moral attitude.

We tend to believe that the ways of moral thinking and the kind or quality of moral feeling is different for someone whose morality is based on the dignity of the individual than for someone whose morality is based on taboos against smoking, drinking, stealing and the like.

For us, it remains an unverified assumption that all values or social attitudes are alike in form or structure, that all are learned by the same social influence processes regardless of their content, and that this learning may be measured by a strength or a "like-dislike" rating.

The "naturalness" of form and content connections in the moral domain is in a certain sense attested to by man's recurring feelings that the moral right is constraining in and of itself regardless of the self's impulses, loves, fears, or the pressures of groups, as well as by man's recurring efforts to derive obligation from reason. In matters of nonmoral social conventions, men have no hesitancy about recognizing the content of the convention as artificial, as not naturally or intrinsically determining the motives or attitudes of conformity inspired by it.

However, the validity of the belief in such natural connections rests on the success of studies such as ours which attempt to isolate them.

CHAPTER II

AN ANALYTIC REVIEW OF SOME GENERAL THEORIES

OF MORAL DEVELOPMENT

A. Theories in the Utilitarian Framework: Hume, Smith, Mill, Stephen

The first serious effort to construct a psychological theory which would give an adequate account of the claims of "duty" and "practical reason" while finding the origin of these claims in simple elements of a general psychological nature was that of the utilitarians.

1. Common Moral Beliefs Based on Practical Intelligence

One task of the utilitarians was the logical or casuistical one of deriving the rules and beliefs of common morality from a few simple principles, a task most completely carried out in the work of Sidgwick (52). These principles, all of which base the worth of an act on its predicted pleasure-consequences, were those of prudence, preferring the greater satisfaction consequences to the self to the less; benevolence, preferring the greater pleasure consequences to others over the less consequences to the self or others; and justice, treating each man or case equally or the same when there are no generalizable relevant differences.

The most striking apparent exceptions to these principles in the common morality of modern Western man seem to arise from either particularistic preference for those related to the self or the fixity of obligations to specific rule' where they conflict with situational

23

consequences. Such exceptions are incorporated into the utilitarian framework in terms of the efficiency of allowing for psychological factors conducive to general conformity to these principles. By including factors like the practical need to promote good habits, to avoid bad examples and to present good ones, to maintain stable social expectations, etc., it is possible to justify most common moral beliefs on a utilitarian basis.

Although a skeptic might claim that with such ad hoc epicycles in the model, it might be made to fit any set of values, utilitarianism remains the only comprehensive effort to deduce general moral beliefs from a small set of postulates which might plausibly be judged to be meaningful cross-culturally. Studies of adult casuistry or moral thinking in Western culture, such as those of Sharp (50), are also quite convincing in terms of showing the extent to which such thinking is of a utilitarian nature. Exceptions to such thinking of an "irrational" nature could always be explained by recourse to the associationistic psychology which was the other side of the utilitarian effort.

2. Morality as Based on Sympathy

In addition to a derivation of morality from logic and intelligence, utilitarians, commencing with Hume, have grounded morality on sympathy, which they conceive to be the basic and universal sentiment which makes man social. Since a moral judgment was viewed by Hume not as a pure cognition but as the expression of a sentiment, and since a moral judgment must be universalistic and secure agreement, there must exist some impartial sentiment which would lead everyone to feel the same way about some object (26). An innate tendency to experience pleasure when

perceiving the pleasure of others or pain when perceiving the pain of
others was considered to provide the ground for common evaluations of
objects. Hume rather ingeniously derives a multitude of terms for virtues from the pleasure-pain consequences of personality traits. His
account of why people attempt to be virtuous themselves rests on an
effort to show that prudence or concern for the self's happiness and
benevolence or concern for society's welfare are identical from a long-
range intelligent point of view.

In the case of justice, by which he means obedience to basic
rules of social order, Hume says we judge others not in terms of the
consequences of their action to some individual but in terms of the
consequences of general observation of the rule for society. Hence the
demand for regularity, regardless of situational consequences, is simply
a generalization over time and space of the prediction of consequences
and the sentiment of sympathy. Hume was enough of a cynic to see the
sympathetic tendency as primarily functioning in our judgments of the
worth of other people rather than as determining our own action. His
treatise is primarily an attempt to explain psychologically the part of
morality dealing with judgments of others, which he views as analogous
to esthetic judgments of objects.

3. Development of Individual Differences in Morality as Determined by Intelligence

From this point of view, both the process of moral development
and individual differences in moral beliefs could be seen as determined
by the growth of practical intelligence. Thus tendencies to sympathy,
and to prefer the greater pleasure consequence over the less could be
viewed as innate. Situation-specific individual differences in values

could be defined in terms of individual differences in assigning utilities
to the specific elements of the situation. General differences running
through individuals and age-groups would be explained by differences in
general ability to predict long-range consequences, to differentiate and
relate means and ends, ability to weigh probabilities, and to abstract
general rules, ability to delay gratification, to anticipate the consequences of action on the feelings of others, etc.

While this may sound intellectualistic, it also seems to be the
core criteria of what psychoanalysts call ego strength or reality-principle
functioning. Actually rather than being intellectualistic, the utilitarian
emphasis on prediction is the result of a hedonistic psychology which denies
the existence of "faculties" of conscience or will and rests choice purely
on the strongest of various conflicting "fore-tasted" pleasures and pains
(58, pp. 42-58). In its essential implications for choice, the utilitarian
approach seems almost as indistinguishable from much of expectancy theory,
Lewinian field theory, and statistical decision theory, as these do from
each other (53).

In any case, if we view morality as a developmental dimension,
the utilitarians would lead us to expect it to be a more or less direct
function of the obviously developmental dimension of IQ and of whatever
other factors may independently extend the range of practical thought out-
ward in space and forward in time. While, in our opinion, no very general
measure of moral development has ever been utilized, the research evidence
does seem to offer some support to the utilitarian view. A recent example
is a study of moral character based on clinical ratings of projective and
interview material which found its highest correlate of moral character to
be intelligence, with a correlation in the .80's (42). The research on the

relations of delinquency to intelligence and time-perspective seems to offer some further support to a view of morality as a derivative of practical intelligence (35).

4. The Problem of Altruism and Sacredness

The criticisms which have been made of the utilitarian approach to morality have been primarily expressed in terms of introspective analysis of "rational" moral experience. The elements of moral experience which Hume denies—sacredness, self-sacrifice, and compulsoriness—are those which pose the general problem for a psychology dealing with introspective experience in terms of individual pleasure and pain, whether that psychology be utilitarian-associationistic or psychoanalytic. Introspectively, neither the perception of my own pleasure-pain nor that of others seems in itself to imply an obligatory or sacred quality.

One answer of the utilitarians was to identify this aspect of introspective experience as simply superstition, as habit and vague fear of supernaturally caused pains. A complete reduction along these lines implies Spencer's conclusion that the sense of duty or moral obligation would completely die out if fear of punishment and beliefs in supernatural forces were eliminated from moral education (55).

A more moderate and eclectic statement with the same implication is made by a non-hedonistic utilitarian: "That moral obligation is commonly expressed in the form of a command and is therefore in the imperative voice is an accident, due to the fact that right action is associated with political, parental, or other authority" (43, p. 109).

However, the problem is not primarily to be phrased in terms of feelings of inner compulsion to be explored by introspection. It is rather the question of whether the elements of self-sacrifice or altruism are remnants of pre-rational associations or whether they are in fact products of development of intelligence and sympathy.

The problem and the utilitarian answer are perhaps best presented in L. Stephen's discussion of 1882 (58). He commences by ruling out parental and sexual instinct which lead animals to sacrifice, since we cannot infer altruistic intentions from altruistic consequences, and altruism has no meaning in a pre-reflective stage (pp. 221-223).

He then goes on to rule out dependency or social conditioning and reinforcement as bases of altruism:

> The simple association of a particular object, material or animated, with certain pleasures may doubtless make us value it as a useful instrument but we do not see how it can change the instrument to an object of sympathy. The child may regard its mother as a fountain of agreeable drink, but so far there is nothing in the association which should lead the child to distinguish between the mother and the bottle [p. 224].

Dependency does not imply anything but a purely instrumental manipulative view of another, an attitude merely concealed rather than contradicted by the child's inadequate usage of the means-end distinction. The same holds true, Stephen says, for factors of common interest or exchange of services and favors.

Altruism implies sympathy, he says, some _essential_ and _unconditional_ tendency of my knowledge of your happiness or pain to promote my happiness or pain, not merely a view of it as instrumental to my own. Such sympathy is the result of universal primitive tendencies to project sentience. It is not only natural but necessary and useful to understand or predict the actions of other people. To know the feelings of others, we must to some extent feel them; we must use our own feelings as representations of his, if we are to think about his conduct.

However, even given a natural tendency for another's pain to be intrinsically painful to the self, Stephen recognizes we still have not arrived at altruism. Why should a person not instrumentally avoid feeling another's pain sympathetically as he instrumentally avoids feeling his own pain? Why should he not shut his eyes and move away so that he no longer needs to feel sympathy with the other's pain, instead of trying to help him?

Stephen's answer to this problem seems to us unsuccessful as well as not being derived from the psychology of hedonic calculation basic to utilitarianism. Briefly, Stephen's answer states that it is impossible or irrational, given a belief in the existence of a sentient object, to deny its feelings. It then goes on to postulate an identification of the individual's welfare with the welfare of the social organism which does not have any detailed psychological mechanisms to justify it.

5. The Problem of the Sense of Justice

Besides the phenomena of constraining obligation, of self-sacrifice, and of concern for another as an end in himself, there are also certain aspects of the sense of justice which the utilitarians have found it difficult to account for. Distributive equality and contract are indeed easy to fit into the utilitarian model of the natural and rational man. The utilitarian view is naturally allied to a contract view of the origin of rules and institutions. Supposing a number of independent individuals bent on rationally maximizing pleasure together with some feelings of sympathy, on what other basis could social agreement or common action be based except the equalities of exchange or distributive equality for all?

A more serious problem was the strong sense of punitive or

retributive justice which seemed to be normal in the Western adult, and which seemed to have an impersonal and obligatory aspect going beyond an expression of hostile impulses or any preventive concern for social utility. Another difficulty was concern about the good or bad desert of an act independent of its actual consequences, and based rather on its motives.

An effort to explain these phenomena within an expanded version of the utilitarian psychology of sympathy was made by Adam Smith (54). His fundamental addition was to include the element of "sympathy" with the agent and motive of the act as well as with the patient and consequences of the act. This self-projection into the actor's role aroused the sentiment of "propriety," our feeling of the fitness of an action. Its emotional basis is a sense of pleasure in finding ourselves being similar to or in agreement with another.

Propriety seemed to Smith to provide a less mechanistic moral sentiment than that of utility since as he says, "It seems impossible that we should have no other reason for praising a man than that for which we commend a chest of drawers." It also provides a less simply hedonistic and more adequate view of sympathy. Thus Smith points to the fact that we are pleased to be able to feel commonness of reaction even when the actor is in pain, as in drama. Again we feel pity even when the other person does not express unhappiness, as in the case of an insane person.

Smith undertook to derive all the virtues from their natural tendency to allow this kind of role-taking. Thus propriety becomes identical with emotional moderation and control, since an observer is unable to sympathize with really violent emotion. This would explain the Golden Mean of Aristotle or the generalized fear of extremes so strong in Smith's day in Britain, or in modern "other-directed" America.

The strongest moral emotion, the sense of punitive justice, is derived both from antipathy toward or "dis-identification" with the culprit and sympathy with the resentment of the victim. Its great strength is a result of the dual identification involved.

In a not very clear way, our judgments of others leads to our own concern as to whether others can take our role. Such a concern gradually develops into an inner "impartial spectator," a "man within the breast." This development occurs because of our experience of the fallibility and unjustness of outer judgments. A concern for rules he sees also as arising from experiences of the fallibility of our own feelings of propriety and the like. We find that the rules coincide with the main trend of our sympathies, and we find these sympathies fallible in particular emotional situations, so we learn reliance on the rules. For the utilitarians in general the force of the rules lay merely in their value as generalizations from, and to, particular experiences.

B. Theories of Morality as Defense against Instinct: Freud and Nietzsche

There was, at the end of the nineteenth century, a revulsion from utilitarian thought in morals, expressed in the development of psychologies of instinct and habit on one side and in the sociologies influenced by Marx or by "culturology" on the other. However, most of such theories essentially denied the existence of moral orientations in the sense in which we have defined them. They do not attempt to analyze any essential or special feature of the moral; the moral is simply the mores and ideology of a tribe or class. The theories seeing morality as an expression of group-preservative instincts also differentiate the moral from other sectors of the personality only in terms of behavior content.

Theories such as Freud's and Nietzsche's which see morality as inversion of instinct and defense against instinct do attempt to explain some of the formal features of morality. We shall not recapitulate Freud's theory of the superego. We may mention, however, that we are not really able to deduce the features of the specifically moral or of the sense of justice from the mechanism of identification itself. Identification as a general process is available as an explanation for the rather fixed holding of many attitudes and values besides the specifically moral as we have defined it. As we have mentioned, even given a "superego," conscience implies an "identification" of the ego with it. The concept of the ego in Freudian theory is sufficiently similar to utilitarian conceptions of the self so that the development of an "ego morality" need not be considered specifically.

1. Morality as Aggression Turned Inward in Nietzsche

The work of Nietzsche, however, offers an interesting bridge between the utilitarians and Freud in its derivation of a view of conscience as pathological or defensive from a set of elements which are mainly those of Smith. Nietzsche starts with Smith's concepts of a natural situational self-projection and resentment, but strips them of any natural moral, impartial, or benevolent cast. He sees a judgment of good as originally merely a projection of what the ego likes to do. He sees the demand for punishment as based on contractual equality. "Justice" is a restoration to the victim by giving him the enjoyment of seeing the pain of his injurer (40).

As opposed to such an ego-morality, conscience is viewed as a pathological development consisting of fixed self-ideals on the structural

side and guilt on the affective side. He bases this development on the
transformation of resentment in the "slave revolt in morals." Ideals are
created when socially inferior persons take "good" to mean, not their own
self qualities as do the nobles, but qualities which are the opposite of
those of the nobles, which they wish to establish as good in order to
judge themselves better than the nobles. This involves sympathy and returning good for evil and the blocking of any direct discharge of resentment, which turns back on the self and becomes guilt, or self-destroying
tendencies.

2. Altruistic Moralities as "Unnatural"

In terms of our general problem, we may say that both Nietzsche
and Freud fundamentally share the utilitarian view of the self or ego as
a machine for maximizing pleasure and control of objects, though it is
underlined by an instinctual substratum. The mechanisms of self-projection
and identification which make the self and other persons social do give
rise to guilt and pathologically fixed standards, and so to some extent to
general universalistic attitudes of altruism, benevolence, impartiality,
and justice. However, these universalistic standards do not correspond to
any natural processes of the adult ego. As natural mechanisms, ego-identi-
fication processes would tend to lead to identification with the lion rather
than with the Christian, with those nearest rather than those distant, etc.

The ideals or virtues with which civilization is linked are not
natural developments of the ego, nor are they "rational"; they are in a
sense pathological—though, for Freud, necessary. They are the result of
the constant need to deny and disguise hostility from the self, a need in
turn engendered by ambivalence, by the feelings of envy or love which are

also felt toward authority. The ideal self is the opposite of what we really are; sympathy is a denial of hostility; the impartiality of "justice" is a denial of vengeance.

In a sense these charges are as old as cynicism itself. However, the Nietzschean version sees the denial of underlying asocial motives, not as the effort of the prudent ego to deceive others, but as its effort to deceive itself about the powerful instinctual forces beneath it. So he more satisfactorily accounts for the binding hold or force of ideals than does conventional cynicism. The value of his theory, in terms of our problem, is in its complete denial that Smith's mechanism of role-taking could ever lead to a genuinely impartial attitude, whether as identification with the strong, pity for the weak, or as vicarious vengeance and moral indignation.

C. Morality as Respect for Society: Durkheim

The purely sociological trend in its dealing with morality is best represented for us in the work of Durkheim. His fundamental thesis is, of course, that the moral attitude is a respect for the "rules," which in turn is a respect for the group's set of collective representations of which these rules are the essential part. Such respect is based on the externality, permanence, strength and universality of collective ideas.

Given such a more or less universal and natural respect for collective representations, the differentiation of the moral attitude from other social attitudes is primarily a question of strength. Just as all collective representations are stronger than individual ideas, moral beliefs and sentiments are stronger than other collective representations. Those beliefs and sentiments which are so strongly held by society that they arouse diffuse repressive sanctions constitute morality (14a, App.).

1. Morality in Mechanically Organized Societies

The concept of morality as respect for any strong collective representation or belief seems especially appropriate in societies where mechanical solidarity is the dominant social tie. In such groups "Society" exists in the form of a common self-image, in the form of common beliefs and sentiments. A deviation from the most strongly held and universally shared of such beliefs constitutes a crime. A crime is perceived not primarily as an attack against the victim but as an attack upon the common system of beliefs and sentiments. That a crime in such a society is not a violation of a formal "rule," but of a collective sentiment, is evidenced in the fact that when written law emerges, it defines the punishment but not the crime. The badness of a crime and the severity of punishment is based not on the consequence of the crime, either to the victim or to society, but on the strength of the shared norm which is violated. Punishment is a passionate attitude of aggression or retaliation designed to extinguish the deviant attitude. This retaliation is felt as springing from the group or its symbol and as giving the group image satisfaction. It is not forward-looking or preventive, since what is reacted against is the group awareness of deviation which must now be defended against, rather than any actual future consequences. The central bad content of the crime is the attitude of rebellion.

There is also a positive attitude both behind obedience to the norm and behind punishment, a desire for group solidarity or maintenance. Durkheim views respect as leading to the attitude of obedience, constraint and duty, while a desire for group unity leads to the attitude of emulation, the ideal and goodness. However, Durkheim never really spells out the psychological relation between respect for collective sentiments and the desire for group unity, nor the details of any of the foregoing sentiments.

Respect for society is learned through the pressure of the older generation on the young, but respect for elders is, in turn, based on their being perceived as representatives of society. Thus, though Durkheim's sociology of morality involves a heavy reliance on emotional phenomena, these emotional phenomena, in turn, seem to be primarily derived from characteristics of cognition of the social structure. Of course Durkheim never deals in detail with the social psychology of the individual. But were he to do so, it would seem he would have to derive intensity of moral emotions from the individual's estimate of the actual prevalence of the collective belief or sentiment and of the relatedness of the given belief to the body of collective beliefs.

2. Morality in Organically Organized Societies

The course of social evolution for Durkheim is from mechanical to organic solidarity. In the more evolved culture, "society" is not a shared body of beliefs and sentiments but a system of functions, united by relations. The bond of obligation in a mechanical society was directly between the individual and the group. Insofar as orientation was toward a person or symbol representing the group, that individual had the full sacredness of the group. Obligation existed in the form of similarity to the group, obedience, and being owned by the group.

In an organic society, obligation is directed toward the individual role-partner. Society's only demand is that the expectations of the partner which it has defined as legitimate be met. Crime is deviation from a

legally defined functional role and punishment is restitution to the
partner. Society enters in, not as the vengeful, willful group whose
sentiments have been violated and aroused, but through its delegated
judge, balancing culprit against victim in order to restore the previously defined relationship between the two.

3. Morality as Respect for Group Rule versus as Individual Role-taking

It is only the result of the organic form of organization which
leads thinkers, such as utilitarians, to see individual role-taking and
functional consequences to individuals, to see individual judgment, "the
man within the breast," as the basis of morality. Behind contract, and
function, and individual rights lies the pressure of the group, though in
a weaker and more abstract form than in a mechanical society.

We may look at the conflict between utilitarians and Durkheim as
fundamentally defining the problem of morality to social psychologists who
have followed. The utilitarians attempt to derive morality from individual situational role-taking and so never achieve the structure and sacredness or objectivity of moral values and codes. Durkheim's morality, as a
preexistent fixed structure of rules never achieves either the internality
or the flexibility of a thinking individual moral self. Both our ideals
and our actual moral experience as individuals deny the fact that our moral
judgments are simply carbon copies of the moral code of society and its
representatives, nor yet are they purely the product of thinking in concrete social situations. If there were either one of these we would deny
them the odor of sanctity we attach to "conscience" and "justice."

Some solution to this problem through developmental social psychology defines the central task for the moral theories of G. H. Mead, J. M.
Baldwin and J. Piaget.

D. Morality as Societally Organized Role-taking: Mead

G. H. Mead's moral psychology, like the utilitarians, is based on role-taking the selves of others. Like the utilitarians he sees the growth of morality as essentially the growth of intelligence (36). However, the meanings of role-taking and intelligence and self are radically different for Mead than they were for the utilitarians.

1. Intelligence and Sympathy as Presupposing Role-taking

The utilitarians held a non-social view of intelligence as quantification and prediction of consequences in the service of a non-social self, thought of as states of pain and pleasure. The moral problem was to get such an intelligent hedonistic self interested in seeking the pleasure of others.

Mead, on the other hand, views all thinking as based on role-taking and intelligence as simply the ability to role-take (36, p. 147). Thought is a result of language, which grows out of communicative situations involving role-taking. Moral thought and decision go on essentially, not through weighing probabilities and hedonic utilities, but through an "inner forum," a process of inner intercommunication among the various persons involved in a given conflict situation. Even thought about physical situations is a process of "role-taking" the physical object through projected contact-experience and resistance. Thus role-taking acquires a highly cognitive but still social definition. It goes on, not in terms of feeling the pleasures and pains of the other, but in implicitly responding to the self's words in the role of the other within an organized social act.

"Sympathy" is the form of such role-taking in a cooperative act of assistance, real or implied. The social act precedes the role-taking; if there is no impulse to assist another, there is no calling out in the self of the attitude of the other, which is what is implied in the concept of sympathy (36, p. 299). For support of this view we might turn to the same fact used by Smith to support his view of self-projection, that we feel sorry for people who are not expressing unhappiness themselves, such as madmen.

Mead would ask of Smith, "How do we get this concept of self which we project into others?" Mead claims that the existence of the self as an object to itself presupposes that we view ourselves from the standpoint of another which presupposes role-taking. The fundamental content of the self as an object are not drives, pleasure, and other bodily qualities but social roles, e.g., social categorized classes of functional and communicative acts involving a complementary role-partner. Thus, as far as morality goes, we do not start by judging others using the self as a standard, as Smith thought, but we start by "judging" ourselves using others as standards. This makes the development of the "impartial spectator," "the man within the breast" more plausible.

2. Moral Development as the Development of the Generalized Other

For Mead this growth of an impartial spectator is identical with the growth of the self as an organized object to itself and with the growth of intelligence. All three developments are different expressions of the development of "the generalized other."

Thus, unlike the utilitarians, the dimension of growth in intelligence upon which Mead focuses is not that of the expansion of the spatio-temporal range of prediction and means-end adjustment, but of abstraction

or generalization of concepts. The development of abstraction or generalization is not represented by the number or range of objects to which
words apply but rather by the number or range of others whose attitude
we take toward the given word or object.

The development of impartiality is essentially a process of ab-
stracting from and organizing the various partner roles whose attitude
the self takes toward a social action. Such a process is closely related
to the learning of rules. Mead sees rules essentially as the organization
of roles and role-taking, not simply as prescribed and proscribed shared
acts. Thus the learning of rules is viewed by Mead as the acquisition
of a generalized other, which is both an impartial spectator of the
self and a universe of discourse for abstract analysis or intelligence.
The emotional attitude toward the rules is not one of respect and obedience, but a group "morale."

3. Moral Development from the Play to the Game Stage

Mead illustrates the development of the generalized other in
terms of the transition from the play stage to the game stage of social
participation. In the play stage, dyadic roles are acted out as if in
a conversation. The child alternately is the buyer and storekeeper,
rather randomly moving from one role to the other. In the game stage,
the child simultaneously takes a set of cooperatively organized roles
toward himself, those of the other eight members of the baseball team.
These roles are organized in terms of the "rules of the game" and around
the shared purpose of winning the game.

This organization or unity of the "others" in the game is also a unity of the self as an acting subject. The counterpart of the game which he uses as an example is the sustained story or novel. In the play stage the child responds to fairy tales or folk tales and responds with an interest in each event. In the game stage, the child sustains a sympathetic identity with a hero, an identity maintained through the rush of events and through the various "others" who react to the hero (36, p. 370).

There is another sort of advance made in the game stage, a development related to matters worked out in more detail by Baldwin and Piaget. This is the identification of the "voice" of the internalized other as either the voice of the self or of some definite outer person. In early stages of development the child does respond to itself in the role of the other, but the response is not himself; it has no relation to the acting self. That is, the child takes the role of the other and comments on his own activity but the commenter is not itself experienced as the self. The actual acting self does not reply to the commenting self; it simply acts. An example is the child who says, "No, no," to himself in the role of the parent but goes ahead and performs the forbidden act. On the one hand, the child has no control over the "inner voice"; on the other hand the voice does not actually control the acting, willing self. The self of action is still pretty much the impulsive biological actor (36, p. 372).

In the later stage the child can more or less use the commenting other instrumentally to guide his own action. He carries on a dialogue with it, using its voice to elicit a line of thought which it in turn responds to, this inner dialogue being the essential nature of reflective thinking. The individual has a set of attitudes or expectancies toward the object toward which it is about to act. He is enabled to test out and reconstruct these attitudes by responding in the role of the other in this dialogue form. Thus these attitudes become clearly identified as merely ideas in his mind, as subjective, rather than as essential parts of the object. The conflict of values is taken out of the object and located in his mind. Where the animal merely oscillates between approach and avoidance depending on proximity to the conflictful object, the child is able to locate the avoidance as the response or taboo of the mother and the approach as his own impulse and in some way resolve the conflict (36, p. 375).

4. The Small Group versus Society as Prerequisite for a Moral Generalized Other

However, it may be questioned whether these "game-stage" developments are sufficient to define morality as opposed to social intelligence and group feeling.

Mead is a little obscure as to whether "character" exists in the stage of the baseball game or whether it requires an orientation to society as a whole. On the one hand, he says:

> The child is one thing at one time and another at another; what he is at one moment does not determine what he is at another. You cannot count on the child; he is not organized into a whole. The child has no definite character, no definite personality.
> There is a definite unity, which is introduced into the organization of other selves when we reach such a stage as that of the game, as over against the situation of play where there is a simple succession of one role after another. The game has a logic, so that such an organization of the self is possible; there is a definite end to be obtained and the actions of the different individuals are all related to that end so that they do not conflict. In playing the game, the child is taking over the morale of society and becoming an essential member of it. The child passes into the game and the game expresses a social situation in which he can completely enter; its morale may have a greater hold on him than that of the family to which he belongs or the community in which he lives [36, pp. 159-60].

On the other hand, mere group participation or group "morale" does not seem to constitute morality. Nor does it in itself imply or

create real "character," i.e., some consistent viewpoint with which to
view the self across situations and in interaction with various "teams."
This would seem to involve some ability to simultaneously relate all the
"teams" or audiences with which one plays and all the "games" or situations in which one acts. The organization of all these teams and games
we term "society" and presumably some orientation to society is required
before an individual could be said to be moral, or have rights and duties.

Thus Mead says:

> Until one can respond to the self as the community responds to
> him, he does not genuinely belong to the community. He may belong to
> a small community as the small boy belongs to a gang rather than to
> the city in which he lives. The degree to which the self is devel-
> oped depends upon the degree to which the self calls out the institu-
> tionalized group of responses (of the community) in himself. The
> criminal as such is the individual who lives in a very small group
> and then makes depredations upon the larger community of which he is
> not a member [36, p. 265].

5. Mead's Account of Rights and Justice

When Mead discusses rights, duties, and ethical obligation, his
discussion is always in terms of society as a whole. He uses, as an example, property rights which imply the idea of appeal to a general attitude of respect for property, one shared by everyone including the self.
The point is that rights are not simply what the community allows a class
of individuals to do. There are "natural rights" in the limited sense,
that certain activities are self-contradictory if everyone cannot pursue
them, as Kant had pointed out (37a). A piece of property is something
that everyone wants or ascribes value to. In making a claim to this piece
of property, the claimant is defining the situation in such a way that he
must also define others as having claims to property.

On the side of the individual role-taking we may say that in

respecting the rights of another, the individual is not merely sympathetically putting himself in the place of the other as by whim. Rather
he is expressing that attitude which he has appealed to or demanded every-
time he sought property himself. Thus Mead gives us a third basis for
role-taking the victim in situations of justice beyond the two advanced by
the utilitarians. This basis is the fundamental reciprocal role structure
of social interaction and communication. This reciprocity, however, must
be backed up by universality, by the "generalized other" before it can
issue into a sense of justice. The basis of justice is not merely the
reciprocity involved in interaction so that the actor now takes explicitly
the role he once took implicitly. The point is that he once appealed to
the group, the generalized other, to support that claim so that now he must
recognize the appeal of the other in his own taking of the role of the generalized other.

On the side of the "rules" and "respect for the group," the
Kantian categorical imperative is not merely based on the factual sharedness of a rule within the group, as Durkheim claims. Rather it rests on
the ability of the individual victim in the situation to appeal to an attitude which is felt as one to which the criminal must necessarily also appeal
as a group member. The attitude is felt not only in fact to be shared, but
to be "logically" or necessarily shared by anyone who is to be a member of
the society. The group attitude on which rights are based is not a fixed
set of taboos or rules but a common thinking and acting subject reacting
to the given situation, a "generalized other."

6. Mead's Account of the Moralities of Mechanical and Organic Societies

Role structures may vary greatly in their being based on rights.

Genuine rights imply that the basis of the actor's claim on the partner, his rights, are the same as the basis of the partner's claim on the actor. This distinguishes the caste society from the organic or functional society for Mead (36). In a caste society, one conforms to and identifies with the same-status group and appeals for support of one's rights to the same-status group. In a functional society one conforms to and identifies with or role-takes the partner for the following reasons:

a) a functional, cooperative or purpose-oriented role demands not simple activity performance but rational adjustment to the partners' roles, which are usually multiple and differentiated.

b) the actor's rights and claims have the same basis as the partner's claims and so their support is based on mutual role-taking.

c) the fact that roles are not fixed, ascribed statuses implies anticipatory role-taking in terms of potential occupancy.

Thus Mead arrives at substantially the same view of the two structures of conformity as did Durkheim, one oriented to a collective self-image, the other to diverse, partner expectancies and rights. Mead takes great and perhaps wishful pains to deny the importance of the collective self-image or "peer" element in modern functional democracies as an important determinant of conformity. He insists that equality need not lead to conformity to a common self-image akin to the old caste or tribal images because of the diversity of functional roles in modern democratic societies.

As opposed to Durkheim, however, he denies the fundamental moral significance of the rules as anything but the structure of situational role taking embodied in the "generalized other."

7. Moral Responses as Determined by
the Social Situation

Unlike J. M. Baldwin, Mead does not attach significance to the "ideal self" and to personal models in morality. This appears clearly in his efforts to explain how an individual transcends or stands up against his own society. This takes place through actual involvement in situations of conflict where various groups conflict and there is no real "generalized other," no established perspective on the situation as a whole. The individual, in his need to act, redefines the situation and so gets a new "self," but his decision as to what he is going to do in the situation precedes any definite self-image. He may appeal to distant posterity, but the value of what he is doing is still defined from society's perspective. Thus moral necessity or compelling obligation is not a property of rules or of an ideal-self, i.e., of a transcendental or ideal end, but of the reciprocity of self and social situation achieved as a resolution of such a problematic situation (37b). This doctrine, close to that of Dewey, appears to be what moral necessity should be, not what is necessarily is psychologically.

It becomes very difficult to isolate any characteristics of morality in Mead which really differentiate morality from any problem-solving uses of social intelligence. No doubt in someone like Mead whose dominant interest was abstract social thinking and whose constant inner audience was clearly an ideal public, this distinction could be personally neglected. The subtlety and abstruseness of Mead's thought is sufficient evidence of the inwardness of the audience to which he conformed. But it takes a very high degree of such "inwardness" before thoughtful situational adaptation has the moral force which Mead simply assumes.

8. Mead's Account of the Motives of Duty and Justice

What are the actual motivational forces for taking and acting on the viewpoint of society or maximizing social value from a reflective standpoint in situations of conflict?

Mead simply says: "The sense which the individual self has of his dependence upon the organized society or social community to which he belongs is the basis of his sense of duty and in general of his ethical consciousness.(36, p. 320). His clearest effort to deal with the motivational side of morality is contained in his article on "The Psychology of Punitive Justice," of 1918, an article which seems related to both Freudian and Durkheimian views (37). He postulates an instinctual aggressive energy which can gain an outlet in relations of functional self-assertion of a more or less competitive sort. In relations of group solidarity there is no such outlet, and aggression must be directed against the out-group. The revulsion against crime or the national enemy is both an exclusion of violators from society, an inhibition of violation and an assertion of the solidarity of the group. Respect for the law expresses the dominance of the group over the individual and its impartiality makes us all equally members.

The part of Mead's treatment which goes beyond Durkheim is his explanations of the disparateness between the intensity of our attitudes toward a crime and toward social defense as opposed to the mildness of our attitude toward positive values and functions in a society based on organic solidarity. One factor is that of concreteness; the enemy outside the wall is definite, the values inside are vague, multiple and abstract. A second factor is that the values within the wall are essentially individual values; they are the goals and welfare of separate individuals. What is shared or common is only a negative definition of the value as a right to be defended, not a positive definition as a common purpose. Respect for the group is embodied in a respect for individual rights, not a respect for the purposes and interests for which these rights are used. The abstractness and individuality of social goals means that the value of society as a whole, and the measure of respect for that society, is thought of in terms of willingness to sacrifice for its defense. Thirdly, the attitude of common defense makes us all equally valid members of society, regardless of differences of status and the like.

The purpose of Mead's article, a reaction to World War I, is to explain why in an organic, functionally rational society, rather emotionally primitive retributive sentiments should be perhaps even stronger than in a simple society. In its developmental implication, it suggests that strong "moral indignation" may not be the primitive phenomena that either Durkheim or the utilitarians suggest. It is just the separateness of the individual identity from the group identity in a complex society which gives rise to moral punitiveness, rather than the simple identification with and subordination of the individual to the group, as Durkheim thought.

9. Summary of Mead's Theory

Let us summarize the implications of Mead's theories for the moral development of the individual. Very early social interaction and language learning in the child leads to role-taking or the "introjection" of the attitudes of others. However, these attitudes stand in no organized relation to each other and to the acting self. Further development rests on participation in organized social institutions. Rules then become not

simply vague "No, no's" but the structure of situational role-taking.
One would expect development cognitively to show an increased number and
organization of roles taken. On the emotional side, developed morality
implies some sense of dependency on society as a whole, on all the roles
one can take.

However, there is another side of development into community membership besides flexible and universal role taking. This is a sense of
rights and of retributive justice. This reflects identification with
society as a whole as a defensive agency represented by the state and society as that which is universally shared as opposed to society as the organization of differentiated roles.

Both sides of this development would be expected to be dependent
on identification with or participation in extra-familial roles, which in
our society are primarily occupational.

E. Formal and Cognitive Characteristics of Moral Development: Baldwin and Piaget

In considering the theories of Baldwin and Piaget, it is important
to recognize that Piaget's works of the twenties dealing with cognitive
development were largely creative empirical elaborations stimulated by
Baldwin's "armchair" theories. While both wrote books specifically on the
development of morality and its interpersonal roots (4, 44), these works
are also very loosely integrated parts of more comprehensive efforts to
describe cognitive and logical development (5, 46). Insofar as moral
development is defined in terms of basic social relations, there is extensive disagreement between them. Insofar as both characterize moral development in terms used for cognitive development in general there is a fair
degree of agreement between them.

In this section we shall consider these more formal and cognitive characteristics of morality as they are embodied in the stages of Baldwin and Piaget. These stages are elaborated empirically in Chapter VI and summarized in Tables 19 and 20 in Chapter IX. In the following sub-section we shall consider the more social and explanatory concept used by the two writers.

1. The Adualistic Stage of Evaluation

According to Baldwin, as well as Piaget and Werner, the young child must develop from a stage in which experience is adualistic (5, 6). In terms of value judgment, there are two chief aspects of this adualism, aspects which may survive in various forms at fairly advanced ages. The first adualism involves the inability to differentiate between subject and object, or between ideas and the objects to which they refer. This Baldwin calls a "projective" attitude. The second adualism is the inability to differentiate the meaning of the object to the self from its meaning to others, the uncritical unconscious assumption that the self's attitudes toward the object are generally shared (6, pp. 56–60). This Baldwin calls a "syntelic" attitude.[1]

Baldwin's original concept of the adualism of subject and object implies that the value of an object is believed to be located in the object. That is, we ordinarily view values or "tertiary qualities" as not really located in the object, as we do primary and secondary qualities,

---

[1]Piaget, in adopting Baldwin's theories, labeled the first adualism "primitive realism" and the second adualism "ego-centrism." In his treatment of moral judgment, Piaget focuses on these attitudes as they relate to conceptions of the roles.

"Moral realism," according to Piaget, is the confusion between rules and things and the ascription of quasi-physical reality and force to rules. "Moral ego-centrism" is the uncritical assumption that all rules, and also the self's perceptions of the rules, are universally shared.

but rather as relative to some subject. Without a person valuing, no values. In the "projective stage," however, value qualities are viewed by the child as actual properties of the object.

Projective valuing leads first to a confusion of the perceptual qualities of an object, or of its consequences, with its value. Secondly, it leads to a confusion of all types of value. Since the question "valuable for whome or for what purpose" is not asked, all forms of value tend to merge. Because a person was well dressed, it might be assumed that he had intrinsic quasi-moral value and should be saved in a disaster ahead of someone who was not well dressed or rich.

A third related expression of projective valuing is the use of perceptual or other value-irrelevant similarities and associations in attributing value to a give object. The goodness of an object is justified by showing that it is similar to another good or liked object regardless of whether the shared characteristic actually forms a basis for the value of the originally prized object.[1]

2. The Instrumental or Dualistic Stage of Evaluation

All such characteristics of projective valuing indicate an attribution of value to the concretely experienced object, rather than making such value relative to something else, to a subjective end or standard. In the case of value the distinction of subject and object tends to take the shape of a distinction between means and ends. Objects or acts have value only as means to some subjective end. The value basically lies in

---

[1]An extreme example of such arbitrary associations is provided by a situation observed by us in which two four-year-olds were comparing their sunglasses. One said, "These glasses (her own) are God and these glasses (the other girl's) are Jesus, and God is better than Jesus." Previously she had cried because her sunglasses had a picture of the Disney dog "Goofy," and she had been laughed at by the others as "Goofy."

the end and only contingently in the means.

Instrumental thinking demands such a distinction for selection of the most economical and effective means in light of a given end. A given object, or act which is to serve as means has an indefinite number of possible values or value-laden consequences. In order to view the object "rationally" in terms of my particular end, one must be able to disregard all such value-qualities which one might attribute to it on other occasions, and consider only the possible manipulations one can perform on and with the object on this particular occasion for this particular end. The value element of the whole situation one must restrict completely to some need or purpose of the self or another subject in the particular situation and make the value of the means completely dependent on such a purpose.

Instrumental thinking is reflected by asking such questions as, "Is this trip necessary?," "Is this object or act necessary for the end I have in mind?," or "Can I use a substitute?" Such questions imply an ability to hold the end completely constant, as being imaginatively there, while considering the consequences of various means. If I have not properly differentiated the means-value of the object from its habitual value, I will get lost in a chain of consequences relevant to other values but not the value I had in mind.

These characteristics of instrumental thought we may see as related to the localization of value experience in the self and the corresponding ability to see external things as pure means, which in turn is one phase of the discrimination by the subject of his own ideas from the objects or states to which they refer.

A closely related development is the discrimination by the subject

of his own perspective or attitude from that of others, an overcoming of
the "syntelic" or egocentric attitude. However, these two discriminations
may be independent. One may be able to view the object in terms of its
instrumental value to needs or purposes felt vaguely to be shared. On
the other hand, one may consistently discriminate his needs or value experience from anyone else's and yet not see objects purely as means to a
specific end or need.

3. Piaget's Conception of the Dualistic or Instrumental Stage

The foregoing presentation of the development of instrumental
thinking from the differentiations or dualisms of self and other and idea
and object we have developed in attempting to apply the rather scattered
statements of Baldwin to our material. While Piaget's earlier works, including "The Moral Judgment of the Child," rested on this concept of
adualism, his later works have given a somewhat different, though complementary, interpretation of the rise of instrumental thinking. Whereas in
his earlier works Piaget speaks of the period from six to eleven as one
in which "egocentrism" and "realism" were overcome, in his later works
he speaks of the period primarily as one in which the ability to carry
out concrete operations in thought is developed.

A comprehension of Piaget's concepts requires some study of his
logical terms and of the examples of children's thinking about physical
situations with which he illustrates them (27, pp. 129-55, 242-50).

A concrete operation is a symbolic transformation of an object
which is "internalized" and "reversible." In pre-operational thought
there is an outer object and there is something done to it in imagination.
Imaginative transformation of the object or the situation is made in terms

of an actual motivated bodily action upon it. This action is not reversible except in the sense that it can physically be undone.

Since practical and moral thinking involves actual human actions or operations, the differentiation of pre-operational and operational thought is less clear and important than it is in the sphere of physical and numerical thought. However, it is a necessity for the ability to use "different points of view" with regard to a situation. Thus a child is asked to use two different modes of classification by being presented with a group of brown and white wooden beads and being asked whether there are more brown beads or more white ones. If he is "pre-operational," he may say, "If I made a necklace with the brown ones, I could not make another necklace with the same beads and the necklace made of wooden beads would have only white ones" (27, p. 133). The concreteness of his imaginative operations prevens him from using simultaneously two perspectives or systems of classification, color and material.

A pre-operational concept of moral reciprocity is the following response of a ten-year-old, following an effort by the examiner to explain the Golden Rule:

> (What would the Golden Rule say to do if someone came up and hit you?)
>
> "Hit him back."

The "operation" prescribed by the Golden Rule is an external irreversible action.

A use of moral reciprocity as a reversible internalized operation is the following response by another ten-year-old:

> (Why is the Golden Rule a good rule?)
>
> Because just feel yourself like you're in their place, the poor people's place if you're rich, and how you would have to be with

those laws. Then sort of go back to your place as a rich man and make laws according to what you dreamed sort of like.

While this is a "moral" use of operational thought, it is equally useful in coordinating various selfish purposes in prudential action. One expression of this is an ordering of values or situational purposes into a transitive hierarchy by the operation of seriation.[1]

4. The Ethical or Ideal Stage of Evaluation

However, purely instrumental value does not seem to be moral value. To reduce value to that which serves desire is not to take a moral point of view, unless the desire be desirable. Thus Baldwin constructs a third or ethical stage to follow his dualistic "intellectual" stage. In the "intellectual" stage, the fact of desire or need was the end point of value. In the ethical stage purposes or needs have some value put upon them beyond their factual strength. Thus at the "projective" and "syntelic" stage, if an activity was perceived as bad for some reason, this meant that the activity was not liked by the subject; no need for it would be perceived. At the "intellectual" stage, whatever needs the self actually had was the measure of the value of objects. One might have an "ideal self" but only in the sense of wishing to possess some trait which would satisfy an experienced need. At the "ethical stage"

---

[1] A related logical development, whose treatment by Piaget in French we have not read, is the development of a concept of probability. Young children in the verbal anticipation of consequences seem to use either the category of possibility or that of necessity. Conformity is justified in terms of an improbable though logically possible concrete consequence or else in terms of some necessary or inevitable consequence. Mor mature ten-year-olds increasingly tend to use categories of probability and to consider only more likely events. In general, predictions of the behavior of others rests on a belief that probably they will conform to the norms for the situation. The importance of such a set for prudential or instrumental thinking is obvious.

ideals exist in the sense that there may be a discrepancy between the desires one consciously does have and the desires one consciously should
have.

Expressed as the development of the means—end dichotomy, an "ideal"
self means the ability to view desires as means. There is a search for
some further end to which various desires are means, and in terms of which
they may be evaluated. Put in terms of objects, there is the concept that
various acts or objects should be desired, regardless of whether in fact
they are desired. This seems in a sense to be a return to the "projective
stage" where objects have a quasi—perceptual intrinsic value. However, at
the ethical stage the intrinsic worth of the object is still the product
of an act of value-judgment by an observer. It is intrinsically "there"
only in the sense that the ideal observer would judge it to be truly there.
Some effort toward "appreciation" of the object is required, some process
of judgment and experience by which the value of the object comes to be
genuinely recognized—some further perspective of it to be gained. The
actual value resides in the standard, and it is subsumption of the experience or object under the standard which gives it value.

5. Conscience in the Ethical Stage

Baldwin defines the ethical stage not only in terms of modes of
experiencing ends and value but in terms of modes of experiencing obligation and conscience.

The concept of "conscience" implies some thinking process in the
mind which exerts a strong force on the rest of the self to follow its be-
hests, but which the self identifies with. That is, the compulsion is
obeyed out of the self's "strength" and disobeyed out of the self's weak-

ness, unlike neurotic or impulsive compulsions. It implies choosing in the "line of greatest resistance" as William James put it. One has only to read any serious novel to be given a description of the experience which our culture denotes by conscience. Victor Hugo presents the classical, if stereotypical account of the conversation between a man and his conscience in **Les Miserables**.

Concepts of "conscience" and "duty" imply a rather subtle mingling of feelings of freedom and constraint in action. They imply that I feel compelled to perform an act, but that this compelling force exists within the self or personality. I am "compelled" to do right in opposition to the remainder of the self, as opposed to impulse, fear, or self interest.

Thus, as opposed to the rest of the self, conscience is compelling. But, as opposed to outside forces, conscience is "free." Just as it must override other forces within the self, it must override external forces. All this is implied in the phrase "ought to," as opposed to "want to" or "have to." When we reify the "ought," when we see it as having a psychic locus, we call it conscience. This introspective reification has had vast meaning in advanced cultures which poses many problems, not reducible to those of the "internalization of norms" as habits of behavior.

Many efforts have been made to explain "conscience" in terms of identification with outer authority, which would lead to a sense of the rules as both "self" and "not-self." However, such explanations are by no means sufficient, since many individuals and cultures seem to have "superegoes" without the least tendency to deify conscience and without even any conception of conscience. The feeling of many adults that they have a higher or better self which can and should guide them would seem to be a product of development rather than simply the remains of early identification.

The experience of conscience does not seem to be subsumable under the concept of "ego-ideal" either. Many of us have had, at least in vicarious and sentimental form, the experience of self-realization in a freely chosen sacrifice for a "higher cause," of which idealists like Royce have made so much and which Mead terms "the fusion of the Me and I." Such a realization of the ideal self is quite different from the realization of the "ego-ideal" in such experiences as successful achievement of social or manly prestige.

It becomes very difficult to think about the phenomena implied by ...science if we do not make it a unitary introspective entity. However, assuming some kind of "directive," a prescription or model of action, and some kind of motive or "sanction," conscientious obligation would seem to involve experiencing both of these as "inner" and as "necessary." "Necessary" implies regardless of irrelevant outer conditions and inner feelings. This more or less implies two other types of experience of obligation which do not fulfill these conditions. Baldwin presents these as three stages of the sense of obligation which parallel his three stages of evaluation:

> First there is the case in which the sanction is objective and unconditional, which we may call "objective necessity." "I am compelled to do this," or, "I must do this for you compel me," is its form. Second, the case of personal selection and decision within a whole of objective or possibly social sanctioning, giving the "hypothetical imperative," "I should do this under certain conditions" or "I should do this if I want this to happen," or "I am impelled by prudence, by my interests, to do this." This in turn passes over, third, into the "moral necessity" of ideal conformity: "I must do this because it is right," or "I ought to do this" [5, v-3, pp. 139-40].

At the stage of objective necessity, the child would say, "I (or you) have to come inside because it's raining." At the hypothetical stage, he would say, "If I (or you) don't want to get wet, I'd better come inside."

In the first case he merely presents some usually compelling event. In the second stage he simply states a means—end relationship and makes action dependent on the existence of a natural motive in the self on the particular occasion.

In the third stage, a person makes assertions that an act should be done regardless of whether there is at the moment a corresponding need or outer press. The necessity is based on a line of reasoning, thought and feeling. The "voice" which does the reasoning does not defer to another self or aspect of the self to make the choice. There is, then, a certain necessity and impersonality about obligation both at the first and the third stage. At this third stage, this impersonality and disregard of the self's needs is that of the conscientious self oriented "only to duty." The definition of duty may be highly personal and strongly focused on providing for the needs and feelings of others. However, the acting subject who follows such a definition of duty must disregard his own feelings to perform it.

At the first stage, it is not the action and conformity of the subject which is impersonal, it is the pattern or object conformed to which is impersonal and indifferent to needs. Outer authority or law may be seen as completely indifferent to the intentions, needs or welfare of anyone, but the self's reason for obeying authority is based completely on the personal need of fear of punishment.

Thus Baldwin's third stage corresponds to what Western culture defines as the experience of conscience, as well as corresponding to the experience of the ideal.

6. Piaget's Account of the Ideal Stage

Piaget does not develop a stage of the ideal in his book on moral judgment. However, in a recent work, he describes the development of concrete operational thought into formal thought, during adolescence, as necessary for the formation of social ideals and principles (27, ch. xviii). Whereas concrete operational thought performs operations upon object-images, formal thought uses operations upon other operations or upon verbal propositions (27, pp. 249-66). Accordingly, every logical possible combination or transformation of concepts can be worked out in hypothetico-deductive fashion. This means that empirically anticipated events are subordinated to logically possible events, so that empirical events are seen as merely cases of some more general formal system.

Piaget discusses the resulting impact on the social life of the adolescent in terms of characteristics of <u>haute bourgeoise</u> ideological concerns. The adolescent becomes interested in ideas, attempts to systematize ideas, has his own opinions, wants to evaluate and change society according to some ideal schema. These ideological trends are in turn related to his own planning of a long-range career. Rather than simply having fantasies vaguely in the future while living in the present, he tries to organize present and future in some comprehensive if unrealistic fashion in which the present gains its meaning as a step toward the future. Without stressing the planning and systematizing of life and society, Piaget says that affect is for the first time felt for ideas and ideals rather than for the particular persons and events which represent them in the child's experience. The adolescent is in love with Sally because he is in love with love, whereas the juvenile is simply stricken with Sally. There may be a concern with moral principles themselves rather than a particular moral situation.

The highest form of personal development Piaget sees when such

ideals are integrated with empirical reality through devotion to a life-
task. This means adopting a work role which is not ready-made but must
be created in filling it. It involves simultaneous expressions of the
self's scale of values in the task and subordination to the task as something "larger than" the self.

F. Baldwin's Conception of the Ideal Self and Its Genesis

Both Baldwin and Piaget see all cognitive development as a moving
equilibrium between trends of accommodation on the one side and assimilation on the other. In social development the trend of accommodation is
described by Baldwin in terms of processes of imitation and of submission,
while the trend of assimilation is described in terms of ejection and
assertion.

1. The Bipolar Social Self

Most of the activities and possessions which the child thinks of
as himself and prides himself on are attributes he first saw in others
and which he imitated from others. Because of this common context, he
has ejected into his concept of others his own feelings and sense of voli-
tion. Thus the self concept which determines voluntary action is a concept
derived from and continually adjusted to the selves of others. The young
child's interaction is social, says Baldwin, because it is based on his
reciprocal conceptions of himself and of others. These conceptions are
social, because concepts of what both the self and others are doing in the
situation are based on a common core image of a general self or person.

Although the young child's interactional self is from the first
social or common, it does not begin to become actually moral until around

the age of five, according to Baldwin. If lacks two features requisite
for morality, a degree of consistency and a degree of altruism.

Considering first altruism, we may ask if all social action is
determined by a self or self-concept, how can any action be unselfish?
Baldwin's answer is that moral action is determined by and enhances a
general or ideal self, as partially described in our discussion of Baldwin's ideal stage and of Mead's generalized other. As opposed to moral
action, premoral or amoral action is determined by a concept of the concrete self with its historically given needs, desires and interests.

Baldwin says that the premoral self is not only concrete, it is
bipolar. Premoral interaction involves an active, assertive, controlling
self and a passive, submissive, imitative self. The child may be either
as occasion arises. With a younger child, or a parent in a permissive
modd, the child himself defines what is to be done and the other is
merely an object to be manipulated, an agent in terms of which the action
may be carried out. With an older person or in a novel situation the
child expects to be the object in terms of which action determined by the
other is carried out.

In either case the self determining the child's action is "selfish."
The act of adjusting to or obeying another need not imply an experience of
self-control and unselfishness since the self controlling the child and
demanding sacrifice of his wishes is not his own self. Though the child's
action may be determined by the dominating self of the other, still that
other self is conceived by the child in its own image as a basically impulsive or need-gratifying self (insofar as motives are assigned to it at
all). The experience of unselfish obligation requires that the two selves
or will be identified or unified with one another, an integration which is

not achieved by motives to imitate or obey in themselves.

The problem of the genesis of the moral self is not solved by the internalization of prescribed habits in the sense of the learning theorists or the associationists of Baldwin's day, as we stated in discussing the utilitarians. Even if the child accepts certain conforming habits or rules as part of himself, this does not guarantee the existence of a concept of a moral or altruistic self as determining action. There need be no difference between a child's feeling of self-assertaion and dominance in carrying out a conforming habit and his feeling in carrying out a deviant or asocial one.

Considering the moral self as a consistent self, the inconsistency of the premoral child can also be defined in terms of the bipolarity of his self. When interacting with another person who appears stronger, who offers something to appreciate or imitate, the child is submissive and flexible. When interacting with a weaker or fully understandable or predictable person, the child appears dominating and inflexible, a kind of rigidity which does not imply real consistency. For Baldwin, as for Mead, consistency of character requires a "social bond of union" for the child's various situational selves or roles (4, p. 40). Whereas altruism reflects the ideality of the self concept, consistency reflects its generality.

2. The Ideal Self

Baldwin characterizes the determinant of moral action as a "self" rather than as rules or as situational consequences in an effort to account for the introspective phenomena connoted by "conscience" just discussed in section B-4. Rules enter into moral decisions, not as habits, but in terms of a general rule—obeying self which is not certain in advance as to what rule really applies in the situation. Sympathetic concern for consequences enters into moral decision not as spontaneous impulse, but in terms of a self which is regularly concerned about others and their legitimate claims.

The concept of a moral self is invoked to account for a set toward altruism and self-consistency which is independent of settled attitudes of obedience to particular rules or sympathetic involvements with particular persons in particular situations. The need to postulate such a set appears most clearly in the way in which thinking and choosing is directed in situations or moral conflict. Where particular rules and sympathies break down, the moral person still has a moral set directing him to reach some morally integrated solution to which his moral self could assent.

Baldwin uses the good Victorian example of a decision as to whether to give a handout to a beggar. One cannot simply sympathize with the beggar and let his self or his wishes determine action. On the other hand, one cannot simply determine action by one's own natural self which would like to spend the money on its own purposes. Rather the decision is made by a self "trying to do right," which attempts to anticipate what an ideal self, an all-wise, purely motivated self would choose or recommend in the situation.

Such a self is general, it is to the actor's mind the same for both himself and the beggar. It is a process of thought and feeling which would justify both the beggar's asking and the actor's giving, or repudiate both.

Though general, it is not simply a rule. In ninety-nine cases out of one hundred, one might refuse beggars, yet the merit of the claim of the individual beggar must be examined if a moral choice is involved.

3. The Genesis of the Ideal Self

How does such a concept of a self which wants to be good and to conform to rule arise?

Baldwin's answer is shaped by the problem as he states it. The difficulty in developing an ideal self is that of getting a situation in which the child conforms, but does not see such conformity as either enhancing his own impulses, or due to his own weakness relative to the other who is enhancing himself. The child must come to see the denial of his own wishes as somehow self-enhancing.

The experience required, says Baldwin, is one in which the child perceives the parent as putting pressure on the child to conform to something outside the parent. Such an experience is not bipolar since the parent wants the child to be like himself vis-à-vis his attitude toward the rule. The fact that the parent's role and the child's role are differentiated on the power dimension is interpreted in light of the desirability of common conformity. The parent's self is seen as simultaneously commanding and obeying. Thus initiating action and conforming are seen as both parts of the same self, a self-controlling self.

Such conformity to a third force might simply be perceived by the child as indicating that a third person dominates the parent as the parent dominates the child. However, the fact that such pressure to conform goes on in the absence of the third person or authority tends to give rise to the concept of a generally conforming self. In addition, the fact that the conformity is shared in the family or group gives rise to a sense of a common self which the child is to become.

Originally such a general or ideal self is largely in the image of the parents. It is ideal to the child, it is what he is to become, but it is largely realized in the parents. This does not mean that there is no differentiation of parents from the rule; the parents are seen as obeying the rule. It does mean that the image of a good, conforming, self which obeys rules is in the parent's image.

By experience of conflict between models and by perception of their failure to incarnate the rule, the self which is the child's model becomes recognized as abstract and impersonal and is embodied as conscience. Even at this stage of conscience there is need to have the approval of others. Such approval, however, is only required because the process of self-judgment requires an imagined social generality. Action conforming to the ideal self is action conforming to a line of thought and feeling, a self, which can guide both the actor and his partner.

G. Piaget's Conception of Autonomous Morality and Its Genesis

1. The Heteronomous Stage

Like Baldwin, Piaget sees imitation and obedience as in themselves inadequate to establish an internalized morality. Unlike Baldwin, he sees a sense of conformity to rule as also inadequate to account for such a development.

According to Piaget, the child feels a "heteronomous respect" toward his parents and elders, a respect composed of fear and love or admiration. This same respect is transferred to or experienced toward rules which acquire a sacred and unchangeable aspect.

Such respect is heteronomous or unilateral because it does not

imply a reciprocal right or wish to be respected by the authority. The
authority's rights are not based on his duties, and any action or command
of his may be viewed as right. Respect for the rule is also unilateral,
it is not based on the function of the rule in serving individuals and
their values.

Such heteronomous respect for the rules combines with the child's
egocentrism to give the rules a fixed, external, quasi-physical cast.
The child's egocentrism or inability to take the point of view of another
prevents him from seeing the rule as serving a purpose for the selves who
created it. There is a confusion of concept and thing, called "realism,"
which leads to a perception of rules as fixed things outside of minds and
a rigid literalistic application of rules. One expression of this is a
judgment of action by its actual consequences rather than according to its
intentions.

Another expression of the quasi-physical nature of rules is a belief in "immanent justice" or of natural events as punishing. In general,
the heteronomous sense of justice is one insisting on inevitable and expiatory punishment.

2. The Autonomous Stage and Its Genesis

Whereas Baldwin and Mead see moral development largely in terms of
increased depersonalization and social generalization of rules, Piaget
sees such development as largely an increased relating of conformity to
individual selves.

Such development occurs in the transition of the child to the
stage of mutual respect or autonomy. Mutual respect implies an attitude
of reciprocal conformity and approval.

In such a stage, rules are seen as the product of agreement and cooperation. Respect for the rules is based on contract and on the group goals they serve, rather than being based on a belief in their intrinsic value.

The sense of justice centers around the attitudes of equality and of reciprocity themselves as manifested in contractual maintenance, exchange and distributive equality. Punishment is oriented toward restitution to the victim rather than to retribution.

The development of the attitude of mutual respect is largely dependent on interaction with age peers according to Piaget. Even though adult authorities endeavor to be democratic, the natural prestige of the elders hinders a full development of reciprocal orientations.

CHAPTER III

PROCEDURE

A. Subjects

1. Rationale for Selection

The selection of our subjects was determined by the foci of the principal theories we have discussed.

Piaget sees peer-group participation as crucial to moral development, participation for which sociometric status seems to be a suitable indicator.

G. H. Mead sees participation in secondary institutions as crucial to moral development, with peer interaction important primarily as providing an easily assimilated model of adult social organization. For such participation, socioeconomic status might be taken as an indicator. It is not as natural an indicator of social participation as sociometric status, however, since it is an indicator of participation in secondary institutions by the parents rather than by the child. However, it was felt that a measure of community group memberships by the child was too superficial a concept of societal participation to take as an index of deep moral trends. A sense of participation in the society as a whole would be expected to be a more diffuse, subtle and pervasive trend than the fluctuations of cub scout membership.

Both sociometric and socioeconomic status are only gross indicators of psychological participation, just as age is only a gross indicator

69

of psychological development.[1]

Three age groups were selected: ages 10, 13, and 16. These ages were used for the following reasons:

a) They seemed to span the period in which peer and societal group membership become important determinants of self-conceptions relatively independent of family roles.

b) It seemed legitimate to expect fairly adult moral thinking at the 16 level while the 10 level seemed to represent about the lower level at which many children could be expected to have the intellectual skills to meaningfully respond to complex moral situations verbally presented.

c) Age development in moral thinking at younger ages had already been explored by Piaget and his followers but the significance of such observations as validating his theories required filling in development at the pre-adolescent and adolescent eras. Piaget's theory seems to require that adolescent development be characterized as primarily a further extension of developmental trends which he observed in the juvenile era.[2]

Finally, it was decided to secure a delinquent comparison group for various reasons, such as the following:

a) Such a group might offer some validation of our concept of moral development in terms of the line of thought about delinquency indicated in Chapter I, section C-2.

b) To provide groups differing in family participation and organization in terms of Baldwin's theory of ideal-formation.

---

[1]Both participation and status would be expected to be related to the more psychological components of motives, knowledge and skills and self-conceptions. A sociometric star would be expected to wish to interact with and be accepted by peers, to be skillful in such interaction, and to conceive of himself as someone who does relate to peers and is accepted by them. Various observations for assessing these psychological components of societal and peer participation were made, but their analysis is not reported in the thesis.

[2]Piaget's sketch of value development toward ideals in the adolescent period only became available as we were completing this thesis. In our opinion, an acknowledgment of this third stage as possible and desirable requires a reworking of his earlier thinking on the social side of moral development. The mere fact of formal thinking is inadequate to generate the ideal attitude, which is also not accounted for in Piaget's earlier account of the two basic attitudes in the latency era (cf. Chapter VII, section C-2.

c) To differentiate the more "motivational" aspects of moral development relative to class differences due to secondary institutional
participation and class sub—cultural differences.

2. Population

The basic population consisted of eighty-four boys filling the following 2 x 2 x 3 factorial design:

Sociometric	Upper Middle Class		Lower (and Lower—Middle) Class		
	Iso-lates	Inte-grates	Iso-lates	Inte-grates	Delin-quents
4th grade (ages 9.6 to 10.4) . .	6	6	6	6	
7th grade (ages 12.6 to 13.4) . .	6	6	6	6	
10th grade (ages 15.6 to 16.4) . .	6	6	6	6	12

The population had the following characteristics:

a) Class.—To facilitate filling our design, two suburban Chicago
areas were selected, one predominantly upper—middle class, the other predominantly "common man" or lower and lower—middle class in Warner's terms.
A dichotomous judgment of a boy's socioeconomic status was based on his
parents' occupation and education, as reported in the school folder. In
spite of our efforts to get discrete groups, we were forced to take children along a fairly broad continuum with a rather arbitrary though conventional dividing point. The distribution of our subjects' parental occupations is presented as Table 1.

b) Sociometric status.—When entering a given classroom, we would

TABLE 1

PARENTAL OCCUPATIONS OF SAMPLE

Class and Occupation	Number of Parents
Lower and lower-middle class (including delinquents)	
1. Unskilled laborer or driver	12
2. Semi-skilled factory, including foreman . . .	22
3. Primarily non-factory skilled crafts—printer, butcher, electrician, machinist .	6
4. Small business (0 or 1 employee) or salesman, without college education	8
Upper-middle class	
5. Small business, accountant, or salesman with college education	16
6. Semi-professional, engineer, teacher	13
7. Executive or professional	7

describe the procedures we would follow, including a "revealed differences" discussion among three boys. Then we asked the boys to write the
name of three other boys with whom they would like to have the discussion. The sociometric test was informally discussed with the teacher
and compared with notes in the school folder before a final selection
was made, in order to somewhat reduce determinants of school and athletic
achievement, temporary fluctuation of popularity, etc.

As in the case of socioeconomic status, we did not have enough
subjects available to get only extreme groups, so that our dichotomy tends
to divide a continuum.

The distribution of our subjects in terms of sociometric status is
presented in Table 2.

c) Delinquency.—Nine of the twelve delinquents in our basic sample and one additional thirteen-year-old were interviewed in a detention

TABLE 2

SOCIOMETRIC COMPOSITION OF SAMPLE

	Number of Subjects
Isolates	
1. Never chosen	18
2. Chosen once or twice, but by no one whom the boy chose (usually by another isolate) . . .	18
Integrates	
3. Two reciprocal choices or three choices, one reciprocal	11
4. Three or four choices, at least two reciprocal	15
5. More than four choices	10

home where they were awaiting trial. The home was located in an industrial city similar in social composition to our "common man" suburb. In this city there seemed to be no tradition of organized delinquent gangs, so that while most of the juvenile crimes were done by small groups, these groups were very transitory. All the boys interviewed indulged in repetitive car stealing, sometimes associated with burglary and robbery by assault.

Of these ten boys, six came from broken homes. Three additional 15-16-year-olds and one 13-year-old were interviewed in a settlement house in a high delinquency area in Chicago. These boys were members of a semi-delinquent gang worked with by a member of the Chicago Area Project.

None had committed any serious crime as far as was known, but they were highly rebellious, aggressive and vandalistic in the school and the neighborhood. The four boys came from Italian Catholic families with fairly strong extended-family ties. Thus these boys were believed to represent more culturally determined delinquent trends, in children from more stable families.

The chief reason for interviewing these boys was to estimate the influence of the institutional setting on delinquent responses to our questions. The extent to which these interviews were successful in eliminating situational reasons for maintaining a conventional front was rather convincingly demonstrated to the investigator by a series of hot-foots and the like, administered to him during the course of the interviewing. However, in spite of such "frankness" on the part of the boys, their interview responses were more conventionally moral than those obtained in the detention home.

d) Religion and ethnicity.—The ethnic and religious composition of our sample is presented in Table 3.

TABLE 3

RELIGIOUS AND ETHNIC COMPOSITION OF SAMPLE

	Number of Subjects
"Common man" group	
Mexican Catholic	3
Slavic Catholic	5
Italian Catholic	2
North European Catholic	4
Italian Protestant	1
North European or native American Protestant .	21
Upper middle-class group	
Native American or North European Catholic . .	3
Jewish . . .	2
Protestant .	31

e) Intelligence.—The thorniest problem in selection of subjects was the effort to equalize intelligence for our class and sociometric groups. In spite of our efforts, we were not able to fully achieve this within the limits of the schools available to us. The results of an analysis of variance of IQ scores for our various groups is included in Table 4. Scores are based on various group tests routinely administered in the various schools (e.g., the Otis and the Thurstone P.M.A.). Popular children in our sample were significantly higher than isolates, and upper-middle-class children higher than "common man" children, though non-significantly so. Accordingly, we have used covariance analyses for our major tests of group differences in morality.[1]

TABLE 4

ANALYSIS OF VARIANCE OF SOCIAL GROUP DIFFERENCES IN
INTELLIGENCE IN SAMPLE

Effect	Group	Mean	Sum of Squares	df	F	Significance
A. Class	Middle class Lower class	109.7 105.9	268	1	2.54	N.S.
B. Sociometric	Integrates Isolates	111.2 104.4	834	1	7.90	.01
Remaining between			120	11		
Within			6338	60		
Total		107.8	7560	71		
	Delinquents	106.5				

B. Instruments

1. Rationale

It is clear that our conception of morality implies or refers to rather complex thoughts and feelings about action in genuine conflict or

[1] Such intelligence test differences probably are largely a reflection of the social participation differences which we want the groups to represent. We quoted Mead's remark that the g factor in intelligence represented role-taking ability. Our conceptualization of the relation of our moral test to an intellectual test is presented in Chapter V, sections A and D.

crisis situations. Accordingly, we decided to use extensively probed open-ended individual interviews about hypothetical conflict situations which posed genuine dilemmas to educated adults. Some of these situations were adaptations of ones used by Sharp (51) and by Stendler (57).

Such an approach runs counter to some popular maxims of what might be termed "Dick and Jane" child psychology. These maxims tell us that we maximize comprehension and involvement by constructing situations with a same sex, same age hero performing activities which the child is likely to perform.

However, equally popular maxims tell us that children want to be adult and that they become involved in matters which appear to have adult importance. It seemed to us that we could not expect children who were fairly mature to show serious moral involvement in situations which they would view as "kid stuff." The kind of involvement we sought was the kind many of the children expressed in statements like "These are murder," "Boy, you've got some tough questions," etc. We felt it would be easier to analyze qualitatively a case in which the situation demanded more than a child could respond to than to analyze a case in which a child wanted more challenge than the situation could provide.

After pretesting, we were able to select a group of questions which seemed fairly challenging, meaningful and differentiating at all age levels. While some children responded at a primitive and confused or apathetic level, we were not able to construct any stories which did not reflect this trend.

An unexpected benefit emerging from the use of situations conflictful even to adults has been a constant shaking up of the investigator's preconceptions as to "good" and "bad" types of response. It is difficult to convey the extent to which a study like the present one forces an investigator to see his dearest cliches in a new perspective and to organized and reorganize his own moral values.

The questions were originally conceived as presenting a conflict between habitual conformity to a rule or authority as against a utilitarian or "greatest good" response to situational values and social value objects. In accordance with the view of Piaget, and the retrospective feelings of many middle-class liberals, it was felt that the dominant trend of moral development in pre-adolescence and adolescence was an increase in latitudinarian, situationally "flexible" and value-maximizing attitudes.

The situations were also designed specifically to elicit Piaget's sense of "reciprocity," i.e., attitudes of exchange and mutual trust, distributive equality and restitutive punishment. In addition, they were hoped to elicit a "generalized perspective" following G. H. Mead. Our original purpose was to see which of these two latter attitudes would be more related to increased utilitarian flexibility and to general developmental advance.

2. Instruments

The situation and probing questions are presented in Appendix A. Interview responses were tape recorded. Probing questions involving obviously uncomprehended concepts were not repeated for each new situation. A subject might be asked, "Did his father have a right to expect the boy to tell on his brother?", and reply, "No. If his father was expecting Alex to tell, Alex might not tell and his father was waiting and waiting and he might forget." In such a case no further questions involving the direct concept of "legitimate expectations" would be used in other situations. On the other hand, individual responses of interest would be probed in an individual manner, wherever necessary.

On three questions (III, VI, VII) the interviewer disagreed with the child and gave an argument to influence the child to change his mind. This argument was designed to be as "low level" as possible, and was based on a ten-year-old pre-test response. If the child maintained his previous response, a second "high-level" argument was offered to the child.

This procedure had two purposes: first, the assessment of independence of judgment, and secondly, the validation of developmental levels. It was believed that children at a given developmental level would tend to discount a line of thinking if it were really at a much lower developmental level; would tend to accept a line of thinking at their own or a slightly higher level, and would fail to comprehend or attempt to reduce to their own level a higher level argument.

After completing the individual interview, the children were assembled in groups of three and asked to discuss the questions and come to agreement. Each child was in the minority at least once in these "revealed differences" discussions and an effort was made to arrange groups so that each child would be in a minority twice. These group discussions have not been quantitatively analyzed for the thesis.

Finally, the children were given two Q sorts presented in Appendix F. The first is a ranking of how much a number of occupational roles are respected, the second, a ranking of how much the boy wants to be various personal and occupational roles. The placement of each item was probed in a manner similar to the moral situations. Additional free questions on the ideal self and on occupational aspirations were asked. This material has not been quantitatively analyzed for the thesis, but it has been drawn on for conceptual and illustrative purposes.

CHAPTER IV

CONSTRUCTION OF A STAGE SCHEMA OF MORAL DEVELOPMENT:
METHODS AND STATISTICAL CHARACTERISTICS

A. Rationale for Developmental Type Construction

1. Ideal Typological Methods

Our purpose was to set up a general developmental dimension of
morality on a basis other than that of content and strength of various cultural conformities. Various efforts at setting up a pr' . 'formal" dimensions of moral development did not seem to work out well. Accordingly, the
appropriate methodology seemed to be some form of developmental typology.
A typology may be purely conceptual, purely empirical, or a mixture of the
two, termed "ideal" by M. Weber. A purely conceptual typology, such as
that developed by Parsons for values, represents the various permutations
and combinations of concepts which seem important to the typologist. A
purely empirical typology would be represented by a simple-structure multiple factor analysis of between-persons correlations. The ideal typological
method involves observing a great mass of more or less qualitative material
and seeking for joint presence of various elements which have some "understandable" relationship to each other. Thus it involves simultaneous willingness to select out and stress empirical consistencies which can be
coherently interpreted and willingness to revise and reform principles of
observation and interpretation as new empirical patterns seem to emerge.

It is a useful technique in a field in which theory and research

80

are not sufficiently developed to convince us that we know what dimensions might be generally important or that we know how to define such
dimensions operationally in a given field. In the study of age development, it seems to be an almost necessary technique for summarizing, selecting, and interpreting a large number of age tends. Developmental
stage concepts provide us with a semi-descriptive, semi-conceptual background requisite for detailed study and explanation of any particular
age trend.

The nature, function and limitations of the method have been most
clearly and thoughtfully considered by M. Weber in his methodological
writings (65). Weber stresses that the method implies the accentuation
of a certain point of view toward a trait and of certain traits. This
accentuation serves the purpose of synthesizing individual objects or
persons into a unified analytic construct. It also serves the related
purpose of stressing those traits and the interpretation of these traits
which bring out the genetic implication of the object, implications as to
what the object will develop into or become. Thus Weber, taking as an
object "Protestantism," in comparison with other religions, stresses
those elements in it and an interpretation of them which were conducive
to capitalism (66).

Although the "ideal" type is ideal, it is not simply a theoretical
construction. The "spirit of capitalism" is not a construct of the same
type as Parsons' "affectively neutral self-oriented universalistic achievement value-orientation." An ideal type refers to and develops out of the
study and interpretation of concrete historical objects. It must describe
concrete traits observed or defined in non-theoretical terms and the type
must show some empirical fit to each object as a whole.

Thus any student of values will be tempted to come up with a typology of creative, conforming, and rebelling or withdrawing types as have Thomas and Znaniecki (61), Riesman (48), Havighurst and Taba (23), and many others. The trouble with such types is that they describe the person externally in terms of his impact on and relation to his culture and to the observer's values. They do not tell us how the individual thinks, what values he actually holds. There are rebels and conformists in every culture but a "creative" or "rebellious" Zulu would have little in common with a "creative" or "rebellious" Frenchman.

2. Methods for Establishing Developmental Relations between Types

A typological method for setting up a general developmental dimension of morality implies that each type be looked on as more or less a "stage" of development or that each child be viewed as successively moving through each type.

What evidence or method could be used to support such a view? The best evidence would of course be longitudinal, but this was unfeasible. Age differences between the various types would offer some support. However, if the types were fairly numerous, the age range limited, and development not viewed as closely related to physical age and perhaps as often permanently arrested, age differences would not be expected to discriminate much more than the top and bottom types.

The relevant rationale seemed to be suggested by the thinking of L. Guttman (18). This thinking specifies some necessary, though not sufficient, conditions for inferring a developmental sequence. If certain tests or items or dimensions stand in a developmental sequence, with regard to one another, then a certain pattern of associations should hold between them. The finding of such a pattern does not prove that the variables stand in a sequential relation to one another, it merely is consistent with or predictable from such a hypothesis.

Such a pattern in quantitative data is called a "simplex" by Gutt-man. We will not be concerned to present Guttman's full conceptions of the simplex as a form of "radex" factor analysis. The basic aspects we are interested in do not depend upon any particular general mathematical or statistical assumptions and rationale.

The simplest form of a development sequence implies <u>cumulativity</u> and would be represented in dichotomous items by a Guttman scale. If a set of dichotomous items represent a developmental order of difficulty, we would expect the items to form a scale. Thus a calculus item would be unsolvable without algebra, so that we might expect all persons who pass a calculus item to pass an algebra item while all persons who pass the algebra item would not pass the calculus item. If there were a set of items in such a relation to one another, we could predict exactly which items an individual passed from his total score on the total number of items he passed. The items would then be said to form a cumulative scale, with perfect reproducibility.

The kind of developmental variable and types in which we are inter-ested would not be expected to be cumulative in this sense. If we are thinking of developmental stages or modes of thinking, we would expect a higher stage to supersede a lower stage. However, we would expect someone at a given level or stage to use thinking characteristic of the next earli-er level more than thinking characteristic of a still earlier level. In general, we would expect a person to show a steady decrease in level usage as we moved away from his modal level in either direction.

The implication is that each level would correlate most highly with its neighbor(s) and its correlations with other levels would decrease steadily as those levels were increasingly distant from its position in the order of levels. If the matrix of these correlations were arranged in this developmental order, the correlations would decrease in any direction moving away from the main diagonal.

If the relations between levels were dependent purely and solely on their relationships to each other in a developmental hierarchy, we would expect that the correlation between any two levels would disappear if we took into account the correlation of those two levels to an intermediate level. We would expect that the correlation of $Level_1$ with $Level_3$ would be a function of the relation of $Level_1$ to $Level_2$ and of $Level_2$ to $Level_3$, i.e., that the partial correlation $r_{13.2} = 0$. In general this condition would imply that all tetrad differences on a given side of the main diagonal will vanish. This is, of course, a stringent condition which we would only wish to demand if we expect that the relations between levels is due to nothing but developmental hierarchy or complexity.

3. Typological and Development Methods as Evaluative

Both typologies and developmental sequences influence the value people set on the traits which such typologies organize though this is obviously not a final method of evluation of the traits. While the value accorded by typologies seems to us more limited than that given by developmental study, it appears to us to be legitimate for certain purposes.

On the surface, such a procedure may simply appear unscientific, or irrational. Thus, a group of social scientists collect a group of traits, some clearly "bad" and relating to the enemy culture and some

others less bad and try to show that they all form some unitary organization, the "authoritarian personality." Since these traits are bad, then
the opposite traits must be good, traits more or less clearly characterizing the social science culture. Is this not an illustration of the fundamental "authoritarian" mechanism of creating some stereotype of a unitary
personal enemy or bad person onto which to discharge the numerous frustra-
tions to which the culture exposes the unappreciated social scientist?

However, it appears to us that typological clues to evaluation are
not mere stereotypes and that they do offer some legitimate guides in the
evaluation of a trait. Thus, it does help us to achieve a clearer view of
some of the value-implications of a trait to see it in extreme form, either
in relative independence of traits which modify it in most people, or in
the context of traits with which it is often associated. Logically, a certain mode or postulate of valuation characterizing a type need not lead to
certain beliefs with a fairly clearly "good" or "bad" character. However,
if these postulates can lead to this conclusion logically and frequently do
empirically, this has justifiable, if limited value -implications as to the
desirability of cultivating the mode, of valuing.

The alternative mode of evaluation to the typological might be
called the quantitative. This approach takes a trait which most people
will agree is good and then assumes the more of it, the better. Thus, on
the whole it is good to consider many features of a situation before acting,
so one may count the number of alternatives considered by a given subject.
However, for such traits there is almost always a "too much," e.g., the
obsessive personality who considers so many alternatives he never acts.
The quantitator may search for some optimum, "considering just the right
number of alternatives," but he can never hope to define such a golden man,

since it varies with each situation and person.

For almost every simple quantitative trait we attempted to set up in our study, we felt that in one typological context or developmental level it might appear good and at another bad. An example is that of resistance to examiner-pressure which at one typological level seemed to mean "negativism," at another "rigidity," and at still another "autonomy."

On a sheerly quantitative level it would be almost impossible to say how much resistance should be considered reasonable autonomy and how much sheer negativism.

As opposed to approaches which assume we know what traits are good and attempt to predict or create them, a typological set toward evaluating traits attempts to reach new perspectives for evaluating traits. This is particularly true of developmental evaluation. The developmental method takes a number of traits and attempts to put them in sequence in which the higher presuppose all the lower. Thus, when we give an individual credit for the higher we can presuppose, to some extent, the lower. Thus, we concentrate not on the general value of the trait in isolated functioning, but simply on its value relative to general development.

Such value is basically of a "present-absent" variety. Some presence of a given trait may be necessary for further development, but this does not imply it is an unlimited good and the more of it, the better. We can all agree that some resistance to pressure sometimes is "good," though we cannot say how much of it is good.

A developmental context of evaluation may take into account the fact that "excesses" of an attitude may serve a positive function in the development of the individual and the group. If we find that a given trait which we would have thought was undesirable seems to be a precondition to a higher trait, i.e., is present to some degree with higher traits and is absent without them, we weigh it accordingly.

As an example, we felt this to be the case with "moral punitiveness," which seems to be controlled or transcended at a higher level and absent at lower levels. But "mercifulness" can be observed or differentiated from a lack of interest in justice or from a costless sympathy only by expressions indicating some familiarity and identification with punitive attitudes. And our developmental "right" to weight the attitude of mercy higher than that of punitive justice is based on the fact that the attitude of mercy, by definition, presupposes that of justice while the reverse is not true. Thus, we can make a developmental weighting of these traits regardless of just how much punitive justice or just how much mercy are desirable in the individual and in society.

What the value of "development" itself is or how heavily any given person's evaluation of a trait should be based on its developmental status is a question beyond the scope of this work. Our method of developmental weighting will probably be responded to in fact by readers as implying that the developmentally higher is the more valuable. We tend to share this assumption in the sphere of morality. We even believe that in some sense the moral right may be defined in terms of the development of the self and of others and that the "highly developed" morality is the morality conducive to further development. However, we wish to justify not the value of the development but the method of assigning developmental weights.

B. Actual Procedures Used in Setting Up
Developmental Typology

1. Case Analyses

When we attempted to construct empirically a developmental type, we selected from a great deal of qualitative material certain age-related characteristics which seemed to cluster somewhat independently of age and to have some understandable coherent relationships to each other. Construction of the type proceeded in terms of the construction of other types, such that there was some plausible basis for moving developmentally from one type to the next.

When we started, we noticed a number of rather striking responses clustering together in more than one individual, responses which did not seem to have a purely conventional coherence or interpretation in the culture or in the group of children as a whole. There were a limited number of plausible "principles" of thought and evaluation of which they could be expressions. We found the individuals possessing this trait-cluster occurring in various age and class groups, so that the cluster seems to represent something more than common exposure to some environmental cluster of stimuli or cluster of cliches.

As we examined the detailed responses which these various tentative types made and considered the types in relation to each other, we of necessity began to revise initial conceptions both of what was important and what was developmentally advanced or retarded in such responses. As we developed new conceptualizations of underlying principles in the types and new considerations as to what was important, we look for new responses as foci of observation and attempt to use other individuals as focal points or to include new individuals in our types. What before seemed a "mixed

type"now seemed a pure type, or vice versa. At the end of this research
stage we had made case analyses of each child, with each case analysis
attempting to support or revise our interpretation of the basic features
of the type to which it seemed closest.

2. The General Schema

The number of types we came out with was eventually rather arbitrary, and undoubtedly determined by the limits of variation of our particular population.

Too few types seemed to us worse than too many, since too many
may be simplified but too few cannot be refined. A two- or three-stage
schema almost implies that the bottom stage includes all the primitive
responses and the top all the advanced, or that one type is simply defined as not having the traits of the other. Too few stages tends to
leave us with purely cognitive age differences, too many with purely cultural and personality differences.

Our final schema is a compromise. On a more cognitive and global
development level, we have three major stages. Each stage is subdivided
into two types in terms of more attitudinal factors. While the content
of the types will be elaborated in Chapters V, VI, and VII, we may present
the type labels here to indicate the schema:

Level I.—Values reside in external happenings or consequences rather than
persons or rules.

    0. Heteronomous authority and punishment orientation.

    1. Naive and egoistic orientation.

Level II.—Value resides in good and bad roles and in maintenance of the
conventional order of reward and punishment.

    2. Approval-oriented "good boys."

    3. Authority system maintaining orientation.

<u>Level III.</u>—Value resides in the conformity of the self to some shared
    standard of judgment and defined rights and duties.

    4. Legalistic classifying or conventional orientation.

    (5. Other-directed utilitarians—later pooled mainly with 4.)

    (6. Contractual legalists—later pooled with 4.)

    7. Conscience, principle, or mutual respect orientation.

The division into subtypes, while primarily representing attitudinal orientations, is also intended to represent some transitional cognitive developmental material. Thus a child dominantly   type 0 would be expected to
develop next into a type 3, but such development would involve some use of
modes of thought characteristic of types 1 and 2, which are implied in type
3 thinking.

3. Coding

    We arrived at this schema, with several tentative "principles"
characteristic of each type, and picked out a few good representatives of
each type. Then we went back to code sheets in which we had listed all
the varieties of response to any given question or sub-aspect of a situation, defining these responses purely in terms of surface content. We took
each such response and tried to interpret it as representing some principle
characterizing one of our types, even placing responses made only by 3 or 4
individuals if they could be given a plausible interpretation. "Cliches"
with no clear interpretation, such as "He shouldn't do it because its against
the law" were counted as only half-units. Such items were assigned to the
lowest level type which used them.

    The resulting placing of idea content is given in Appendix C which
gives our coding schema, somewhat abbreviated for the sake of presentational
economy. On this basis we coded or assigned to a type each thought content
produced by each individual on the moral judgment question. The range of

the sum of such coded contents for completed interviews was 43 to 117. Six interviews were used which were incomplete for various reasons.

4. Rating

We wished to be able to determine the relations of each of our moral situations to the other. Accordingly, we made up sheets to guide a global rating of each total response to a given situation as belonging to one of the types (Appendix C). These ratings are based on intuitive weightings by the rater of the various elements included and imply some feel for the types as a whole and some experience of the range of possible responses.

5. Reliabilities in Coding and Rating

Measures of interjudge agreement between global ratings by the investigator and by another rater of children's responses to a given situation are presented in Table 5. Time allowed only two situations and about one-half the children to be jointly rated.

There is a fairly noticeable difference between agreement on the two questions, which is probably not random. This may be due to the differential values of the questions in representing the typology.[1] It may also be due to increased learning of our system by the second judge, since it was rated last and after considerable discussion.

In a study in which the investigator systematically rates subjects already intensively studied, it is important to limit and assess the halo effect. While this could not be done systematically, we did inspect the scattergrams of association between the two questions in the ratings of

---

[1]The more agreed upon question better represents an individual's total performance as indicated by its loading in the factor analysis presented in Table 9.

TABLE 5

PRODUCT MOMENT CORRELATIONS RELEVANT TO THE RELIABILITY
OF MORAL JUDGMENT ASSESSMENTS[a]

	N	Correlation	Significance
Inter—judge agreement on global rating of question II	44	.64	.01
Inter—judge agreement on global rating of question VII	36	.79	.01
Correlation of total score on detailed coding system and on global ratings	.87	.91	.01

[a]The measure is based on the assumption that the types may be assigned numerical values as a developmental scale.

each judge. The two questions seemed to be no less correlated in the blind ratings of the second judge than in the ratings of the investigator.

The coding operation, as opposed to the ratings, appeared to be concrete and objective enough to obviate assessing reliabilities. The close relationship between the two methods of assessment is indicated in Table 5.

C. The Degree to Which Our Ideal Types Actually
Describe a Population of Individuals in
a Representative Fashion

1. Typological Selectivity and
Theoretical Selectivity

Like any scientific description, ideal types are selective. Thus the types we developed are focused on responses which seemed to be in the moral domain, which seemed to have genetic implications, and which seemed relevant to the various moral theories we were considering. While selective they are not abstract and a priori in the sense of conceptual types such as these mentioned previously or even Piaget's moral types. We started with apparent consistencies in individuals rather than starting with a theoretical schema.

The primary "bias" in our ideal-typological selectivity probably stems from the fact that some people are more consistent, understandable, involved in our subject, and theoretically interesting than others. Accordingly, "the principles" in the thinking of such persons are stressed more in a typological conceptualization than are those of other persons.

Such "bias" does not have the implications of bias in a survey of distribution of attitudes in the American population. We are not interested in the actual proportion of the population which falls in each of our types or fails to fit any of our types.

The representativeness we require is one which allows us to take the principles and analyses useful in comprehending development in our "extreme" or prototypical cases as more or less useful in comprehending development of any American child in this age range. A "genuine" type might be very rare and superficially quite unlike most of the population yet be very important in explaining development in general. The use made by Freud of the now rare hysterical type in explaining personality pathology in general is a case in point.

2. Recurrence and Representativeness

In succeeding chapters, we shall analyze our types and consider the implications of these analyses for moral development in general. We will present sample responses to justify such analyses. How "representative" are such responses?

It is very difficult to specify criteria for this kind of representativeness. The most illuminating and "quotable" responses are usually
the most unusual or idiosyncratic. A principle of thinking we believe
common to the type is caught in one response to one question in one child,
in another for another. The coding schema represents an effort to systematically interpret or classify fairly recurrent responses in the interviews. However, the more recurrent and "cliché-like" the response, the
more must any interpretation of its underlying meaning be questionable.
This interpretation rests largely on the simultaneous expression of a wide
variety of such responses included in a single type, together with the
illuminating remarks made by children scoring high in the type. It
seemed to be a fact that quantitative consistency in the type was associated with qualitative extremeness in expressing its underlying "principle,"
as the cases in Appendix D will illustrate.

3. Selectivity in Typological (Q) and in Dimensional (R) Methods

This "bias" in typology at the qualitative case level is similar
to the "bias" or selective factor in quantitative methods of typology
like Q technique (59).

As opposed to R technique, typological methods imply an interest
in consistencies which are not inferable from manifest similarity in content of various responses. In typological work, the fact that a number
of persons made both responses A and B is interpreted in terms of some
general knowledge about these persons and a whole host of other responses
which they have made. Associations between persons would be expected to
stress "formal" similarities in modes of thought and evaluation which
could be applied to any content situation or question. Such modes or

"orientations" might appear more clearly in response to one item for one member of the type, more clearly on another item for another member of the type, so that an interest in items is secondary.

The responses which tend to be ignored in analyses based on a Q typology are those of persons who belong to "mixed types" or to no type at all. These persons tend to be unilluminating, however, since they tend to be apparently inconsistent or random in their responses to the material. Some kind of intrapersonal consistency is a precondition for a high correlation with other persons and may be lacking in people who do not correlate with others.

This selection of consistent persons for descriptive purposes in "Q" may be contrasted with the selection of "consistent" items in "R" factor methods (63). R factors based on associations between items in moral judgment would be expected to stress similarities in content of the items, similarities perceived by or responded to by all subjects. Just as in "Q" associations, persons who are inconsistent across items would tend to be ignored in "R" associations, items which are "inconsistent" or diversely interpreted across the population of persons tend to be ignored. For some types these items might be highly associated with each other, for others they might be negatively associated or unassociated. Thus the items which were best or most important from a typological or person-defining point of view might be worst from an "R technique" point of view.

In typological methods, we start with relatively few persons and many responses and use procedures to further reduce the number of persons considered to define the area of interest. In R, we start with relatively few items and many persons and use procedures to further reduce the number of items considered in defining the area.

4. Application of Typological Concepts to
New Cases and in Theorizing

However, the functions of and criteria for an ideal typology are clearly quite different from that of Thurstone's multiple factor analysis, whether used on persons or item correlations. The practical function of Thurstone's multiple factor analysis for future work is to reduce the number of tests to be given to an individual in order to predict his scores on a battery of tests.

The function of typological reduction or selection of persons is not really that of economizing future observations. It is not important to use the same persons, or even the same items, in future work. Rather it allows us to select focal persons and observations to develop principles of interpretation in a given domain.

Weber says that every genuine application of an "established" ideal-typology to a new individual implies a detailed study of the particular individual and of the empirical relations which hold in a particular case, relations which held up or were testable independently of assumptions about the type. The type functions as a selective frame of reference and background of interpretation in such study of relations in the individual. It is the latter which is explanatory, not the act of subsumption under the type.

Thus ideal type-construction implies that the types will be used to interpret further cases observed in full detail, perhaps using different techniques of observation, not that the typology will be used like R factor analysis to reduce the number of observations or the analytic interpretation of them requisite for further cases.

Thus the criterion of descriptive parsimony basic to multiple factor analysis is inappropriate to our typological efforts. So are criteria of truth and predictability applicable to experimental theories.

What is important is rather that the consistencies derived from our conception of our types be in some sense "real" consistencies and not artifactual ones. This does not mean that we assume a one-to-one relation of our types to individual personalities. We do not expect all the variances in a person to be deducible from his dominant type-membership. We do assume, however, that the important strains to consistency within individuals is largely describable in terms of the consistencies of the types. Stated differently, we assume that many of the traits related in our type conceptions are genuinely related to each other and not merely joined by accidents or ecological regularities in the environment.

The reader's conviction that this is true must rest necessarily largely on unquantifiable impressions.

Appendix D and the detailed interpretation of the types in later chapters will allow the reader to get a general sense of the degree of unity to the various orientations in cases favorable to the typology. The cases in Appendix D allow the reader to see these orientations with regard to a particular situation and also to follow some representative children through the series of situations. In Appendix E, we have reproduced a set of interviews in Little Rock on desegregation to illustrate the wide applicability of the types.

D. The Reality of Stages and Criteria of the Validity of a Developmental Scale

In concluding our methodological discussion, it should be noted that the question of the reality or descriptive power of our types is independent of the validity of our situations and coding schema as a test or assessment of moral development. Claims for the latter may to some extent hold regardless of any views about stages or types. Intelligence test items have value as such regardless of whether they indicate stages in the development of thought.

The only requisites for a test of moral development are the same as those for intelligence, e.g., the following:

a) That it be developmental in nature or developmentally differentiating.

b) That various tests or situations for its assessment intercorrelate substantially and fairly uniformly so that it cannot be broken down into other factors.

c) That the test have some face relationship to the concept at issue, e.g., morality.

d) That it show some correlation with whatever external criteria be available, though no such criteria can be definitive either for morality or intelligence since these concepts are not defined by any external criterion.

The remainder of this chapter and the following chapter are devoted to analyzing the degree to which our test and concept of morality meets these requirements, and the implications of such a variable of morality.

Chapters VI through VIII are devoted to elaborating the types as types, and exploring their implications for theories of moral development. The reasoning of these chapters is partially based on assuming that our types are genuine types.

E. Statistical Characteristics of the Developmental Typology

1. Developmental Characteristics of Type Intercorrelations

The first and most important question we may ask is "To what extent do our six types represent a developmental sequence or hierarchy?"

In order to ascertain this we calculated the product-moment intercorrelations between the types as required by the rationale presented in section A-2. The results are presented in Table 6-A. These correlations represent the relations between percentage use of one type response and percentage use of another type response by each individual in our sample.

The correlations are unlike those described by Guttman between abilities in that they are often negative. These negative relations would be expected from the fact that the scores being correlated are based on percentage of total responses, since we did not wish the correlations to be heavily biased by the factor of general verbality or number of responses. We were not interested in the absolute size of these correlations, but in their pattern or relationship to one another.[1]

The basic aspect of interest in the matrix is the general tendency of the correlations to diminish as we move away from the main diagonal.[2] We had had conceptual and operational difficulty in differentiating original Types 5 and 6 from Types 3 or 4 in a systematic general way. Since the correlations of Types 5 and 6 did not add particular clarity to the picture, we decided to ignore them or treat them as equivalent to Level 4 in subsequent analyses. Type 5 (original Type 7) on the other hand was a fairly clearly conceptualized type with fairly clear "high" developmental aspects so that it was retained.[3]

---

[1]As there was no major purpose for which it was important to know the "true" amount of association between any two types, there seemed no reason to derive correlations from the actual frequency of response in each level rather than from percentaging and eliminating one degree of freedom.

[2]The negativity of these relations makes it impossible to apply the test of the vanishing of the tetrad differences. However, if only same-sign correlation tetrads are considered, these do not tend to vanish, though they are quite low.

[3]The correlations of Level 5 are "distorted" by the low population mean upon it, compared with its high standard deviation. This reflects a

TABLE 6

INTERCORRELATION MATRIX FOR PERCENTAGE USAGE OF
TYPES OF MORAL JUDGMENT

A. Original Matrix

	0	1	2	3	4	5	6	7
0	x							
1	55	x						
2	-41	-19	x					
3	-52	-41	18	x				
4	-52	-58	09	00	x			
5	-60	-58	-03	14	37	x		
6	-48	-56	-30	13	45	39	x	
7	-37	-43	-29	-07	23	41	68	x

B. Reduced Matrix of Finally Selected Levels

	0	1	2	3	4	5
0	x					
1	55	x				
2	-41	-19	x			
3	-52	-41	18	x		
4	-52	-58	09	00	x	
5	-37	-43	-29	-07	23	x

In this smaller matrix (Table 6-B) we notice that the expected decrease of correlations away from the main diagonal either going down columns or across rows. The only two exceptions in the fifteen relative positions which a developmental order would generate, are the correlations

bimodal distribution with the major mode at 0 and the other mode at the high extreme of the distribution, expressing the typological nature of the variable. Thus we would expect the correlation of 5 with 0 to be more highly negative, but while the sum of the cross products on an interval scale to 11 is only 19, Level 5 mean is so low relative to its standard deviation that a high negative association cannot result. The scattergram distribution has the form of an L rather than a negative slope.

of Type 5 with Types 0 and 1 which are algebraically higher than those of Type 4 with these variables.

We may also note in Table 6-B that the only positive correlations are between Types 0 and 1, Types 2 and 3, and Types 4 and 5. This offers some justification for our looking at these couplets as sub-types within three over-all developmental levels.

This fit to our schema is not too surprising since we undertook throughout our type-formation and informal analyses of data to set up levels which seemed to have such developmental properties. The fit is that of intuitive conception of empirical relations in a body of data to a systematic quantitation of these relations in the same data.

Additional evidence of the developmental nature of the coding schema is provided by the analysis of variance of age differences presented in Table 7. In this analysis, we have weighted percentage usage of each type by the score of the type, i.e., from 0 to 5. The resulting age differences on this score are significant beyond the .001 level.

An interpretation of these age differences as not merely representing superficial verbal sophistication rests on several kinds of evidence, which are more fully considered in the next chapter. The first is evidence of within-type consistency implying that the levels indicate not mere familiarity with adult cliches and modes of thought. The second is the evidence of sequentiality between types. If certain concepts and attitudes must go through sequences of qualitatively differentiatible levels, these levels cannot be looked on as simply levels of familiarity with cultural cliches. The third are various forms of behavioral evidence.

TABLE 7

ANALYSIS OF VARIANCE OF GROUP DIFFERENCES ON
MORAL JUDGMENT SCORE[a]

Effect	Group	Mean Score	Sum of Squares	df	F	Level
A. Class	Middle class Lower class	222.0 196.5	11,679	1	5.23	.05
B. Sociometric	Integrates Isolates	252.0 166.4	131,256	1	58.8	.001
C. Age	10 13 16	130.2 238.4 259.2	231,208	2	51.8	.001
A. x B.			1,390	1		
A. x C.			829	2		
B. x C.			901	2		
A. x B. x C.			13,925	2	3.12	.10
Within			133,945	60		
Total		209.2	525,133	71		
Delinquency	Delinquents Lower class 16's	155.8 240.6		22	t- 3.28	.01

[a]Bartlett's test indicates that the heterogeneity of variance is
well within the limits of chance (p = .50).

2. Typological Characteristics of the Developmental Levels

To what extent does our 5-level coding schema represent a set of 5
unitary orientations and to what extent is it merely a collection of various independent bits of verbal behavior of varying degrees of complexity?

One aspect of the question is the extent to which the bits of verbal behavior cluster meaningfully together with regard to a particular situation so as to imply some central unitary orientation. The second aspect
of the question is the extent to which such an orientation is carried
through various situations.

We have not yet performed statistical analyses to answer the first question, since it seemed to have a lower priority than other statistical problems.

A slight idea of the degree to which a type label really may characterize individual children's orientations to our situations is provided by Table 8. Table 8 indicates the amount of usage of a type by children for whom that type was modal. A rough judgment of this table may be provided if we consider a "null hypothesis" that no children have any set toward any of the six levels. In such a case, we would expect the frequency of usage of any level by those for whom it was modal to differ little from the total sample population mean for the item. Such is clearly not the case. Classifying each person in terms of his modal type implies, with a few exceptions, that the person is at least one standard deviation above the mean in usage of that type. If we assumed normality, this would imply that he is in the top .158 per cent of the population on the given level. Since there is a six-variable classification available, we would expect a good classificatory system to be able to place each person classified in the top one-sixth of the population on the variable used to define him. The relatively low correlations between our six levels offers some further evidence for viewing them as independent categories or types.

3. Factor Analytic Evidence for Moral Development as Trans-situational

Assuming some unity within each of our six moral orientations within any given situation, and assuming they form a developmental hierarchy, we may ask to what extent such orientations are consistent across situations. We are concerned not so much with typological consistency as with developmental consistency. Is someone often "high" in moral development also

TABLE 8

NUMBER OF CHILDREN FOR WHOM EACH MORAL TYPE IS MODAL
DISTRIBUTED ACCORDING TO PERCENTAGE USAGE
OF THAT TYPE

Type	0	1	2	3	4	5
65–70%	2					
60–65%	3	2				
55–60%				1		
50–55%	1		1	3		
45–50%			2	3		
40–45%	4	2	5	5	2	
35–40%	3	3	7	5	2	3
30–35%	1	2	8	5	2	
25–30%	1	1	5	2		
Total N = 86	15	10	28	24	6	3

B. Percentage Usage of Types by the Total Sample						
Mean	17.2	15.6	20.8	19.0	10.5	4.3
Sigma	16.8	12.6	10.5	12.6	11.6	11.0

often "low" within our schema?

The matrix of intercorrelations of the global ratings of nine situations and an unrotated centroid factor analysis of these correlations is presented in Table 9. We have left our first factor unrotated as a best approximation to a G factor. Its rather uniform and fairly high loadings indicate a high degree of trans-situational consistency on our rating system.

If situations have no general importance in defining the moral orientation, we would expect there to be only one significant factor. Our second factor is certainly not very impressive.

TABLE 9

INTERCORRELATION MATRIX FOR MORAL JUDGMENT SITUATIONS AND
LOADINGS OF THE FIRST TWO UNROTATED FACTORS

	I	II	III	IV	V	VI	VII	VIII	IX	Factor I	Factor II
I	x	.59	.62	.64	.45	.40	.50	.49	.75	.67	-.47
II	.59	x	.44	.44	.28	.31	.48	.37	.33	.58	-.21
III	.62	.44	x	.59	.63	.56	.69	.44	.62	.80	-.11
IV	.64	.44	.59	x	.40	.56	.53	.51	.51	.73	-.15
V	.45	.28	.63	.40	x	.64	.44	.66	.55	.71	.22
VI	.40	.31	.56	.56	.64	x	.71	.75	.57	.79	.46
VII	.50	.48	.69	.53	.44	.71	x	.52	.41	.75	.11
VIII	.49	.37	.44	.51	.66	.75	.52	x	.51	.75	.35
IX	.75	.33	.62	.51	.55	.57	.41	.51	x	.76	-.18

To assess its significance we used the easily calculated, though conservative criterion recommended by P. Vernon and given in Thomson's text (62). This criterion is that more than half of the loadings of a factor be at least twice the size of the standard error of that loading. The standard error is given by Burt's empirical formula:

$$\frac{(1 - l^2)\sqrt{n}}{\sqrt{N(n - r + 1)}}$$

where l = loading, N = number of persons, n = number of tests, r = ordinal number of the factor. Only four of the nine loadings are larger than twice their standard error, so that by this criterion, the second factor should be rejected.

Whether or not we should reject the second factor, the factor analysis does seem to indicate a relatively content-free dimension involved in our global ratings.

CHAPTER V

INDIVIDUAL CONSISTENCIES AND SOCIAL GROUP DIFFERENCES AS
EVIDENCE OF A GENERAL MORAL DIMENSION OF DEVELOPMENT

In our first chapter we rested the whole case for the psychological usefulness of the concept of the moral on the existence of some individual consistency in moral level across various value situations or items.
The case seems to us somewhat analogous to that of intelligence. If there
were not something like a g factor in various intellectual tests, it would
be pointless to invoke a concept of intelligence, however such a concept
be ultimately defined and explained. Without the empirical existence of
such a factor, we would perhaps conceptualize and measure intellectual
functioning in terms of reaction times, habit strengths and the memory
drum as was done before Binet and Spearman.

We do not dream that our first factor represents an order in the
domain of values equivalent to that which Binet and Spearman found in the
domain of abilities. Were such wide ranging consistencies to be found in
the values domain, they would have appeared long before the present research. Nevertheless, the consistency we have found may aid in providing
some focus in a field in which roughly the same items have been used to
indicate the existence of different class subcultures and values (12),
the intellectual level of the child (1), and fundamental social development
of the child (44), etc.

Before considering the actual implications of consistency in our
developmental "scale" of morality, some analysis along the lines just

106

mentioned is required. In particular, we need to clarify the relation of the consistency of moral level we have found to the consistencies we would expect from various cognitive or emotive conceptualizations of verbal morality.

A. The Intellectual Conformity Approach
to Verbal Morality

We considered in our first chapter, utilitarian views of moral development as the development of a general practical intelligence which is often considered today as an aspect of "ego strength." From another view, responses to our questions may be purely verbal, so that we might expect them to represent a general ability to learn and use cultural cliches or concepts correctly. From either of these points of view, any general intercorrelations found in verbal moral materials should be accounted for by one or more factors of intelligence in general.

The reasonableness of an interpretation of moral verbalizations in terms of intelligence appears when we consider that some of the concepts or explanations required of our subjects are used in intelligence tests. The comprehension subtest of the Wechsler Intelligence Scale for Children asks such questions as "Why should one keep one's promise," "Why do we have senators and congressmen," "What should you do if you break a borrowed plaything," etc.

The legitimacy of viewing responses to such items as indicating intelligence rests on the fact that everyone in America is confronted with the same laws, the same government, and the same basic prohibitions. The answers scored corred on the W.I.S.C. are those which imply seeing these institutions "objectively" or "from the point of view of society," in terms of slogans with general currency and import.

Insofar as everyone may be assumed to have a set toward finding general or objective reasons for social usages, differential success on the W.I.S.C. Comprehension Scale could be based on differential reasoning ability in ascertaining consequences of general import related to these usages. Our interest was rather in ascertaining whether the individual had such a set, and in defining it. The intellectual skill involved in implementing the set was rather irrelevant to our purpose.

However, it might be argued that the difference between our levels which we saw as qualitative differences in set were really merely differences in skill in conforming to the objective set expected in our culture. Alternatively, it might be argued that genuine moral level or set differences did exist but that they simply reflected differences in intellectual level. In either case, the consistency found in our items would be a byproduct of general intellectual ability.

1. The Difference between a Moral Set and an Intellectual Test Set to Verbal Moral Choices

The notion of a pure ability factor implies that the individual's feelings about an object or symbol have nothing to do with his handling of it. It implies that the verbal choices of our subjects would be made relatively independently of their actual feelings toward the social objects and acts involved.

In addition, an individual's set to ability tests is situation-specific. In each question he is out to win, regardless of what he did in the last situation. If an individual insists on the same mode of solution to two problems, he is merely being "rigid" or showing "the Einstellung effect."

There are qualitative indicators in our interviews that the individual's orientation to our problems is in part a cognitive or test-taking one. In its most naive form, this is indicated by the 65 per cent of the 10-year-olds who, when asked "Is there a right answer to these questions and who knows it?" replied that "You know the right answers because you have them in the book there behind the questions." In spite of initial explanations of "research" and the researcher's status, several asked if they were being graded. For such children, questions might be hard, not in the sense of implying difficult moral decisions, but in the sense that, as case 10 says, "They don't get them right if they're not good thinkers, or if they are always worrying about stuff or just play with things like I'm doing with the microphone now and then they don't get their answers right."

While there are cognitive and affectively neutral elements to a moral set toward the right, they are obviously different from this. A moral set involves doing justice to felt values in the situation rather than the achievement or success in the display of ability regardless of such felt values. It involves consistency of one decision with decisions made in other situations, even at the cost of appearing externally in error. Moral difficulty implies difficulty in making a choice which will maintain values believed in by the self in a conflict situation. Test-taking difficulty implies difficulty in predicting the response marked correct by the tester.

We would expect the predictive or test-taking set toward our moral questions to be related to a general tendency to choose in terms of getting the external reward which is best for the self in a particular situation. When the boy just quoted is asked whether to tell on a brother, in question II, he answers, "In one way he shouldn't tell on him and in one way he should.

If he doesn't tell, his father would be made and if he does tell, his father might get mad too and give both of them a licking." The difficulty in choice is simply the difficulty of predicting punishment; it is not the difficulty of maintaining values which contradict each other in a particular situation.

2. Expectations as to Choice Patterns If These were Determined by an Intellectually Conforming Set

While such a boy is oriented to "getting the right answer," he is very naive as to what the right answer is in the moral sphere. It is possible that a more intelligent or an older boy might have the same basic set, but realize that it is not acceptable to say that he merely wants to guess the examiner's answer or that he is motivated mainly by punishment avoidance in conforming to others. Primary differences between boys would not be differences in set to the various choices involved, they would be differences in ability to implement this set.

How can we ascertain whether the dominant set of most of our subjects to our choice situations is really that we have called the intellectual conformity set?

In purest form, such a set presupposes that there is some cultural right answer to each of our choice situations, in spite of its denial by the critical and scholarly. Surely if most adults and adolescents are motivated to seek a "right answer" outside themselves to such questions, it is likely that a high degree of consensus or a "right answer" will exist for our conflict situations. The very difficulty which the author had in finding conflict situations in which one alternative was not overwhelmingly chosen indicates such consensus.

Given the more ambiguous choices involved in our situations, we could treat the "right" answers as those given by the majority of our oldest group. This is essentially the logic used in scoring the less precise answers in an intelligence test, such as the Comprehension subtest of the W.I.S.C. If we found strong age differences, and found a pattern of uniform intercorrelations between the actual dichotomous choices on each of our situations, we would feel fairly justified in inferring that the cognitive task set was the dominant one operating in our verbal situations.

C. The Emotive or Values Approach

At the opposite extreme from the cognitive approach would be an emotive view of moral judgments as simply expressing the habits and feelings of the judger about the acts or objects in question. In the case of a choice between objects or acts, the one which is more strongly valued by the self is chosen. One would tend to make this assumption if one were studying moral choices from the point of view of learning theory, psychoanalysis, or culturology or any theory primarily concerned with content or attitude strength.

1. The Meaning of the Values Approach
to Moral Choices

The basic datum of choice in such a view we might term neutrally a "value." By a value is meant merely a definable class of objects or class of acts which has a valence, whether this valence be viewed as derived from a drive, a habit strength, or whatever.

Such a value can be defined both in terms of the individual and in terms of a group or subculture. Groups or subcultures would be expected to have different values or assign different modal preference strengths to various classes of acts and objects. Individual differences in values

would be expected to be determined by the strength of the value in the
child's subculture, and by the effectiveness of the training of the value
in the child by relevant socializing agents.

Usually users of the values approach assume in addition that a value
is oriented to as desirable as well as desired, and is to some extent ration-
alized, generalized, and systematized. In ordinary use of the term "values,"
we imply an orientation intermediate between sheer factual desire and a
moral orientation. If we say we value art, it means more than saying that
we desire to look at or buy paintings, as we desire to eat, sleep, or
scratch ourselves. We feel that it is good that others, too, like art and
that there are reasons for liking it which more or less form part of a
system organizing our preference.

On the other hand, we do not feel it is a duty to like art, and
perhaps feel that our artistic activities have no claim to interfere with
our duties. We do not condemn a person who is indifferent to the value of
art. Neither do we ordinarily feel a need to be rigorously consistent in
our values. The experience of rating such a set of values as Morris's
"Paths of Life" is convincing as to the disparity of value-orientations
which can be simultaneously appealing. As opposed to choosing between
alternative courses of action in a moral situation, such ratings seem almost
like selecting among divergent ethnic dishes for a cosmopolitan dinner.

The particular level at which the value orientation is most apparent is that of sub-group differences within a society. The mixture of a
feeling of legitimacy to our own group-organized and systematized preferences together with some tolerance for the organized preferences of other
groups seems usually to be connoted by the concept of "value."

2. The Values Set to Our Items

We may raise the question then as to whether the set of our subjects was one of expressing "value-orientations," whether as to the desired or the desirable.

Since our items are not "projective" nor even questions of "interests," we cannot assume a determination of choice by value strength. However, it might be that the set of many children to our choices was simply one of allowing expression to their own existing values and emotional attitudes.

Such a set would involve disbelief or lack of interest in a culturally general right answer to our choices. Indeed, many of our 13- and 16-year-olds, especially lower-class children, did say that "Everyone has their own opinion" about the questions. Such children might say to the interviewer, "Wouldn't you do it? or "I don't know whether you're a Catholic or not, but that's a sin." Such remarks indicate that the boy sees the interviewer as another person with his own possibly differing biases, and has no interest in justifying his own attitudes on an "objective" or "absolute" or "rational" basis. Choice is determined by the given values of the self or of the sub-group, with no effort to adapt them or to justify them in the given situation. The response is not adjusted to or "correctable by" an expert as is an answer to an intelligence test item.

With such a set, our items would not be expected to elicit any verbalization that our choice situations are difficult. There would be some need to maintain the self-attitudes, but no need to make a "correct" decision as opposed to a decision that the self with its given values would want to make. The test would be "Would I and other normal, noncriminal people want to act this way?" not "Am I doing justice to all the values I believe in which might be operating in this situation?"

An example of this former attitude would be this 16-year-old's response by case 59 to question III about stealing a drug for one's wife:

> "Yeah. If my wife was dying, I'd do the same thing too."
> (Is it his duty?)
> "No, but if my wife was dying I would."
> (Would a good person do it?)
> "What do you mean, good?"
> (Trying to do right?)
> "Well, I don't know. It depends on how much he likes his wife."

Where the first set toward choice was purely predictive, this set seems to be purely expressive of the attitudes and values in fact held toward particular objects. In general, the boys expressing this set so directly are quite impulsive and frankly egoistic in their thinking. However, it is conceivable that the values expressed be less impulsive and yet the basic set the same.

3. The Significance of Establishing Respondent Set in Studying Group Differences

The significance of the difference in our concepts of desire orientations, value orientations, and moral orientations is illustrated by the endless controversies about the conformity of lower-class children to "middle-class values." Studies, like those of Havighurst and Taba, reveal that lower-class children are rated lower in "moral virtues" like honesty, service, loyalty, responsibility than are middle-class children. To this the sociologist, striving to be impartial, replies that these are middle-class values, and that the moral conformity of the lower-class children should be evaluated in terms of lower-class values.

The difficulty to this approach is to establish the conditions under which class differences in behavior and verbal responses indicate differences in value systems. Surely because there are class differences in ratings of the virtues mentioned, we are not justified in saying that the lower class has a value system organized around the values of dishonesty, disservice, disloyalty and irresponsibility.

Since sociologists are middle class and educated, the value dimensions or polarities they set up may tend to be those around which value controversies center among the educated.

Repeated efforts have been made to structure lower-class attitude response in terms of middle-class dichotomies and patterns of thought, whether of political "liberalism-conservatism" or child-rearing "permissiveness-authoritarianism." Because the lower class may favor control of certain economic functions or allow children to stay out later at night they are assumed to be more "liberal" than middle-class groups. On another question or in another study it appears that the lower class is more "conservative" or "authoritarian" because they believe in repressing civil rights of dissidents or in spanking disobedient children.

The actual conclusion to be drawn may be that the thought structure or dimension "liberalism-conservatism" is largely irrelevant to characterizing class differences. The important difference is perhaps that the middle-class person tends to have basic modes of thinking and valuing which tend to lead him to dichotomize the world in liberal-conservative terms, whereas the lower-class person tends to have other modes of thought and feeling insofar as he is psychologically "lower class."

Even efforts to see the lower class as having different value-categories than the middle class seem to end up reading in middle-class interpretations to lower-class responses without much empirical justification.

We may give as an example the stimulating and important work of

Cohen in which he suggests that the lower class has an ethic of reciprocity as opposed to the middle-class "Protestant ethic" of individual responsibility (12). By the ethic of reciprocity, he apparently means the
liberal ideology of group belongingness, togetherness, warmth, and mutual
aid.

The lower-class boys are more willing to let a friend pay their
way to a group event without repaying it (12, p. 106). Cohen interprets
this as indicating that the lower class is oriented to a spirit of spontaneous giving and guiltless acceptance as against being oriented to
rational exchange and individual responsibility.

However, the value configuration which may lead the liberal to
feel warmly toward the communalistic behavior of primitive, rural, or
lower-class groups, need not be the ideology of these groups themselves.

We do not question the greater frequency of undeliberated giving
and taking in the lower class, but its significance in terms of values is
not clear. Perhaps the lower-class boy, rather than being oriented to a
"groupy" belief in spontaneous giving and mutual aid is oriented to an
individualistic belief that "If someone is enough of a sucker to give me
something, why shouldn't I look out for myself and take it?" Our own work
would lead us to think that both these thought patterns and several others
were involved in Cohen's situation.

Before group differences in responses can be interpreted in terms
of value-systems, some stable pattern of responses with an understandable
coherence must be isolated.

3. Contrasting Expectations as to Choice Patterns
Derived from the Values and Intellectual
Conformity Approaches

In order to apply the values approach, we must assume that value dimensions are not purely idiosyncratic for each individual and involve classes of situations. We must further assume that values interact in some simple additive way in each particular choice or conflict situation.

> This assumption can be expressed most clearly in terms of the concepts of multiple factor analysis. It would state that for N people responding to n dichotomous choice situations there are a smaller number of reference attitudes or values from which we can predict these choices. A particular choice is predicted as a linear function of an individual's score on these values and of the loading of the given situation on them. The values are then defined in terms of a subset of the n situations or action alternatives for which preferences are correlated, so defined as to be linearly independent of other reference values.

Thus our nine situations call for choices which might be classified in different ways. A boy must choose between stealing a drug or allowing a wife to die, between saving his family or saving the lives for which he has delegated responsibility, etc. What the relevant values involved in the choices were we cannot know a priori. They might be love versus punishment, they might be the one versus the many, they might be the family versus the public.

If some values do underlie our choice situations, they would be revealed by clusters or factors in the association between choice on the nine situations. In the case of the intellectual conformity approach, we would expect a single general factor. However, if strength of value dimensions determines choice, we should expect more than one factor, since our situations clearly do not involve one general value object pitted against nine other specific ones.

These value dimensions might be expected to define differences in choices between our various social subgroups. In any case we would expect considerable sub-cultural difference in frequency of the various alternative choices, differences by class, sociometric status, delinquency, religion, etc.

In the intellectual conformity approach, we would expect sub-group differences to be relatively minor and to be determined by the cultural sophistication of the subgroup. An order of sophistication would explain subgroup differences, which would decrease with age and increased exposure of all to the general culture.

If different sub-cultural value systems were involved we would expect each group to have a somewhat unique value system. Differences between the values of sociometric integrates and isolate would not be expected to coincide with differences between middle and lower class, or delinquents and non-delinquents. These differences would perhaps be expected to increase with maturity as each individual learned his own subculture better.

C. Results of Application of the Intellectual Conformity and Values Approaches to Dichotomous Choice Data

In the preceding chapter we discussed the properties of our relatively complex and qualitative coding of responses to our moral conflict situations. However, we did not directly use in this coding the simplest and most "objective" data we had, e.g., the actual choices our subjects made to the conflict situations. In each case they were asked whether the actor should or should not perform a given action.[1]

---

[1] In many cases it was very difficult to categorize which alternatively a boy chose, since he was constantly in conflict. He would change and revise his decision as he would start explaining it, either because

In our presentation, we have defined items in terms of the mature responses, i.e., the alternative favored by the 16-year-olds. These responses are indicated in the footnote to Table 11.

The fourfold point correlations between our nine items are presented in Table 10. They are not such as to support either of the modes of analysis just described. Only five of the thirty-six associations are significant to the .05 level. The associations are not only negligible but they are not patterned in a simple fashion.

If the items were similar to intelligence test items, we would expect associations between them indicative of some general factor having orthogonal value systems.

Thus we see that there is a class difference in response to question IX, which seems to indicate that the lower class is more familistic or particularistic in a choice between looking after one's family or staying at one's post in an emergency. However, an interpretation that this implies a subcultural value of familism must be qualified by the fact that the younger children are more familistic, as are the isolates, as are the

of further considerations or in response to what a boy would see as "hints" in the probing as to what might be the answer preferred by the examiner. If one probes the reasons for a choice sufficiently, almost inevitably this probing is seen as implying that the choice is inadequate. Only in a few cases would a boy refuse to indicate which of two evils he would side with "if he had to say." In this the children were unlike a number of educated adults who, when interviewed, would simply get angry and refuse to make a choice, deny the empirical situation could exist, etc.

Our chief problem in coding was the decision as to whether to code an initial impulsive response based on some misunderstanding or ignoral of aspects of the situation for the choice, or to code a later response after the interviewer redescribed the situation. The former alternative was adopted in line with keeping this part of the analysis as much like a standard paper and pencil test as possible, with the idea that trends in this kind of data could be followed up with a much larger sample if they appeared genuinely interesting.

TABLE 10

ASSOCIATIONS BETWEEN CHOICES ON MORAL JUDGMENT ITEMS

A. Fourfold Point Correlations between Choices

	I	II	III	IV	V	VI	VII	VIII	IX
I	x								
II	.00	x							
III	.17	.11	x						
IV	.27[a]	.11	.17	x					
V	.21	.16	.04	.05					
VI	.08	.01	.08	.09	.12	x			
VII	.29[a]	.27[a]	-.08	.00	.20	.12	x		
VIII	.37[a]	.27[a]	.00	.04	.08	.04	.12	x	
IX	-.04	.16	.09	.09	.01	-.17	.21	.04	x

B. Associations between Items Expressed as Cross-products[b] before and after Correction for Age[c]

	I-IV	I-VII	I-VIII	II-VII	II-VIII
Before	.06[a]	.05[a]	.09[a]	.05[a]	.05[a]
After	.03	.02	.04	.01	.01

[a]Significant at .05 level.

[b]Cross-products are the observed minus the expected proportion of response in a given cell or $P_{ij} - P_i - P_j$.

[c]The age corrections can be made following MacRae's procedure, by taking the expected joint positive frequency as:

$$n_{ij} = \sum_{k=1}^{B} n_k P_{ki} P_{kj}$$

where n_{ij} = expected number of boys giving mature answers to both item i and item j; n_k = number of boys in the kth age group; P_{ki} = proportion of boys in the kth age group giving mature answers to question i and P_{kj} = proportion of boys in the kth age group giving mature answers to question j (33).

TABLE 11

LEVELS OF SIGNIFICANCE OF SOCIAL GROUP DIFFERENCES[a]
IN CHOICE ON MORAL JUDGMENT ITEMS

Groups	I	II	III	IV	V	VI	VII	VIII	IX
Age[b]	.05	.05	..	..	.05	.20	.10	.20	.05
Class	.10	.05	..	..	..	..	..	..	.01
Sociometric .	..	..	..	..	..	..	.01	.05	.20
Delinquent . .	..	..	..	..	..	..	..	..	.05
Catholic . . .	..	..	..	.05	..	..	..	..	..

[a]All differences of the more privileged groups are in the age
positive direction. The age positive responses were those favored by
the 16-year-olds and were the following:

I Refuse to give money to father   V Go on suicide mission himself

II Don't tell on brother   VI Send sick man on mission

III Steal drug to save wife   VII Worse to cheat

IV Don't mercy kill   VIII Don't report reformed convict

     IX Don't leave post for family

[b]For the age breakdown, the sixfold tables were always collapsed
into fourfold tables of age 10 versus ages 13 and 16 in order to save
time in calculating and correcting for continuity.

delinquents. Caution is further induced by the low association of IX

with other items, especially III, which represent conflicts between

family welfare and societal rules. Is it not equally plausible that

these differences all represent differences in sophistication as to the

culturally agreed upon answer? The other class differences are on I and

II and reflect a greater or more uncritical acceptance of paternal author-

ity by lower-class children, again in line with the more "immature" re-

sponses.

If a lower-class value system were operative, we would expect

increasing class differences with increasing socialization experience.

As children grow older they should increasingly learn their own group value system. If the class differences reflected differences in social exposure to the general symbolic culture as the "intellectual conformity" approach would postulate, we would expect class differences to decline with age. An inspection of class differences at our various age levels does not indicate any pattern of increased class differences with age. Such a pattern would be reflected in an increasing profile dissimilarity for the two groups in choice frequencies across the various items. To indicate this, we present in Table 12 Cronbach's D measure of profile similarity between the two groups at each age level, taking as "scores" the percentage of "mature" responses (13). The D's, measuring the dissimilarity of profile of the two classes, do not markedly increase with age.

Again, evidence for a lower-class value system operating in our material would be offered if lower-class sociometric integrates were more dissimilar to the middle-class boys than were lower-class isolates. We would expect leaders in a subculture to represent subcultural values better than followers or isolates. Again this is not borne out. Table 12-B presents the D's for lower-class integrates and isolates, each compared with the middle-class group's profile. The table indicates that the choices of the lower-class integrates are more like the middle class than the isolates.

3. Sociometric Differences

We might view sociometric integrates not as leaders in a class subculture, but as members of a "peer culture" or a "youth culture." If such were the case we would expect an interaction of sociometric differences with age as we did for class differences. We would expect as boys

TABLE 12

D SCORES INDICATING INTERACTIONAL RELATIONS
BETWEEN GROUP DIFFERENCES IN CHOICE[a]

A. Differences between upper-middle and lower-class groups at various ages:

Age 10	Age 13	Age 16
.705	.697	.831

B. Differences from Middle-class choices among lower-class integrates and lower-class isolates:

Lower-class Integrates	Lower-class Isolates
.454	.732

C. Differences between integrates and isolates at various ages:

Age 10	Age 13	Age 16
.908	.650	.755

[a]D is Cronbach's measure of profile similarity (13). It is the square root of the sum of the squared differences between two groups. These differences are between the proportions of the two groups favoring the "mature" response. The smaller the D, the more similar are the two groups in their preferences on the nine situations.

moved into adolescence, sociometric group differences in choice would become more pronounced as the peer culture became more salient and organized. The D's between the two groups at the various age levels presented in Table 12-C do not indicate this.

As in the case of class, the content of the significant sociometric differences could be interpreted as referring to "peer values," but it is difficult to carry such an interpretation through in a consistent fashion. Thus both questions II and VIII involve "squealing," but in II the situation is a particularistic one of brother versus father, and in VIII it is an impersonal one of benevolent stranger versus the police.

we would expect question II to differentiate attitudes of peer loyalty better, yet it is VIII on which sociometric differences appear. It would be more in line with plausible group values were the sociometric differences on II and class difference on VIII.

4. Religious Differences

Finally, when we consider religion, we again fail to see any general evidence of the operation of a sub-cultural value system. On a point of specific doctrine for both, mercy-killing, we do find a difference between Catholics and Protestants.[1] However, the specificity of this difference only points up the absence of evidence of the diffuse operation of some general religiou value system, of a "Protestant ethic" in our material. The differences on mercy-killing can just as well be interpreted by the intellectual conformity approach in terms of knowledge of a specific religious rule which is also a legal one.

5. Group Differences as Ordered by Degree of Sophistication

In Table 13 we present an anlysis of the frequency of each group's choices in each of our items, which allows us to compare their general fit with the "intellectual conformity" approach. We assigned a score to each group on each item, this score being the percentage of "mature" responses in the given group (where the "mature" response was that preferred by the 16-year-old).[2]

---

[1] The mercy-killing difference falls below significance if the six Catholic delinquents are judged to be responding with the answer dominant in the delinquent group rather than with the answer dominant in the Catholic group.

[2] Items III and IV were omitted, since they showed no age trends and were almost equally chosen at age 16; hence no nature answer could be defined.

TABLE 13

MEAN RANK OF·EACH SUBGROUP IN TENDENCY TO CHOOSE IN
THE MATURE DIRECTION IN MORAL JUDGMENT ITEMS[a]
(The mature direction was that favored by age 16)

Group	Mean Rank
Age 10 Lower—class isolates	1
Age 10 Middle—class isolates	2
Age 10 Lowe—class integrates	3
Age 13 Lower—class isolates	4
Age 10 Middle—class integrates	5
Age 16 Lower—class delinquents	6
Age 13 Middle—class isolates	7
Age 16 Middle—class isolates	8
Age 16 Lower—class isolates	9
Age 13 Middle—class integrates	10
Age 13 Lower—class integrates	11.5
Age 16 Lower—class integrates	11.5
Age 16 Middle—class integrates	13

Kendall's W = .341

$$X^2 = 28.6 \text{ with 12 df } p < .01$$

[a]Items III and IV were omitted in calculating mean rank, since no mature direction could be
defined for them.

These scores were then ranked from low to high for each question
and the groups arranged in the order of their mean rank in preference of
the "mature" response. Kendall's coefficient of concordance of .34 is
significant at the .01 level and indicates that the ranking is not due
to chance. This coefficient shows the degree of association among all
13 groups or the degree of divergence of the rankings from a perfect
agreement in which all questions ranked the groups the same way. If there
were such perfect agreement, represented by a W of 1.00, one single factor
or reference vector would completely order the relations of the groups

to one another on all our questions. The order of the groups shown in Table 13 certainly would support the interpretation of such a factor as representing the degree of maturity or sophistication by our various groups.

6. Implications of the Foregoing Analysis

The foregoing certainly suggests the limited power of a "values approach" to order our particular choice situations with our subjects. It says nothing about the fruitfulness of the values approach "in general."

From the point of view of the individual trying to measure value, our negative findings would hardly be disturbing. He would simply throw out our items and find better ones.

We originally chose items which we believed were not primarily determined by either intelligence or values in order to study a special moral domain. The negative findings we interpret as evidence that they do indeed tap such a domain. The positive findings reported in the previous chapter support this interpretation.

The intellectual conformity approach orders the choice data somewhat better than the values approach. We interpret this better order as due to assumptions shared by interpretations based on intellectual conformity and those based on moral development. Both classify individuals developmentally. However, the failure to find a general factor in the associations between choices indicates that these choices are not determined by knowledge of the right answer. Choices are not determined by a general American value system which people reproduce according to the degree of their sophistication. We may also rule out a utilitarian hypothesis that choice is determined by the application of practical intelligence maximizing value consequences in our situations.

(Original article mispaginated.
No page 127 in original.)

E. Consistency in Choice and the Moral Set

1. The Concept of a Moral Set

We have considered two general "sets" toward our choice questions
and the kinds of individual differences and consistency we would expect
within each set. In Chapter I we defined in abstract fashion a "moral
orientation" and in Chapter III vaguely identified it with the higher types
in our scale. In Chapter II, section F-2, we saw that Baldwin's concept
of an ideal self implies a general moral set in decision making and exem-
plified some of the characteristics of such a set.

Such a moral set involves, on a higher level, both elements of
the "values set" toward expressing the self's values and the "intellectual
conformity set" toward adapting values to the appropriate in the given
situation. In its full sense, a moral set implies an orientation toward
a right decision, a decision which an ideally good or wise person could
make, though perhaps a decision which no individual could actually attain
and of which no one could actually be sure. The solution must do justice
both to what the self believes and yet meet the situation. Thus the choice
is difficult in the sense mentioned before, the difficulty of doing justice
to all the values which the self believes are true and important, not the
difficulty of guessing the right answer to a test item.

Some elements of such an orientation are indicated by the following responses by case 65, a 16-year-old:

(Is there a right answer to these questions? Would most people
agree about them?)

In every one of them, there's been a question of the lesser of
two evils. I don't think in most of them there is an answer. In
that one just now, whether the robber should go or the one that
was dying, I don't think there's any answer to that.

(Is there a right answer for any of them?)

For quite a few of them; like the one about the family and the camping trip. Some were opinions but most of them were right and wrong.

This boy attempts to discriminate between controversial situations which are "matters of right and wrong" and those for which there is no answer, because they are the "lesser of two evils." For the preceding sets we mentioned, all decision is a choice of the lesser of two evils, such a choice of evils does not imply a solution that is not absolutely "right" or a situation where there is no answer. To say that a choice of the lesser of two evils cannot be really right means a conflict in the boy between the need to maintain some "objective" or "absolute" values and the need to make a sensible choice of the lesser situational evil. The right means both upholding an accepted value under all conditions and making a choice or decision which does justice to the particular situation. The concept of a conflict between principles and situation is a meaningful interpretive concept for a boy with this set.

Here is an example of case 37, a 13-year-old, in the throws of such a conflict about mercy-killing, attempting to do justice to the demands of both of the rules as personal values or principles and of the situation as he ought to comprehend it:

If I was the doctor, I just wouldn't like to kill people, but in a way he'd be doing her a favor. These are murder. I really don't know, but I can't see anybody being killed . . . I don't think a person should be killed like an animal, it wouldn't be any compliment to that person, but then she wanted it. I'm trying to put myself in the shoes of the doctor and I don't think anyone can imagine the pain. If it were absolutely necessary, if they were sure she would die and she were out of her mind, they would do it in a painless way.

We have opposed for this boy two values which have probably never before been seen as conflicting, the value that people should never be

killed and the value that people should not suffer. If we attempted to
rank the strength of the two values, we would find that he, like almost
everyone else in the world, would habitually think it was worse to cause
death than to cause suffering. What seems more important is his effort
to find the right way of looking at the situation, to reorganize and
integrate his values with regard to this particular situation. Of course
he never finds such a reorganizing perspective in this situation to his
own satisfaction. But the effort, made anew in each of our conflict situations, prevents us from predicting his choices from value strength or
measuring value strength from his choices. Thus this boy, like case 59
quoted in illustration of the value-expressing set, says a husband should
steal the drug to save his wife. But for case 59 this choice is based on
the fact that one's liking for one's wife is stronger that one's objection to stealing. For case 37, the situation is one of injustice and of
"a matter of life and death," of a responsibility that exists regardless
of one's objections to stealing, and holds even if a friend is involved.
Thus the situation for him hardly indicates that he values retaining a
wife more than avoiding stealing; he tells us elsewhere that he does not
intend to get married.

2. Implications of Different Sets

We have sketched out three different sets to our questions, the
test-taking, the expressive, and the moral. Each set seems to suggest a
different model of the relations of choices in our various situations to
one another and of the nature of age development with regard to such
choices.

The first type is consonant with the view that choice is determined by an effort to predict the answer of the examiner or of the culture in general. With such a set little inter-situational consistency would be expected except that due to general level of sophistication in guessing the right answer. Within such a set or type, age changes would be increased in the number of acceptable specific beliefs and specific choice solutions which were known by this child.

The second type is consonant with the view that choices are determined by the relative strength of personal values. With such a set, inter-situational consistency should appear in the form of consistent preferences for some value objects as against others. Within this set or type, age changes should reflect an increase in the strength or internalization of various cultural values.

The third type is consonant with the view that choices are determined by efforts to realize the good or right in general, in each case involving reorganization of particular values in the situation in terms of the right in general. With such a set, intersituational consistency of choice in concrete content preference would not be very apparent, but there would be a general consistency of approach or principle to all situations. Reasons would be consistent, not content chosen, whereas we would expect the second type to adjust his reasoning to justify the choice of a value which was stronger on an a priori or arbitrary basis.

Within the third type, age development would be primarily a matter of developing principles or perspectives for reorganizing and reinterpreting his values, principles for the choice and derivation of values.

In our subsequent description of our types, these three crude sets roughly corresponding to our three major moral levels, are broken down and elaborated.

The point is that the major consistency represented by our g factor
in assessing our nine situations is a consistency of set. The kind of
cross-situational consistency involved is a function of the developmental
level in which the child stands. Individual differences in intelligence
or in values mean something different at each of our levels of moral development.

F. Behavior Conformity and Moral Level

1. General Conformity and Item Choice

In Chapter I, we consider a specific form of the values or trait
strength approach. This is the approach which views morality as a generalized behavioral disposition to conform to rules and cultural norms.
Our assessment of morality puts no premium on either statements of conformity or statements of independence, rating them in terms of developmental quality.

Influenced by Piaget, we originally did have a set that, with age
development, choices would increasingly reflect situational leniency or
personal independence with regard to rules and authority in general. It
is easy to view such leniency as having rational connotations in terms
of "flexibility" and simplified utilitarian concepts of maximizing situational value.

While some greater willingness to stand up to authority is indicated by age differences in Table 11 on questions I, II, and V, it is hard
to view this as simply a decrease in sacredness of authority and rules, a
greater leniency in general. We had defined our situations primarily to
appeal to considerations of "justice" as reasons for modifying obedience,
rather than to considerations of the needs of the self or of others with

whom the self sympathized. Qualitative material indicates that our questions appeal to both. However, there is some evidence that development is in line with greater concern for justice rather than a greater utilitarian leniency towards the rules. The cases in which violation of the rules least involves justice, III, IV, V, and IX, show either no trend or a trend toward greater obedience to the rules.

The item—intercorrelations also do not reveal a general conformity-strength dimension, whether such a strength dimension be viewed positively as "morality" or negatively as "rigidity."

2. Moral Consistency as Based on Conformity Strength or on Development

From the point of view of consistency in terms of developmental level, we would not really expect to find any such dimension of generalized conformity strength.

Efforts to test the generality of moral conformity have almost always assumed a model in which conformity means inhibition of a need, impulse, or class of "bad" acts. The first question raised has been as to whether such an inhibition constitutes a "trait." Do people who exhibit stealing or cheating in one situation tend to do so in all? The second question raised has been whether all the inhibitions constitute a unity. If an individual strongly inhibits aggression, does he inhibit cheating or sexuality or whatever?

It may be said that the work of Hartshorne and May and Havighurst and Taba indicate some cross—trait generality. Since the initial cross-situation validity of the traits appears to be so low in children, however, there seems to be little point to looking for higher—order generality of a trait variety.

Cross-situational generality of moral development, however, is quite a different matter than cross-situational generality of inhibition of deviant acts. At each level of development, particular kinds of deviance and inhibitions become redefined and are derived from new central concepts of deviance and conformity.

We might use as an example a "temptation situation" such as was used by Hartshorne and May or the Harvard Human Development Laboratory. A boy is offered a sharpshooting medal for achieving a certain score with a play gun and he is given an opportunity to cheat apparently unobserved. From the point of view of our schema, both forces in the situation are designed to appeal to an equally immature developmental level. Thus belief in the value of an economically worthless badge won by cheating is "projective" and "syntelic" in Baldwin's terms. On the other hand a belief in any strong "badness" to cheating in such a socially meaningless situation strikes us as almost equally primitive, projective or syntelic.

In both cases there is an undifferentiated concern for outer labels. The idea that one should never lose and the idea that one should never cheat may both have the same sort of "generality." On a higher developmental level, it is not a taboo on cheating which is general, but the demand to fulfill one's obligation in a social situation. Whether such duty involves obeying or violating a given rule in our situations is secondary.

Each developmental level in our schema tended to have its own pattern of choice in our nine situations. The relation of these patterns could not be termed one of increasingly "rigid" conformity to rule nor one of increasing lenience. Rather each level defined the conflicting forces in the situation in increasingly moral terms. The "increase" in our developmental hierarchy is an increase in the number of aspects of the situation which can be included in a relatively "pure" or differentiated moral attitude.

3. Moral Development and Behavior Ratings

It is obvious, however, that in most situations, such development does imply sanctionless conformity to rules, since most reasons for deviance are trivial and impulsive. Thus we would expect a correlation of developmental assessment with teacher's ratings of our subjects.

We were able to have thirty-four of our subjects rated by their teachers on eight personality variables including strength of conscience, obedience, independence of judgment, fair-mindedness, effort, ambitiousness, response-seeking, or dependence on the teacher and response-seeking from peers. The rating scales for "strength of conscience" and "fair-mindedness" are presented as Table 14. The correlation of our pooled ratings and coding score on moral development with teacher's rating on strength of conscience was .46.

The description for the rating of "conscience" is pretty much in terms of a behavioristic or learning theory conception of internalization, one which also seems to coincide with natural ways of thinking for a teacher. It is not a description which parallels our own formal and developmental view of morality based on children's thinking, but one which was designed to get at an antecedent variable important in determining development. It might better be termed "reliable conformity."

Thus the teacher's ratings are fairly age-independent while our moral development dimension is not.[1] The main "deviant cases" in the

[1] The lack of any age trend in teacher's ratings of reliable conformity in the years 10 to 16 is indicated by the study of D. Harris, et al. (20).

TABLE 14

TEACHER'S RATING FORM FOR STRENGTH OF CONSCIENCE AND FAIR-MINDEDNESS

A. Fair-mindedness

4	3	2	1	0
Very fair	Generally a good sport	Unconcerned	Selfish	No sense of fairness
Defends the rights of others and wants everyone to share equally; "puts himself in the other fellow's shoes."	Tends to share—to respect others' rights and to stick up for his own—except when he gets angry or excited or wants something very badly.	Usually knows what the fair thing is but doesn't care too much about others' rights or his own.	Does what he wants; only thinks about rights when he wants his share or turn.	Doesn't seem to know his own rights or the rights of others.

B. Strength of Conscience

4	3	2	1	0
Completely trustworthy	Reliable	Conforming	Unreliable	Untrustworthy
Can always be depended on to do whatever he knows right regardless of what he wants at the moment.	Usually does what's right even with no one around to check up on him.	Follows rules mostly in order to keep out of trouble and/or to win approval.	Can only be depended on to follow rules is someone is around to check up; e.g., might cheat if he thought he could get away with it	Is always trying to get away with something.

correlation are 10-year-olds rated high on strength of conscience.[1] We would view reliable conformity as a necessary but not sufficient condition for good performance on our measure. Everyone of the top third of the boys in moral judgment are above the median on reliable conformity, but so are other boys who are fairly low on moral judgment.

This stresses the initial difficulty described in our first chapter, the difficulty of securing agreement upon, and behavior measurement of, morality defined in a positive sense as more than absence of deviance. Presumably situations of the order of those used in our stories would be required to separate out the upper reaches of morality in terms of gross behavior conformity and deviance.

The correlation of our moral judgment score with ratings of "fair-mindedness" was .45. This rating was meant to get at a sense of "rights," equality and peer reciprocity, while the conscience rating was meant to get at a sense of "duty," task commitment and reliability with regard to authorities. These behavior ratings seems to correlate more highly with our moral judgment measure than did any of the other eight traits rated by the teacher. (This statement is made in part on the basis of visual inspection of the scattergrams of our moral score with the eight ratings.) Table 15 indicates that the correlations with "conscience" and "fairness" are clearly higher than the correlations with obedience and school work effort, the variables with which "conscience" might be expected to be confused in a school situation.

3. Delinquency and Moral Development Ratings

We might consider a lower score by the delinquents on the moral

---

[1] The 10-year-olds were a disproportionate part of our rated sample of 34 boys.

TABLE 15

CORRELATIONS OF MORAL JUDGMENT SCORE WITH BEHAVIOR
RATINGS BY TEACHERS
(Correlations are product moment and are
based on 34 subjects)

	Correlation	Significance
Moral judgment and conscience or reliable conformity	.46	.01
Moral judgment and fair-mindedness . . .	.45	.01
Moral judgment and obedience	.24	.10
Moral judgment and effort	.03	...

judgment as offering some additional behavioral confirmation of the scale.
In Table 7, the mean score for delinquents is compared with the mean score
of the non-delinquent lower class 16-year-olds. The difference is significant at the .01 level.[1]

As we shall see in Chapter VI, some of our delinquents tend to
verbally advocate "exaggerated" obedience to authority, while more of them
verbally advocate disobedience. But in either case, their verbal choices
rest largely on self-interest and impulse checked by fear and they tend
to be insensitive to higher-level values.

While we get this clear differentiation in terms of how the delinquents think, their dichotomous choices themselves, as reported in Table
11, hardly give support to any general differentiation of delinquents from
more conforming children.

On the other hand, our analysis of choice content failed to support

---

[1]The IQ's of only 5 of the 12 delinquents were available but the
mean of these was slightly higher than that of the non-delinquent lower-
class group, so that we can fairly confidently rule out intellectual level
as a determinant of the differential performance of the delinquents.

the notion that general differences in our material could be accounted for as a "delinquent subculture," or even a veneer of "verbal conformity" rejected by the delinquents, though we would not deny the existence of these factors.

Thus we would tend to consider the delinquent as someone who is at a very low level of internalization of norms or conformity pressures in general. As our earlier discussion has indicated, this does not mean that he would be expected to violate every cultural norm but that the quality of his conformity would be expected to be generally low.

G. Social Group Differences and Moral Development as Determined by Social Participation

1. Results

In section C-2 of this chapter we considered social group differences in actual choices made in our situations. We concluded that though few clear-cut extensive differences appeared in our small sample, what differences appeared could fairly well be ordered in terms of the differential exposure of the groups to the general culture.

Our typological assessment of moral development also manifests this differential exposure trend. The analysis of variance presented in Table 7 indicates significant differences favoring the (upper) middle-class children over the lower- (and lower-middle) class children, and favoring the sociometric integrates over the sociometric isolates. The sociometric differences are much stronger than the class differences. None of the interactions between sociometric status, class and age appear noteworthy.

Remembering the existence of group differences in intelligence presented in Table 4 and the correlation of intelligence with moral judgment, we see the need for a covariance analysis. Such an analysis allows

us to see whether the group differences in moral development disappear
when the effects of differential intelligence are controlled for.

The results are presented in Table 16. The sociometric differences remain very substantial. The class effect remains significant if
we accept a one-tailed test of the hypothesis, which seems legitimate due
to the fact that we predicted the direction of differences in our original
research planning.

TABLE 16

ANALYSIS OF COVARIANCE OF CLASS AND SOCIOMETRIC DIFFERENCES
ON MORAL JUDGMENT, CONTROLLING FOR INTELLIGENCE

	SS.MJ	C.P.	SS.IQ	Corrected M.S.	df	F	Level
Sociometric Within	131,256 133,945	10,484 10,376	834 6,338	87,570 116,959	1 59		
	265,201	20,860	7,172	204,529		44.18	< .01
Class Within	11,679 133,945	1,770 10,376	268 6,338	6,330 116,959	1 59		
	145,624	12,146	6,606	123,289		3.19	< .10

2. General Interpretation

As we stated at the beginning of Chapter III, each of our groups
may be seen as differentially participating in society. Each kind of differential participation we saw as related to the kinds of role-taking
stressed by Mead, Baldwin and Piaget. The fact that all the group differences are significant seems to justify the assumption common to all three
theorists. This assumption is that moral development is dependent on role-
taking ability and on general social participation rather than on the
learning of specific habits or values.

148

The fact that all our groups differ, and the fact that the differences are global differences in developmental level prevents us from clarifying which of the kinds of role-taking stressed by our theorists is most significant.

As we stated in section B of Chapter III, we originally endeavored to construct dimensions of role-taking to represent each theorist, e.g., "generalized perspective" for Mead, "reciprocity" for Piaget and "internalization" or "ideality" for Baldwin. In attempting to elaborate such dimensions in application to our data, we seemed to find that either aspects of such dimensions were joint or closely linked expressions of general development or else they seemed unrelated to development and rather artifactual. The presentation of our developmental types in later chapters will perhaps make it clear why these dimensions appeared too artificial and formalistic.

However, our findings that group differences in moral development seem related to differential role-taking is important both in clarifying the basis for group differences in values and in supporting our general conception of morality. The "moral set" is a role-taking set. Whereas group differences in responses made with a "values set" or an "intellectual conformity set" need not be based on differential level of role-taking, this is not true of moral responses.

The focus of thinkers like Baldwin, Mead, and Piaget on sociality as role-taking stands in sharp contrast to the superficial but popular dichotomy between the "social-emotional" are of social psychology and the intellectual area of biological psychology. This dichotomy appears in its baldest form when we see that modern "integrations" of the dichotomy are conceived of in terms of specifying how one separate area influences the other, e.g., how needs or the group influence perception and conception.

A major purpose of the analysis reported in this chapter was to indicate the nature of a moral set and the ineffectuality of the cognitive-emotive dichotomy in analyzing such a set. However, our very effort to distinguish kinds of sets, e.g., the intellectually conforming, value-expressing and moral, implies a different concept of sociality than the usual. There have been many efforts to differentiate "social" from "non-social tasks" in terms of content, e.g., with regard to whether items overtly refer to people or not. In terms of our focus or set, all three approaches to our task are social. They differ, however, with regard to the level of social development from which they spring. In this sense, the moral set is "more social," it represents a higher degree of social role-taking, however such role-taking be defined.

3. Interpretation of Class Differences in Morality as Due to Differential Participation in and Perspective toward Society

Our finding of class differences is in line with the findings of E. Lerner and D. MacRae, that middle-class children differed from lower-class children in giving the more mature response to dichotomous Piaget items, with intelligence controlled for (29, 32).

We may point to the study of Schatzman and Strauss as indicating the superior role-taking skill of the middle-class adult in an interview situation (49).

Our own analyses indicate that different modes of thought in our material do tend to be differentially favored by different status groups. We claim that these modes of thought reflect not so much different class value systems, but differential social participation and resulting development.

As we stated in section B-2, positive characterization of a lower-class "value system" has been quite unsuccessful. We believe this is because no one has been able to find any fundamental organized institutions in which the lower class participates more than the middle class.[1]

In the case of morality, it is obvious that subgroups in a society are exposed to and in some way assimilate and value the same basic content, the same laws and institutions. Insofar as rules and institutions vary from subgroup to subgroups in a homogeneous and mobile society, these variations tend to remove such content from the sphere of the moral to the sphere of opinion and taste. Accordingly, subgroups differences in moral values arise not so much from prizing of different fundamental behaviors and institutions, as from the effects of differences in level of participation, exposure, aspiration and responsibility with regard to these fundamental behaviors and institutions.

At the same time we do not view class differences in morality as differences in personality traits in the usual sense. We do not say that all children "see" or are exposed to the same standards and therefore that differences represent personality controls or ability to conform or be virtuous in terms of them (behavioral conformity approach). Neither do we say that differences in "seeing" are based on differential intellectual skill in cognizing these patterns (intellectual conformity approach).

Fundamentally, the class differences are differences in the posi-

---

[1]The only such obvious "institution," the corner gang, does not in itself contain any value determining features differentiating it from the middle-class clique except its indifference or hostility to other institutions. Certainly efforts like Cohen's to assimilate it to the liberal middle-class concept of the group do violence to the tendency noted by many observers for the structure of the corner gang to be a reflection of some of the cruder features of the power and status hierarchy in the outside world of secondary institutions.

tion or situation from which the individual views society. This position tends to determine the kind of value accorded to the various fundamental institutions.

The operation of society is largely unknown or irrelevant from a lower-class perspective. If the arbitrariness and indifference of society appears great, the tendency is to focus on the concrete, the immediate, the egoistically gratifying.

From what might be termed the lower middle-class perspective, the operations of society are largely unknown but they are seen as offering values and opportunities to the self, and hence as valued. The combination of unknownness and value tends to lead to a "moralistic" perception of all society. Society is seen as an apparatus designed for legitimately rewarding and punishing individual virtue. Virtue consists largely in displaying respect for social institutions, authorities and their symbols, since one cannot directly do much to cause the institutions to achieve their goals.

From what might be termed the upper middle-class perspective, the operations of society are oriented to directly rather than symbolically. Rather than a general value aura enveloping an institution or its leader, the specific functions and values of the institution are focused upon as to be "rationally" chosen and implemented.

In section C-1 of Chapter VII, we elaborate class-characteristic ways in which status or achievement is crystallized into various virtues. For the lower class status tends to be seen as largely a product of luck and connections. For the lower middle-class it tends to be seen as the product of quasi-moral virtues of conformity, discipline and respect for the social order. For the upper middle class, achievement tends to be seen as the product of intellectual and social abilities which become major "virtues."

Social position tends to determine, not only the relation of status to virtue, but the entire perception of the bases of conformity.

For a multitude of structural reasons industrial societies still tend to rest the maintenance of conformity among the lower class on the policeman on the corner and the weekly pay check at the factory gates. While the normal lower-class boy outgrows the child's subordination to similar incentives in the family and small group, the mere existence of a remaining set of externally coercive rules probably tends to hamper the more personal conformities from taking on a fully internalized or autonomous form.

The lower-class father is exposed at work to a standardized pattern of supervision, coercion and payment. The system of personal relations and personal esteem which does exist at work is largely in conflict with, or indifferent to, the actual functions and rules defining the job role, and, accordingly, tends towards irresponsibility. This tends to lead the lower-class father to present himself to his family either as someone who submits to the formal pattern for the sake of their approval of him as the good provider, or as someone who enforces the same pattern of fixed non-empathic authority on his family as is enforced upon him at work. The arbitrary and impersonal necessity of his work role will complement a view of the family as a biological given independent of consensus, choice, or virtue.[1]

---

[1] An alternative pattern is one in which the mother runs the home and "disciplines" the father as she does the children and as he is "disciplined" at work. Here outside norms of justice and responsibility are even less relevant and the moral standards of the home may be at the level of justice appropriate to the toilet training of infants.

Society confronts the lower—class person with a situation in which the personal virtues of "character" or even the ability to put up a good front are relatively useless. Accordingly, unless the lower—class father is bent on making his children different and more successful than he, he is not likely to pattern his parental role as one of training some set of personal virtues seen as needed for a successful and useful adult life in the family or outside. Whether lenient and limited or severe and extensive, the focus of moral training will tend to be prohibitions of classes of acts which lead to punishment by civil or religious authority, or which displease the parent himself.

We need not detail the contrasting way in which family, work, and community conformity all tend to be oriented to choice, agreement, responsibility, contract, "group goals," personal abilities and virtue, judgments of personal approval and esteem and respect and the like in the middle—class world.

4. An Example of Differential Participation and Moral Level as Determining Values

Although core institutions and the moral concepts defining them may be commonly oriented to by all subgroups in a society, what of the mass of more specific culture patterns and values held by various status and ethnic groups? Here, too, we may find a link between societal participation and subgroup differences in preference by focusing on our moral dimension. We may take as an example the "value," art. It is well known that an interest in or positive evaluation of art and other cultural activities is positively correlated with socioeconomic status. It may be that such a correlation expresses nothing more than does a similar correlation of status with fox hunting and polo whose cultivation is facilitated by being idly rich and which serves to prove one's idleness and richness.

We found all our Midwestern suburban boys almost universally indifferent to art as a matter of personal interest and enjoyment, a reflected in the fact that none of our 16-year-olds had any wish to be an artist or said they enjoyed art. However, class differences appear in the extent to which 16-year-olds see the artist as a socially respected person.

As examples we may give the following "extreme" responses to the question, "Why are(n't) artists respected much?"

Case 59—16 LC Is. 96 (father carpenter, mother factory assembly).

I don't know nothing about their paintings. People don't care about paintings, they don't think about them.

Case 54—16 LMC Int. 104 (father electrician and district representative for Bell).

Guys who are just starting, who aren't known for their great paintings, they haven't done much work and you think of 'em as a bum sort of. A well known painter is respected for his education and for what he is doing for humanity like he painted something that influenced everyone to give to the March of Dimes.

Case 65—16 UMC Int. 115 (father bank V.P.).

There was a time when a good artist, a fine sculptor was about the highest thing you could possibly have. I think nowadays an artist is still highly respected for his insight on the culture of the world.

In this case, each sees the value of the artist from completely different grounds. For the lower-class boy, the artist represents some one whose claims to respect don't have to be conformed to. He presents no force, no appeal to impulse, to overcome ignorance. For the lower middle-class boy, the artist is evaluated in terms of internalized "moral" standards of hard work, clean living, education and concrete helping of others. While he cannot evaluate the artist in specific value-orientation, he can judge him as conforming to general rules and symbols. For the upper middle-class boy, the artist's claim is respected because of his ability to cognitively or expressively represent aspects of culture or society in general.

While qualitatively so different, there is certainly no question as to the relative scope or level of societal participation involved in each of these perspectives. It would be very difficult, however, to establish any quantitative or additive concept of social participation by which these differential levels could be measured. It is a very different problem than counting the number of groups to which someone belongs.

It also seems apparent that the lower middle-class statement is indicative of a more moral orientation than the lower-class statement. On our over-all score for moral level, the upper middle-class boy happens to score the highest of the three in moral level.

The point is that the more developed moral orientations to some extent allow the individual to give various aspects and values of society their due regardless of group or personal values or interests. The example also makes clear that it is in part through differential participation in broader meanings and values of society and culture that fundamental moral concepts gain their differential meaning for various subgroups.

5. Sociometric Differences

Whereas there have been a large number of studies of class differences in values and few of class differences in role-taking and interactional tendencies, the reverse is true for sociometric status. These sociometric studies tend to show relationships between popularity and cooperativeness and behavioral conformity as well as between popularity and role-taking skills or empathy (10, 31, 7, 15).

We were not able to isolate any distinctive component of moral development of an egalitarian small-group nature which corresponded to sociometric differences, such as Piaget's sense of reciprocity. To some extent our moral material seemed to differentiate our isolates into two familiar groups—the withdrawn and submissive (related to Moral Type 0) versus the impulsive and egalitarian (related to Moral Type 1). This differentiation works out best in the lower-class group.

Such a dichotomy of isolates could be complemented by a dichotomy of integrates into "integrated conformers" (Moral Types 2 and 3) and "leaders" (Moral Types 4 and especially 5). To some extent, such a four-fold typology represents successive points on our sociometric measure, as well as on our moral scale. However, the qualitative differences between the types suggest the futility of seeking a single dimension or moral attitude as linked to peer group participation.

H. Conclusions as to Individual Consistency in Our Data

Our analyses seem to provide strong support for a developmentalist approach to morality. The usefulness of the concept of the moral and the developmentalist approach seem intertwined.

The developmental approach allows us to abstract the moral from specific situations and values as is indicated by the general factor in our moral situations.

Such abstraction from the situation is not through the invocation of personality traits, e.g., needs, habits, and intellectual abilities. The constancy across time and situation implied by a personality trait is a constancy based on a fixity or ignoral of the situation.

As opposed to such constancy across situations, morality is a matter of consistency through integrating situations. We can predict moral level across situations not because moral attitudes ignore specific or unique elements in any individual situation, but because they require that justice be done to each and every situation of moral import.

Presumably we can predict over time from our knowledge of moral level, but such a prediction is not based on an expectation of constancy of moral attitudes. Rather it is based on the expectation of continued development, which has a cumulative or sequential character.

The trait approach takes constancy for granted and only seeks specific causes for change. A developmental approach tends to take development for granted and only seek specific causes for constancy or arrest of development. In the case of a variable like mental age, the reasonableness of the latter supposition seems obvious. In the case of morality, a trend toward greater adequacy is more questionable since morality is not obviously useful in serving the individual's needs as is intelligence.

Baldwin, Mead, and Piaget offer various bases for such a trend, bases which remain problematic. However, some such trend seems postulatable given some basic motivation to conform and the continuous expansion of social participation and conformity which comes with age.

CHAPTER VI

THE FIRST TWO TYPES AND PIAGET'S THEORIES OF

MORAL DEVELOPMENT

A. Introduction

In the lengthy discussion of the next few chapters, we have attempted to combine the tasks of description of our types, interpretative analysis of concrete material and consideration of implications for theories of moral development. In addition, we have made some comments relative to the degree of morality and the degree of adequacy of each of the types in terms of justifying our arrangement in an order of increased morality as conceptualized in Chapter I.

1. Scope of Type Descriptions

Due to these several functions of the following discussion, ready comprehension of the types as a system of description becomes somewhat difficult.

Our conceptualization of the six types is summarized in Appendix B, and operationalized in the coding schemes of Appendix C. References to these appendices through the lengthy discussion of the next chapter may enable the reader to keep this discussion in perspective. The basic headings in the summary, useful for quick comparison, are subordinated in the discussions to a more organic and theoretic presentation. The description of the orientations of the types to justice is presented in Chapter VIII and summarized in Table 17 (see page 326).

151

It is important in following the discussion of examples to have a fairly clear conception of the conflict situation as presented in Appendix A. Probably the easiest way for the reader to group and remember the meanings of these conflicts is to drop the social scientific role for a moment and think how he would himself answer it. The responses to question III in Appendix D, and the newspaper interviews on integration in Appendix E provide material for a good "feel" for the types.

2. Overview and Basic Theoretical Problems Raised by the First Two Types

Piaget has gathered various evidence that the young child is orientated to avoiding punishment and obeying authority in his moral thinking and that he displays various cognitive rigidities, immaturities and absolutisms in such thinking. His basic explanation, which is also a basic assumption in his interpretation of qualitative material, is that this pattern of childish response to moral questions is a reflection of a moral attitude of heteronomous respect.

The exact meaning of "respect" or "heteronomous respect" is elusive and will be explored during our discussion. However, Piaget's concept implies some of the sense of sacredness of authority and the rules, some of the elements of a sense of guilt and a moral indignation present in clear form is the adult "authoritarian" or "moralist."

The punishment orientation of the young child might, however, be interpreted as evidence of the child's failure yet to have developed a sense of respect for authority and rules. Rather than reflecting awe for parents and the moral order, a concern to avoid punishment and a focus on punishment-related labelling may reflect merely a wish to avoid a painful, shameful event. The fact that punishment is oriented to rather than moral motives and consequences, may indicate a failure to respect the moral order and authority in itself.

Piaget's answer is that punishment is oriented to as a tangible symbol, as representing the moral order and disapproval by it. The child bases choice on punishment only because he cannot trust his own ideas as to the basis of that order and authority. Because of the vast superiority of the authority, the child cannot predict the authorities' reaction or take his role in terms of his own thoughts and feelings. Just because the child has an exaggerated internalized emotional regard for the order or authority, his cognitive view of authority is externalized and does not involve role-taking and self-projection.

The plausibility of the belief in the child's heteronomous respect rests largely on data collected by Piaget as to various types of "rigid" adherence to rule joined to a susceptibility to adult influence, both seeming to fly in the face of "rational" instrumental self-interest. However, such phenomena may be explained purely in terms of general cognitive immaturity, as Piaget partially does in terms of "egocentrism." This we have described in our account of Baldwin's "Adualistic Stage" in Chapter II, section E-1, and summarized in Table 19, Chapter IX.

The assumption of heteronomous respect is fundamental to Piaget's interpretation of development into the autonomous stage. Thus the autonomous stage is characterized cognitively by an overcoming of egocentrism in favor of an instrumental and relativistic perception of value. Piaget believes that this cognitive advance is not due merely to greater experience, sophistication and awareness of self-interest where it conflicts with the interests of others. Rather it is due to experience in pursuit of common goals and in voluntary conformity. Piaget believes that instrumental flexibility is in large part a product of the attitude of mutual respect expressed in moral concepts of reciprocity.

Piaget's concept of the basic trend of moral development as one of flexibility toward the rules and the "levelling" of respect, rests on the interpretation of the more primitive stage as one of sacredness and heteronomous respect. If his concept of heteronomous respect and its vicissitudes is incorrect, the development of moral sacredness, of ideals and moral absolutes, in the adult, remains to be accounted for.

This problem bears on our types, both in the sense that these types offer a partial test of Piaget's hypotheses, and in the sense that a correct interpretation of them and of our developmental schema rests on consideration of these hypotheses.

Our Type 0 does display many of the features Piaget attributes to the heteronomous stage of moral development. The dominant motive or sanction is punishment, and punishment avoidance is an end in itself. Type 0 children tend almost always to choose the line of conduct to which punishment is not attached, regardless of other considerations. Avoidance of punishment is very frequently the end term in their verbal justification of any rule or action.

Even where punishment is not directly involved they are often oriented to obedience, regardless of other considerations. Some of them have a sense that age, status and possessions make a person "intrinsically" more valuable.

They believe that a forbidden act is bad in itself and to be punished regardless of its situational value or intent.

In spite of these parallels to Piaget's type, we find it difficult to see out Type 0 as having an orientation of heteronomous respect.[1]

Our Type 1 also bears some relationship to Piaget's autonomous type. Choice is based primarily on situational consequences assessed in terms of natural needs and impulses. No great weight is assigned to avoiding punishment or obeying authority. There is much usage of exchange.

In spite of these resemblances, our Type 1 does not seem to us to have an orientation of mutual respect.

The problem we attack is not "Are there children with attitudes of heteronomous or mutual respect?" but, "Are such attitudes the basis of the moral beliefs and cognitive styles described by Piaget and embodied in our first two types?"

Our attack upon the problem rests in part upon according a status to our types of the sort outlined in Chapter IV, section C. A summary of our analysis of the problem is contained in Table 20, Chapter IX.

B. Attitudes of Respect and Concepts of the Social Order

1. The Meaning of Piaget's Concept of Unilateral Personal Respect as a Basis for Conformity to Rules

The existence of strong attitudes of dependency toward adults in most children seems unquestionable. The recognition by the child of the adult's ability to do things he can't do, and the importance of this differential also seems unquestionable. But does this mean that the child "has respect" for adults? Such questions are very difficult to answer, or even to define clearly.

---

[1] One crude support for this conclusion are the low ratings of reliable conformity received by Type 0 children. Piaget would, however, claim that these children might genuinely respect the rules and still break them through an egocentric failure to perceive this inconsistency.

As Piaget indicates, the other side of an attitude or respect is an attitude of obligation. Obligation implies the side of the attitude which constrains to do something, to make action conform to some requirement or model independent of the actor. Respect implies the side of the attitude directed toward a social object from which the requirements or models of action emanate. It implies an attitude that the object conformed to has some generalized value justifying such conformity.

According to Piaget, who follows Bovet, the attitude of respect in some sense precedes any regular obedience and imitation:

> Without respect, the rules would not be accepted and the rules would have no power to compel the mind. . . . It is a fact that the child in the presence of his parents has the spontaneous feeling of something greater than and superior to the self. This respect has its roots deep down in certain inborn feelings and is due to a sui generis mixture of fear and affection which develops as a function of the child's relation to his adult environment [44, pp. 377-79].

We may note as a problem that ambivalence, or fear and love, do not in themselves suffice to constitute an attitude of respect in the sense of "looking up to," a feeling of something greater than or better than the self. Thus they need not, as is claimed for respect, lead the young child "to attribute to his parents the moral and intellectual qualities which define his ideas of perfection" (44, p. 380).

Such attribution of perfection is usually called "idealization" and implies a need to attribute a general worthiness to a person in order to justify feelings of love or dependency. It implies usually also identification with the other so that his victories and perfections are felt as enhancing the self.

That most young children feel both dependence and fear toward their parents we need not question. That the child is not only dependent but also rather uncritical in his assessment of what he and others can do

also seems unquestionable. Whether there is in the very immature child
any dynamic linkings between the two of the sort usually termed "idealization," as Piaget thinks, is an open question. We certainly may need
and fear someone without idealizing him, though many adolescents and
adults clearly do "idealize."

The concept of "respect" essentially seems to refer to a tendency
to believe that our attitude or actions of obedience, imitation, dependency or fear are or should be deserved by the object or person toward which
they are directed. It implies that the person is in some general sense
worthy of being given or shown conformity at some cost. It is obvious
that it is possible for a child to obey or imitate without any attitude
that the person he obeys or imitates needs to be worthy of such conformity,
beyond the fact that he can get it.

It is possible to attribute positive value to a person without respecting him, as when such value is instrumental to some need of ours. It
is possible to think someone is better than the self in some regard without respecting him, unless all envy and competition are respect. Respect
means something more than thinking someone is better than the self in some
or several regards. If it does not, "mutual respect" becomes a meaningless
concept. Mutual respect only becomes meaningful in terms of the other's
conforming to a valued standard, which is still in some sense "higher." As
Piaget says, "Respect implies (at least as regards mutual respect) admiration for a personality precisely insofar as this personality subjects itself to rules" (44, p. 92). However, to the extent to which such a statement is true, it seems difficult to derive respect for rules from a primary
respect for persons, as Piaget does.

2. Baldwin's Concept of Personal Respect

We may contrast this derivation with that of Baldwin and of Durkheim who, though in different ways, derive respect for persons from a respect for the embodiment of the culture. The concept of respect for both Baldwin and Durkheim implied an attitude toward a person as something more than a person, as representing something beyond what any individual self could be. To Baldwin, this was an "ideal self." When the individual respected someone, it was not only because he could do this or that, but because there were an indefinite number of virtues and abilities which he also represented. To Durkheim, when the individual respected someone he represented the group or the culture which stood behind him. This holds true even for "mutual respect" which implies for Baldwin and Durkheim respect for personality as such, the respect which one feels toward anyone insofar as they are human. It is respect for the "general" of humanity which the individual merely represents, insofar as they are members of society. It occurs through generalization of "unilateral respect" to everyone as a symbol of the culture rather than originating from concrete egalitarian social ties (though the latter might be necessary for such generalization to take place).

Baldwin defines three stages of development in terms of respect or dependence (4). At the earliest "projective" stage, there exists a physical dependence and a "respect" for superior force or for the control exerted by the parent. At this stage the intellectual interest of the child is in "who does what" in the physical and social world and an interpretation of the world in terms of quasi-human quasi-physical forces. This stage Baldwin illustrates in terms of primitive animistic religions, in which there is no orientation to any central order or purpose in the world.

In the next or "intellectual" stage, the child "respects" intelligence, the fact that the adult has purposes, predicts, and adjusts means to ends better than he does. At this stage the interest is in planning, and in finding a teleological purpose or design for everything. The child feels dependent in terms of his own inability to explain and design things and actions, and feels admiring in terms of an interpretation of others as possessing more of what intellectual ability he feels he has.

At this stage the child sees no differences in basic self, no differences in purposes and motives between himself and the person he admires. He interprets the other's purposes in terms of his own general motives, in terms of a natural selfishness and he is not interested in purposes which cannot be interpreted in this way. Accordingly, at this point the attitude of respect does not imply any reluctance to get around the respected person. Baldwin illustrates this in terms of pagan religions in which there are propitiation and exchange relations with the Gods which do not rule out mutual deceit. As one of our 10-year-olds says, "If you don't believe in God, he won't help you."

The third or ethical stage of respect, Baldwin says, occurs when the child respects someone for being a better person or self, for being good, having good purposes and attitudes, for wanting and knowing how to conform to standards of conduct better than the self. The sense of inadequacy is more or less one of moral inadequacy and a need for guidance.

Such an attitude need not imply any utilitarian dependence on the person respected. However, it does imply that the respected person can judge the self in the same way that the self tries to judge itself. As a form of this on the religious side, Baldwin mentions the various phenomena of adolescent religious awakening which seems to have been taken for granted as more or less universal by late nineteenth century psychologists.

Such a description of the development of respect implies in a sense
that the more realistic is the comparison of self and other, the greater
does respect become. It implies that personal respect is engendered from
a sense of inadequacy in comparing the self with an ideal or norm, so that
in a sense the "respect" for the norm precedes the respect for the person.

3. Circularities in Piaget's Method

Piaget hypothesizes an emotional attitude of heteronomous sacredness, respect and obligation which collaborates with and helps produce conceptual realism and a quasi-physical rigidity in perception of the social
order. However, the only material he uses to indicate the existence of the
emotional attitude of unilateral respect are the cognitive naivetes of the
heteronomous child which they are designed to help explain. To indicate
that rules are felt to be "sacred" and "untouchable" he shows that the
child has a belief in the fact that they cannot be changed. To indicate an
attitude of "awe" for parents, he indicates a child's belief in their unlimited age and knowledge, or his identification of father and God (cf. 44,
pp. 46–48).

However, such beliefs may be due to the child's having no need to
limit the abilities of anyone for lack of any "respect" for the unlimited.
Others may be seen as knowing all, but knowledge may not be seen as of tre-
mendous difficulty or value. The father may be seen as no different than
God, but the child may have no feeling of the divineness of God in any adult
sense. The father may be seen as knowing all, but so may the self. Thus
Piaget himself quotes remarks like "Then Daddy couldn't know everything
either nor me neither?" (45, p. 215).

Primitive equations of a "higher" concept with a "lower" concept may always be read in two ways. If a child or a primitive man equates father or God with an animal, we may believe this to be a mystic or magical attribution of higher qualities to animals or we may say that the child attributes animal-like qualities to the father or to God. If a child says a culprit should be punished with death, we may believe that this indicates that respect for the rules is so strong it demands that the ultimate value of life itself must be sacrificed or we may believe that the child sets no high value on the concept of life. Our assessments of conscious values are always limited by the fact that they are based on the comparison or choice between two terms which may both be unknowns.

Having learned by a slow process of development, a process of respect for society, God, duty, parenthood, and the like, it is difficult for us not to automatically read this respect back onto the child who is from an external point of view so weak and dependent. Would we not feel this respect in the child's situation and with his beliefs?

The same difficulty in interpreting equations appears in Piaget's belief that the immature child is oriented to a purposive and sacred social order. Piaget has obtained evidence to show that there is a confusion of physical regularity with social or moral regularity in the young child. Such evidence is a two-edged weapon with regard to Piaget's general thesis. Does it indicate that the child has a mystical reverence for nature or does it indicate that he has a physicalistic, impersonal attitude toward the moral world?

While such ambiguity in equations cannot be eliminated, our own interpretations endeavor to minimize it by considering a whole series of responses which given children make. This necessarily leads to a discursive analysis.

4. Verbalizable Concepts of Respect as Limited to Outward Obedience in Type 0

We first asked our children the meaning of the word respect. Our Type 0 children gave answers of overt obedience; respect means, "Do what they say" (Obs. 1).[1] Even after attempting to explicate the word in terms of "looking up to" or "thinking they are good," most of the children kept with this concept. Thus if asked whether "you could do what the teacher said and still not respect her?" many gave answers like: "Yes, if she told you to open the book to page 128, you could open the book but turn it to a different page."

With this concept of respect, Type 0 children tend to think that people only respect persons to whom they are in direct relationship of subordination. Thus when asked whether people respect someone with a lot of money, they say that they would be respected by their servants, but not by others. In some of the lower-class children, this is even carried to the point of saying that one respects one's immediate superior in a hierarchy more than someone higher up, e.g., "I don't think civilians would respect the senator as much as the policeman because he only gives orders to the high officers like the judge or policeman."

Where Type 0 respects a power figure projectively or regardless of what need he is a means toward (Obs. 1), Type 1 respects a person only as an irreplaceable means to serving some need (Obs. 2, 4). Where Type 0 respects a person syntelically in terms of vaguely shared attitudes, Type 1 sees respect as relative to the individual respecter and his relation to the authority figure (Obs. 3).

---

[1]The numbered observations or interview extracts are located at the end of this chapter.

A few of the middle-class or middle-class oriented children gave "projective" responses to property as well as to power, i.e., attributing some intrinsic value to the possession of property, which is fused with the authority and functional usefulness of the individual. How far this may go may be seen in Case 9's response to the value of life as based on furniture-ownership in question III (Appendix D). For Case 9, there is a "projective" evaluation of power and wealth, so that a powerful or wealthy person is valuable in general, without qualification.

Does this projective value of status imply an attitude of sacredness or respect? It does insofar as a child may be said to "respect" furniture to which Case 9 reduces status.[1] "But still it seems impossible that we should have no other reason for praising a man than that for which we commend a chest of drawers," as Smith said. Smith's comment was a criticism of the utilitarian view that moral value was basically of the depersonalized instrumental sort expressed in the Type 1 responses. But it would seem to hold equally for the impersonal but "intrinsic" value of Type 0.

Thus the "sacredness" for Case 9 of furniture and its possessors does not seem to be because these represent or symbolize some vague being or order felt as greater than the self. There seems to be nothing "behind" the value of furniture as a respected object as there is for the moral respect postulated by Baldwin or Durkheim. While property is desired and protected by parents and other beings more powerful than the self, it is not "respected" as a symbol of them since they are subordinated to it.

---

[1] The interpretive problem is, "Is furniture overvalued because it symbolizes a mystically respected status?" versus "Is status valued simply as a complex of overvalued physical traits like possessions?"

In a sense, this absence of symbolic value is indicated by the very equation of activity value and person value which leads both to the exaggerated value of "the important person" found in some Type 0 thinking and its instrumentalist denial in Type 1 thinking.

Case 9's uncritical equation of status and general vague value is typical of only a few of the Type 0 children. For most of the children authority and privilege do not involve any vague superior personal value; it is simply a fact. However, Case 9 is typical of all the Type 0 children in seeing a sort of one-to-one relation between the value of an activity and a person.

5. In Contrast Respect for Authority Is Symbolic of the Social Order and Is Based on Knowledge and Responsibility in Types 2 and 3

In Types 0 and 1, there is no consideration of a person's value except in terms of his performance of a specific role activity. Whatever a role occupant does, he knows how to do best (Obs. 5). In Type 2 or 3, authority is related to some general concept of superior knowledge in general, i.e., intelligence or wisdom with regard to matters outside his role, or in the subordinates' role (Obs. 6). Thus, in regard to respect, Type 0 and 1 show none of the thinking the Type 3 boy is discounting when he says: "The head of the company would be the guy who ran the financial end, but they'd think of him as directing all the branches, transporting all the food, but he wouldn't really be doing all that."

On the side of social organization, Type 0 has little concept of responsibility, in the sense that the authority is responsible for everything done by his subordinates, a Type 2 concept (Obs. 7). This concept of responsibility fuses with the concept of superior ability in all roles to produce the Type 2 response that the superior should undertake the risky job rather than ordering the subordinate (Obs. 8 and 9).

The respect of Types 2 and 3 is in part Baldwin's "ethical respect" in the sense that it is respect for the willingness and ability of the authority to fulfill his duty or responsibility. It implies one respects someone who does something the self finds difficult and unpleasant, something the self does not want to do (Obs. 10).

For Type 3, as for Type 0, one's evaluation of authority is intrinsic as opposed to Type 1's view that the value of an authority is relative to what he can do for you. For Type 0, this intrinsicness is because he does what one would like to do, for Type 3 it is because he does what one wouldn't like to do even though it is good.

Thus the Type 3 children tend to say they do not want to take the authority or high-status roles which they respect because of the responsibility.

In contrast, some of the Type 0 children see escape from pressure as lying at the top, and hence want to be president or the like. The obligation of an authority is limited to taking orders from the next highest up in the line (Obs. 11).

6. Absence of the Notion of a Social Order Distributing Roles According to Merit in Types 0 and 1

Piaget seems to say that the heteronomous child sees the world as a moral order in which all aspects of the social structure, all social differences, have a moral meaning. At the same time, he says, the social order is confused with the natural order so that it might be expected to have some impersonal feature.

As in Case 22, several of the Type 0 children see authority as

ownership of the subordinate (Obs. 12 and 11). This is perhaps the extreme in a depersonalized view of the social order. But we do not see
why such depersonalization implies sacredness. This order itself seems
to be almost without value and without norms; it is simply a matter of
fact. No judgments of value support the relation of one role to another.

Thus views of payment tend to be in terms of the quasi-physical
distribution of some fixed intake (Obs. 13 and 14). This seems to reflect
the lack of any judgment of value in determining pay, any sense that the
rich are deserving of being rich, though a "projective" value may be
attributed to them. It seems to imply the absence of a central intelligence or purpose which creates and organizes the various roles.

On the other hand it also reflects a lack of some conception of
varying personal abilities required of roles (Obs. 16). Undoubtedly the
boy knows that a person existed as something else before he became a
senator, etc., but he has no concept of a general selection process beyond
variations in what individuals want to be. The concept that the person
who became a policeman does not have to meet as difficult requirements as
the judge is not meaningful to most of our 10-year-olds.

This cognitive difficulty in separating person from roles means
that status cannot be related to personal value attributes beyond the activity itself. This comes to acquire diverse meanings in Stage 1, so that
"respect" for a judge is the "respect" most of us feel toward the hangman.
In general, the role is simply a bundle of activities which are compulsory,
rather than a set of personal qualities.

7. Children's Concepts of Role Organization and the Status Order in Other Studies

Some of these characteristics of immature concepts of role and status which we have described are in line with the findings of other research on development of such concepts. Thus on the purely conceptual side, Hartley, et al., find that the role "American" was defined as some martial or parade activity for the youngest children, by activities or simple location in the 6–8 year old range, and by personal virtues like bravery in the 8–10.5 or oldest group (21). Again, their youngest children could not separate person and role at all; one person could have only one role. With successive development, children came to conceive a person as having a disposition or potential to be in an alternate role while being in a given role.

On the value or status side, Stendler's study indicates both the "projective" value interpretations young childre make of money along side of a quasi-physical "non-moral" distribution of money (56). Thus, in first grade, 78 per cent of the children associate "good behavior," portrayed on cards, with being rich but at the same time most saw jobs as "rich" because they actually handled money, or because of amount of actual activity rather than viewing it as a moral reward. In other words, "the goodness" of the rich does not seem to imply a concept of merit.

8. The Privileges of Age or Authority Are Not Justified by Virtues in Type O

Turning to our own material on the relation of virtue to adult authority in Type O, we may note that though certain good behavior may be predicted of status roles, there is no feeling of any necessary or required relation between virtue and authority.

Few go as far as Case 7, who says it's worse for a son to break a promise than a father because "the father is older and he can break

promises and the son is smaller." This example would perhaps be interpreted by Piaget as indicating the authority is of such prestige that he
should be above the law. We would read it simply as a statement of the
fact that authorities can "get away with it."

It does not seem to us to represent too much of a difference from
Case 7's moral evaluation to say, as does Case 9,

> It's worse for the father because his father is older and if he broke
> his promise he'd be excused the first time, but not after that. But
> the boy could do it lots of times and they'd excuse him. The father
> is older and should know better not to do it.

This child definitely does conjure up a vague external punitive agency enforcing conformity. But the father no more "represents" this agency than
he does represent personal virtue. Both responses define the expectation
of adult virtue in terms of how able the adult is to "get away with it."
Adults may be expected to have more virtues since they have more of everything else, but it is not required of them to justify the respect of the
child. Thus Type O children never attribute any moral virtue to an authority as a justification for any attitude or conformity of their own toward
him.

9. For Type O the Fixity of Culture Patterns through Time and Situations Is Not Due to Their Sacredness and the Sacredness of Age

Just as we see Type O children expecting status figures to have
privileges without these being merited by the virtues of the status-
occupant, we would expect these children to express beliefs in the inflex-
ibility and everlastingness of social behavior patterns without this implying anything about the sacredness of these patterns. "It has always been so"
can be an easy way out of a difficult question, reflecting the absence of
a need to justify behavior rather than implying the sanctity of the past
and the status quo.

Piaget gets such responses from his children. The children trace knowledge of a game or other bit of knowledge backward in time perhaps to creation and God. Piaget makes the assumption "that this simply means that the rules are sacred and unchangeable because they partake of parental authority" (44, p. 48). Piaget presupposes the sacredness of the rule and the sacredness of the father or of age, and then, by the logic we have criticized, interprets the statement as a projective or affect—determined effort to link the two.

However, our interpretation would be different. In our view, the child sees the conventional response, not as a cognitive adjustment to a concrete situation, but simply as what people do, and what they learn from each other. Hence, if asked about how someone learned the correct response, the child simply sees an unending chain of imitation or social learning. There seems to be no reason to assume that the child attributes any sacredness to ancientness, nor to the transmitter of the response nor to the response itself, simply because he sees it as endlessly transmitted.

We have obtained the same sort of responses from 10-year-olds who obviously felt no mystic sacredness or unchangeability about either authority or rules. Here is one example from Case 10:

(Who knows the right answers to these questions?)
"You, 'cause you made them up."

(How do I know my answers are right?)
"You could check with the University."

(Whom would they check with?)
"Could they check with the mind reader?"

(How would that be?)
"He reads big people's minds to find out what's the answer to those things. I saw one last night on TV."

(How would that tell him the answer?)
"Well, if the man who was going to think of the answers, if he was thinking of them, the mind reader could read the answer in his mind."

This boy starts out saying that the interviewer made up the answers when he made up the questions, and then is pushed back step by step to the mind reader. The right answer never has an origin as a response to a situation, probably because answers are verbal entities, rather than adaptations.

Such responses seem to have no relation to any kind of sacredness of right activities, or even of "big people." His concepts of respect for age and of fixity of tradition in the family area are given by the following:

(What would your brother do if he wanted to tell on him?)
"They'd say, 'If you tell on me, I'll whip you with my belt real hard.'"

(What would you do then?)

"Well, if I was to tell my Dad if my brother Butchie was still hurting me, my brother Butch would go find another house to live in."

In our view, then, the "unending tradition" is essentially an acceptance of the arbitrary nature of social responses, whether that arbitrariness arises from invention or simply limitation and obedience.

All our observations suggest that the more immature children are completely forward looking in their thinking and in the factors they consider in choice. Obligation is almost never based on the prior in time, as we shall discuss in relation to the concept of obligation as "debt." This may be a function of the American culture. But as long as conformity is viewed as being to something external, it seems almost logically necessary that it be adjustive, predictive and present or future oriented.

As we hypothesize in our discussion of Type 3, it is only when the child feels he knows and has been taught what is right, and that he must resist illegitimate external influence, that he may really become conservative. This in turn presupposes some of the thought and experience

which we attribute to Type 2. This consists of an orientation of parent
and child to a common situation about which the parent knows more and
some realization that parental directives or "the right" represents some
effort of the parent and of others to orient or adjust to such situations.

It is the indefiniteness of what the subordinate needs to know
which is probably a major basis of conservatism as an emotional trend, the
unpredictability of a departure from authority and past tradition. Not
knowing all the reasons, not having all the wisdom of the past, we cannot
change established patterns of response to an indefinitely complex situation. A related basis is the fact that as an adult, the conservative
finds no person as wise or able as he felt adults or parents to be when
he was a child. But a mere responsiveness to existing external authority
such as we find in Type 0 children need not lead to conservativism in the
child or the adult.

We would not deny that many young children have a wish that a
sanction system remain unchanged or be regularly applied to everyone.
It is rather that we question that young children are predisposed to feel
a sense of respect or sacredness for age and tradition which is quite another matter. Neither primitive desire for repetition nor feelings of
relative powerlessness before "big people" seem to us to imply any value
orientation toward age as such. Given that a habit is established in the
self or in the environment, the immature child has no concern about its
pedigree and lineage.

10. Summary and Conclusions in Our Analysis of Heteronomous Respect in Type 0

Piaget makes two fundamental assumptions in his study. The first
is that a young child's orientation to rules can be described as one of

respect and that this respect derives from the respect he feels toward individuals who teach and maintain the rules. The second related assumption
is that such respect is heteronomous, i.e., it implies the vast superiority
of others, a mystical concept of their attributes and of the organization
and purposiveness of the social order in which they are located.

These assumptions are probably not directly testable and Piaget
uses them as principles of interpretation for connections in children's
thinking rather than attempting to support them by direct empirical evidence. However, we have attempted to consider such connections more criti-
cally.

To summarize our empirical analysis so far, we see "respect" conceived as an act of obedience by Type 0 children, an obedience having
little relevance to any value of the other. Judgments of the value of
roles, however, can be made, but these do not discriminate any personal
value behind the role from the value of the role activities themselves.
Particularly in the case of authority, there is no concrete value to authority activities except perhaps some primitive value of power activities
as such. Authority is not seen as knowing how to perform subordinate roles
better and being responsible for them, so the authority does not seem to
represent symbolically the value of the institution as a whole.

Neither do these children invoke the superior knowledge of the
authority as a reason for conformity, as was stated earlier. They do not,
as do the Stage 2 children, say that one should conform to one's parents
because they know what is best for the self or for the family. The authority's knowledge consists only in the fact that he knows how to give the
command or the punishment, not that he "knows" the situation to which the

subordinate or child making the choice is oriented.[1]

Respect in the usual sense implies admiration for such attributes of the other which allow him to act appropriately. There are, of course, other bases of "respect," physical attributes which are shared with things, e.g., physical power, possessions, and beauty. These are attributes which do no one any good but their possessor, and hence to value their possessor for them is projective and syntelic.

It is the non-instrumental character of such valuing of physical characteristics which tempts Piaget to explain them in terms of the awe which an adult might have toward a mystical or magic figure. However, if an emotional attitude of heteronomous respect underlay such projective valuing, we would not expect instrumental modes of thought to completely wipe out symbolic respect as it seems to in Type 1.

Those implications of valuing physical qualities which we would stress take their cue from Baldwin's analyses. First, such qualities do not lead to a social relationship of identification. Physical qualities are not transmittable from the admired person to the self except in magical thinking. If a boy admires the physical strength of his father or of adults, he will be anxious to grow up physically but not imitate, learn from and conform to his father or other adults. We saw boys who admired the quasi-physical power of authority and its "gravy-train" position, and wanted to have it; but gaining it did not involve learning from and conforming to the authority.

---

[1]We stress knowledge because, although knowledge has various meanings for various personalities and cultures, it is probably a transcultural universal that the division of labor and the justification of differential role behaviors and rewards rests largely on concepts of differential knowledge and skill, or on concepts of differential moral virtue, primarily on the former. Even the most authoritarian concepts of status rests on such a basis though the concept of knowledge may be one of revelation.

The second related implication stems from the fact that all admired non-physical qualities imply some conformity of action to norms of
appropriateness, conformity or adjustment to something outside the self
of the actor, while physical qualities do not.

Of course, admiration for the greater cognitive ability may and
probably does precede a generalized concern to conform to the culturally
appropriate. However, there is no reason why this should imply an attitude
of respect though it need not deviate from such an attitude as far as the
following remark of a six-year-old boy to us:[1]

> I'm going to knock your brains out. Then they'll go into my brains
> and I'll be twice as smart. You've got twice as much brains because
> you're twice as big.

Respect for the ability of another requires shared values. When
we say someone "knows what to do," we mean that he has some concepts, rules,
ideas, or experience by which he adjusts his action to the situation. However, a more primitive meaning of "knowing what to do" seems to be simply
knowing some definite response which has been made before by others to the
situation. This seems to be the conception of at least some of our Type O
children.

It is not that these children do not see some particular socially
transmitted activities as difficult, as involving effort and perhaps "smart-
ness." Thus to be a teacher "you have to know writing" or "making numbers"
or "you have to holler at the kids," which is hard. However, such socially
transmitted activities do not involve a common situation or object to which
both teacher and learner are oriented. The teacher is not someone who is
seen as knowing when to write and why to write and what to write; i.e., the

---

[1]This illustrates how "identification" with reference to physical
qualities is not only magical but non-social.

application of the activity to a situation the child will face or does face. The learning situation is not one of mutual role taking. The Type 0 child is a crude behaviorist who sees roles and culture patterns as simply "there," and as learned by imitation and obedience.

Instead of speaking of a common situation, being absent in Type 0 thinking, we could speak of the absence of a common tradition, which an authority must know. Insofar as someone has authority, there is a vague mass of norms and knowledge which he possesses which have a bearing on what the subordinate should do or on what the subordinate is to become. A teacher must be seen not only as someone who knows how to write but as someone who knows what it is the child should do to become "smart" or to become a grown up or to become a worker or perhaps to become "good." If to learn what the school teacher knows is only to learn to become a school teacher, there will be little respect for the teacher.

Her activities as a model and as sanctioner must be viewed as oriented to this vague mass, "the culture," which may be looked at as knowledge or adaptations to situations, as purposes, or as models of ideal persons. We require someone's advice or approva just insofar as we feel there exist norms or knowledge beyond what we know and understand which have some bearing on the issue confronting us, and which the other knows. We may feel this vague mass to be a personal creation of the individual authority or to be his by right of longer or higher membership in some group or culture. But it is just the indefiniteness or unlimitedness of that which must be brought to bear on a situation which creates a sense of personal authority. If a doctor is someone viewed as having authority, he must not only be someone who knows how to give shots, but someone who knows how the patient should protect his health.

Thus our usual concepts of emotionalized respect for personal authority do seem to depend on the individual's respect for the culture, which in some way the authority embodies better than the self.

Accordingly we are led to say with Baldwin and Durkheim that the attitude of conformity to the culturally appropriate precedes personal respect in Piaget's sense. For Piaget, moral sacredness is based on such personal respect which is based on emotional ambivalence plus cognitive adualism. If we substitute the word "identification" for respect, we may say the same for psychoanalytic theory. The implication of Baldwin's position is that even if we wish to see conscience as a product of respect and identification, we must study in detail the development of the child's conceptions and of his values and conformities. Only as these acquire certain properties can the child's "identification" and "respect" acquire the properties making possible the internalization of parental and social norms. Reciprocally, the internalization of parental norms increases rather than decreases some forms of respect and dependency. The normal latency child who needs his parents' approval of his conformity to social norms **feels** more dependent than the young child symbiotically dependent on the mother to gratify his needs.

C. Children's Conceptions of Rules through All the Types

1. Piaget's Concept of Respect for Rules

There is a third hypothesis fundamental to Piaget's concept of moral realism and heteronomous respect for rules, in addition to the concept of heteronomous respect for persons and the derivation of respect for rules from such respect. This is the hypothesis that children's modes of conceiving of duty, good, and right may be defined by some kind of respect for rules. This third hypothesis has more to do with the actual concepts of children and is more easily verifiable empirically.

Piaget says: "In the first place, duty as viewed by moral realism is essentially heteronomous. Any act which shows obedience to a rule, or even to an adult, regardless of what he may command, is good" (44, p. 106).

This raises the image of a child as judging whether an act fits or is in obedience to some standard or generalized command. Is this in fact the way in which obligation presents itself to the young child?

While rules are obviously important in children's games, it is rather questionable whether many obligations of the child appear to him in a form analogous to games. From the adult observer's point of view, the child is always conforming to rules, and we may talk of the child's orientation to rules in the loose sense in which we might talk about a dog's orientation to the rules his owner lays down. Naturally the young child goes much further than this in consciousness of rules; he may verbalize "Don't do that" or "we do things this way," i.e., he is aware of a pattern of activity he does share with others or wants to share or is supposed to share with others. However, such verbalizations are not formulations of rules in the full sense of the term.

Piaget introduces the concept of rule "in the full sense" when the consciousness of obligation is added to the pleasure in regularity of the motor ritual. He says,

> The element of obligation or, to confine ourselves to the practice of rules, this element of obedience intervenes as soon as there is a society, i.e., a relation between at least two individuals. As soon as a ritual is imposed upon a child by adults or seniors for whom he has respect (Bovet) or, as we would add, as soon as a ritual comes into being as the result of collaboration, it acquires in the subject's mind a new character which is precisely that of a rule [44, p. 23].

Let us consider in what sense it may be said that once a pattern of activity or a ritual is socially imposed or imitated, the child then feels that he is "respecting" or "obeying" that pattern of activity. Piaget would not say that the child "obeyed" or "respected" his own motor ritual or habit. It would seem to us that the primitive concept of a rule as an activity and not as an idea in people's minds makes it impossible for the individual to feel he is obeying a rule, rather he feels he is imitating or obeying a person.

It appears to us that a child can only acquire a respect for rules when concepts of rules have most of the usual features adults assign to them. These important characteristics of rules, Piaget notes as developing in the third stage of development of the game and attribute to "autonomous" peer group attitudes and experience. They are:

a) the demand that rules be held in common,

b) the use of rules as standards against which an act is evaluated,

c) conceptions of rules as forming a role system defining the game as an "institution."

2. Type 0 Does Not Seem to See Obligation and the Social Order as Defined by Rule

One approach to this problem was to ascertain the meaning the child gave to the words "rule" and "law," the functions he assigned to rules, and whether he believed that rules or laws could ever be bad or wrong.

This has obvious limitations akin to those involved in asking when and why roles are respected. However, some interesting data emerged as appears in the examples.

In Observation 17 Case 10 assimilates a law to a concrete command of a storekeeper to a little boy. There is nothing fixed or universal about it; it does not hold for all situations or all people. In Observation 18, Case 10 also assimilates the concept of rule to a sort of prudential or technological directive, to "safety rules" for staying out of trouble. Though Case 10 is oriented to avoiding punishment, he does not see punishment as resulting from violating a rule (Obs. 19). Rather, certain actions lead to punishment and the rule is advice to avoid such actions. Punishment preceded the rule. In Observation 22, Case 22 also seems to imply that you do not obey rules; you obey persons, since the rule seems to be a warning or piece of advice to obey persons. In Observation 20, Case 10 says you don't need laws if you just mind the law and the Bible, so that minding the law must mean obeying the police, not following rules.

These responses do not indicate the expectancy of regularity and stability of the punitive order which many Type 0 children have. But they do indicate that respect for such an order is not respect for rules, and that the order is not perceived in terms of the concept of general laws or commands.

In a sense, these observations justify Piaget's belief that children confuse physical and social laws. However, the confusion lies in the direction of reducing the social order to mechanical regularity rather than reducing the physical order to the regularity of moral rule. As in Observation 22, a society in which disobedience is punished is just "there," it is not organized by rules. The rules are simply good advice as to how to orient to such a quasi-physical structure, they are not its basis.

These observations also make it clear how far Type 0 is from an "authoritarian" regard for the government as the central source of right and wrong (Obs. 21).

3. Type 1 Sees Laws as Instrumental Commands by the Police

Some cognitive advance seems to be indicated in Case 19's Type 1 response, which sees rules as to be obeyed and rule violation as the basis of punishment (Obs. 22). Such a response indicates an ability to take the perspective of the rule maker as differentiated from that of the rule obeyer and as able to make the rule instrumentally in terms of a definite purpose.

An intermediary stage in such differentiation is illustrated in Observation 23. Thus, Case 36's rule of "avoid trouble," is partly at- tempting to take the role of authority and forbid crime, but ending up as "advice" which assumes a fixed punishment structure to define "trouble."

However, the Type 1 conception is highly relativistic in seeing a law as guiding the punishing behavior of the police, rather than a universal shared norm made by a benevolent authority trying to define the right for all. Case 4, who spontaneously suggests making a rule, sees a law as a role norm for the police (Obs. 24). Being "worse by law" for him means that there is a rule that "the law" or the police shouldn't do it.

As far as judgment of "wrong" goes, this is not decided by correspondence to the rule but by the prudential consequences (Obs. 25).

A typical response of Stage 1 is Case 12's response to Question IX, that it's right to leave your post to protect your family, and it's also right to punish the man because "there's probably a rule that says to." He also says that the law has no business legislating about such things as mercy killing or charging for a drug because it isn't the law's property. In other words, "the law" is just seen as the rules or activities of one group of people among other groups, with no supreme authority or responsibility for anything but catching thieves. In terms of punishment, some Type 1's view punishment as to be determined by the victim and his family. Where a bad activity and a law are opposed in both Stage 0 and Stage 1, the children say one should break the law.

3. In Types 2 and 3, Laws Are Oriented to as a Core of a Generally Good Social Order

In discussing our next two types, we are endeavoring to focus on attributes absent in Types 0 and 1. These attributes seem necessary on the cognitive side if moral judgments are to be based on comparison of action with a rule. They seem necessary on the motivational side if respect for the social order in general, and of all rules, is to be embodied in respect for a particular rule. These two bases of the rules seem necessary to create an orientation of "the sacredness of the rules."

Our discussion of these aspects of Type 2 and 3 is supplemented in the next chapter where the types are discussed for their own sake rather than to provide perspective on Types 0 and 1.

In Type 2 we seem to see some of the derivation of respect for rules from respect for persons which Piaget hypothesizes. Laws are seen as good, because of the superior wisdom of the authorities who make them (augmented by tolerance and the wish not to get hung in Observation 26).

Such a conception seems to be related to a conception of the common good or common welfare and an acceptance of rules as generally helpful or protective as a matter of faith. Type 2 has a basic justification of the status quo used in all succeeding stages. This is the awareness of the good in most cases as justifying conformity in the atypical particular case, and the good of the many as justifying the conformity of the one.

In Type 2, such conceptions may be yet indistinct and are tied to that "naive" trust in personal authority which Piaget uses to account for the thinking of Type 0. This in turn is based on a belief in the general agreement of all good people in what is expected (Obs. 28).

Type 2 does not yet see loyalty and conformity to authority and the social order as primarily expressed in conformity to rule. Vague images of being good, role stereotypes, and sensitivity to the wishes and approval of accepted authority are more important definers of conformity to Type 2.

Type 3 tends more to see conformity to parents, God and the social order as the maintenance of fixed general rules and expectations.

A "transitional," or mixed type child, indicates the "being good" concern of Types 2 being subordinated under the concept of rule (Obs. 29). Such rules are seen as a comprehensive system, perhaps even to the extreme in which deviation from one may have the force of deviation from all (Obs. 30).

It is in these types, and usually among the 13-year-olds, that religious interest or conceptualization in moral matters appear. There is a concept of man's relationship to God as defining relation to other men. At earlier stages, religious acts and taboos exist, but as a few of the many social taboos rather than as providing a general basis for conformity (cf. Obs. 20). Among the older Type 0 and 1 children, the "religious" reference is illustrated by Observation 31.

The religious conceptualization of rules by some of the Type 2 and 3 children seems remote from Piaget's interpretation of the stage of "codification of rules" as being a product of game-like experiences with the peer-group.

4. Types 4 and 5 Show Autonomous Orientations to Rules

Piaget says that the autonomous stage of respect for rules is represented by a sense of the need for agreement as to prescribed actions for the sake of group goals or the functioning of organized activities.

We classified as Type 4, this respect for the agreed upon together with a sort of functional acknowledgment that the attainment of agreement might necessitate some unoptional content.

Type 4 believes in a complete conformity to the idea of law itself, regardless of its content, as the shared expectations and judgment of society, which must be taken as final, and which may define action in any situation. Type 4 may expect an individual to deviate naturally from the law under certain extreme circumstances but there is no perspective from which such deviation could be said to be actually "right."

Many of the type identify law and right with majority opinion (Obs. 32, 34). Some of the "other-directed" representatives of the type suggest peer-group good sport analogies.

The stress upon agreed upon rule is associated with a sense of the function of the rules in defining expectancies in any social context (Obs. 32). This broadened scope increases the importance of law and rules while making its content more secular and less limited to basic taboos.

Our Type 5 classification of rules includes the following characteristics:

a) Conformity to law as a procedural or methodological principle, i.e., it is in some sense right to conform to law though the law does not make the action completely right (Obs. 35).

b) Conformity to the majority as a methodological principle, i.e., it is not that the majority always is right, but that majority rule is the best principle to make decisions on (Obs. 35).

c) There is a law and a type of conformity higher than legal law, usually expressed as "principle" as "God's law" or "the moral law." This is associated with the individual's judgment or conscience, preferably with the idea that higher law should or cannot be enforced punitively (Obs. 35, 36). Deviation from law is not justified on the basis of natural impulse or situational consequences but in terms of "principle."

Type 5 responses are rather rare among our children and concentrated in four of them. Perhaps it becomes more frequent in maturity, though one of our four representatives of the type is only ten.

We might add that various recent surveys of American adolescents support the notion that few of them have a notion of "ideal" or "higher" rights or laws or principles as opposed to de facto law (47).

5. Summary of Implications of Our Study of Developing Concept of Rules

As we follow through the concepts of our six types, we note a successively clearer definition of obligation in terms of rule. Associated with this conceptual trend there tends to be a progressively increased respect for rule and law as a formal matter. In Type 5 this is manifested in a respect for universal principles which are more "truly" rules than statute law, but there is no denial of rules as such. In this context it becomes very difficult to interpret the rigidities of Type 0 as a punitive sort of literalist legalism, as Piaget does. There is a fixity of punishment and of bad activities, but it is misleading to see such fixity as one of rule. The implications of this for Piaget's concepts of a primitive "morally realistic" sense of objective responsibility will be considered in the next section.

D. Modes of Valuing and the Sense of "Objective Responsibility" in Types 0 and 1

1. Piaget's Conception of Objective Responsibility and the Studies Based on It

The points in Piaget's theory with which we have dealt so far have been postulates which he did not endeavor to test. The kind of data which

Piaget gathered relative to the heteronomous stage involved an additional deductive step to lead to the hypothesis that the young child has a "sense of objective responsibility."

Thus we may extend the quotation of Piaget made in Section C-1 as follows:

> Moral realism possesses at least three features. In the first place, duty, as viewed by moral realism, is essentially heteronomous. Any act that shows obedience to a rule, or even to an adult, regardless of what he may command, is good.
> In the second place, moral realism demands that the letter, rather than the spirit of the law, shall be observed.
> In the third place, moral realism induces an objective conception of responsibility. We can even use this as a criterion of realism, for such an attitude towards responsibility is easier to detect than the two that precede it. For since he takes rules literally, and thinks of good only in terms of obedience, the child will at first evaluate acts not in accordance with the motive that has prompted them, but in terms of their exact conformity with established rules [44, pp. 106-07].

Piaget made up a series of items in which the child had to judge the badness of well-intentioned or non-intentional acts with bad consequences as opposed to acts based on bad intentions. These items have been shown to be age differentiating on both sides of the Atlantic by Piaget (44), Caruso (11), Lerner (29), and MacRae (32).

Such items have not, however, stood the test of defining a "morally realistic" or "heteronomous" type. MacRae got low associations between them with age held constant, and negligible associations of such items with other aspects of moral judgment (32, 33).

Piaget himself admits obtaining little individual consistency across such items, and explains this by saying that a child can be at various developmental levels in various situations or in various tasks.

Piaget's justification is not adequate, however. His conceptualization implies some individual consistency, though it does not imply the child is always at the same level. His items obviously have a culturally correct answer, it is this which has made them appealing to other investigators. Failure to find individual consistency beyond that due to age suggests that development with regard to such items merely reflects a process of moving from ignorance to knowledge of cultural cliches, rather than a process of moving from one level of thinking to another. To put the objection from another point of view, there has been little evidence presented to indicate that such items have anything to do with moral growth as opposed to the development of intellectual sophistication. We have endeavored to show that these objections cannot be raised for our moral types or levels in earlier chapters.

Our contention is that his questions about intentions versus consequences do tap typologically consistent orientations, but not if they are scored dichotomously as "chooses intentions vs. chooses consequences."

The modes of thought involved are much more complex, with each of our types having differing conceptions of the value of intentions and the value of consequences.

We interpret the failure to obtain individual consistency on "objective responsibility" items as reflecting confusions in Piaget's interpretation of a consequence-orientation as due to a rule-oriented legalism.

It might be added that the importance of a detailed analysis of this problem does not rest only on the importance of validating Piaget's theories. It is also quite crucial to any of the other theories we have described, since it is of necessity a major focus of any analysis of moral judgment. In a sense, the domain of moral values may be defined by the fact that intentions are of concern to it, alone among all the kinds of value judgment such as the scientific, aesthetic, political, economic, etc.

2. The Intrinsic Value Attached to Moral Labels in Type 0 Usage Does Not Indicate a Rigid and Literalistic or "Morally Realistic" Orientation toward Rules

The conclusion of our earlier sections was that young children were not oriented to rules as fixed concepts against which situations or actions were evaluated. Our Type 0 appeared to be oriented to bad activities, to obedience to persons and to bad or punitive consequences. All these aspects of the Type 0 orientation are "situational."

Type 0 is not rigid in the sense of the legalist who has fixed rules which must apply to any situation and who disregards aspects of situations which do not fit in order to maintain the rule unweakened and unchanged.

In our next chapter we shall see this mode of orientation at work in Types 3 and 4.

In our opinion there is nothing especially "rigid" about Type 0's failure to consider intentions. An example of a "situationally flexible" adaptation of judgment which ignores intentions is Observation 38. From the point of view of a rule, both cheating $500 and stealing it are equivalent as taking money. From the point of view of intentions, the cheating is worse. The fact that "asking" approaches less to the form of stealing shows a concreteness in the concept of stealing but no rigid set toward a rule.

The concern for the empty form of asking is pretty clearly not related to the sacredness of a stealing rule, but to an assessment of the punitive consequences, evidenced by the thought that the person who was asked might not do anything about it. A primitive instrumental set is indicated by Case 7's willingness to justify lying as a part of the "asking permission."

It is true that in addition to an instrumental avoidance of the anger and punitive reactions of the other, Case 7 is also attempting to instrumentally avoid the label "stealing." He probably must feel this label is bad in itself. It does not seem that it is completely reduced to need consequences, which we shall see happens in Type 1.

We know that young children think that being labelled with a bad word is bad "in itself." A kindergarten child says to the teacher, "Make him stop calling me that" whether the label is true and applicable or not. Thus Observation 39 seems to be saying, "Although it isn't fair to call someone a bad name, if it isn't true, it still hurts just as much."

Intrinsic concern about being called a bad name is not intrinsic concern about violating a rule however. The mere process of going through instrumental acts like telling teacher to stop the other from labelling the act, or as in Observation 38, lying and asking permission in order to avoid being labelled as stealing indicate that the only thing wrong about violating a rule is getting labelled and caught. This is reflected in Type 0's indifference to whether people think an action is bad apart from what they say and do about it (Obs. 40).

Piaget says that the child confuses the name with the act so that the name acquires the badness of the act. Here we seem to see that the name is worse than the act, it is the labelling which is to be avoided. The "intrinsic" negative value of the name seems to arise from its association with punishment and hostility, not with the badness of the action. The primitive and basic Type 0 meaning of "bad" seems to be "to be badly treated," "to be punished," or "to feel pain." The "slip of the tongue" in Observation 41 is an illustration of this.

Names or labels are not rules. We can "obey" or "respect" rules but not labels. Some cultures do indeed respect names of deity and treat them as sacred by not using them. The name is a symbol of the deity. This has nothing in common with a Type O orientation to the "projective" value of the name.[1] The projective value of the moral label does not spring from the value and respect accorded to its adult user.

The projective value of the name reflects the inability to separate the pain felt by the self or the punitive reaction of others from the name itself. It is the confusion denied when children say, "Sticks and stones can hurt my bones but names can never hurt me." It has little to do with any rule, sacred or otherwise

3. The Concern for Consequences in Type O Indicates Not Moral Realism but the Failure to Make Categorical or Rule—Oriented Judgment

Piaget interprets the child's concern for material consequences of action as indicating a process of comparing the act to a standard, a process of assessing, whether it "exactly conforms to established rule."

Actually a legalistic set ignores not only the motive, but the consequences. "Stealing is stealing," "Lying is lying," "It's just plain wrong" would be the judgment of the rigid regard for rule. This type of response, completely absent in Type O, involves a definite set to disregard some factors in the situation in order to secure fixity or regularity of judgment. It is a rather puzzling piece of reasoning by which Piaget associates the very situational and variable or "flexible" concern with consequences with an orientation to fixed rules.

It seems more plausible and logical to deduce a concern for consequences with our hypothesis which is the exact opposite of Piaget's. The

---

[1] See Chapter I, section E-1 and Chapter IX, Table 18 for the elaboration of this concept.

Type 0 child orients to consequences because he is not oriented to rules at all in his judgment.

In the last section we said that the question "Was this man wrong or bad?" was not interpreted by the child as meaning "Did this man disobey a rule?" but meant "Would he be punished or called bad names." In addition to these punitive consequences, other bad consequences are also included in Type 0's judgment of an act as bad.

4. The Punitive Meanings of Good and Bad Ignore Standards and Intentions

The punitive basis of an evaluation of action as bad are either the "projective" repugnance to the act itself as in "dirty" and "perverse" actions or else consequences whether judged "projectively" or consciously in terms of pain and frustration. Objects and persons are "judged" as bad in the same way as acts, as having aversive, unpleasant characteristics or consequences.

Essentially such judgment is from the standpoint of someone outside the person or thing, but being affectively aroused by it. It does not involve either a denial of one's own interested reaction or a role-taking of the other and, therefore, the question as to whether the other deserves to be labelled bad is irrelevant.

Bad is not a judgment, it is a description of one's feelings and a prediction. A bad or mean person is someone who is likely to harm you. Our Type 0 and 1 children did no retrospective labelling of people in our stories as good or bad, they seemed to have no motives to praise or blame someone who had not affected them.

The developmentally more advanced judgments of good and bad imply a personal model or standard of comparison. It is this type of concept which is required to judge the actor's intentions as good. It involves role-taking the person judged and finding him worthy of imitation, as conforming in the way the self would try to conform in the situation. It involves sharing his expectation of approval. These are the judgments of the Type 2 "good boy" orientation which are absent in Type 0 and 1. They imply role stereotypes, or images of a generally good and conforming self.

5. A Concern for Consequences as Implicit in Type 0's Primitive Meanings of Right and Wrong

A concern for intentions, "goodness" and conformity to a general role model is one basis for eliminating consequences in judging action. As we said, another basis for ignoring consequences is a categorical judgment of an act as conforming to rule, as right or wrong.

On the motivational side, such a judgment seems to imply taking the role of the authority, or the judge, of the member of the community concerned about and able to condemn or punish. It implies someone with an interest in seeing that people conform. The implications of this set are developed in our description of Type 3.

The basic primitive meaning of right seems to be cognitive and instrumental as follows:

a) Right means a label applied by some authority to a response on a basis I do not understand.
   "Teacher marked it right" analogous to "He called me a liar" (Obs. 42).

b) Right means a response which corresponds to the teacher's judgment, a cognitively correct prediction of what is rewarded (e.g., "Sydney's response" in Obs. 42).

c) Right means any action which gets the person what he wants, i.e., an instrumentally appropriate action (Obs. 43, 44).

Such meanings of right involve role-taking of the actor and his wishes, whereas the primitive meanings of good look at him as an object.

However, it is not specific rules which are shared with the actor or determine role-taking, it is rather a general set toward success and punishment
avoidance.[1]

It is characteristic of the judgments of cognitively and instrumentally correct that they are concerned with consequences and results, and
are adaptations to concrete situations.[2]

This is because they imply concern with the actor's self-seeking
intentions rather than a morally categorical ignoral of them. The authority is fixed and ignores the actor's situational adaptation, but the child
does not in judging the actor wrong.

The categorical judgment of wrong is one kind of judgment by intentions, an assertion that the actor should be oriented only to obedience to
rule. The Type O judgment of wrong is an assertion that the actor is predicting incorrectly that he can avoid punishment or bad happenings.

Thus an alternative way of stating that the child is not oriented
to rule is that he does not discriminate the moral right and good from
other forms of right and good.

---

[1] The Type 5 or "highest" judgment of moral right is also cognitive
and involves role-taking the actor in the situation. However, it presupposes the actor is motivated to conforming morally and asks, "Was the actor's line of thinking as to what was morally right correct?"

[2] It is easy to see how issues about intentions versus consequences
may be reduced to questions about cognitive versus moral meanings of the
word "wrong." A judgment "by intentions" implies realizing that an act is
cognitively "wrong," but "morally right."

As an illustration, we may quote an adaptation of one of Piaget's
items used in MacRae's study (32):

"A boy who didn't know the names of the streets very well was not
sure where Cambridge Street was. One day a man stopped him in the street
and asked him where Cambridge Street was. The boy answered, 'I think it is
over there.' But he gave the wrong direction and the man lost his way.
Was this a right thing or a wrong thing for the boy to do?
    1. Right because he tried to help the man.
    2. Wrong because the man got lost.
    3. Wrong because he shouldn't have told the man if he wasn't sure."

6. Concern for Quantity of the Consequences in Type O
   Does Not Indicate a Literalistic Orientation
   to Rules But Indicates Projective Evaluation

One of the indeces of "moral realism" used by Piaget is a quantitative and materialistic approach to the judgment of badness. The sheer size of the act or of its material consequences determines how bad it is.

Piaget finds that young children "realistically" think the worst lie is the biggest lie in terms of sheer deviation from reality, regardless of intent. An example from our Type O is provided by Observation 45. Here the child has a view that the bigger the lie is, the more detectable it is, or the harder to get out of or undo.

An example of a judgment in terms of materialistic quantitative consequences from our Type O is provided by Observation 46. Here again we see a concern about the restorability of the consequences, which is no doubt looked upon as closely related to the punishment.[1]

In all the concreteness about size and material characteristics of the act, we see no hint of Piaget's assumed process of a literalistic assessment of whether "an act exactly conforms to established rule."

In each of our types there is some concern for choosing the "greater good." The differences lie in what is the good to be maximized and why it is good.

In Type O, size per se tends to be equated with value. We are all

---

[1]Here we see that a restorative view of punishment does not lead to a judgment by intentions. Piaget's thinking that a concern for quantitative consequences is linked to an expiative view of punishment, whereas the reverse seems to be true. Concern about quantitative damage done is natural if you have to make it up, not if you have broken a system of sacred rule. Concern about quantitative damage is also characteristic of a view of punishment as vengeance, as being "paid back" by the victim. This type of reciprocity is also not characteristic of Piaget's concept of heteronomous expiative justice. All this seems to be further evidence that a concern for consequences has no relationship to a heteronomous concern for rules.

familiar with the urge of the young child to be and have the biggest and
most, regardless of the value or use of the bigger object.

Such a mode of evaluation is projective, it is an equation of the
comparative value of an object with its perceptual characteristics. A more
advanced concept of comparative value used extensively by Type 3 is that of
importance. We saw this used projectively by some Type 0 children in the
concept of the greater intrinsic value of important people. While naive,
this strikes us as closer to a moral orientation than a concern for size,
per se. It indicates some concern to inferentially judge the value of
things in terms of what is of concern to other people rather than a lack of
any effort to differentiate the self's reactions from that of others.

E. Duty and Choice in Type 0

1. The Sphere Denoted by Conscience and Duty

In our discussion of respect and of objective responsibility, we
have focussed on the way in which Type 0 evaluates other people and their
actions. It may be useful to shift our perspective to the way in which
Type 0 experiences obligation and choice. The distinction is that between
the moral evaluation of another acting object and moral experience as an
acting subject.

The assumption of almost all moral philosophers in every culture
has been that such experience is that of "conscience," the meaning of which
we elaborated in Chapter II, section E-5.

Our assumption is that moral experience becomes more conscience-like
with succeeding stages of moral development. On the one hand we do not feel
conscience can be reduced to a primitive "internalized" behavioral conformity when the policeman is not around. On the other hand, we do not think

it is merely a complex concept or system of verbalizations developed in sophisticated cultures.

The kind of phenomena which we have taken as making possible a suitable ground between these extremes are the reactions of our children to explicit and implicit questions as to:

> What is a duty?
> What tells one the right thing to do?
> What makes one do it?
> What choice does one have in moral situations?

Needless to say, our results are as limited and incomplete as those in our discussion of that other "sacred" attitude, respect.

2. Obligation as External Necessity in Type O

In our discussion in Chapter II, E-5, we found that both Piaget and Baldwin agreed that the most primitive sense of obligation was the heteronomous one of "external necessity," though they disagreed as to the sacredness of this necessity.

We shall present a series of observations which indicate that in at least some cases Baldwin seems to be more correct than Piaget. In these cases "obligation" denotes the compulsion of external forces, even when these forces are not those of authority and the rules.[1]

---

[1] Many of our observations are quotations from Case 8, a lower-class Mexican boy. Probably these are related to the fatalism and passivity before external forces of the Spanish-American cultures described by the Harvard Values Project, as well as to the condition of powerlessness and alienation in the face of social authority experienced by lower-class immigrants. However, this in no way changes the status of these observations as indicating thought patterns of a level of development, as our discussion in Chapter IV argued. In most Type O children the obligation of external compulsion is more closely linked to legitimate authority. Case 8 is useful to indicate that this need not be the case, as Piaget thought. It seems to illustrate the physicalization of the moral rather than the moralization of the physical.

Thus in Observation 47, the doctor has to do what the wife and husband tell him, and what the situation demands to avoid bad consequences without special regard to rule. The element of personal command is even more absent from Observations 48 and 49 in which the "have to" is that of Piaget's concept of reciprocity or autonomy.

Instrumental and heteronomous meanings of the right are not inconsistent. If all an individual's ends are constrained or given from without, the only realm to do right or wrong is in the choice of means. One is wrong for choosing the wrong means (Obs. 52). Or perhaps, as for case 8, it is right because it is necessary (Obs. 48).[1]

For Case 8, illegal acts like the stealing, are not performed by bad people with bad motives. The criminal, like the authority, is governed by external necessity (Obs. 53). One's father might possibly steal like any one else (Obs. 54).[2]

The forces which can restrain someone from committing crimes are completely external for Case 8. An external figure must block one (Obs. 55).

Case 8 is typical of several Type 0 children in his heavy reliance on the semi-fantasy prediction of bad events beyonds the actor's control as a justification for conformity. Such a style of argument has three interesting features. First, it is completely predictive, one's espousal

---

[1]This is another illustration of the consistency of a Type 0 orientation with what Piaget would call a judgment by intentions. The discrimination between causing bad consequences through accident or through pressure of others and causing such consequences through voluntary action is entirely consistent with a heteronomous equation of the wrong with the voluntary. The young child's excuse "He made me, he told me to" is entirely Type 0 (Obs. 51).

[2]There is another striking case of how the heteronomous obedience to the father shown in Obs. 49 is not based on the sacredness of the father as hypothesized by Piaget.

of the cause of conformity never rises from the passive to the imperative
voice. Secondly, it assumes that the person warned is equally passive,
warning being in terms of evil possibilities and habits out of the actor's
control. Thirdly, it assumes great separateness between the motives and
knowledge of the arguing self and the other argued with. The "you" who
shouldn't steal is a sort of unlistening monster from the movies who
doesn't know he might be punished, but at the same time is someone with
whom one is identified (Obs. 55).

We may for speculation's sake imagine whether this style of thinking could form a dialogue of the boy with himself. There is the self as an
actor in a situation, a "Me" in Mead's terms. There is also a warning
"generalized other," which is not itself actually identified with the police
or other community or authority roles. It passively predicts what will happen to the deviant acting self which ignores these predictions until it is
punished when it says "I've done wrong all my life."

There seems to be in all this a complete lack of any part of the
personality which is self-constraining or self-punishing. The closest
activity to "conscience" would seem to be processes of fantasying punishment from outside. In Baldwin's terms, we would say that Case 8 has a
bipolar self in which the conforming self is merely passive and submissive.
As such, it cannot be self-constraining or controlling. As this is manifested externally, there is no shared self between the moral speaker and
the person spoken to.

In general, Type 0 does not verbalize anything which would indicate
conformity controlled by inner forces or processes.

3. Obligation without Choice and Susceptibility to Pressure in Type 0

The verbalizations we have quoted have indicated that the right action is not a chosen act, it is a constrained one. This seems closely linked to the indifference to evaluating the motives of action, as Piaget stressed. If the right act is one compelled by superior forces, the motive for it is irrelevant.

It should be stressed that such an attitude is quite distinct from the prizing of respect and obedience to authority as good motives, a prizing displayed by some of our Type 3 children. It is very compatible with an egoistic or prudential set. The direction for action comes from without, the motive for assent is a prudential one.[1]

Thus when these children change their answers under slight pressure, this is not out of "respect for authority." There was no conflict about it, since there is no egoistic motive or reward to maintain one's answer; whereas one can get the right answer by changing. It indicates little more respect for authority than cheating on a new game taught by an authority. Most see nothing wrong with changing their mind for money (Obs. 56).

4. Concepts of Rights for Type 0

These children do not have a concept of rights, in the sense of a sphere of freedom of choice. For some "having a right" to do something seems to be an unfamiliar phrase and means "being right" in doing something, e.g., avoiding punishment. Others have a fairly generalized concept of ownership rights meaning the right to control assigned property. These are the children who see authorities as owning the people they control.

---

[1]This distinction was elaborated in Chapter II, section E-5.

F. Type 1 and Piaget's autonomous Stage

Our presentation of Type 1 may be much more succinct since we do not need to interpret a variety of "illogical" patterns of thought as in Type 0. Aside from our typological and descriptive purposes, our interest is based on the hypothesis that it is possible for Type 0 modes of thought to develop naturally into Type 1. If this be true, it indicates that Type 0 does not really contain the core of adult morality, even of a heteronomous variety.

1. Dualistic Value Modes and "Intentions" in Type 1

A response which provides a sort of smooth transition to Type 1 is provided in Observation 57 which may be compared with the more Type 0 Observations 38 and 46. Observation 57 indicates a complete reduction of rules and consequences to the implications for the eogistic needs of the actor.

Such an instrumentalism would have to be called "intensions-oriented" in Piaget's dichotomous scheme. The wish or need justifies the act, e.g., "He didn't want to pay him back, so he didn't."

For Type 1, the value of the act is completely determined as means to some purpose or need. But there is no discrimination or evaluation as to which are good purposes or needs, and which are bad. It is not that a purpose is good and therefore an act is good, but that any act is good which serves a purpose or need. There is no idea that this purpose or need be considered good or be shared by others. The excusable or justified act expresses a natural need, not a good or conforming self.

In our discussion of respect we saw that Type 1 valued persons only as means. Now we see that the same is true for action.

The extent to which such thinking may be carried is indicated by Observation 58. Quotations such as this seem equally remote from "delinquent subculture" sociology as from "unconscious conflict" psychology.[1] Presumably the boy is putting up his most conforming front to the world since he is role-playing alternately being a probation officer or being himself, talking to the probation officer about delinquent acts he actually performed. From his point of view, stealing really isn't any reflection of a bad self; there's nothing bad about riding horses and cars. It isn't that he likes to steal, it's that he likes to ride bikes. The extant to which he is unable to even understand punitive or conventional or evaluative attitudes is confirmed by his role-playing as his probation officer.[2]

The focus of evaluation, of the good, is on liking. Doing what you like is good. In Type 0, the right was an action instrumental to meeting some external constraint or avoiding a sanction. In Type 1, it is an action instrumental to meeting some need or liking of the self.

In the younger and non-delinquent representation of Type 1, being good also means being liked by the role partner or doing something he liked (Obs. 59).[3]

---

[1] With such a child, one almost feels that the techniques he recommends in the role of the probation officer, offering alternate means for his wishes and taking him fishing, would keep him out of trouble although they are hadly curative.

[2] We note an attitude, typical in our delinquent sample, that the reason the parent objects to stealing is that it gets the boy in trouble which in turn is a nuisance to the parent's self interest and to the interest he may have in the boy.

[3] Case 11 espouses both Tannenbaum's theory that delinquents are boys acting on their social definitions as "bad," and psychoanalytic theory of delinquency as displaced aggression against the father. It is only our more developed morality which makes it necessary for social science to tell us these things. In Case 11, these tendencies imply the projective value equation (bad = badly treated) as well as Type 1 instrumentalism.

2. Relativism of Value and Role-taking in Type 1

In considering concepts of value, we see that Type 1 children tended to reduce values to relativistic selfish needs, sharply differentiated objects and persons as means from egoistic needs as ends, and realistically predicted consequences of deviance on the same basis as consequences of conformity. If we accept Baldwin's and Piaget's hypotheses of a primitive tendency toward adualism, this represents a certain cognitive developmental advance from "projective" to dualistic value.

We would expect this instrumentalism to be linked to a relativism of value as opposed to the syntelic perception of value in Type 0. For each person sees the right as what coincides with his own interests (Obs. 60, 61).

The boy is himself able to sympathize with each person, but he does not see each as trying to, or being obligated to, consider the viewpoint of another. Each person is seen as being oriented to his own interests or to the habitual functioning of his role, not to the interests of the role partner.[1]

In Observation 62, a philosophical delinquent, in a sense oriented to "rationality," denies the existence of an impartial spectator's viewpoint. It is clear that these children are not without an ability to role-take others. There may even be a rudimentary judgment of propriety in Smith's terms, an evaluation of the other in comparison with the self's reactions to the situation. Thus Type 1 children may respond to such a

---

[1]This boy presents this relativism more clearly than the delinquents because he is compliant and empathic enough to move from role to role under the pressure of the interviewer or spontaneously. Most of the delinquents simply take one selfish role in the story, ignore the others, or if they are forced to move from role to role in the situation, show no concern or awareness of discrepancy.

question as stealing a drug for one's wife by asking the examiner, "Would-n't you do it?" Such self-projection takes place in terms of spontaneous, more or less selfish, interests rather than good motives.[1]

These cases dramatize the difficulty of theories like Hume's or Smith's in which morality or the viewpoint of the impartial spectator naturally develops out of the play of sympathies.

They also dramatize the difficulty of the view that the conscious-ness of the relativism of values constitutes in itself an important achieve-ment in the development of morality, a view of Piaget and Lerner (30) well enough accepted to have become textbook doctrine (39).[2]

If spontaneous sympathy need not lead to a "generalized other" or impartial spectator, neither do rules in themselves. A graphic illustra-tion is provided by Observation 63, a case whom we have previously used to indicate thinking which seemed transitional between Types 0 and 1. Obser-vation 36 dramatizes the inadequacy of "rules" or authority in themselves to establish any role-taking at all, much less impartial role-taking. Case 36 knows and accepts the rules, but there is no "generalized other" which the rules represent, or who represents the rules.

---

[1] Thus out of the twelve delinquents questioned, about punishing the doctor for mercy killing, five recommended a death sentence and two said death would be all right without having spontaneously recommended it. On the question of stealing a drug to save one's wife, ten advised not punishing the husband at all.

[2] These writers recognize that the relativism of sheer egoistic interests is not the sort of effort at integration of multiple-role tak-ing and the sense of tolerance which they value. Unfortunately the em-pirical techniques of Lerner which we also employed would seem to repre-sent egoistic relativism primarily, if interpreted according to a simple schema. Thus, Lerner asked the children how each person in a situation would judge a given act, and counted the number or diversity of such judgments. The resulting dimension of "number of perspectives" hardly corresponds to the organized perspective of Mead's generalized other.

What is right for each is to avoid punishment. The valuation or judgments of right and wrong made by each individual are based only on his own interests, but there is a partial meshing of each individual's selfish judgments in terms of each anticipating the response of the same punitive order. The giving of punishment cannot even be reduced to a subjective judgment of wrong by the judge. Nor does it involve a choice of the storekeeper versus the robber, both must anticipate punishment.

3. Obligation as Conditional or Hypothetical in Type 1

We would expect from the foregoing that "duty" would be in the voice of the hypothetical or conditional imperative in Type 1. Our example of relativistic role-taking indicated the same passivity and distance between the self as respondent or cognizer and the self as role-taking the actors which we found in Type 0. The self could sympathize with the other but it could not tell another to do so.

In general, Type 1 tends to refuse to use an imperative or unconditional statement as to what another should do. The typical statements are, "If I were him, I would," or, "If he wants this, he could or should do it," rather than, "He should do that." In Type 0, "should" tended to mean "have to" which tended to mean "external forces and reactions compel to." When the interviewer asks, "Does a good person have to?" these children reply, "He doesn't have to do anything," i.e., no one can force him.

In part this seems to mean that if you are willing to take the painful consequences of punishment, you can do what you please (Obs. 64). In part it involves a more conditional expectation and evaluation of punishment. Thus when punishment is used as a determining influence for choice, it is in a situation in which no natural or selfish interest opposes it, as in mercy killing or informing on a reformed convict.

The right, as we saw, meant "instrumentally in accord with self interest," although only the most "extreme" boys would say that the only right is "to look out for Number One," or to maximize self interest (Obs. 66). But many others would say that a failure to violate self-interest in the interests of another is not wrong (Obs. 65).

4. Concepts of Rights in Type 1

The observations we have analyzed seem to go somewhat beyond the mere factual assertion that people can do what they want. They seem to contain a quasi-normative feeling that they have the right to do what they want. "God gave everyone the free will to do as they please," as one 10-year-old says in regard to whether something is a duty.

This seems to lie behind the assertion of "responsibility" as purely negative, as avoiding actively harming or interfering with another individual (Obs. 66). Responsibility is limited to that which the actor causes or owns (Obs. 66 and 67). Even the law should not interfere in other people's business (Obs. 68).

This negative concept of responsibility also takes the form of saying that it is all right to deviate if the other deviated first. One form of this is retaliation. The other is to say that if someone is "sucker enough" to expose himself, it isn't the actor's fault if he takes advantage of it.

All of these concepts seem to imply role-taking the victim as another selfish actor and asserting that he has nothing to complain about. They also seem to imply a sense of reciprocity in relation to their own resentment of authority, e.g., "Do not interfere with the freedom of another as you do not want your freedom interfered with."

When we consider Type 4, we shall see that to some extent an actual system of obligations may be built on rights. This is not the case for Type 1, however. Before rights may lead to duties they must become legitimate shared expectancies. Where question of rights are simply "your arbitrary freedom vs. mine," it is clear that no duties can result. Even the concept of law as having the function of protecting rights is outside the thoughts of the older Type 1 children.

5. Choice and Susceptibility to Pressure in Type 1

Turning to the related matter of "autonomy" in the sense of resistance to pressure to change opinion, we find what we would expect. The children do not yield to pressure by the interviewer as readily as the Type 0 children. However, most of them say that they would pretend to agree with me if given a dollar, but they really wouldn't change their minds.

In terms of people agreeing on the right, they say, "Everybody has their own opinion," often with some expression under probing that people never really come to agreement and everybody should go their own way. They do not see diversity of opinion as differences of norms or of background, but simply as dependent on conflicting interests and wishes.

Essentially their resistance to social pressure is largely a function of the need or self interest involved. Some of these children, including 16-year-olds, would spontaneously change from a pro-parent to a pro-child response when the question I or II were put to them in a discussion with two other peers, even though the interviewer was still in the room. However, most of them seemed to have more of a sense that accepting suggestion or pressure made the self inferior unless there was a rational egoistic reason for it, such as money.

G. Two Extreme Cases

1. The Representativeness of the Two Cases

Our Type 1 represents children showing very varying degrees of both intellectual consistency and sophistication as well as varying degrees of resistance to conformity.

As our discussion has suggested, it is hard to view either Stage 0 or Stage 1 thinking as representing a value ideology. Insofar as we view these stages as concrete personality types, most just don't or can't care about making moral judgments. Their morality seems to be pretty much of a matter of situational forces, external forces for Type 0 and need arousal for Type 1. There is little impetus to select and organize the forces responded to except as they are related to the self and the immediate situation. They would not be expected to have organized opinions.

However, since we shall present some "personality types" for the sake of exposition of our later stages, here we wish to present a Type 0 and a Type 1 as illustrative of extremes in the use of such thought models. These children are not typical representatives of children scoring high in their respective modes of thought. They are both 16 and use some of the higher modes of thought, though their highest score is in the given category.[1] They are more conflicted, more explicitly at war with society, and more reliant on their own thoughts about the matters we have dealt with,

---

[1]Their scores on category usage, expressed in percentage of total response, and on global ratings of questions, expressed in numbers of questions receiving the rating, are:

		Type 0	Type 1	Type 2	Type 3	Type 4	Type 5
Case 70:	category usage	23%	20%	20%	21%	6%	...
	ratings	4	2	3			
Case 75:	category usage	11%	31%	13%	22%	16%	2%
	ratings		7	1	1		

than any of the other high-scoring children in these types. Thus they represent these types, not as normal developmental stages, but in their potentiality for forming "schizoid" pathological types, the only manner in which the types could crystallize into ideologies.

Each is an extreme in behavior as well as thought. Case 70, our Type 0 case, was our most isolated of all possible sociometric isolates. Case 75, our Type 1 case, is as delinquent as any of our delinquents, while being a definite leader among them.

2. Our Type 0 Case

Case 70, age 16, is so isolated a boy that, according to teacher's report, he had never spoken to any of the other children in school at least as far back as the fourth grade. He is an adopted child from a middle-class home with an IQ testing from 80 to 100 on various occasions.

In his thought, he reflected trends which would be apt to be called "paranoid schizophrenic," though there is no need to judge him as actually psychotic. We would expect paranoid schizophrenics to use Type 0 evaluation modes to an extreme, to make projective stage value judgments based on a vague syntelic unity of people's behavior or perception, to experience obligation in terms of objective necessity and perceive good behavior (and bad, also) as based on control by outer forces.

What would distinguish the paranoid in moral thought would be chiefly his discontent or feeling of badness about this outer control and these projective values. "In my house," Case 70 tells us, "there is Communist rule, dictatorship," but his mother "can get mean, a perfect little devil so let's not put it all off on Pop," and his brother is a "little Dillinger," because he is always stealing cookies.

Such use of concepts of public malefactors to express the self's

feelings about the family represents a usage of "projective evaluation."[1]
The only concepts of badness which he can employ with regard to his family
must come from the realm of public punishment. There are other indications
in his record that "bad" means likelihood of being punished (Obs. 41). The
very need to see a disliked authority as "Communist" indicates an inability
to reduce value experience to subjective interests and judgments or even to
definite standards. Such Stage 0 "projective" and "syntelic" modes of
evaluation of bad acts and persons, however, provides no guarantee for
acceptance of the social order itself. Criminals may be bad but this is
no guarantee that the order of authority is not bad. The mere fact of
power, either in the family or outside, need not mean the authority does
his job or is good.

Thus Case 70 sees the social order as completely based on authority,
but is concerned and confused about the fact that authority may be bad in
general. At one moment authorities make the country like Russia, at the
other moments they prevent it from being like Russia. He says,

You have to respect the judge more or less because you have to go
along with the verdict more or less; there shouldn't be any corrup-
tion. You need a fair judge because you have to put away those
dangerous ones. Without the judge and police we'd be like Russia.
Of course they have the secret police there but you can't trust any
of them. Plain citizens you could, some of them, some might be
working for the government, some not. Policemen are good in some
cases, bad in others. They can be just as good or bad as any citizen.

---

[1]In the course of the interview in expressing such hostility, he
continually referred in a "joking" fashion to the fact that "maybe the
room was tapped," "even the walls have ears," or he would ask me to stop
the tape recorder when a question was asked which aroused some derogatory
idea. Such ideas of reference again seem to imply some vague "syntelic"
unity of the various authorities of the outside world, together with a
confusion of inner auditors with outer one. However, Baldwin's projective mode should not be confused with paranoid projection of disowned
impulses.

Type O thinking provides no answers to such doubts. On the one hand, the social order is not a system of rules and fixed roles to which the individual authority must conform; it is simply a chain of persons. On the other hand, authorities do not have any particular kind of self in terms of which they are selected. There are no shared standards, no shared self, and no processes of mutual influence which could prevent deviance. The deviance of authority is not seen in terms of being selfish, "purely out for themselves," as it is for Case 75. It tends to be rather seen as the performance of projectively bad acts or as being in league with bad people. This involves a perception of them externally as objects, more or less externally controlled.

In general, we may note in this boy the split between judgments of value and the sense of what is constraining or of the social order. Judgments of value are made by the self in terms of the mere possibility of projectively bad events occurring; they are not made on the basis of conformity to rule or to the social order. The social order, on the other hand, is not organized in terms of value-judgment; it is rather an external quasi-physical set of activities of control. Hence the conflict between one's self and society can take the form of suspecting the authority of doing criminal things.

3. Our Type 1 Case

Our Type 1 ideologist, Case 75, a boy with an IQ of 130, is in a certain sense a leader among delinquents. In response to "being a good leader" he says,

> To be a good leader, you gotta be good yourself and being good's too much of a headache. But I'm a leader naturally. Kids around town always follow me around and give me stuff and whatever I feel like doing, they all want to do. I understand how they're made and I just pull the right strings and make monkeys out of them.

This self-report is fully born out by observers in the detention home.

His father "has gotten married umpteen times and I've got a fifth stepmother now." He tells us, "I don't trust nobody or nothing unless I know," and when probed, says, "Oh well, when I was a little kid my old man made a promise and didn't keep it and all that stuff. He'd say we'd do it and it would be just the same as if he didn't say it because it just depended on how things turned out, whether he felt like it or not."

We have already considered his concepts of duty (Obs. 65). He systematically denies the existence of any unselfish or impartial motives in the world, but then explains natural evil-doing in terms of "Watsonian" environmentalism. Thus he replies to "Would you need rules or laws in a country with all good people?"

> None whatsoever. Laws are made by cowards to protect themselves. But if it would start out good. Everybody is a crook at heart. But you take a child from birth and raise him to be any type of character. His whole personality was made up out of his environment. We've been brought up to think it's right to fish and hunt, that's killing, but we think it's perfectly right. We could be brought up to knock off people just like fish.

In one way he tells us he's like everyone else in being selfish but then the next moment, he's the one who is different, since he breaks the laws. Thus he replies to, "What would be an ideal society?"

> If it were possible to have one that people would follow without such a strong attitude of get everything when you can and the hell with everyone else. I didn't start that way but that's the way it is and so I'm that way too. Take what I can and have fun. I certainly can't fight it. Isn't it possible that the majority of the people could be wrong? Some people don't fit the majority. They're the ones that get run over. I'm the one that doesn't fit the majority, that's why I'm here.

He makes the same criticisms of the punitive attitude of the impartial spectator which Nietzsche did, that it is just frustrated or displaced vengeance and desire for superiority. Thus he replies to, "Why should the law make it worse to steal?"

I don't see that they have a right to decide anything. Who are they? They weren't there, they didn't get robbed, they don't do the stealing. It's vanity and pride. They like the feeling of saying what's right and what's wrong. All punishment is bestowing unhappiness upon you, pain and suffering—just returning evil for evil.

The only standards he accepts are those of exchange and distributive equality. With regard to distributive equality, he tells us in response to Question VIII:

All lives are just like so many peas in a pod; they're all equal. If I had a choice of having my life knocked off as against two other guys, even if I value my life four times as much as those two, I'd think it would be fair to die. Of course, I'd raise a hell of a fuss, but I'd think it fair.

He goes on to elaborate a form of what Piaget calls "equity" or equality proportionate to need. Thus he replies to: "Is a human life worth more than an animal?"

In my consideration, it's just a life and one is worth as much as the other. Maybe I could get a lot more fun out of life so I should live, but maybe he should have a little more fun.

Such extreme cases as these show both the logical appeal of concepts of equality, but their inadequacy purely in themselves to lead to actual moral obligation. Thus he is hardly dedicating himself to revolting against social inequality. He says, "I plan on being an absentee landlord of some sort or other, like my uncle who's got three taverns and two gas stations. He's getting money for doing nothing."

Thus the form in which this boy sees his conflict with society is simply as a conflict between purely egoistic selves. He does not see himself as different from anyone else except perhaps as being more intelligent and frank in his selfishness. This is a different conflict than that of Case 70, which we may perhaps see focussed on the question of whether he is projectively bad or the authorities are, on some feeling of difference between himself and others. Case 75, on the other hand, tells us that he is just like others such as his unreliable father in being bad. As he has been manipulated so he manipulates others.

The contrast may be illustrated in their responses to, "What would the Golden Rule tell you to do if someone came up and hit you?"

Case 70: "He was wrong in the first place. Why should you do something wrong? Just forget about it. Let him enjoy it but don't do it back."

Case 75: "Well, that hitting me would be against the Golden Rule. Therefore, that Golden Rule didn't stand and therefore, I would disregard the Golden Rule and lay him out. It would be the Golden Rule in reverse; treat him as he treats me. If a buddy of mine loans me something, I would do anything for him. If he double crosses me, I'll do anything against him."

G. Examples from Interviews to Illustrate Chapter VI

1. Adualistic and Dualistic Modes of Respect (Section B-4)

Type 0 — Case 9, 10 UL 125 Is.[1]
Obs. 1 — Respect as obedience. Respect as projective evaluation of power.

(Why do people respect a policeman?)[2,3]
Well, he directs traffic and when you're on the corner he blows the whistle and you're supposed to respect him; you're supposed to go.

(Who is respected more, a policeman or judge?)
A judge is more popular than the policeman, because the policeman can't do everything the judge can. Like the policeman can put him in jail but the judge can say he doesn't have to.

Type 1 — Same boy, one year later.
Obs. 2 — Respect as based on the other as instrumental to need.

A lifeguard, policeman, schoolteacher, they're not too important. The kids 1 to 4, they don't go to school, they don't cross the street.

---

[1]Identifying data for the child is abbreviated. The first number after the case number is the age, as in this example, 10 yrs. old; the following two letters indicate lower-lower, upper-lower, lower-middle, or upper-middle class, and is in this case upper-lower class; the next number indicates the IQ; the last abbreviation is for isolate (Is) or integrate (Int).

[2]Interviewers' questions are enclosed in parenthesis.

[3]Responses are replies justifying the Q-sort placement of occupational roles. The instructions for the Q sort were: "Whom do people in general all over the country respect the most?"

The older kids get taken by the mothers and when they grow up they should know better themselves and that's why you don't need a policeman.

Type 1 – Case 15, 10 UM 116 Int.
Obs. 3 – Respect as based on the particular needs of the self.

A lot of people resent being sent to jail these days and the ones that get out, they couldn't respect the judge very much.

Type 1 – Case 24, 10 UM 112 Is.
Obs. 4 – Value of the ends is not the value of the means.

(Why do you say people don't respect the farmer very much?)
The farmer raises the crops. He isn't the one who is the crop or anything like that.

(Why don't they respect a mover too much?)
They can move themselves.

2. Status and Authority as Based on Knowledge and Responsibility (Section B-5)

Type 0 – Case 11, 1C UL 109 Is.
Obs. 5 – Knowledge as activity-specific.

(Replying to question I—Should the son give his father the money he earned for camp?)
The boy should give his father the money because the father knows more than the boy.

(Is there a law that boys should give their father money they earn?)
Yes, because they need it for the food. Like the fathers give the mothers the money for the food. The mothers know what to buy.

Type 2 – Case 16, 10 UM 108 Int.
Obs. 6 – Knowledge as wisdom in considering the other's welfare.

(From I—Should the son obey the father if the father was wrong to ask?)
Yes, because it may turn out that he should have followed his father's direction. If he asked his father's permission to go boat riding and his father said "No," and he didn't listen to him and the boat had an accident, and his father wouldn't know where he was and then it might be too late.

Type 2 – Case 15, 10 UM 118 Int.
Obs. 7 – Authority implies responsibility for the subordinate's action.

(Who gets more money, the judge or the policeman?)
The judge. It's like the manager that works on the road. He just watches the men. But he gets more money because if something happens, it's his fault.

Type 2 - Case 18, 10 UM 124 Int.
Obs. 8 and 9 - Authority as having skill in and ultimate responsibility
        for the subordinate's role.

(From VIII—Should the captain who knows the way back send a man
on the suicide mission or go himself?)
I think he should go himself. He probably has more experience and
he can make it better than a recruit. He's got a sargeant who could
lead the others.

(Have a right to?)
Yes, but a good captain would risk his own life for his men.

Type 3 - Case 18, 10 UM 124 Int.
Obs. 10 - Respect for filling an unpleasant duty. Respect for attributes
        antecedent to the role.

People who were convicted wouldn't be so fond of the judge,but he's
doing his duty. Gotta have a good education to be that job. Learn the
laws and what you should do in a case like that.

Type 0 - Case 22, 10 UM 105 Is.
Obs. 11 - Authority as ownership. Escape from responsibility at the top.

(If you could be anyone in the world, who would you like to be?)
The president. He kind of owns the U.S. while he has his term.

(Why don't you want to be a private?)
Well, I'd like to be a general more than a private. A general
can give more orders. When I give orders, I don't have to do what
the man that I gave the orders to does.

Obs. 12 - The same in the family.

(Would being a good son and obeying your parents come under the
Golden Rule?)
Yes.

(Should they obey you?)
No, they shouldn't obey you. They practically own you. Like if
you're working, you gotta obey the boss or you could get fired.

Type 0 - Case 10, 10 LL 90 Is.
Obs. 13 - Relative income determined by who is closest to the source of
        supply.

(Who gets paid more, the judge or the policeman?)
The policeman, because they get paid out of the meters that you put
pennies in and they get paid by taxes.

(Do they keep the money in the meters?)
Not all of it; that goes to all the policemen, some to the judges
and to all the men in the organization.

Type 0 — Case 9, 10 UL 125 Is.
Obs. 14 — The same.

(Are jobs which pay a lot always high or important jobs?)
No. Like a doctor, he's got a big job; he takes care of people
but he doesn't make money on his job.

(What would be a job that makes money but isn't high?)
A printer; he could make a lot of money. Someone who wants to be
in the paper, he has to pay so much a word.

Type 2 — Case 25, 13 LM 109 Int.
Obs. 15 — Salary determined by merit.

Are jobs that pay a lot always high or important?)
I think so.

(Are there some jobs that are important that don't get paid much?)
I think so. Maybe the company doesn't see all the man has done.
Take my Dad for instance. . . .

Type 0 — Case 13, 10 UM 116 Int.
Obs. 16 — Inability to understand prerequisites of role antecedent to
         filling it.

(Which is harder to become, a senator or a judge?)
The senator. A senator takes more work and the judge may not have
anything to do for a month.

3. Conceptions of Rules Do Not Define Obligation and
        the Social Order in Type 0 (Section C-2)

Type 0 — Case 10, 10 LL 90 Is.
Obs. 17 — A law as a concrete command.

(Can there be a bad law?)
Yes, like if a woman in a store was to say that you can't come into
the store any more to buy anything.

(Would that be a law?)
Sort of a law and a rule.

(Who makes the law?)
I think the commissioner and the mayor or the judge.

Obs. 18 — A rule as a prudential directive.

(What is the one best rule?)
I'd make a rule that all the kids should be in the house; the
smaller kids my age at 8:00, and the bigger boys at 10:00.

(Why would that be best?)

Well, if they stay out till about 12:00 or 1:00, they'd probably go rob some place, a beer joint or something.

Obs. 19 – Inability to see a law is necessary to proscribe bad action and to prescribe punishment.

(Then wouldn't the first rule be not to steal?)
Yeah.

(Why would that be best?)
Well, they could take care of their kids easier and keep track of them better, won't have to get the police after them or find them.

Obs. 20 – Same. Religious commands as one of many social taboos.

(Could someone be a good person without laws or rules to follow?)
If they tries, they could go to church on Sunday and mind the laws and pay taxes and do their job right and not drink or gamble, obey the Bible and do what the Bible says.

Obs. 21 – The wrong and punishment not determined by general law.

(Should you obey a law if you think it is a bad law?)
If it was a law about stealing. I'd break the law; I wouldn't steal. I don't steal anymore like I did with that candy bar. I put it back and then I didn't steal anymore because I got a licking.

Type 0 – Case 22, 10 UM 105 Is.
Obs. 22 – Rules as specific and not as the basis of the social order.

(What would be the one best rule?)
There's gotta be two rules, one for the kids and one for the grown ups. The grown ups most of the countries outside America have kings; they should obey the king. And children should obey their father and mother.

(Why are those best?)
In some countries, if you don't honor the king, they maybe put you up to the firing squad.

(Would those be the best rules in any country?)
Like you said, you could only have one rule, so you gotta have it only in one country.

4. Laws as Instrumental Rules of the Police in Type 1
(Section C-3)

Type 1 – Case 19, 10 UM 103 Is.
Obs. 22 – Rules as to be obeyed and as prescribing punishment.

(What is a rule?)
Something you should obey.

(What is the one best rule?)
Thou shalt not kill. Or people would go out and walk up to a guy and go KaKaKa and kill a guy and they'd do nothing about it.

Mixed Type 0 and 1 - Case 36, 13 UL 101 Is.
Obs. 23 - Confusion of perspective in rule-making.

(What would be the one best rule?)
Not to get in trouble. Because if you said not to tell a lie, they might start stealing. And when you say not to get in trouble, that means not to lie, not to steal.

Type 1 - Case 4, 10 UL 95 Int.
Obs. 24 - The law is a rule of the police.

(Question VII—Which is worse according to law, cheating on a loan or stealing?)
I think cheating. Maybe that's a rule for the police, that they should never cheat.

Obs. 25 - Wrong is not the violation of the rule but its prudential consequences.

(Should you obey a law that you think is a bad law?)
I guess so. There's a penalty against you if you break it.

(How about in Russia? Would it be wrong to disobey there?)
Well, if you couldn't get away with it, I guess it would.

5. Laws as the Core of a Good Social Order in
Type 2 and 3 (Section C-4)

Type 2 - Case 16.
Obs. 26 - Laws as based on superior wisdom and on the welfare of others.

(Should someone obey a law he thinks is bad?)
Yes, because maybe he didn't think it was a good law to steal and he went ahead and then he found out it was a good law, then he might change his mind.

(How about in Russia?)
It would be wrong to disobey the law there because everyone's got their different opinions and they have their way of thinking how it should be run, and the person that made the law was trying to make it fair and maybe they were trying to make it better for everyone. And in this country, all they do is put you in jail, but maybe in another country they didn't know and they hung you.

Type 2 - Case 25, 13 LM 109 Int.
Obs. 28 - Correspondence of personal respect and respect for rules.

(Why would the commandments be the best rules?)

Because we have the rules and it's God's rules too, that we should respect other people like our fathers and mothers. It just goes together like.

Mixed Types 2 and 3 — Case 33, 13 LM 119 Is.
Obs. 29 — Equation of being good with guidance by rules.

Do unto others. I think that would be the most important because it would apply to everything.

(Would you need laws or rules in a country of all good people?)
Well, in order to be good they have rules. They'd practically all have to, because—of course if they were all good, it would be like a rule in their own mind not to do it.

Type 3 — Case 69, 16 UM 113 Is.
Obs. 30 — Rules as a system. Deviation from one rule is deviation from all.

(Which is worse, robbing or killing?)
Robbing is, actually, supposedly not as bad as to kill; punishments are less for robbing. But morally I don't think there is any difference, you actually disobeying God's law in either case. If we're guilty of one law, we're guilty of all. No difference in the sight of God; we're still doing something wrong.

Type 0 — Case 84, 15 LM ? Int. Delinq.
Obs. 31 — Confounding of religious and secular taboos and punishment.

(Question IV—Should the doctor perform the mercy killing as she asks?)
That is a mortal sin of mercy killing; it is a federal offence and a church offense.

6. The Law as Representing the Group Will or as Representing Principles of Conscience in Types 4 and 5 (Section C-5)

Type 4 — Case 28, 13 UL 115 Int.
Obs. 32 — Law as defining expectancies of the role partner, i.e., of what the patient may expect and what the doctor may anticipate will be expected.

(Question IV—Should there be a law allowing mercy killing?)
No. There'd probably be a lot less doctors because it's awful hard for any doctor to do a thing like that.

Obs. 33 — Law as representing group agreement as defining the right.

(Should the doctor be punished for doing it if there was a law against it?)
Well, if other people had agreed on not letting somebody and made a law against it and everybody agreed to that, he'd have to go to jail and he would have been wrong.

Type 4 — Case 66, 16 UM 112 Int.
Obs. 34 — Law as representing majority opinion.

(Is it wrong for someone to disobey a law if he thinks it's a bad law?)
I don't think anyone should disobey any law. A lot of people must have thought it a good law to pass it, a minority thought it was bad.

(How about in Russia, would it be wrong there to disobey a law you thought was bad?)
If the rules are just made by the leaders and the people don't have anything to say about it, I think probably most of the people would be against the laws and they probably wouldn't obey them.

(Would it be right or wrong to disobey then?)
Hard to say like in Russia. I don't know.

Type 5 (and 4) — Case 65, 16 UM 116 Int.
Obs. 35 — Legality and majority rule as a methodological principle rather than as guaranteeing the rightness of action.

(Should someone obey a law they think is bad?)
Yes, especially in this country which is supposed to be the best democracy in the world. It's still the will of the people; it's supposed to be made by the majority. If you think it's bad, nevertheless obey it until it's changed.

Obs. 36 — Sense of the "higher right."

(How about returning an escaped slave before the Civil War?)
I would say yes even though I would hate to, if the law says so. Even though I feel it's wrong, I would return him. However, there is a point like if the U.S. were to say you could kill or declare anything legal which the Lord says isn't legal.

Type 5 — Case 18, 10 UM 124 Int.
Obs. 36 — The right as higher than the law.

(Have you ever talked to your parents about these questions?)
Yes, like the one about stealing or cheating being worse. And my Dad said, "You should have said stealing is worse; it's worse by law." But I said, "In God's book it would be worse to borrow it," and I said, "It would be higher to follow God's laws than the laws down here."

(What did your Dad say then?)
He said, "That's a tough one to figure out; I don't know," and he turned out the light and I went to sleep.

Obs. 37 — A principle for making laws.

(What is the one best rule?)
There's a lot of rules from the Bible that are excellent. Would be pretty hard to pick 'em out. But "Do unto others as you would have them do unto you" would be about the best one.

(Why that the best?)

Because just feel yourself like you're in their place—the poor people's place if you're rich, and how you would have to be with those laws and then sort of go back to your place as a rich man and make the laws according to what you dreamed sort of like.

7. Concern for the Label Is Not Concern for the Letter of the Rule in Types 0 (Section D-2)

Mixed Type 0 and 1 - Case 7, 10 LC 104 Is.
Obs. 38 - Ignoral of intentions combined with a "situationally flexible" classification of action in terms of punishment probabilities.

(Question VII—Who did worse, Alex who broke into the store and stole $500 or Joe who borrowed it saying he needed it for an operation?)
Alex, because he didn't ask if he could borrow it; he just walked in and stole it.

(Why isn't it so bad when you ask?)
Because they might think you're going to pay it back to them.

(Who was the meaner person?)
Alex, because he didn't ask permission and Joe asked for permission by saying he was sick.

Type 0 - Case 9, 10 UL 125 Is.
Obs. 39 - Labels are of concern as things said. Unfair or untrue labelling still hurts.

(Question II—Would Joe think Alex was a bad brother for telling?)
He'd be made at him but he wouldn't be a bad brother. Joe might do it on Alexander sometime and Alexander wouldn't say that.

Type 0 or 1 - Case 22, 10 UM 105 Is.
Obs. 40 - Labels or what someone thinks depend on what they can do.

(Question II—Would Joe think Alex was a bad brother for telling?)
I think he would if he was bigger than Alex.

(Why?)
Because if I told my brother and he was bigger, he might beat me up.

(Wouldn't his father thinkhe wasn't a good brother if he didn't tell?
He'd have to read a mind to do that.

Type 0 - Case 70, 16 UM 90 Is.
Obs. 41 - Being bad means being badly treated.

(Why does someone want to be a good father?)
Maybe he was treated bad when he was little and when he grows up, he's going to be especially good to make up for it. But just because he was bad—I mean badly treated—I suppose he'd take it out on his wife when he got married.

8. An Orientation to Consequences Implied in Primitive Concepts of "Right" (Section D-5)

Type 0 – Case 7, 10 UL 103 Is.
Obs. 42 – A "right" moral choice is one anticipating the stamp of the authority.

> (Who knows the right answers to these questions?)
> Sydney.
>
> (How does he know?)
> He's probably smarter.
>
> (Wouldn't I know?)
> Yes, because you have it right there.

Type 0 and 1 – Case 9, 10 UL 125 Is.
Obs. 43 – Wrong as the unsuccessful.

> (Question III—Is it still wrong to steal if it's too late to work for the money?)
> Yes, because he might get caught and he'd have to put it back and he'd be in jail and he wouldn't be able to raise the money.

Type 0 and 1 – Case 10, 10 LL 90 Is.
Obs. 44 – Same.

> (Question II—Should Bob tell his father what his brother had told him?)
> Well, in one way he shouldn't tell and one way he should. The way he should, his father might get made and give both of them a licking. And so Joe wouldn't do that ever again. The way he shouldn't, his brother might not like him any more if he told.

9. A Materialistic Concept of Relative Badness Indicates Projective Evaluation and Concreteness, Not a Literalistic Orientation to Rule (Section D-6)

Type 0 – Case 10, 10 LL 90 Is.
Obs. 42 – Badness of a lie depends on its physical quantitative deviation from reality, on its "bigness."

> Like they say they're little white lies.
>
> (What's a white lie?)
> Like you say, "There was a robber in that store there," and if it was a black lie, you'd say, "There were about a hundred robbers and the cops were surrounding it and shooting it."
>
> (Why would that be blacker?)

Well, the second one, you'd be so deep in lies, you wouldn't be able to confess it and then if you didn't go to confession or Holy Communion, God might not take you to heaven.

Type 0 - Case 8, 10 LL 90 Is.
Obs. 46 - Badness related to quantitative consequences. This in turn related to restorability.

(Question VII—Who did worse, Alex who stole the money or Joe who borrowed with no intention of paying it back?)
Both of them. Joe said he would pay the $500 back and he didn't. Alex broke in and stole the $500 and he didn't pay it back either. Both stole. I think Alex did worse; he broke in and lowered the windows and that would have to be replaced.

(Why shouldn't someone steal?)
If you steal, they'll check fingerprints.

10. Obligation as External Necessity in Type 0
(Section E-2)

Type 0 - Case 8, 10 LC 90 Is.
Obs. 47 - "Have to" as social situational pressure independent of rule.

(Question IV—Should the doctor mercy kill?)
He should give her a drug to put her out of her pain. If she wanted to die—she can't stand the pain.

(Is it up to the doctor, what he thinks is best?)
No, he's got to have Heinz's permission. That's her husband.

(If the husband agrees?)
Well, she has to go.

Obs. 48 - Right as bowing to necessity. Heteronomous necessity can be based on situational need.

(Question III—Is it right to steal the drug?)
If you had a wife with cancer and you only had half the money and you had to break into the store for your wife. You have to like your wife.

(Was it right?)
If your wife was dying.

Obs. 49 - Heteronomous reciprocity. (Above continued)

If you were dying and she broke into that store and got the drug. That's the same way you have to repay your wife.

Obs. 50 - Heteronomy of choice in every area for Case 8.

(If you could be anything at all, what would you want to be?)
Whatever my father orders me to do.

(Why?)
Well, he's my father and he works for the railroad. If he wants
me to work for the railroad, I have to work for the railroad.

Obs. 51 - The actor is not wrong or responsible for any action he has
been pressured into.

(From Question II—Was his father right to punish Alex for not
telling on Joe?)
No. If Alex didn't tell him, it ain't Alex's fault, because Joe
told him not to tell.

Obs. 52 - Wrong as the instrumentally inefficient consistent with heteronomous constraint.

(Question IX—Was it right or wrong to leave his station?)
Wrong. It was a long way home. He could have got on his fire
engine and went faster instead of walking.

Obs. 53 - Crime as based on external necessity.

(Why do some people want to rob?)
Like if I had; if you had a real sick brother and have no mother
or father, you need $1,000,000 for the operation, so you had to rob
a bank.

Obs. 54 - Authority as compatible with crime.

(What would his father think of Alex for keeping quiet?)
He wouldn't be mad at Alex if he wanted to pay back the favor.
Maybe he had been robbing and he told his sons and they kept quiet
and if Alex kept quiet that would be paying back.

Obs. 55 - Moral argument as prediction. Criminal identified with but seen
as being unknowing and uncontrolling.

(What is the one best rule?)
Teach them not to steal. Not to kill. If you kill, you have to
go to the electric chair.
If you killed, and then kept on killing, and killing around 40
people until somebody told him, it would be too late. Someone should
tell him right away before he started.

(What harm does it do to steal?)
Well, it harms yourself. If you stole from a lot of stores and
you got a real lot of money, over a million dollars, then they start
realizing they never caught you. Then you say to yourself, "Why did
I steal?" And then when the police find out where you live and you
had a wife and you shot two policemen and they had to shoot you back
so they killed you. Then you realized you done wrong all your life.

Obs. 56 - Suggestibility.

(Would you change your mind about one of these questions for 50¢?)
Yes.

(Why?)
I'd just feel like changing it.

11. Dualistic Value Modes and "Intentions"
in Type 1 (Section F-1)

Type 1 - Case 21, 10 LM 103 Is.
Obs. 57 - Complete instrumental prediction set in which rules or labels
are irrelevant. Egoistic needs justify the ends.

(Who was worse?)
Alex who broke into the store. Because he could have got caught
and Joe didn't want to pay him back so he didn't.

(Why shouldn't someone steal from a store?)
Because the storekeeper might know you and recognize you in the
police mug book.

(What harm would it do?)
Well, like the story you told me, maybe the owner, the father had
promised his son he could go to camp. Then he couldn't go.

(Would Joe be worse or better if he cheated a very good friend
instead of an acquaintance?)
Worse. The one who didn't know him too well might not be able to
identify him.

(Which is worse for the country, stealing or cheating?)
People stealing. The police would catch up with you and put you
in jail.

Type 1 - Case 87, 13 LL Delinq., Negro.
Obs. 58 - Egoistic needs justify the means. The only reason not to steal
is that there are alternate means to gratifying these needs,
and the possibility of trouble. Authorities warn but do not
disapprove.
(Role-playing scene in which interviewer plays role of boy's probation
officer accusing him of his actual misdeeds.)

(Why have you been getting in so much trouble?)
I just don't want to stay home all the time. If I stay home all
the time, I have to do so much work.

(That doesn't mean you have to steal bikes.)
I steal them because I like to ride. I want to go somewhere. I
was figuring on going West and have a ranch when I get big.

232

(Why did you have to steal a car then?)
You can't travel on a bike that way so I'll just get a car.

(Well, it looks pretty bad stealing bicycles and cars. It looks like you are pretty bad.)
I'm not so bad. I just like to ride horses and cars. I asked my mother to let me drive the car sometimes, but she'll never let me.

(What does your mother think about it?)
She said if I get in some more trouble, she's going to send me to boy's school.

(Role playing response, interviewer as boy, boy as his own probation officer. Interviewer as boy in parentheses.)

I want to talk to you about what you're going to be when you're big. I'm going to try to get you a job so you won't get in so much trouble. Why do you like to steal bikes? You don't have to take them to ride them. You can ask your mother for one.
(That's going to be a long time.)

You can wait. You don't have to steal other people's bikes.
(That only happened once.)

You stole three. You get into trouble stealing other people's bikes. You could get shot.
(Do you think I'm a bad boy?)

Yeah, I'm going to try to make you a good boy instead of a bad boy.
(It's too late for that now.)

It's not too late. I want to get you some kind of job so you won't get in so much trouble. I want you to be a nice boy. Maybe I'll take you fishing with me some day if you be a good boy.

Type 1 — Case 11.
Obs. 59 — Being good in a role means doing something liked by the role partner. Role conformity as exchange. Delinquency as frustration—aggression.

(Could you be a good son and a good brother at the same time?)
No, you can't. Like he was keeping a secret from Dad but he was doing good for his brother. Or he could be good to his Dad and get his brother in trouble.

(Why would you want to be a good son?)
Be good to your father and he'll be good to you.

(Why does someone want to be a good father?)
They don't want their son to grow up bad. If they treat them bad, the son won't like that and they'll be bad. Like they don't give them money and they can't have it, they'll grow up to steal it.

12. Relativism of Value and Role-taking in Type 1
(Section F-2)

Type 1 — Case 34, 13 LC 101 Is.
Obs. 60 — Wrong as relative to self-interest and affect.

(From I—Was it wrong for the father to break his promise to his son?)
Not to himself, but it broke the kid's heart.

Obs. 61 — Same.

(From IV—Should the doctor give the woman the drug to let her die?)
According to how you look on it. From the doctor's view it would be "No." It could be murder. From his view of looking, she just wants to die, she's suffering so much pain.

(Which view should he look at it from?)
From his view.

Type 1 (as a philosophy) — Case 75, 16 UL 128 Int.
Obs. 62 — Right as maximizing self-interest. A non-interested right does not exist.

(Question III—Is the druggist right to kill someone who's robbing his store?)
Certainly. He's taking the chance. He accepted the risk with full knowledge of the results.

(Should Heinz shoot back?)
If I were in his shoes, I would.

(Would it be right?)
As far as deciding right I wouldn't know. I could say what I would do in both places, what I considered right for each but there would be no equilibrium between the two.

Mixed Type 0 and 1 — Case 36, 13 LC 101 Is.
Obs. 63 — Relativism of the right combined with heteronomous attitude to punishment.

(From III—Was it wrong for the storekeeper to shoot Heinz?)
Yes. Because if the druggist killed him, he'd have to be put in jail.

(Would it be wrong for Heinz to shoot back?)
Yes, he would have to be put in jail for killing and stealing both.

(Would the judge think Heinz was wrong?)
No. Yes, I think he'd think it was wrong. The druggist would think it's wrong because he wants the money. He doesn't want to lose his merchandise.

13. Obligation as Conditional in Type 1—Rights
(Section F-3,4)

Type 1 - Case 88, 10 UM 112 Is.
Obs. 64 - If willing to take the punishment, have free choice implying no
duty.

If he really wanted to go bad enough and he knew he'd get punished,
but he didn't care that he got punished, he just wanted to go to camp.
It would be his own responsibility. It's up to him, but if I were him
and I knew I'd get punished, I don't think I would.

Obs. 65 - No duty to oppose self-interest.

(Replying to VIII—Would it be wrong if the captain didn't go himself on the mission?)
No. It wouldn't be wrong. Well, if there was somebody out beside
the road and there was car coming and he couldn't get up because he
had a sprained ankle, it wouldn't be wrong for me not to get him. Because it's up to me whether I want to go out and risk my life or not.

Obs. 66 - No responsibility for that you do not cause or own.

(Suppose you wouldn't be risking your life?)
It wouldn't be wrong not to go because it wouldn't be my fault that
he was out there in the first place. I didn't have to save his life if
I didn't want to.

Type 1 - Case 75, 16 UL 128 Int.
Obs. 67 - Duty only to the self.

(In response to III—Would it be a good husband's duty to steal it?)
Well, as far as duty goes, I would eliminate that completely into a
sense of whether he wanted to or not. If he wanted her to die, there
ain't no use keeping her alive. He can marry someone else, some young
good-looking thing.

(Would she have the right to expect him to?)
Yes. He is the provider, but she picked a provider in that economic
level. He can't afford it and he's honest. She picked it. If I was
her I would expect anything; I would go to any lengths, for my preserva-
tion. But as far as anyone else goes, I wouldn't expect him to violate
the law, the majority rule always abides. This someone else is stealing without a gain, but she's got a reason for her stealing. She's
saving her life by it.

Type 1 - Case 12, 10 UL 95 Is.
Obs. 68 - Responsibility and authority limited to that which one owns.

(From IV—Is it a doctor's duty to mercy kill?)
Well, if they knew she was going to die, it isn't paying her to
live anymore if she's just going to be in pain.

(What if her family doesn't want it?)
It's up to her because it's her life.

(Should there be a law allowing it?)
It's up to her because it's her life.

(Should the doctor do it if the law didn't allow it?)
I think he should be able to do it because it's the person's life, not the law's life.

CHAPTER VII

THE FOUR LATER TYPES

A. Type 2, the Good Boy Orientation

1. Introduction

Our presentation of the remaining types will be more descriptive,
and will tend more to follow the outline of Appendix B. The plausibility
of the interconnected features of the type will probably rest partly on
sympathetic introspection by the reader, since most of us probably can at
least recall having had most of the attitudes and beliefs involved.

While Types 2 and 3 do not correspond to concrete ideologies,
they contain elements familiar both from social science and literature.
It should be remembered that our images of extreme or ideal types are not
meant to be representative descriptions of the population but intuitively
clear illustrations of the way in which the general elements of the type
may hang together to form a distinct and unitary whole, or a concrete
"personality type."

Thus in its extreme form Type 2 implies an orientation to a system of cliches we all know as the "good boy" or "good girl" orientation.
The following adolescent essay quoted in Blumer's work on the movies
should vivify the cliche system for those readers who may have escaped
direct contact with it:

I remember once I had had trouble with my mother. I said that
everything that was done in the house I had to do. I was very down-
hearted and thought how cruel they were to me. That night I went
to the movies. I do not remember the name of the picture but it hit

229

237

the nail on the head. It concerned one girl who did not get along with her family and one who did. The one girl was so good that everyone loved her, and her life was very happy. The other girl was not happy, and people did not like her because she was not sweet, good, and kind to her mother like the other girl. This made me think that I was just like the girl who was not good. I always wanted to be liked by everyone and to be happy, so I went home that night with the intention of being as good as possible to my mother and of trying to make family life as happy and pleasant as possible both for myself and mother and father. It has been a good many years since I saw this picture, and I am still trying to be that kind of a girl. I have succeeded some, but not enough yet [9, p. 174].

There are perhaps two essential features of Type 2, features which seem to overlap or be opposite sides of the same coin. One is an orientation to conforming to a stereotypical role image. The other is an orientation to approval.[1] Both tend to lead to a focus on parental approval and family roles.

2. The Sanction—Approval

It would seem that all of us are responsive to role stereotypes and approval, as is the girl quoted. However, these elements do not define our moral ideologies as they do hers. She is distinct, not in the strength of her approval needs, but in the way they are equated with ultimate values. Such an equation does not mean she would necessarily be at the top of the distribution in behavioral or projective measures of approval-seeking.

When we speak of approval-orientation we are not speaking of a behavioral tendency so much as we are speaking of a basis for ordering and understanding social claims. As mature people we presumably accept

---

[1]The diffuseness of what we call "approval" would lead Parsons to call it "esteem" (41). The latter term is usually used to refer to respect however. The point about "approval" as we use it is that "esteem" depends on approval of each specific act, and the standard of approval of a specific act is the esteem of the significant partner.

our need for approval but we do not judge something right because it
gains approval and wrong because it does not.

Thus for Type 2 children approval appears to be the strongest or
highest sanction for action, in our conflict situations, as punishment
was for our Type 0 children and need satisfaction was for our Type 1
children. It is more difficult to offer adequate objective evidence that
approval is an ultimate sanction in Type 2 than it was for the previous
sanctions. In the case of a conflict situation, approval is involved at
both horns of the dilemma and there may be individual differences as to
whose approval is more desirable.

In our conflict situations, the younger Type 2 children reflect
a good deal of uncertainty, which does not necessarily appear to be particularly upsetting. "In one way" stealing a drug is right because "it
is helping your wife," and "in another way it is wrong," because it is
"wrong" or "not very good" to steal. There is a desire to be good or
approved of in all ways.

3. The Equation of Approval with Goodness Implies That the Parents are the Ultimate Approvers

In general, role conflicts tend to be resolved in terms of the
approval of those nearest and dearest on whom the self is most dependent.
Thus the vagueness of moral directives of helping and approval-seeking
does not lead to too much uncertainty or deviance because there is a natural shared order of who is liked best and whose approval is sought. This
order culminates in the parents, who are wiser and more responsible.

Thus we are told by an immature Type 2 16-year-old in reply to
Question II:

If it was me, I think I'd tell. If my father finds out later, he
won't trust me.

(How about your brother?)

My brother wouldn't either, but I wouldn't have a conscience that he didn't. To be lying to my Dad and just be standing up for my brother—I wouldn't feel right about it at all.

"Conscience" means primarily sensitivity to disapproval, such sensitivity is based in part on the performance of some act generally considered bad vis a vis the partner, but it rests also on the actual knowledge and disapproval of the act by the partner.

We would interpret this dependence on sanctions not as a purely motivational phenomenon, but as reflecting cognitive uncertainty as to the good as well. There are a general mass of good actions whose core is primarily a general conformity to the wishes and welfare of a partner. However, what is good in any particular situation is not clear, especially if the situation involves conflict between various ways of "being good." In the concrete situational definition of the good, the child must depend on the actual or predicted reaction of the parent or of some other interested, helpful, and liked person.

A core meaning of good as personal conformity does not imply performing activities which are inherently good regardless of sanctions. It prescribes rather a responsiveness to the directions and more or less mild sanctions given by the parents and others. To be good is to be responsive to relatively mild and distant wishes and sanctions, to "not having to be told twice." Being good is not primarily resistance to temptation, nor making right decisions; it is exerting a little more effort in the established ways of conforming than one would without prodding or without wanting be good. Thus the boy who "wouldn't have a conscience" about his brother's distrust tells us in regard to "being a good son" that:

You obey your parents, you do things for them. They've always done things for you. I try to do everything she says, don't get her worried, don't get her mad, do the things she tells me, try to please her like she wants me to be a doctor and I want to too, and I want to get up there and she's helping me, so I try to get to be that. Just be good.[1]

4. The Standard—Role-Stereotypes

Before considering the child's sanctions and sense of obligation further, let us consider the normative or cognitive bases of evaluation which make approval-seeking something more than attempting to please the selfish whims of others. This basis we can in part describe as that of role stereotypes.

Neither Stage 0 or Stage 1 could be called a role-stereotype. We noted earlier that at Stage 0, children tended to view roles in terms of specific prescribed activities, more or less purposive, which classes of persons performed, rather than viewing roles as a set of personal traits, virtues or vices, i.e., of a view of the various role activities as expressing some type of self. Secondly, such a stereotype involves some degree of fusion or confusion between fact and norm, between what occupants of the role are like and what they should be like. On the one hand there is a tendency to attribute to the actual selves of role occupants traits or motives which would lead to performance of activities they are obligated to perform. Mothers must take care of children; therefore they probably all naturally do love children. On the other hand there is a tendency to attribute quasi-normative value and obligatoriness to purely accidentally modal qualities of the group of role-occupants. Thus to follow E. Hughes' discussion, a doctor is viewed as possessing a desire to help people in fact and he is viewed as someone who ought to be white, middle-class in his bearing, and the like (24).

---

[1]It may be noted with regard to the boy's mother-orientation that his father has been long dead and he now has a stepfather.

There is a third feature of thought required by role stereotyping, presupposed by the attribution of abilities and motives and in the fusion of fact and norm. This is the use of some concept of a probability or an average. Thus to say that people respect policemen because they catch burglars is to base respect on a more or less necessary or universal role attribute. To say that people do not respect policeman because "he might give you a ticket when you didn't do anything" is to base respect on a purely accidental individual but possible role attribute. To say that people respect the policeman because "most of them try to be helpful" is to base respect on some conception of probability or average. It allows for a margin of deviation around a normative concept. This means on the one hand a vast expansion of the number of traits which become normative together with a vagueness in their actual application.

The confusion of what most people do (fact) with what they should do (norm) in role stereotyping corresponds to a similar confusion of fact with norm in making approval the final criterion of conformity. Approval seeking implies that what is approved of should be approved of. It also tends to imply that self-interest and approval coincide. One's long-range interests depend on the good will of others.[1]

5. The Content—Helping, Liking, Getting Along with and Thinking of Others

The chief role—conforming trait, particularly among the lower middle-class children, is liking of and desire to help the role partner.

---

[1] These confusions have long been recognized as typifying the American value system. On the national level, we give aid to foreign nations because we think it is good to help others, because we think such help makes us liked, and because we think it is to the national interest to be well-liked. The confusions between helping others, gaining their approval and serving self-interest are perhaps fatal to actually accomplishing any of these objectives effectively.

This is viewed as a fusion of probable fact and norm. It is of course most conspicuous in the definition of family roles. Concern for the welfare of another member of the family is seen both as final motive for choice by the actor and is expected of the various partners involved. A study of Type 2 responses in Appendix A presents this clearly enough, most strikingly presented in Case 25's response to family roles.

Thus definition of role performance as based on positive attachment to the partner leads to a view of the basic role function or virtue as "helping" the partner. Thus the same conforming action of a child which might be seen as "obeying" by Type 0 children, and "doing a favor to get something in return" by Type 1 children, would be seen as "helping" by Type 2 children.[1]

6. Respect Orientation toward Parents

On the side of the child, this concern for helping is seen as motivated by liking based on past care or services by the parent, by a desire to be liked and approved of, and by some belief that the parents know what is best for the self's own welfare. On the side of the parents, these children say parents want to be good parents because they like their children.

---

[1]Type 0 and 1 children of course also have the concept of "helping" which is probably learned as good earlier than obedience. But they do not see the activities of fixed roles as actually set up by and motivated by the desire to help, particularly in the case of extra-familial roles. "Helping" simply means performing a fixed activity that happens to be useful to others. Thus a policeman is respected because "he helps to catch robbers," or a nurse is respected because she "helps the doctor." The role is helping to carry on an activity rather than implying an orientation to the welfare of other people. "Helping" is seen in terms of consequences, not as an expression of intentions. Thus the Type 2 response to question V about the deservingness of an escaped convict who has built a hospital is in terms of his "doing good" as a vague general "helping other people," while Type 0 and Type 1 responses are in terms of "doing good" as "keeping out of trouble," "making a good business," and "the hospital will close up without him."

Such an orientation does not imply absoluteness, unlimitedness or mystic sacredness about the parents. One is a good son primarily because "my parents are nice to me." The 10-year-old Type 2's, when asked "Who would know the right answers to these question" replied that, "No one is perfect."[1]

The Type 2 child relies on the judgment or approval of the parent then, not because his parent is wiser than all other mortals about affairs in general but because of all mortals, he is most likely to know what is good for the child and because it is good and natural for each child to rely on his own parents. This is illustrated in the following Type 2 response by a 10-year-old lower middle-class integrate with an IQ of 133:

> (Would anybody know the right answer to these questions?)
> No, I don't think anyone is perfect.

> (Do you go along with other people if you disagree with them about what is the right thing to do?)
> I think I go along with them.

> (Would you go along with your parents more?)
> Yes, because my parents, they took care of me and they know more about me, and they know what to do with me.

Primary responsiveness to parental judgment and approval.

7. Concepts of Authority and the Social Order

The concept of helping tends to be read out from the family into all roles in those most highly defined by this type among the 13-year-olds. Case 25's concepts of roles, such as of "President Eisenhower practically working himself into the grave to help other people" represent this trend in its extreme (Appendix D). In a boy like 25, there is a complete fusion

---

[1] "Perfection," in this and other contexts, seems to imply never having a little lapse, making a mistake or incurring disapproval with regard to the usual conformities, rather than referring to some higher or ideal wisdom or virtue.

of all the common meanings of the good; e.g., "being good" is getting ahead, which is helping others, which is helping the self, which is helping the family, which is doing what others want you to do, which is getting approval, which is being liked, which is having the family help you, which is naturally what most people actually want to do. As a number of these children say with regard to being someone "who works hard to get ahead in life": "He's the kind who helps other people at the same time he's helping himself."[1]

On the one side, these children are urged by their parents to do things so that they will get a "good job," so that getting a good job implies a responsiveness to parental wishes, a pleasing of the parents, and an actual helping of the family in financial terms. On the other hand they project such a helpful, conforming self as the typical occupant of such roles, i.e., a status role implies a conforming "good" self to fill it. In more advanced Type 2 children we may say that roles are seen both as more or less chosen by a self who has motives to perform its functions, and as more or less given to a deserving self as a reward.

However, this role ascription by merit is limited by a failure to completely separate role and self. That is, the role is not yet seen as a fixed set of duties defined independently and in advance of the self which occupies them and which the self takes on and is bound to, more or less contractually.

8. Approval and Stereotypical Role Conformity Leads to an Orientation to Intentions

As a result, role duties are defined only in the general sense

---

[1]As an interesting sidelight, the few children who want to be scientists tend to view occupations in terms of helping others while helping the self and, in general, are high in Type 2 thinking.

of helping the partner. Thus in ambiguous situations, the right is defined by what most persons in that role would probably want to do in terms of natural emotion toward the partner and by what most partners would want done. This implies that the natural family attachments tend to take precedence over the law or over secondary roles in crisis situations (III and IX).

An example is case 33's response to IX:

I think he should owe it to his family first. He loved his family and everything. Other people might die on account of him but his family is more important to him. I don't see what difference it would make if he saved his own family or somebody else's.

A 10-year-old's example of this tendency, together with the difficulty in separating the self behind the role from the role, is the following response to question IX about whether it is wrong to leave one's post to help one's family:

"Half and half. He would be endangering some people's lives but maybe other people saw the fire and could rescue the people.

(What would the other men think?)
That he was a good father and husband.

(Would a good family man have to?)
There's no law that says he has to.

(What would a good citizen do?)
He'd rather be a good family man.

(Could he be a good citizen and not a good family man?)
Yes. He could help the people of the city and let his own house burn down.

A good role is equivalent to helping the partner, e.g., a good citizen is "helping the people of the city," but a good citizen "would rather be a good family man."[1] In both this and the preceding response

---

[1]It may be noted that this child's spontaneous responses in terms of "good roles" may well be the result of previous questions in which the interviewer introduced these concepts. However, even intelligent Type 0 and Type 1 children did not pick up this usage.

there seems to be some sense that it!s good to be concerned about any
other person or citizen but it is more good to be concerned about one's
family.

We also notice that stereotypical role conformity is supported
here by a reliance on other people to "see the fire and rescue the people."

The preference for the natural role is part of a general tendency
to favor role conforming intentions over consequences where these are seen
as conflicting. This involves the naive trust or reliance on superiors
and the social order to do good and the lack of actual responsibility for
the welfare of others characteristic of these boys as children.

More fundamentally, however, it rests on the approval and role-
stereotyping orientation itself. This leads to the empathic judgments of
propriety through projection of the conforming self into the other's situation discussed by Adam Smith. Primary group approval tends to be given
on the basis of role-taking intentions. This is true both of parents
with an educative or encouraging set and of peer groups which base liking
on similarity.

As our illustrations from Question IX indicate, the primacy of
intentions may hold both against rules and against utility consequences.
Both the latter are involved in judgments of right and wrong, while judgments of intentions are judgments of good and bad, of approbation.

The primacy of judgments of approbation over rules is indicated
by responses to Question III about stealing the drug. These range from
"I wouldn't blame him" to "Anyone would do it" or "No one would blame him."

9. Empathic Definitions of Value

On the side of the value of objects and events, value is defined
in personal terms, people have a greater and different value from physical

objects, activities and needs, and they are not reduced to these latter values. This value tends to be defined in terms of the affection or prizing of some other individual.

Characteristic of Type 1 thinking was a reduction of the value of a person to his value for himself as "number 1," or to his value to the needs of some other individual. This value, in turn, tends to be reduced to pleasure and pain. "I would want to die if I were in pain," or "there's no use living if you're sick like that," are responses of Type 1 to question IV about mercy-killing.

Case 9, when asked why one should mercy-kill animals but not human beings, says:

> There's more animals than people. Like a pet dies, you can always get another one, but if his wife died and he married another woman, he wouldn't have a wife just the same as the one he had.

In Type 2 children, the value of a person beyond this Type 1 hedonic value lies in the empathy and affection of other people for him, primarily the family.

As this affectional value begins to emerge, it is hardly distinguishable from either the selfish or projective value put on a person by others, as in the above. Thus, in regard to a doctor mercy-killing, a 10-year-old tells us:

> If he didn't want to wait and she died, they'd have to bury her. Her husband wants to look at her a little more, wouldn't you say?

The implication is that the woman is as good dead as alive for the husband except that he can't see her.

From this type of thinking, the next step toward an empathic value basis appears to be:

> A dog isn't exactly a part of you; he's just a pet I guess. Like a human being is part of your own flesh and blood but a pet is just a companion.

From such a stage in which the value of life is seen in terms of role-taking the family response, we might see the next stage as assessing the value of human beings in terms of their capacity for eliciting an empathic response in general.

Such statements, differentiating mercy killing animals from men, are:

> They mean more to us; they're your own kind; you just feel different about people than animals.

Such statements, which we characterize as Type 2, are still far from a sense of an absolute universal dignity or worth of personality. The relativism implied is sometimes recognized by some of these children who add, "Of course maybe to the dog a human life doesn't mean more." That is, human value depends still on the natural response of empathy of a typical member of the group.

10. Conscience and Duty are not Categorical

On the whole, the Type 2 children assume a "nice" world and a "nice" self, an assumption which coincides with the lack of need to make a sharp judgment of right and wrong.

"Conscience," particularly in the younger Type 2's, tends to speak in the persuasive voice, as in this response to whether it is worse to cheat or steal:

> I'd say Joe because he went to this man who loaned and wouldn't pay him back. I don't think that would be very nice.
> Stealing isn't very good business because the money doesn't belong to you. The people work hard for the money and if they steal, those people can't get anything for it.

The voice here is neither simply the voice of prediction of fact or of what the self would do, which we heard in Type 0 and Type 1, nor is it the voice of the judge of "right and wrong." It is the voice that doesn't want to offend, which assumes that we all mean well and like good things. A reminder that it isn't very nice to steal and that it isn't good business should suffice. The use of persuasive adjectives of understatement and overstatement, suggest that the boy is actually speaking to the potential thief rather than reporting and justifying his judgments to some impartial spectator, and that he views the auditor or potential thief as another good boy. There is no effort at this stage to demonstrate, the approach is rather to appeal to shared sentiments.

A few of the children actually openly respond to the situation as a test of their incorporation of the attitudes which they have been taught. Thus they respond as if the questions were temptations or accusations, e.g., "I have some money saved up for emergencies and I'd never steal like that." The major emphasis is on the self's goodness and not on convincing or affecting others.

Thus Type 2 refers to examples from his own experience as convincing him of the wisdom of moral precepts and of the social order, experience perhaps where his doubts turned out to be unjustified. He makes generalizations of the sort just quoted that "It's never good business to steal."

This style is quite different than the Type 0 prediction of unlikely possibilities. The Type 2 boy has been convinced in the past, he need not raise dire contingencies for every act of conformity and compliance.

11. Conflict and Modes of Coice in Type 2

All this seems to imply that these children live in a world in which there is a high degree of unity in the conformities involved in various roles to various partners. Conformity or goodness to one is goodness to all. They expect, as Case 25 says, "a good father to congratulate you on that good report card."

Most of the Type 2 children, especially the 13-year-olds, find it difficult to envisage a situation in which a conflict in conformities would exist. Thus no matter how arbitrary the authorities portrayed in our stories, these children may tell us that culprits should be reported and the like because the authorities will deal fairly with them, etc. (Appendix D, Case 25).

In general, there is a great tendency to see people and the world as providing a good outcome if the actor conforms to convention.

As we mentioned earlier, at the younger ages Type 2 tends to resolve conflicts by focussing approval sensitivity on parents.

This focus persists among some of our 16-year-olds, especially among upward mobile boys in a lower-class neighborhood.

In such cases, it seems to reflect the absence of any "good" sources of approval outside the family.[1] Four Type 2 16-year-olds tell us that if there were a country with no rules, the one best rule to make would be "to stick together in the family."

Sometimes for the working class 16-year-olds, under pressure to be upward mobile, the conflict is not resolved in favor of reliance on family approval. As one boy says,

> I think a person who'll do a thing just to make his family proud of him isn't doing very much. The family might like him more, but he might be hurting other people doing it. Like between two men for a job, maybe one guy went and told on the other to get the job and make his family proud and really the other guy was worse off and needed the job more.

---

[1] The 16-year old who identified virtue with pleasing mother was very confused and suggestible in his replies to the questions and immediately accepted the interviewer's pressure to change his mind. However, once having been given the "authority's" response, to the interviewer's shame and consternation, he staunchly argued for it while being violently heckled by two of his good friends in the "revealed differences" discussion. This boy's rectitude depends on "correctly" distributing his sensitivity to approval and suggestion.

When such a general conflict between various approvals and role-stereotypical conformities is recognized, these boys become acutely confused and indecisive on our conflict situations, and tend to "relapse" to Type 0 and Type 1 thinking to make a decision.

Techniques of compromise are frequently and often unrealistically suggested, as the coding form indicates (Appendix C). Rather than coming to a decision, these children tell us all the attitudes the actor should take which they are sure are good. Thus, after much discussion and probing on Question I, Case 25, a 13-year-old, ends up saying:

> I think that Joe should think on both sides, of what his father has done for him and of his fun and then maybe he could decide which one he would want—to give his money to his father first or for himself.

Another manner of handling conflict is to focus on one's own virtue regardless of its actual effectiveness in improving the situation. This is a Pharisaic rigidification of the naive intentions orientation. It involves elements of a Type 3 rule-orientation in addition to Type 2 elements.

An example would be the following:

> (Question III—Should the husband who was robbing the store shoot back if the owner was shooting at him and wouldn't stop?)
> No. If the storekeeper didn't have brains enough not to shoot, then I think the man who stole should have brains enough not to shoot back. Let that other man take his life but he doesn't have to take another person's life. That's just too bad for the other man; he doesn't know any better or something.

Thus we see the same "Look out for number one" and "You can't blame me if I do nothing" attitude on a much lower level in some of our Type 1 children. The difference is that the interests of "number one" lie in the paths of conformity and approval. The approval that such a young Pharisee seeks is still outer; it is still the judgment of someone else, even though death may be recommended in pursuit of it.

Thus we are hardly surprised when the same boy tells us that you shouldn't steal because:

> It's not right and he'll probably try it again and he'll get caught for it, and then he'll really be in trouble. He's hurting the storekeeper too; he'll be out of money, but worse than all, he's hurting himself.

In addition to focussing on one's own virtues, these quotes indicate a characteristic attitude toward evil of Type 2 which ranges from "Pharisaism" to "Christian Science." This is the set that bad people or events are to be avoided rather than to be changed through help or active resistance and punishment.[1]

12. Implications of Type 2 for Theories of Empathic Approbation as Resting on Primary Group Relations of Equality

The conformity of our earlier types we saw as controlled by outer sanctions and directives, but there was no felt inner dependence upon outer authority. We argued that in the earlier types, sanctions were an end per se. They were not _symbolic_ of the fact that the self stood in a good relationship to a moral order, or that he had acted optimally in a situation. The persons who dispensed sanctions were not symbolic representatives of a moral order either as exemplars to be imitated or as personages to be respected. Clearly sanctions and authority are so symbolic in Type 2.

To say that such symbolic meaning is completely absent in one stage or type and present in another is of course an artificiality, as the

---

[1]It seems to us that this boy invokes the certitude of sanctions not to maintain his own conformity which is reliably trained into him, but to dispel his envy of others who may deviate. If this be true, he is a transitional type to Stage 3 which actually identifies with or acts to represent and maintain the social order, in part punitively, rather than merely demanding or hoping that it be there to reward him if he conforms and to punish others if they deviate.

types themselves are. However, it does allow us to see the implications of such symbolic meaning at quite a different level than that described by Piaget or Durkheim. On the level which we have described, there is the potentiality for such symbolic dependence to develop further into conscientious judgment, as Piaget thought in characterizing an approval orientation as "autonomous." As we saw, such an approval orientation is associated with Piaget's intentions orientation, with ability to role-take and approve and disapprove of others as described by Adam Smith.

Neither Piaget or Smith stress the dependence on authority and the symbolism of a moral order of conventional roles implied in this orientation. The egalitarianism and instrumentalism stressed by Piaget and Smith we saw as belonging to a different orientation, that of Type 1. We shall see it operating on a much higher level in Type 4.

At the Type 2 level we did find a group of six upper middle-class children at all three ages who were almost caricatures of Riesman's peer-oriented "other-directed" types. Space limitations forbid us to describe or explain their very interesting differences from the "good boy" types. But in terms of our concepts of developmental level of morality, they seem to have the same basis of judgment in terms of generalized conformity, approval seeking, and role-stereotyping as the "good boys." Instead of being a familistic approval-orientation of "helping other people," however, it is a job and peer group orientation of "being intelligent" and getting along with other people. This leads to greater situational flexibility, decisiveness and utilitarian rationality in adapting means to ends for the sake of the immediate goals of the individual or the group. However, it also lends to an even greater dependence on what other people actually do and want as determining what the individual's ends are to be.

Our impression, elaborated in our discussion of Type 4, is that in part these children represent an upper middle-class sociable and social climbing ethos of achievement, associated with a characteristic lack of personal identification between parents and children. In any case it was hard to believe that the orientation arose from spontaneous peer interaction as Piaget might hypothesize.

B. Type 3

1. Relations to Previous Types

Insofar as Type 3 is viewed as an extreme type, it seems to represent not a development from Type 2, but a development from Type 0. Type 0 moral thinking was more or less compliance with external force and an avoidance of punishment. Type 3 represents an "identification" with authority and the social order which was merely complied with in the earlier stage. Such "identification" is expressed in tendencies to actively maintain the social order, and to punish the self and others if they do something which is a violation of that order, tendencies going beyond a mere wish to play a power role.

As far as its over-all "moral goodness" as an actual type goes, we would not consider Type 3 superior to Type 2. However, there are definite modes of thought we have classed in this type and used by extreme scorers which do represent an advance over Type 2 within our conception of morality. In addition, a number of the children in this extreme group are able to use the "good boy" perspective and discount it along with lower perspectives whereas the extreme "good boys" are relatively unable to use a Type 3 perspective and are unable to discount any perspective.

We may give two illustrations of a discounting of Type 2 perspectives. Such discounting has an element of narrowness or "rigidity" which is at an opposite pole from the Type 2 eagerness to include all cliches and approval:

Case 14, age 10
    (In response to V—If he were just thinking about being a good citizen would he tell?)
    If he was just thinking about how he was being a good citizen to tell, he was only trying to get a little self-praise for himself and maybe a little money on the side, just because he wanted to show he was a good citizen.

Case 54, age 16
    (In response to III)
    Well, in that case it would be natural for him to steal, but just because he wanted to or it was natural, I don't think it was right.

Thus regardless of its goodness it seems to be more developmentally advanced than Type 2, and to persist as a stable orientation through adult life.

2. Background Characteristics of High Scorers

We shall first present the type as an extreme or "personality" type in terms of nine children who constitute the top decile in Type 3 scores and then try to extend this extreme picture into a "stage" with wider developmental implications.[1]

One of the nine children was 10, two were 16, and the rest were 13. With one exception, our nine upper-decile children were classed as "stars" as opposed to isolates. However, unlike the other-directed children, only one is a "true star" of his class, the others being merely

---

[1]It may be mentioned that in this case, as in our others, the type was first established and scored in terms of rather refined features of the conflict situations, and only later were "personality" materials considered in any systematic way. However, it is easier to communicate more or less familiar or striking personality features to create a sense of the type than it is to enter into refined verbal moral distinctions.

"popular," having been chosen by three or four other children in the class. Their peer activities seemed to be focussed on organized games, in which all but two were highly interested and competent. Their IQ's were in the 100-120 range. One was an actively thinking 10-year-old, the others 13 and 16. Four of their fathers were in traditional craft trades, the remainder being two accountants, one army officer, a coach and a non-college trained executive. All were clearly presented by their children as hard working. Thus they might be viewed as part of the "lower middle-class ethos" as this has often been conceived.

3. The Sanction—Punitiveness and Fear of Chaos

We may say that as a "personality type," upper decile children have a few of the features of the "Authoritarian Personality" (2), features which differentiate them from our other children and which they seemed to share.

Turning to "authoritarianism" characteristics, we may note first the "punitiveness" which we have already mentioned. This is indicated by a response on our questions II and V that the "culprit" should be reported in order that he be punished, regardless of other considerations. Stage 0 and 2 responses to such questions would justify reporting the culprit so he or the self would avoid punishment or disapproval, not because he "ought to be punished" or "shouldn't get away with it," or because "he did something wrong and it should be corrected."

A hypothesis of "The Authoritarian Personality" is that such "punitiveness" is largely due to the fear that if others are not kept in conformity, the self will follow their example and deviate, and the belief that people conform only through fear of punishment.

These children give many expressions of related ideas such as, "If you steal, others will start stealing (in vengeance or because they see you get away with it) and it will get worse and worse until there is war." Thus the concept of example and the possibility of the end of the social order is added to the Type 0 idea that "If you steal once, you will steal bigger and bigger things and then you'll really be in trouble."

There is a fairly clear demand for regularity and generality of both conformity and punishment, both in the sense that "If you do it once, there is no place to stop" and in the sense of "What if everyone were to do it?" This generality works both ways. On the one hand, the self must conform, since as we noted in our discussion of rules, they say, "Everyone must obey the rules so you shouldn't disobey." On the other hand, there is the demand that others conform or that others should not "get away with it."

4. The Standard—Fixed Rules and Discipline

In its extreme form, a stress on clearly defined expectancies or rules implies a distrust of the natural self which is at the opposite role from Type 2's belief in stereotypically good role occupants. This in turn seems to be closely related to the more renunciatory and painful nature of conformity in the eyes of our Type 3 children. Approval and "what most people do" are not final norms, others can only prescribe as demanding common obedience to the social order. Four of our top nine children give us the rare responses that "you shouldn't be too good a sport "or" too good a friend, "because people want to stay out late— they don't think certain things are wrong" or "If you're hanging around with a bunch of rough guys and they were playing poker or something, you would naturally hang on to that."

There are other expressions that majority or peer behavior is not a proper model for action. Perhaps the potentiality of others for leading the self astray is the explanation of the interesting oddity that seven of the nine boys spontaneously choose for an occupation a solitary outdoor activity, e.g., forest ranger, farmer, rancher, whereas only one boy in our sample chooses such an occupation. (Other trends were to choose to be a soldier and definite expressions of a desire not to get married.) One might see these careers as both a desire for manly discipline and an escape from various social temptations.

Three of these children sharply distinguish and accept violence in the service of a "cause," e.g., the country. This seems to parallel some preoccupation with anger and revenge as a bad but natural thing to be differentiated from punishment.[1]

5. Respect for Authority

These children showed little desire to take either authority or high status roles, in spite of the conviction that they should work hard. This is usually connected with their invoking too much responsibility, and in four of them, with the possibility of making a mistake and doing some great harm. Thus, "identification with authority" seems to be in terms of maintaining the authority system, not as wanting to be an authority.

There seemed to be little question about the unity and importance of authority for these children in every sphere. Six of the nine chil-

---

[1]It should be noted that this differentiation of legitimate and illegitimate aggression seems to be a developmental advance in some respects. Thus many of our Type 1 children were preoccupied with vengeance. Punishment as vengeance was more or less legitimate but so was any other form of vengeance. The Type 3 child on the other hand had no desire to take "the law into his own hands," as he says.

dren describe a good father in terms of fair but strict discipline, a
quite rare response. They say being a good son is "always thinking your
father is right." However, paternal authority is not merely personal
obedience as in Stage 0. The perception of the father in the disci-
plinary role is part of a perception of parents as teachers of respect
for the social order outside the family.

Sometimes there is a definite conscious equation of legitimate
authorities which appeared in none of the previous types, i.e., a
teacher "was like a parent," etc. These children also talk about action
as "showing respect" and say that someone ought to be respected, unlike
any of the previous types. Respect for outer status is based on representing the state and the law, and on the hard work required for the job.
Thus respect is claimed by and awarded to representatives of "the moral
order."

6. Concepts of Rights

Turning to more developmental moral aspects rather than personality elements of the extremes, we may note first a quite strong sense
of rights.

In the previous types discussed, insofar as rights existed apart
from "doing right," they simply meant the right to control one's self and
one's property or to do certain acts. "It's not yours" or "It's none of
your business," or "Who said you could do that?"

In Type 3, rights seem to mean, "I have deprived myself of something by conforming or working, and the social order should see to it
that I have not been deprived in vain." A right is a claim for some
positive action by another. It is a legitimate expectation as to the
actions of other persons or of the social system. In general these

claims rest on being _earned_ by the claimer, on having given up something with the expectation of a return.

Thus there is little sense of natural or universal inherent rights. For instance, whether or not Negroes have a right to something would rest on one's judgment as to whether they had "earned" it.

The rights of others imply some renunciation and conformity on the part of those who respect and maintain them. Thus duties correspond to rights or claims by others, including authorities who have a right to expect one to complete delegated tasks.

Type 3 is our first type to interpret general types of deviance as the violation of rights. Perception of stealing as taking away something from someone who had worked hard was coded as Type 3, if it seemed to imply a definite role-taking of the victim's indignation or a sense of indignation at disappointed strivings. Some examples are: "You'd be pretty made if you worked for something and someone took it," or on a higher level: "Someone works for something and someone else comes along and takes it, that isn't right at all." The distinction is between role-taking the needs of the victim (Type 1), role-taking his disappointment and disapproval (Type 2), and role-taking his resentment at infringement of his rights, an infringement in which he represents or has the punitive force of authority and the social order (Type 3).

Thus, we did not wish to imply that the imposition of conformity and punishment upon others are tendencies first born in our fourth type. What characterizes this stage is rather a sense of conformity and punishment as the maintenance of legitimate expectancies. The demands of authority and the rules are not only external forces which all should obey, but they are efforts to main.ain a set of claims which the self also makes. In stage 3, the regularity of punishment is not only a fact but a desirable state. At stage 0, punitive tendencies might be based on "If I'm going to be punished, so should he be." At stage 3, the thought would be "My whole life is based on the fact that I have learned to conform, I cannot allow a situation in which conformity and the renunciations I have accepted are useless."

In stage 0, regular role behavior was seen as resulting from impersonal routine and external compulsions, in stage 1, from habit and need, in stage 2 from concern for role partners. In stage 3, it tends to be seen in terms of the claims individuals make on one another. People not only hope to be rewarded for conformity, but they conform in order to constrain others to give them what they may legitimately claim. This leads to quite a different sort of "rigidity" than that of stage 0. At stage 0 any way of doing things might seem as necessarily fixed, e.g., "mothers should always buy the food." At stage 1, not activities but claims and social expectations are fixed.

7. Concepts of Value and Responsibility for Consequences

There is, for the first time, a clear though narrow sense of duty and responsibility in the Type 3's. By this is meant that there is a clear awareness of and concern for a definite delegated set of consequences for which the self is responsible, a concern relatively independent of the actual implications of the situation in terms of sanctions, law, approval and self-interest. In other words, there is a "have to" or "must" or "wrong" independent of the self's wish and of actual compulsion and sanctions. (This, perhaps, can be better conveyed through the examples in Appendix D.)

"Duty" is not simply a situational pressure as in Type 0; no amount of situational pressure changes the demand to conform to the fixed order (III) or to perform assigned tasks with important consequences (IX).

There may be a demand for cognitive certitude before performing a possibly deviant action, rather than a "projective" Type 0 concern for consequences. That is, the actor has an obligation to consider the consequences for which he may be held responsible or blamed. A rather "unrealistic" example would be that a husband should be sure a drug would work before stealing it for his wife.

We might expect a Type 3 parent to take a rather punitive, moralistic attitude to mistakes and carelessness in their children. Thus this group tends to be "consequence oriented" rather than "intentions-oriented" like Type 2. These consequences tend to be viewed in terms of damage to life and property or in terms of pain. The distinction between the concern about consequences in this type and in Type 1 is a subtle one, and hard to really differentiate in some of our questions. It is the distinction between a last-resort choice of evils and an "ends justify the means" attitude. The contrast may be illustrated by the two following brief responses about mercy-killing by 16-year-olds:

Type 1: If there's no chance of her living and she's not enjoying life anymore, they should. He would actually be saving her.

Type 3: If there's no cure, there's no reason to torture a person if they're going to die anyway.

The first asserts that the value of life lies in its being enjoyed. There is no reason to live except for pleasure. It goes so far as to say that the doctor is really saving her by delivering her from pain. One gets no sense that the woman's pain is an intolgerable condition to the doctor, forcing some suspension of rules but rather that the doctor is acting in an instrumentally rational or intelligent fashion. It asks, "Why shouldn't he kill her?"

The second does not assert that a painful life is a valueless one. It asserts rather that the doctor is responsible for causing pain without reason since her life will be lost anyway. It asks, "Why should he cause pain?"

In extreme cases of Type 1, we saw that one was only responsible for the self and for what the self actively caused or initiated (Chap. VI, Sec. E-4). In Type 3, one is responsible for bad events happening to others and for one's own inaction in the face of it. Thus doing nothing for the woman is torturing her.

From what has been said earlier, it should be apparent that Type 3's concern for consequences is not a utilitarianism, but is sharply restricted by rules, delegated authority, etc.

8. Concepts of Duty

The basic image behind the Type 3 concept of obligation seems to be the job role, just as the basic image of obligation in Type 2 seemed to be the family role. Thus work obligation implies a contract or delegation assigning responsibility for a set of consequences. It includes less than the diffuse personal conformity of Type 2 but implies a more definite and decisive sense of responsibility.

We see both Type 2 and Type 3 children as on a level of "role" morality. Both conceive of obligation as to an assigned individual "role, partner expectation," rather than to an abstract principle or purpose with some logical claim. The partner's expectation is seen as based on his own natural sentiments or on what he may claim, though the claim be irrational or egoistic.

We may say that the motive for conformity is inner but the order or content conformed to is "outer," one conforms to the actual expectancies of others, expectancies which are vague and diffuse for Type 2 and fixed and rather narrow for Type 3. One conforms to outer expectancies because one has learned a generalized respect for the expectancies of authorities and for other legitimate claimants, of whom the parents are only individual symbols.

There is an internalized tendency to respect and value the social order and its basic rules. Beyond this the definition of the situation rests on the edicts of this order.

9. Choice as Categorical

Type 3's conformity to the external social order does not mean a suggestible adaptation to adult authority.

Our extreme Type 3 children tend to be very decisive in the conflict situations and consistent and fairly unyielding under pressure. This would seem to justify the adjectives of either "rigid" or "autonomous," depending on one's evaluative set. In any case, their answers reflected a consistency absent in the unyieldingness of Type 1 children, who could be characterized as "impulsive" and "negativistic" due to inconsistency.

However, Type 3's lack of careful consideration of the situation or of the interviewer's argumentation would prevent one from considering the decisions to be "principled." In part their lack of involvement in the moral situations probably represented impatience and annoyance over the implicit challenge and questioning of the certainty of the conventional order implied in them. Where the good boy might be stimulated to say "I'd never do something like that," Type 3 might be stimulated to anger. We have noticed in a few "Type 3" adults a perception of the examiner as a

devil's advocate, dreaming up unlikely and dubious situations and making
an intellectual exercise out of the right and wrong.

Thus we might expect this type to quite earnestly endeavor to
make a right decision if the situation were a real one in which they were
involved rather than one made up in the spirit of "asking for trouble."

10. Another Image of Type 3

We linked our extreme representatives of Type 3 to some of the
mechanisms hypothesized in the "Authoritarian Personality." The actual
character stereotype provided by that work leaves a warped view of even
the extreme members of our Type 3. The type is not necessarily disposed
toward ethnic or racial prejudice, though it tends to be "prejudiced"
against criminals. It is not naturally antidemocratic. Though it relies
on a strong government and respects legitimate authority and force, such
a government or authority may be preferred to be democratic.[1]

A more representative stereotype than that of the authoritarian
personality is given in section D-5 in terms of Victor Hugo's character
of Javert, the police-inspector. Another portrait of the type in relation to the duties of work may be based on a charter sport-fishing boat
captain we know who runs the boat with his adolescent son. He enjoys
fishing and the social interaction with his fellow fishing boat captains.
However, any Hemingwayesque attitudes toward the sportsman's code and
feelings of superiority to the "unmanliness" of his customers are tempered
by their symbolic status as customers and of higher status in the society.
Thus undoubtedly he has a tendency to get upset at their whims and

---

[1]Several express an abhorrence of dictators which only reinforces
their sense of need for rules and order. Type 3 is differentiated from
Type 0 by knowing and feeling the difference between "dictatorship" and
"authority."

blunders which prevent them from landing fish. He seems a little over-critical of the minor mistakes of his son. However, he accepts the whims of his customers as defining his "duty," since he stands in a payment relation to them. His duty includes seeing that his customers catch something even if he must go well beyond the hours he has contracted for and will be paid for. He feels the weight of their expectations even though he cannot and has not contracted that his customer be successful.

Thus the payment relationship raises the play activity to a quasi-moral level. Property implies moral symbolism in other regards. He feels, as he says, the heavy "responsibility" involved in the boat and its upkeep.

He is rather severe in teaching carefulness of task-performance and "respect" for his customers to his son. He pressures the boy to do well in school because he does not want him to be a "dumb fisherman" like himself. He recognizes he chose an occupation which he enjoys, but one in which his kind of hard work cannot bring him much income, status or social usefulness, which tend to be vaguely blended in his mind.

His own rights and duties as an authority to his son are rather independent of his socially defined status and wisdom, as well as of his feelings for the boy. Rather they rest on his being responsible for his son's welfare and his conformity. It is easy to see that in spite of his wishes for the boy to advance in status, the boy may well grow up to be like him and perpetuate the same stable pattern.

C. Type 4—The Contractual Legalist Orientation

1. Overview of the Type and Sub-types within It

It is rather difficult to characterize a complex of sentiments and values characterizing Type 4, since the essence of Type 4 is an impersonal rationalistic orientation to morality which largely excludes the self's sentiments. The Type 4 rationalization is essentially an orientation to that which is socially agreed upon or can be agreed upon. It usually involves a fairly conscious limitation or exclusion of the sentiments and stereotypes of Types 2 and 3. Originally we treated as separate types three orientations included in Type 4. The first orientation is merely a conventionalistic or legalistic predictive set. For this orientation the generally known rules constitute the right, regardless of their bases or of their implications in a particular situation. This type merely predicts what the law is, what the jury probably would decide, etc.

The second orientation or kind of legalism sees as right that which coincides with law and majority opinion, regardless of individual principle or sentiment. However, the second orientation bases such conformity on some "methodological principles." The fact that rules and conventions are based upon agreement and are necessary for agreement and organized social activity justifies them, rather than their being justified per se. For the first orientation, the rules would be equally justified if they were the arbitrary edict of a king, since they would still be generally known and enforced. For the second type, the fact that they are based on general agreement makes them right.

For the first orientation, the rules are simply accepted even though doing violence to the good and just in an individual case. For the second orientation, the rules are accepted though they do violence to the good in the individual case because in the long run their consequences are good and because they are agreed upon. Both accept an element of arbitrariness in moral judgment since those judgments are based on consensus, but the second orientation sees the element of arbitrariness as more or less logically necessary as a starting point for agreement. The recognition of the necessary arbitrariness and hence "non-sacredness" of particular rules is just what impels Type 4 to stick to them even in extreme cases. Agreement starts with the premise, the rule, and is led to the conclusion, the judgment of the individual case.

This may reach an intellectualized development as the belief in codes of rules logically derived from a few more or less arbitrarily agreed upon postulates.

The acceptance of arbitrariness may be associated with leniency in the case of individual deviance. While the authorities must hold to rule, the individual may do the expedient as long as he is acting ex officio. However, the "right" remains law and majority opinion, which coincides with majority welfare. The laws are always right but they are not sacred, and in the perspective of a lawmaker, the orientation is flexibly utilitarian.

The third orientation rests strongly on a sense of contract with some sense of universal individual rights. Respect for individual rights involves a willingness to ignore the individual case which deviates from the good, just as does generalized conformity to law. Such respect implies a willingness to allow someone to do things which are not good for himself and others and to grant an individual certain benefits regardless of actual merit.

A sense of contract implies a sense of responsibility as based on agreement, as does democratic respect for law. Again it implies an "arbitrary" delimitation of duty in terms of an actual situation.

As we mentioned in Chapter III, we originally separated these three orientations, the conventional, the democratic-utilitarian, and the contractualistic.[1] On the basis of our original intercorrelation matrix we decided to pool these types. This decision was based also on difficulties in viewing each orientation as a definite type with regard to individual cases. In addition, there were coding difficulties in differentiating whether or not a reference use of contract and law was purely conventional or was based on democratic-contractual sentiments and ideas. In a less democratic culture, it would doubtless be easier to separate these types.

2. Piaget's Concepts and Type 4

In our discussion of Piaget's theories in Chapter II, we discussed two points of departure for defining the determinants necessary for development into Type 4, one more cognitive, the other more social. The more cognitive determinant is the adolescent's capacity for formal thought, his ability to orient to concepts in the abstract. Piaget stresses this development as making possible social ideals, a development we shall consider in Type 5. In the case of Type 4, we see formal thought as embodied not in ideals but in a democratic bureaucratic formalism. We shall spell out some of the specific implications of formal thought for social values in the next sections. However, we might say generally that it tends to

---

[1]Thus a contractual rights orientation is oriented to the individual, the democratic legalism is oriented to the group. The contractual rights orientation tends not to have a utilitarian expendiency set to law-making, the democratic legalist does.

transform moral concepts and concerns into political concepts and concerns. Rights and duties are seen as the results of the groups interacting and deciding on policies.

Morality tends to focus increasingly on relations of groups of persons to one another qua groups. Social relations are relations between roles at all stages of development but they tend to become group relations in adolescence. Thus in adolescence, the conflict between parent and child may come to be perceived as the conflict between generational groups. The conflict with other age mates is perceived as a conflict between cliques or status groups.[1]

As social relations become perceived as relations between groups, there is a tendency to see the crucial moral ties and rules as those which are needed to govern relations between groups rather than those natural relations between members of small groups which may be left to themselves. The extent to which this politicization of morality may go seems indicated by the attitudes of some liberal educated people. Such people seem to display strong moral indignation over a few social issues like political and racial civil rights but never seem to display moral indignation over acts of personal and individual injustice in family, work or acquaintanceship relations.

Besides the cognitive influence of formal thought, the social influence discussed by Piaget is that of peer relations and "mutual respect." This he feels to be the source of respect for rules agreed upon

---

[1]Our sociometric assessments and interviews indicate a tendency to perceive peer relations as clique relations after age 13. The 13-year-old boy low in popularity may still say he likes the classroom star the best because of various personal attributes. The 16-year-old boy says of the star that "he belongs to a group that think they're hot and try to run everything and he and his friends don't pay much attention to them."

by the group and of respectfor the equal rights of individuals. We have
considered various elements of Piaget's autonomous stage of morality
which we attributed to Type 1 and to Type 2. However, the basic value
system of the "autonomous type" would seem to be that of Type 4. The
fact that we see it as the complex resultant of determinants of previous
types suggests the limits of peer group interaction in itself to lead to
this type. We shall discuss sociometric and social class participation
as determining the type in section

3. Type 4's Modes of Conceiving Roles—Roles as Defined by Rules

One side of Type 4's formal thinking is a clear perception of
roles as concepts defined by rules.

We saw both Type 2 and Type 3 as "role-oriented," that is, as
seeing obligation as fulfilling prescribed functions, stereotypical motives, and partner expectations. Type 2 tends to define role functions
in terms of the wishes, approval and welfare of the concrete role partner. In the case of Type 3, role obligation is defined somewhat more
impersonally and contractually but still essentially in terms of conformity to the interests andexpectations of the individual partner.

As opposed to such concepts we may contrast an orientation to
role-obligations as obligations to rules. Most of us, whether layman or
sociologist, tend to conceptualize social roles as parts of a formal
organization. We can view roles as a system of positions in a "Table of
Organization," positions quite independent of the persons in them. We
think of the administrator or legislator as first setting up and defining
a system of positions whose functions are defined by rules, and then going out to find individuals who will fill these positions. The occupants,

in endeavoring to fulfill their obligations, will be oriented to these specifically agreed upon or defined rules.

A simple example classed as Type 4 would be the determination by law of whether the doctor should mercy-kill, with the law, the patient, and the doctor mutually oriented to each other's expectation and to the need for a fixed definition of the situation. For the same case, we have also viewed as a stage 4 response the idea that the doctor's role is defined by a code made by his occupational peer group.

In contrast, we classified as primitive Type 3 the response that a doctor should mercy-kill if requested, because the patient is "paying him for his services." Another Type 3 response would be that the doctor should get permission from the authorities to mercy-kill, reflecting an orientation to the legal system in terms of personal role.

For Durkheim's view of organic solidity and obligation, it is of extreme importance that the child should acquire the Type 4 capacity to see complementary functional roles as defined by a set of rules backed by the authority of society.

4. Role as Differentiated from Role-Occupant

The other side of the definition of role in terms of specific rules is the perception of roles as simply fixed classifications independent or separate from the persons who fill them. This has important implications for evaluating individuals and the roles they occupy.

We saw as characteristic of stage 0 the equation of a role and an activity, developing in stage 2 to the equation of a role with a stereotypical personality modally filling it. We considered stage 3 a concern with occupational roles as "earned" by hard work, implying a more differ-

entiated relation between the value of the individual role occupant and
the value of the role. Also the role is seen as awarded by authorities
to a person who they think capable and trustworthy and hence the person
is to be respected because he was chosen by authority. We consider as
stage 4 a perception of the respect accorded to a role occupant as determined by the occupant's free choice of the role. It is the choice
of the role as a situation by the person which is to be respected as
implying something about him as a personality. A rather immature or
stereotypical reflection of this is case 66's response.

> Some people think that a farmer must be a dumb person who can't
> do anything else. They think that's all there's left for a person
> to do if they became a farmer.

A response more clearly employing the concept of role choice is case
63's response:

> I think a teacher's the worst job in the way of money-making.
> Where a person goes to school for eight years for a master's and
> end up making $4,000, you gotta be a pretty wonderful person to
> go into something like that.

5. Concepts of Natural Rights

Our conception of the development of "rights" was both complicated
and sharpened by the fact that the more mature and thoughtful 10- and 13-
year-olds tended to answer questions about such rights in the negative.
For them rights were primarily maintenance of "earned expectations."

As we mentioned earlier, however, the Type 1 children were quite
ready to deny authority the right to do any conflict-involved activity.
"Individual rights" meant for them merely the fact that one could control
oneself and one's property.

The more mature concept implies in addition that one should have
such control. It implies a sense of a situation about which the authority

is naturally and legitimately concerned but about which he should do nothing. An individual right is not what the group cannot do, but a manifestation of an attitude which the group ought to universally recognize in each of its individual members (cf. our discussion of Mead's concepts in Chap. II).

We have classed as Type 4 a beginning and somewhat vague concept of such rights of the individual person as "natural rights." In part we mean by individual rights, a distinction between the rights of a person as a role occupant, e.g., as a son or as a soldier, and his rights as a person not fully defined by any single role. In part we mean also rights of "privacy," of some inner sphere which should not be tampered with even by well meaning authority. Case 66 presents some examples:

> (VI—Does the troublemaker have a right to refuse to go on the suicide mission?)
> According to the rule of the army, I guess he'd be wrong, but as a person in the world, I think he may have a right not to go.

> (II—Does his father have a right to expect Bob to tell what his brother told him?)
> I don't think he should have a right to try to make someone else tell something. If the other person had trusted the person with the information, I don't think he should try to pry it out of him.

6. Role Conflict and Choice of Loyalties

We tend to think of a role conflict situation as one in which a person must "stand outside" both roles and go through a process of selection of the one to which he will adhere. The earlier types showed no tendency to see role conflicts in this way. In Type 2, the role occupant was a stereotypical natural role self in a concrete situation. A good citizen "would rather be a good family man" in a situation of role conflict. The person is in the family role at the moment of choice.

We interpreted Type 2 as oriented to one basic role, "the good son," as being equivalent to being a "good boy" in general. Such a role tends to be pervasive because the "being a good son" tends to mean conforming to parental expectations about matters outside the son role itself, and because the expectancies of others besides the parents were mediated through the parents.

We described some expressions by older Type 2 children of conflict between family expectancies and other expectancies. Such conflict tends to be limited in Type 3 by an orientation to specific concrete task obligations, and by the expectation that everyone should accept and be subordinated to the general order, or the authority hierarchy.

Type 4, on the other hand, thinks of our "role-conflict" as implying a choice between loyalties. It implies to some extent a general conforming self outside of both roles and able to choose between its natural dispositions in the one or the other. It implies that this self can see the issue from the "point of view" of a citizen and of a husband.

In Type 4, such choice of roles by the general self is largely determined from a private or prudential view, there is no moral principle of choice used in the solution. Thus role conflict may be defined in terms of individually chosen preference for one partner as opposed to another. Which partner is liked the best and whose disapproval is most feared is taken not as naturally given by one's status, it is something which varies from individual to individual and expresses a free evaluation by the actor.

We may give some examples of various levels of Type 4 perception of role conflict in terms of the loyalties of a choosing self outside a given role:

Case 29 - Type 3 & 4
    (Replying to II—Should he keep quiet if his brother had kept quiet for him?)

Well it would be right in the way they think, its being loyal to each other, but to be right, they should tell their father. You should tell the truth to your father. It's better than being loyal, doing something for the other person if he did something for you. Your father is older than you and he could give you better advice if you were in trouble or something.

Comment: This example represent a precursor of a Type 4 choice. For this boy "loyalty" is identified with exchange rather than being seen as a generalized definition of role conformity. The conflict is not one between loyalties but between moral authority and the basic welfare of the self on one side and the peer role point of view on the other. Thus there is a "really right" which is not just the son role point of view and a "right in the way they think." This latter role-defined expectation is more than simply a selfish or emotional attitude as in Type 1 or 2. It is a shared mode of thought with some legitimacy.

Case 66 (Replying to question II—cf. Appendix A):
If his older brother just found out he had lied, maybe he should tell his father. But if his brother just trusted him I don't think he should tell.

(Would it be wrong?)
Just a choice of what he wants to do. If he likes his brother a lot he shouldn't tell.

(Why should it be different than if he were just a friend?)
A family has a close relationship and they knew each other and the father is head of the family. The two brothers would have to have some sense of loyalty to the father and a neighbor wouldn't.

Comment: Maintaining a peer confidence is here one factor in a situation in which "some sense of loyalty to the father" is another. But these are only limits within which individual choice has to take place on arbitrary individual and situational grounds, on the basis of degree of liking. Obligation does not imply unlimited conformity to either role partner, yet there are certain role conformities which must be met. These conformities seem to involve only general role requirements, not requirements dependent on stereotyping of role occupants and situations as in case 29's reference to to the superior wisdom of the father.

Case 63 (Replying to III—Was it wrong to steal the drug for his wife?)
Well it's against the law to rob someone else's property. I suppose that makes it wrong, but I expect he feels just in his mind, because he's gotta save his wife. In the law's eyes it would be wrong, but in this man's eyes it would be something to save his wife.

(Is it a good husband's duty?)
I feel a husband's duty is more to his wife than to the law. He can serve 5, 10, 20 years, whatever the law is, he could still spend the remainder of his life with his wife.

Comment: Although the legal wrong is essentially the last judgment of wrong, it is reduced to an enforced expectation, to a weaker "duty" than toward his wife. The law is the last social appeal, but it is not the ultimate command or a social taboo. It is a fixed social sphere to which the individual has a duty. Ultimately the claim of the law on the individual chooser here is reduced to a prudential view of punishment on the basis of which the decision is made.

7. The Choice Process and Relativism of Perspective in Society

In contrasting the 16-year-old Type 4 boys with boys who seem like their counterparts at 13, one is struck by their increased caution about committing themselves, their unwillingness to be "boxed in" on the moral judgment questions.[1]

Such caution is different from that of some of the 13-year-olds and some of the Type 2 16-year-olds who showed considerable conflict and attempted to be "covered" on both sides of the question. They expressed

---

[1]Thus when asked if the husband was really right, case 63 replies: "I can't actually say that he'd be right, but in my eyes, he'd have just cause to go out and do it, but in the law's eyes, he wouldn't. I can't answer it any other way."

conflict more than caution, based on a sense of a correct answer which they would like to reach, but of which they were not sure, or to a concrete involvement as to "What would you do?"

Type 4 cautiousness toward our questions seems to spring from a perception of "the right" as not a simple matter of individual judgment. Rather, "the right" is seen as the judgment of society as an abstract system, a judgment framed by experts or specialists following specific lines of thought and then accepted by people in general.

In the family and peer group there is no delegation of this sort. While an authority may make the decision, it is because the authority knows what is good and right in general and for all in the situation. The authority is not supposed to respond in terms of some limited point of view in which he is an expert, e.g., from a "legal point of view."

Again, in the small group there are no decisions which can't be made. Some decision is necessary in any concrete problem-case. In the case of a society or secondary institution an uncertain or methodologically incorrect decision is for many reasons worse than no decision at all. These reasons vary from those of bureaucratic accountability to those of establishing bad precedents to those of infringing on rights. But in any case there are strong pressures only to make decisions within a framework of universal consensus.

Because of the strength of the need to belong in a small group, and because of the concreteness of the decisions involved, it is possible to obtain such consensus. Thus the more mature 13-year-olds essentially seem to have a small peer group view of democracy. The agreement of the majority is equivalent to universal consensus since in the small peer group, the incentives to be a "good sport," to be accepted and to keep the game going are sufficient to get the minority to at least overtly

accept the majority view.

From such a small group view, the life of society is quite simple.

We may quote the response of case 72, a predominantly Type 2 16-year-old:

> Like that colored girl thrown out of school down South. I was
> thinking they could get a vote of the whole United States whether
> they should let colored children into white schools.

He also thought that a mercy-killing decision should be settled by a

family vote.

At the more mature level we have classed as Type 4 there is some

recognition of the law as an abstract perspective shaped by the interac-

tion of various individuals or groups with various more or less idealogi-

cal differences. Thus case 63 tells us,

> At one point, the law has no concern about personal feelings,
> at the next point it's got every personal feeling. I suppose the
> laws are made by many different groups of people with different
> ideas.

From such a point of view, diversities of opinion are permanent and or-

ganized, they are not solved simply by a vote.

The clear recognition of diversities of opinion goes as far back

as stage 1 in our schema. However, at that stage such opinions tended

to be sheer expressions of habit and interest and to be situation specific,

not ideologies. We analyzed this level of perceived relativity in the

individual in Chapter V, but we may quote case 72, our advocate of the

vote, making a Type 1 response with regard to the relativity of group

opinion:

> (Was slavery a bad law?)
> Depends on whether people wanted people free or not. If you
> wanted Negroes free, then it would be a bad law, but if you were a
> plantation owner and you needed slaves to work in your fields,
> they'd probably think it was a good law.

(Who would really be right?)
The owner would probably have more say in the government. The laws the government makes are usually right.

Stage 4 recognition of diversity on the other hand is the diversity of groups of men thinking about the common good, each with their own conception of that good, and each trying to convince the other. It presupposes some stable common basis from which divergent views may be worked out. A good example is case 66's response to, "What would be the one best rule if there were a country with no rules at all?"

I think they should follow all of the 10 Commandments, if you want to classify them under one big rule. Because most of them have to do with man, how to get along with each other. Like you're supposed to love your neighbor, love yourself, and it depends on your faith. Maybe they might not have a God to love, but in the United States most of us do. They say over in India, lots are Buddhists and all other kinds of religions. But in the United States, I suppose those are the best rules.

Such a response in its tolerant recognition of diversity, also indicates a certain acceptance of an arbitrariness in what is conformed to. Even when asked to legislate for a country with no rules, he seeks some existing creed to which to tie. It seems to be a matter of opinion whether God exists or He doesn't. Insofar as a general "principle" is elicited, it is "getting along with each other," which any set of rules may achieve.

Tolerance, if it is not an aspect of a positive effort at justice and impartiality, is not a moral principle itself, however desirable as a personal attitude. Thus a usually unnoted corollary of tolerance is the acceptance of the status quo. If one feels all value systems are equal, one naturally selects the one closest at hand, or the one accepted by the majority or the one which coincides with inclination and self-interest. Thus, in our opinion, a more "principled" attitude toward diversity of values, is the belief that everyone has a right to his own values (within the usual limits with regard to the rights of others), not the belief that all values are in fact equal.

8. The Standard—Law and Majority Opinion

In Type 4, the recognition of various points of view tends to be associated with an attitude that the right is defined by the law and/or the view of the majority. This can be seen in Case 66's views as to whether it is ever right to break a law. As was mentioned in connection with conceptions of rules, Case 66 not only believes that it is right that the majority rule but in some sense the majority opinion is correct. In connection with disobedience in Russia, he relies on what the majority would do without being able to say whether the law is right or the majority is right when they are in opposition.

However, we consider as Type 4, also at its "highest," the recognition of a partial sense of individual rights as prior to the law, as in Case 66's reply to whether it was right to defy the law to aid escaping slaves:

> That has to do with people, and I don't think any people should be ruled by somebody else who's supposed to be better than them. All the races are equal. I think they should have hid the Negroes who escaped. I think this is an exception to the rule actually.

On the other hand, we would also consider as Type 4 the more relativistic reply of Case 63 to the same question:

> There again it's in that someone's mind. The majority of the people in the North helped the slaves but on the other hand the majority of the people in the South would return them. So I think it was just your personal feelings.
>
> (So it's neither right nor wrong?)
> Yeah, in most cases like that where it's a real debatable subject, because you've got two sections of the country feeling different.

For this boy the debatability of a subject is the degree to which there is a 50-50 split on the Gallup poll on it. While one might say he lacks "principles," such a boy is at least capable of participation in political and cultural issues. Such participation requires some sense of alternative "positions" on an issue shared by various groups and to be identified with in terms of which is vaguely best for some larger whole. In his thinking, the fact that one is Northerner, or Southerner, poor or rich, does not settle the choice per se as it did for Case 72, quoted earlier.

9. Peer Group Conformism vs. Intelligent Achievement as the Core Values of Type 4

The best representatives of Type 4 are 16-year-old upper middle-class integrates who are oriented to worldly achievement as business men or engineers. Occasionally, one is tempted to apply the label of "Philistine" to them. At ages 10 and 13, they would probably have been clear representatives of our "other-directed" sub-type. Age has, however, brought more realism to their stereotypes for approval, and widened the peer group into vox populi. Interestingly, the only 16-year-old who fitted the earlier model of other-directed was an upper lower-class Italian boy who wanted to be a politician.

However, it seems likely that many of the Type 2 and Type 3 middle-class boys will develop Type 4 characteristics even if they were not strongly oriented to peer status at an earlier age. Probably more important than such a peer orientation is a high evaluation of intelligent achievement for its own sake.

Both contractual legalism and utilitarianism are efforts to set up morality purely on the basis of an appeal to individual intelligence.

As opposed to the "natural" stereotypically motivated conventional self
of Type 2, legalism and utilitarianism appeal to the achievement-oriented
reasonable or intelligent self. Thus Type 4 implies an acceptance of the
law as an arbitrary starting point for the sake of agreement is different
than a Type 3 respect for the law as representing a higher power or the
whole social order. A utilitarian orientation to individual wish implies
the need for an unambiguous measure on which all may agree as opposed to
the natural sympathy and role-taking which secures consensus for Type 2.

Insofar as there is any sentiment of individual "respect" behind
legalism or utilitarianism, it is a respect for another equal logical and
prudent ego. This is the self which each assumes the other has for purposes of logical argument. For the sake of argument and prediction in
social and moral matters, we make some simple assumptions such as that
each self wants to maximize its own interests.[1]

10. Type 4 Concepts of Respect for Status

Thus Type 4 tends to see respect for others as based on intelligence or ability. Everyone is assumed to be oriented to income and success. The higher the income and status of a job, the more ability the
person must have had to win it. The upper middle-class children tend to
see all jobs as interchangeable prizes in a race which the smartest or

---

[1]This self bears a good deal of relationship to the self which
the delinquent and the non-conforming 10-year-old sees himself and
others as having. However, the self-interestedness, the emptiness, the
arbitrariness, which the delinquent ascribes to people is not a matter
of assumptions for the sake of logical argument and secondary institutional participation. Persons are not selfish and impersonal because
they are being rational or smart; that is just the way they are.
Both our Type 1 and Type 4 children tend to orient to jobs in
terms of income. In Type 1 this reflects little concern about what
other people think of one's occupation compared to manipulateable impersonal gratifications. In Type 4 it reflects the need for an impersonal
standard of achievement which everyone can acknowledge.

(Original article mispaginated.
No page 277 in original.)

most able person wins (cf. the quotation in section C-4 of this Chapter).[1]
In addition to intelligence, role competence involves "knowledge of his
field," i.e., delimited expertise. There is a distinction between matters of formal knowledge and of opinion or value. In the former, one
depends on the expert, in the latter on one's individual judgment or on
majority opinion.

We have already discussed the role-person differentiation which
the Type 4 involves. It involves seeing the role occupant as choosing
the job in an instrumental fashion in terms of generalized career rewards,
while the boss or institution chooses the individual in terms of generalized ability.

However, the Type 4 point of view on respect for adult job roles
involves in addition a change of viewpoint, based in part on the boy's
increased concern for his own adult identity. Whereas earlier stages took
the perspective of the partner in evaluating the respectedness of a role,
Type 4 takes the view of another person comparing his job with that of
the role. "Respect" in this sense is the polite but sincere envy of the
runner-up for the winner.

11. Class Differences in Concepts of Achievement and Virtue

In the lower class envy is not respect, since the loser never

---

[1]Type 2 or Type 3, on the other hand, saw roles as implying personal virtues rather than general abilities. If a role involved helping
others, the occupant was respected for wanting to help others. If it involved hard work, the occupant was respected for wanting to work hard.
Knowledge was a rather diffuse wisdom as to how to handle value-involved
situations.

Associated with the perception of role occupants as virtuous was
the perception of them as delegated representatives of society or the
moral order in general. Persons were respected because they represented
or symbolized the government, etc. The individual role occupant somehow
had attached to him the value of the institution as a whole.

could enter the race. Thus Case 58, age 16, tells us about the head of a company, whom he rated low for respect:

> Most of the common people would have a grudge against him. He made good really. That would make some of them try harder though. If he was just a head or something and didn't do nothing for nobody, just spent his money foolishly, people wouldn't respect him.

Case 61, a middle-class boy, age 16, whose score on moral judgment is about the same, presents a bridge from this attitude to a Type 4 attitude:

> They respect the head of the food company just for the position he has. More of jealousy than respect. They respect the artist because the respect anybody who has a talent for things that are hard to do, that most people can't do. They respect people for doing things they can't do themselves.

For this boy jealousy of the head of the company is respect, whereas for the lower-class boy it was disrespect; The transformation of envy to respect rests on a comparison of abilities. For the lower-class boys, differential status was either due to fortune or perhaps to aspiration ("make them try harder").

Thus we see how a peer orientation to competitive achievement and to status in game-like situations can be generalized much more easily to occupational achievement in the upper middle-class.

At the same time, for the upper middle-class group, achievement is more divorced from personal moral virtues. Whereas for the lower- and lower middle-class child, achievement is an expression of strong character and values, and choices; in the upper middle-class it is a matter of ability.

For the lower middle-class child it is the choice of going to college and the work required to do it; it is the choice of the right virtuous friends and resistance to temptations of dalliance with the peer group, etc. For the upper middle-class it is the ability to do well in school—not respect for education which counts. It is the ability to get along well with the peer group (who are the models of your later customers and colleagues) which counts—not picking virtuous friends.

This is so much the case that while the upper middle-class peer integrates and athletes have a higher level of occupational aspiration than the middle-class isolates, the lower-class integrates and athletes do not have a higher level of aspiration than the lower-class isolates.[1]

We may say that for the lower middle-class parents who have upward mobile aspirations for their boy, the test of achievement is in the vague distant future. In childhood, the parents can only reward signs of virtue, of the capacity to delay gratification until status is achieved. The inculcation of cleanliness, obedience, thrift, industry, temperance, honesty, and similar virtues are the duty of the parent to insure his success. Not only are these virtues necessary for upward mobility; they are themselves expressions of middle-class respectability.

The upper middle-class boy, on the other hand, does not need to be so selective in his response to his environment. He will not move out of his class and neighborhood. He learns how to succeed, not through emotional and symbolic transmission of virtues from the parent, but by "doing" with peers, and in school. His immediate success in school, in athletics, in peer-group prestige is taken by his parents as indicating his "intelligence," his "leadership," his ability to get along with others, etc. He is called upon to prove abilities, not to perform acts symbolizing his possession of virtues.

---

[1]The lower-class 16-year-old isolates, however, include two groups, a high aspiration good boy group and a low aspiration rebellious with withdrawn group. The integrates tend to aspire to slightly higher statuses than their fathers and to be more "realistic" than the isolates.

The social "virtues" prized by our upper middle-class children seemed to be little more than the ability to achieve interpersonal status. Like the ability of "intelligence," so important in our upper middle-class group, these social abilities are measured by success. The content they do have seems to be not offending others by being hostile or "conceited," and "being a good sport." Leadership means in addition "willingness to take responsibility." However, responsibility often has the meaning given to it by Case 61:

> (Who has more responsibility, the senator or the judge?)
> The senator has. He has the responsibility of getting everybody to vote for him.

These concepts have no particular relation to the value of people. One is polite and gets along with them, but this does not imply that one needs to "respect" or care for them as individuals. The most the boys say is that they "like people" in general, implying that such liking has nothing to do with the individual liked.

As the lower middle-class child proceeds through high school, he may begin orienting to success rather than "symbolic" approval. Hence he may come to look more like the way the upper middle-class child has looked for a long time.

An upper middle-class child may learn the idea that all "virtue" is skill in achieving, which is competitive fun, at a very early age. We can illustrate this in a 10-year-old upper middle-class integrate, Case 16, whose concepts of why he wants to be a good parent and husband are expressed in the following definitions:

> Someone who makes his family proud:
> A good husband would make his family proud of him. If he's doing something like winning a prize, that would make his family proud of him.

<u>A good father:</u>

To make your kids like you and be proud of you and if you're a good father you'll have fun and they'll think you're a good father. You go out and play tennis with them and you'll be a good father and have fun doing that besides being a good father.

(Which is more important, being a good citizen or a good husband and family man?)

A good citizen because that helps to make a lot of friends and maybe like saving a baby. He might get credit for it. And if he rescued his own family he wouldn't get anything but maybe his wife would say thank you or something.

12. Class Differences in Respect for Parental Values

A similar "amoral" view of family relations is seen in Type 1 lower-class children, with few achievement concepts. However, as opposed to such lower-class children, the different persons in the upper middle-class world are oriented to each other sufficiently to make their approvals overlap. The typical 16-year-old upper middle-class integrates' response as to why a boy should make his family proud is that if you make your family proud, probably everyone else will be proud too. Usually in describing the "good son" or "family proud" the upper middle-class boys include peer interaction characteristics. Rather than orientation to personal approval, theirs is an orientation to "reputation." Peer group, school and home, each orient to the boy in terms of the others.

This consensus of role partners and the necessity of conformity for achievement makes an emphasis on internalized morality less necessary for the upper-middle class.

We have said that, for the upper middle-class child, the parents' approval and values tend not to be sacred but that they do count because they are integrated with the rest of the boy's world. They are not, however, the legitimately delegated role representatives of the moral order which they tend to be in the lower-middle class and among Type 2 and Type 3 children generally.

To express it in yet another form, the parents are not perceived as "identified with." The child's moral actions and values are not taken as either derived from his parents or as expressing his positive relationship or loyalty to his parents. The lower middle-class child tells us he wants to make his family proud, "to make them feel they've succeeded in bringing you up right." He wants to be like his father because his father has been good to him.

The upper middle-class child tends to see his parents from the "outside," objectively, in terms of their successfulness, and identify on that basis rather than in terms of his own ties to the parents. As a 13-year-old class president, Case 30, puts it:

(Why do you want to be like your father and mother?)
I've been around them so long I know pretty well what they are like. They seem to lead a pretty happy life that I look forward to.

The 10- and 13-year-old "other-directed" children quoted seem hardly ever to have gone through a stage of personal moral meanings defined by Type 2 and Type 3. One might guess that for these children, people or personal traits probably never represented goodness or right-ness in any symbolic sense.

However, our Type 4 seems to include boys who were once definable as Type 2 or Type 3. As children move into adolescence, it seems likely that the social structure is no longer seen in terms of personal morality, in terms of the intrinsic moral goodness or badness of actions and persons.

D. Type 5

1. Introduction—the Status of Type 5 as
a Developmental Type

The majority of our 16-year-olds seemed to use no general modes of moral thinking not present at age 13 or even age 10, whether or not such modes could be included in Type 4 or Type 5. The only general characteristics of the 16-year-olds seemed to be a tendency to be more conflected and unwilling to make decisions. We described this in the case of Type 4 as a sense of some formal social definition of the situation. In part, however, it seemed to be plain confusion and buck-passing, either by invoking what is usually done, leaving it up to the actor or looking for loopholes in the situation.[1] (There was also generally a more limited willingness to submit to parental authority, resting on no new modes of thinking, however.)

We "needed" to find a type with some ability to resolve such outer-directed confusion through an orientation to ideals and moral principles with a claim to rationality. We saw Type 4 as "rational" to a large extent but with a morality even more bound by current public opinion and law because of their rationality.

---

[1] In general, the negative comments of Havighurst and Taba, particularly about the absence of principle in the moral thinking and attitudes of a larger sample of mid-western 16-year-olds seem much more relevant to our materials than the sweetness and light of Gesell's comment about his 16-year-olds. Gesell evaluates his subjects primarily as growing but well-behaved children, in terms of the perspective of a benevolent parent, as the kind of data he collected on moral development makes clear. Havighurst and Taba view the children from the perspective of a high school teacher and find them wanting in a sense of direction and consistency in the school and community. Our perspective, in a sense, sets the 16-year-olds against the dilemmas and principles of Western moral thought in terms of which we might expect them to seem inadequate.

Such a type is perhaps less definable as a developmental stage than any of our others. It seems to be more a personality type, not simply rationalistic but autonomous, responsible and morally creative. As a general "stage," it perhaps exists more as a personal image admired by mature persons than a characteristic pattern of thought used by them.

A synthesis between the rationalistic tolerance of Type 4, the moral conviction of Type 3 and the aspiration to personal goodness of Type 2 should be a possibility for those boys who have reached stage 4. Type 5 is intended to represent such a synthesis of public norms and personal feelings, of what can reasonably be expected of others and what the self believes.

We see such a synthesis achieved and expressed in Type 5's guidance of moral judgment and responsibility by moral principles, by the judgment of one's "conscience," by public and objective modes of values, by a sense of the absolute value of the individual and of human life, by a sense of personal task and by a grounding of obligation on personal trust.

It was our claim in the first chapter that usage of the concept of morality in Western thought implied some of the attitudes and concepts which we attribute to Type 5.

A synthesis of conformity to public norms and of personal feelings has been termed autonomy by Piaget, Fromm, Riesman, Foote and Cottrell, and others. However, the concept of autonomy as a personality trait as developing and maintaining personal tastes, goals, and opinions in the face of pressures to conform is not adequate for the moral domain. We would hesitate to enter the realm of Kant's moral metaphysics which equates autonomy with universalistic morality or duty per se. However, we do view Type 5 as "morally autonomous" as well as moral.

2. Type 5 as an Embodiment of Baldwin's Theory as Opposed to Piaget's

In describing Type 5, we have tended to stress aspects relevant to Piaget's theory on the one hand and Baldwin's on the other. Both agree on a normal stage at around 6 in which morality focuses on respect for the parents. Both agree on the importance of reciprocity of self and other and of role-taking in the higher stages of morality.

For Piaget, moral obligation is always oriented to something outside the self. The process of development after the age of 6 is the increasing sense that what is respected and conformed to is another equal self with equal rights. Such an equalizing process occurs through the whittling of adults down to size, through increased concern about peer approval and peer solidarity, and through increased role-taking skill.

For Baldwin, respect for the adult is, by the age of six, already oriented to an "ideal self" or an ideal "other." The adult is respected only as he himself represents a vague mass of rules and values and obeys them. But the child may respect himself equally insofar as he represents or obeys the rules. At this early period, the child realizes that the adult has difficulty conforming just as he does; it is just the concept of such effortful conformity which is "being good." As he grows up, the child expects to embody the "ideal self" as adequately as do his parents. The process of development leads to an increasing differentiation of the "ideal self" from the actual expectations of the parents. But the sense of dependency on the ideal self remains as a sense of obedience or responsibility to one's own conscience. Such dependency is not simply a rigid imposition of one's own moral habits since conscience or the ideal self must be able to guide the conduct and judgment of both parties in the situation. For this reason the judgment of conscience remains both flexible and sensitive to the imagined legitimate judgments of the others. To put it more concretely, the conscientious person is concerned about the judgments of others, because he needs some agreement to feel he is right, even in disapproving of himself. Such agreement is necessary because of the nature of the moral right or the ideal self as applying to everyone in the situation.

The existence of the two types, together with several others, suggests that neither of these very abstract models of development should be treated as final.

3. The Standard—Moral Principle

We saw Type 4 as more clearly aware of a margin for individual choice within the structure of established rule. It is the existence of such a margin which requires filling in by "moral principles."

It is difficult to make any precise differentiation between a moral rule and a moral principle in everyday non-philosophical thinking, just as it was difficult to differentiate a moral rule from taboo attitudes toward "bad things." However, we can perhaps indicate a polar concept of "principle" from which persons are more or less distant. Essentially, a moral principle is a rule of choice and a principled choice is one which fulfills the criteria of regularity, universality and ideality (cf. Chap. I, Sec. A-4).

a) A moral principle is a rule or method of choosing between legitimate alternatives.—A rules says "Don't do that," or "Do that,"— it prescribes an action. A principle is some "rule" which tells us how to make a choice between two more or less legitimate or ruleful alternatives.

A rule tells us we must not steal and a rule tells us we must maintain the lives of others in our family, but there is no set rule which tells us which to prefer if we must choose one. A rule for such choice must prescribe a way of thinking or evaluating.

b) <u>Moral principles imply consistency in such choices.</u>—For most of our children the verbal basis for such choices could not be termed "moral principles" since they are not highly consistent from situation to situation. To use a complex example, four of our children tell us the fire warden should leave his post because "Your first duty is to your family." However, all four of them say a husband should not steal a drug to save his wife. Whatever the basis of the latter there is an inconsistency demonstrating that "one's first duty" is not really used as a principle.[1]

c) <u>Moral principles imply a universalistic basis for choice.</u>— Besides regularity or consistency in use of a reason for choice, a principle implies the universality and ideality of such a reason. The basis of choice is one which it would be desirable for all to use. "One's first duty is to one's family" is more generalized than "Keep out of trouble," it is more often an adequate basis for choice. However, in the case of leaving one's post in an emergency, primary responsibility for one's family obviously does not meet the requirement of being a desirable basis for everyone's choice.[2]

---

[1]There is empirical consistency in such choices though not principled consistency. If a sixth child were to tell us on question, "Your first duty is to your family," we would expect him to say the husband should not steal the drug in question III. Such predictability we might call "typological consistency" if there is some understandable basis for it.

[2]Consideration of the desirability of generalization with regard to overt actions, though not with regard to choice, enters by stage 3 at the latest. Type 3 says that certain actions should be forbidden in gen-

d) <u>Moral principles do not involve external coercion.</u>—Since one can never coerce others to think or decide in any given way, the generality of principles cannot be coercive. One cannot legislate or coerce others to choose the happiness of the many over the happiness of the few or to do unto others as they would be done by. Accordingly, a principle of choice must appeal to "reason," for its acceptability. It must seem to command assent intrinsically. By this is meant that it seems to follow from the nature of good and right in general, independently of the consequences of acting upon it or of the authority promulgating it. It must appeal for acceptance on the grounds that it is appropriate for "a reasonable being" to adhere to.

e) <u>Principle as a mode of valuing—the greatest good as a principle.</u>—Perhaps the two most popularly quoted principles in our culture are the Golden Rule and "The greatest good of the greatest number." Both principles are either quoted or used in some form of development at all our levels. Below Type 5, they are not actually used as principles, as consistent and general rules of choice.

We may take as a clear example of use of "the greater good" as a principle, the following response of case 65 to question IX about leaving one's post:

> I think definitely you should put the safety of the many over the safety of the few. No matter what he was, volunteer or what, even just a passer-by, I would think that if he was able to help more people than he could at home, he should stay on. Even though he'd be miserable the rest of his life, I still think you should put the safety of the many over the safety of the few.

---

eral because in general they are harmful. At this stage, the generality is limited to action only and it is restricted to avoidances and negative consequences. While from stage 2 on, there is a concern for the generality or sharedness of motives for action and choice; this concern is for what most people do want and choose, not what they ought to want.

First, such a statement impresses us becuase of its sense of categorical duty going beyond the outer rules. The boy uses the "many over
the few" as a principle of action, regardless of the actor's status. In
the situation the principle is used in many other situations by the boy,
in a consistent and thoughtful fashion (cf. Appendix A for his record).[1]
Second, he enunciated the "greater good" as an actual principle of choice.
The man is not wrong because "probably a lot of people would die," an
earlier response. He is wrong because he evaluated the situation wrongly,
because "He put the few over the many."

Thus the actor is evaluated in terms of intentions, not consequences. But the intention is of a different order than "loving your
wife" or the like. It is not simply a virtuous habitual disposition.
It is a "just" evaluation of a particular situation and of the probable
consequences. Thus the modality of "principle" transcends the conflict
between intentions and consequences present at previous levels, by evaluating choices, not habitual dispositions.

The disposition to choose in favor of the many may in itself be
a primitive disposition. We have presented question IX to a few 6- and 7-year
olds, and elicited some responses indicative of this. A 6-year-old told us
that fire warden should stay at his post, not only because he had been told
to (he equated the situation with air raid alerts at school), but because
he would save a lot of people, "whereas if the air-raid warden left he
would just save a few people like Mother and Aunt Joan." Such responses,
however, we would see as primarily indicating a "projective" and "syntelic"
equation of number or size and value, which usually leads children to want

---

[1] Thus, unlike the "family-firsters" in V who are against stealing,
he says that the husband should steal the drug on III, at least partly in
terms of life as the highest value.

to have and do the biggest and the most, which we discussed for the quantitative consequences orientation of Type O.

The normal processes of cognitive growth lead to the differentiation of both the egoistic value and the approval value of an action from the "public" projective and syntelic value of its object. Awareness of this differentiation leads our Type 1 children to see the public value of an object or person as a negligible factor.

In Type 2, there is no real conflict between public and private values. Public value is defined by the role-taking of individual members of a public. Accordingly, no one is expected to disapprove of a man putting his family before others, since such judgment is oriented to his natural shared motives. Type 2 may be oriented to doing the most good but this is essentially wanting to be good in all ways or to have all the approved virtues.

Types 3 and 4 are oriented to public rules but not fully to public values. That is, the prescribed ends of the individual in Type 3 and Type 4 are essentially legitimate private ends, but he must respect the rules and the rights of others in achieving them. The rules themselves are seen by Type 4 as essentially oriented to public welfare or values, but the moral individual is not.

4. Conflicting Role Expectations Resolved through
Expecting Each Moral Individual in the
Situation to Role-take the Others in
Terms of Public Value

Type 4, in seeing obligation as limited to institutionalized roles, leaves a wide area of legitimate conflict in role expectancies which the individual is not required to solve except by prudence.

For Type 5, on the other hand, all good people are expected to

be oriented to the right in the situation, that is to go through a process of more or less reasoned evaluation. As a result, legitimately conflicting expectations tend to be scarce, since an expectation which does
not involve consideration of the legitimate expectations of everyone else
involved in this situation is not itself legitimate.

Thus, Case 65 tells us in situation IX:

(What if the fire warden were just thinking about being a good
family man?)
I think he'd still go to his station because I think his wife
would respect him more for trying to save many people than saving
themselves. Just think how terrible he'd feel if he went home and
found his family was perfectly all right. And without him, maybe
10 people died in the burning building. He would feel worse and
his family would respect him less for it. People in these burning
buildings are somebody's loved ones too.

This boy defines a good family man in terms of the legitimate
situational expectations of the partner (as does Type 4) rather than in
terms of either stereotypical dispositions (you love your wife), or fixed
status requirements (your family comes first). However, these expectations are those of an ideal partner oriented to the same individual value
situation as the actor. The family is expected, not only to take his
role, but to adjust to the same objective value situation in which all
are involved. The actor's relation to his family is not irrelevant to
him as a person, he is oriented to their respect, but it is irrelevant
in the determination of public or objective value. His love for his
family does not make them more objectively valuable, "even though he would
be miserable for the rest of his life" since "people in the burning building are someone's loved ones too."

5. The Value of Life as Public and Principled

The value of life is objective for this boy in the sense described
by Baldwin and explicated in Chapter II, E-4. Although his sense of duty

is oriented to the individual value situation, rather than to rules, his sense of the values in the situation is based on his sense of duty, rather than on actual sympathy and utility. Before the "principled" stage, if the examiner increases the number of people who might die, or reduces the probability of the family dying in IX, he can usually get the child to say that the actor should not leave his post. This indicates that the decisions of such children are not based upon a principle of evaluation but on a vague sense of the badness of consequences. Projective value, sympathy, community opinion, utility, all combine to say that it is worse to be responsible for the death of ten than the death of two.

It is a principle of justice, however, that the lives of each should be treated as of equal value, regardless of sympathy, community opinion, utility, etc.[1]

Case 65 expresses the irrelevance of merit and utility to the right to life in response to question VI about whether to send a company troublemaker or a fatally sick man on a suicide mission:

> There's one question that you couldn't say. One man is going to die and I don't think you should send a man to meet his death even though he is a bad egg. Sure he's been a bad guy, but you shouldn't take advantage of a war situation like that and say, "O.K.—you go out there and get killed."

Although case 65 takes this non-utilitarian stand toward the choice, he thinks the captain should order someone else under the condition that his own presence is essential to the survival of the company.

---

[1]In its less developed manifestations, this sense of equality rests on assertions that everyone is in fact equally useful, equally worthy or equally valuable to society.

Such reliance on questionable matters of fact is a sign that the sense of equality or of rights has not fully reached the stage of principle. Whether in fact Negroes have higher or lower IQ's or delinquency rates than whites is completely irrelevant to the moral issues involved in failing to accord them equal rights.

A more common attitude to V and VI which is classed as Type 3 is that the captain should go himself, even though this may doom the whole company. This is usually joined with the invocation of utilitarian criteria if the choice must be made, e.g., the troublemaker should not be sent because he is more useful to the company or that it is better to lose one man than two.

Thus both Type 3 and Type 5 are oriented both to a rule (don't order a man to his death) and to considerations of utility (act so as to cause a lesser loss of life as opposed to a greater). For Type 3, however, there is a limited range of responsibility with regard to the death of others.. The captain would be responsible for the death of the man he directly ordered on the suicide mission. He is not responsible, however, if he makes a decision (going on the suicide mission himself) which leads to the death of the whole company.

This is analogous to Type 3's emphasis in question IX in sticking to an assigned and agreed upon task as opposed to Type 5's emphasis on responsibility for a decision causing the loss of lives of others, regardless of role.

In our view, the utilitarian standard may be either a just standard or an unjust standard. Thus it is just that one individual's life should be sacrificed for the many's, since it is just to treat all lives as of equal value. However, it is unjust to reduce the value of any individual's life to his value to the group. It is unjust to measure the value of the life of any other person, and it is the injustice of such measurement which leads us to say every individual's life should count as one.

Thus the dilemma in question V is, to us, not a dilemma as to whether one person should be compelled to go on a suicide mission to save the many.

The inapplicability of the utilitarian standard appears in regard to choosing a concrete individual whose life should be sacrificed. The difficulty of such a choice is that it implies a judgment of some individual's worthiness to live relative to others, a judgment which men should not make. It is in this sense that drawing lots does offer a solution to the dilemma of questions V and VI.

6. Respect for the Rights of Others versus Respect for Their Value or Dignity

The objection to ordering someone in V is not so much that it is a violation of his will, as that it implies a judgment as to his worthiness to live. Thus it implies a respect for the "absolute value of human life" going beyond the value assigned by the will of the possessor. From this point of view, there is, in a sense, something higher than "rights" in the moral realm. "Rights" are the highest concepts in the legal realm, but morality implies in addition some sense of duty beyond respect for the legitimate claims of others. We ought to respect other individuals beyond respecting their "rights" or not violating their wills.

The Type 4 orientation to questions V and VI is a contractually developed form of the Type 3 attitude. It clearly recognizes the utilitarian desirability of ordering someone, but sees such an ordering as deviating from a general rule not to violate the will of another. Thus even drawing lots does not resolve the issue, since, as Case 63 says: "If one person didn't want to draw, then I don't think he should be forced." Such an orientation in its reduction of respect for the life of the other to a negative formalistic respect for his will may sometimes be the

highest expression of the attitude "I am not my brother's keeper." This
is more obvious in the mercy-killing situation, where Type 4 may see the
value of the woman's life in terms of her will alone. The restriction of
value to will for Type 4 is apparent also in its definition of obligation
to society in terms of what the majority wants or thinks, rather than to
what the individual may think ideally is most valuable for society. Type
4 orients obligation completely to the actual will of equal others outside
the self. For this reason there can be no obligation for it higher than a
legal obligation. This is not the case for Type 5, which sees a higher
moral right, which tends to be identified with a vague "God's law" (Chap.
VI).

In the case of respect for life, Type 5, if he has a religious
background, tends to be oriented to some vague and unrationalized respect
for life related to life being in the hands of God as a higher power. The
response of Case 49 is an example:

God's got that only right because no doctor can go into a hospital and look over the list and say, "One of them is going to die in
nine months," and say, "Well, I guess I'll take her life."

(Why does God have that right?)
There are a lot of things about God we still don't know, we can't
explain.

7. The Sanction and Experience of Duty and the Deification of Conscience

From a Type 4 point of view, one might consider such a Type 5
orientation to higher ideal authorities and to absolutes as authoritarian
and mystical. However, Type 5's references to God certainly do not give
the impression of being references to an external rewarder and punisher
whose commands are to be obeyed. Type 5 may invoke God against utility
in situations where life is involved, but not in such matters as stealing

a drug. One does not feel the Type 5 absolute in God's commandment, "Thou shalt not kill," but rather that it is the value of the individual life itself.

References to God seem to be used to support certain basic inner feelings in the face of both external authority and logical reasoning. We see it as part of a general feature of Type 5 morality, the "deifying" of individual conscience.

An orientation to conscience implies more than a feeling that one's conscience would bother one if one broke a rule or taboo. Such an attitude, expressed by Type 2 and Type 3 children implies only that "conscience" is a punishing agent, not a rule-making and choosing agent. It does not even necessarily involve an experience of self-judgment as opposed to vague anxiety or depression about violation of a taboo. Such a "conscience," if strong, is something to be placated, not to be followed.

Though such experience is not adequately represented by the ego ideal, it does tend to focus on sacrifice in the name of freedom, love, and the ideal, rather than in the name of rules and authority.

The conflict between individual deified personal conscience and the "superego" or identification with fixed rules and authority has been given a classic portrayal by Hugo. He presents it in terms of the conflict in the mind of Javert, the police inspector, between the claims of a concept of justice which we would call Type 3 and the claims of "mercy."[1] (25, Jean Valjean, Bk. IV.)

The conflict occurs after Javert has released Valjean, the saintly escaped convict whom he had been trying to capture for many years:

---

[1]The resolution of the conflict indicates the relative discrepancies of psychology and of literature from life. Whereas our resolution would have been to give Javert a mixed score of 3 and 5, Hugo's resolution is to have Javert commit suicide.

He saw before him two roads, both equally straight; but he saw two; and that terrified him—him, who had never in his life known but one straight line.

. . . .

To owe life to a malefactor, to accept that debt and to pay it, to be, in spite of himself, on a level with a fugitive from justice and to pay him for one service with another service; to allow him to say: "Go away," and to say to him in turn: "Be free"; to sacrifice duty, that general obligation, to personal motives and to feel in these personal motives something general also, and, perhaps superior; to betray society in order to be true to his own conscience: that all these absurdities should be realized and that they should be accumulated upon himself, this it was by which he was prostrated.

One thing had astonished him, that Jean Valjean had spared him, and one thing had petrified him, that he, Javert, had spared Jean Valjean.

. . . .

There was in him a revelation of feeling entirely distinct from the declarations of the law, his only standard hitherto. To retain his old virtue, that no longer sufficed. An entire order of unexpected facts arose and subjugated him. An entire new world appeared to his soul; favor accepted and returned; devotion, compassion, indulgence, acts of violence committed by pity upon austerity, respect of persons, no more final condemnation, no more damnation, the possibility of a tear in the eye of the law, a mysterious justice, according to God, going counter to justice, according to men. He perceived in the darkness the fearful rising of an unknown moral sun; he was horrified and blinded by it. An owl compelled to an eagle's gaze.

. . . .

Javert's ideal was not to be humane, not to be great, not to be sublime, it was to be irreproachable. Now he had just failed. He asked himself: "This convict, this desperate man, whom I have pursued even to persecution, and who has had me beneath his feet and could have avenged himself, and who ought to have done so, as well for his revenge as for his country, in granting me life, in sparing me, what has he done? His duty? No, something more. And I, in sparing him in my turn, what have I done? My duty? No. Something more. There is, then, something more than duty.

. . . .

respectful, by instinct, toward the established church, he knew it only as an august fragment of the social whole; order was his dogma and was enough for him. . . . He had a superior, M. Gisquet; he had scarcely thought, until today, of that other superior, God. God, always interior to man, and unyielding. He, the true conscience, to the false; a prohibition to the spark to extinguish itself; an order to the ray to remember the sun; an injunction to the soul to recognize the real absolute when it is confronted with the fictitious absolute; humanity imperishable. . . .

In the passage, Hugo puts the law, society as order, punitive

justice and duty as obedience on one side and individual judgment, society as brotherhood, mercy, and obligation as inspired example on the other. Bergson develops these orientations as the two types of morality in a fascinating book (8).

In fact, it seems likely to us that a conscience-oriented Type 5 might waver between stern justice and mercy just as Type 4 may waver between legalism and more or less expedient utilitarianism, like the Eisenhower administration.

8. Conscience as Task

Thus there is a conception of stern and impersonal duty which is not necessarily authoritarian, a concept of duty as a life work, familiar to social scientists as "The Protestant Ethic." Again we may quote a literary example of this orientation and its origins, a perhaps autobiographical statement by Kierkegaard.[1]

> Let the casuists be absorbed in discovering the multifariousness of duties. The chief thing, the only saving thing, is that in relation to his own life a man is not his uncle but his father.
> . . . .
> When I was five years of age I was sent to school. . . . I made my appearance at school, was introduced to the teacher, and then was given as my lesson for the following day the first ten lines of Balle's "Lesson-Book," which I was to learn by heart. Every other impression was then obliterated from my soul, only my task stood out vividly before it. As a child I had a very good memory, so I had soon learned my lesson. My sister had heard me recite it several times and affirmed that I knew it. I went to bed, and before I fell asleep I catechized myself once more; I fell asleep with the firm purpose of reading the lesson over the following morning. I awoke at five o'clock, got dressed, got hold of my lesson book, and read it again. At this moment everything stands as vividly before my eyes as if it had occurred yesterday. To me it was as if heaven and earth might collapse if I did not learn my lesson, and on the other hand as if, even if heaven and earth were to collapse, this would not exempt me from doing what was assigned to me, from learn-

---

[1] The statement is put in the mouth of a representative of the "ethical stage" of development, a stage which is eventually transcended by the "religious stage," which again represents an orientation to divine mercy rather than "duty."

ing my lesson. . . .   I may smile at a little urchin of five years
who takes hold of a thing so passionately, and yet I assure you I
have no higher wish than that at every time of life I may take hold
of my work with the same energy, with the same ethical earnestness
as then. It is true that in later life one acquires a better con-
conception of what one's work is, but still the chief thing is the
energy. I owe it to my father's serious-mindedness that this event
made such an impression upon me, and if I owed him nothing else,
this would suffice to put me eternally in his debt.
. . . .
    I can say that in this respect my childhood has been fortunate
because it has enriched me with ethical impressions. Permit me to
dwell upon it a moment longer; it recalls to me my father, and that
is the most precious recollection I possess, and being by no means
a poor and unfruitful memory it gives me occasion to illustrate
once again my dictum that the total impression of duty is the principal thing and not by any means the multifariousness of duties.
If the latter is made prominent, the individual is reduced and
ruined. Now in this respect I was fortunate as a child, for I
never had many duties but generally only one, but that was a duty
in earnest. . . .   I knew it was my duty to go to school, to the
school where for good and all I had been sent. . . .
. . . .
    When I was sent to this school and the prescribed schoolbooks
had been bought, my father handed them to me with the words, "William, when the month is up you are the third in your class." I was
exempted from all parental twaddle. He never asked me about my
lessons, never heard me recite them, never looked at my exercise
book, never reminded me that now it was time to read, now time to
leave off, never came to the aid of the pupil's conscience, as one
sees often enough when nobleminded fathers chuck their children
under the chin and say, "You had better be doing your work." When
I wanted to go out he asked me first whether I had time. That I
was to decide for myself, not he, and his query never went into
details. That nevertheless he was deeply concerned about what I
was doing I am perfectly certain, but he never let me observe it,
in order that my soul might be matured by responsibility.

    Kierkegaard's account of the origins of "guilt" brings out a num-
ber of interesting features. Duty is for his hero a matter of complete
identification of the self with one thing, one task.

    Although the duty is imposed by the father, it is not an identi-
fication with the father as a person, it is an identification with a task.
Indeed he must take his father's place, in the sense that the father trusts
him to perform the task on his own. But this indicates that the task is
his, not his father's , and that the father is oriented to an already
existing image of him as good.

Again, the identification is not with a rule: A rule is not something which in itself can be identified with, as can a task. Like a rule, a task is impersonal. But a task is individual, it is delegated or it is chosen. It is up to the individual to fulfill it or to achieve it, which cannot be true of a rule unless it be an ideal rule.

A task morality may be stern to the self but it cannot be punitive or authoritative. Each person must have or find his own task, just as each person must have his own conscience and the task requires intelligent service. The basic rules or taboos can be more or less taken for granted by such a task morality, they are presupposed by it. Insofar as a rule becomes defining for such a morality it is perhaps that against lying and deception, a trying to get out of an accepted task, a trying to be something that one isn't. Such an orientation to "truth" is quite different from Type 4's orientation to "reality" or the "agreed upon." One thinks of the devotion of a Freud or Weber to his work and to the concept of truth, as an heroic expression of this morality.

It is clear how far such a conception of task is from the contractual—legalistic view of Type 4. For Type 4, a task is a fulfillment of a rule—defined role on the basis of contract. "Devotion" to a task is heteronomous submission of the self to others, e.g., "the boss." A task is not part of the personality, it is not to be identified with. Generalized goals for success and prestige constitute the personality together with specific "interests." Task roles are entered or left in terms of their contribution to such goals, and stability of identification is based on contractual agreement. Obviously the Type 5 orientation is more suited to a European semi—hereditary <u>haute</u> <u>bourgeoisie</u> with a sense of <u>noblesse</u> <u>oblige</u> engaged in cultural or commercial small enterprise while

Type 4 orientation is more suited to a perpetually upward mobile American middle-class working in large organizations.

9. A Case Example of Task-Morality

Let us compare Kierkegaard's caricature of a child's sense of duty with some aspects of our top-scoring 10-year-old, Case 18. His conception of higher principles is notable in that he invokes "God's law" in arguing with his father. Like "William," he is impressed with the importance of school. He put as a top role in what he wants to be like "someone who works hard to get ahead," saying:

> If you don't get ahead in life, you don't get nowhere, cause everywhere they want kids with good educations.

When asked why people want to be good fathers, he says:

> Life every year, you need more good-educationed kids and you can't get all your education in school. You get some from experience and your father has experience and he knows what's what.

The themes of his father as teaching from experience and his belief in his father's prestige as based on work, not authority, are continued in regard to "being the head of a large food company":

> All he does is give orders and stuff. He doesn't really do the work. A lot of money for sitting around talking.
>
> (Isn't that what your Dad does?)
> He has to show men, he doesn't just tell them. He does it for them and then they get the idea.

Thus identification takes place through example in work. Like some of the Type 2 children he sees achievement and doing good as fairly synonymous. However, he sees both achievement and social usefulness in terms of hard creative individual effort at a chosen task rather than in Type 2's terms of "getting a nice job."

> Pilot 1. You have to learn pretty lot to be a pilot but after you learn, there isn't very much to do. I'd like to have a job where I learn something every day.

Doctor. I want to take after my father and be an engineer. And
how can I be an engineer when I'm a doctor?

(What would you do if you had a lot of money?)
Oh give a lot to a cancer fund, because my best friend's father
died of that. Have a nice house and do a lot of things for other
people. Might even start an organization or a company, an orphan-
age or something like that.

This boy gives one the sense of having very strongly and posi-

tively identified with parental expectations on a moral level while al-

ready discounting the need for any actual status and approval-seeking or

conformity:[1]

(someone who makes his family proud 2)
You don't have to be any hot shot to make your family proud of
you. Just be a good boy and they aren't going to feel any different about you. If you do something to make your family proud, it's
nice, but it's not real important.

(someone who takes after father)
Well, it's nice but you really shouldn't take after somebody unless he's real good. You shouldn't have your own mind and your own
feelings, if you act exactly like your father; you just sort of get
the habit of following other people. They might be doing something
bad.

(But you want to be an engineer like him?)
Yeah, but not in the way he walks or something like that.

We can perhaps complement our discussion of Case 18 by present-

ing a daydream of Case 65 in which he is self-liquidating king. The re-

sponse is to "Who would you like to be if you could be anyone in the

world?"

If we could move everything back a couple of hundred years, I'd
like to be a king of a country of which the previous king had been
a wretched king and the people were in dire poverty. I would like
to take them out of that and build the country up, give everyone a
fair trial and introduce democracy.

---

[1]Many type 3 boys also tend to discount approval seeking re the
parents as "unimportant." However, they tend to have a rather ambivalent
sense of owing them something which must be paid back, not through being
good but in the way of giving them something they want, a sort of cash
exchange. They are aware of the dangers of unlimited conformity to
others, but the recommended solution is not to "follow my own advice" as
Case 18 says, but to follow the proper authority.

We may perhaps take this as a myth of the origin of this boy's strong and genuine type of conscience. Inheriting the strength and authority of the "previous king," the boy out-achieves the father not only by building the country up but by yielding up control over others in the name of individual rights. What is retained is the power over the self indicated in the voluntary yielding of these powers.

10. The Sense of Responsibility and the Sense of Task

Case 18 has a keen sense of what is important or for what he is responsible in the way of conformity. A genuine sense of responsibility implies a dual orientation both to the "rules" of task delegation and to the actual important consequences in the situation.

On Question IX, like many of the other 10-year-olds, he initially says that the fire warden should go to his family and quickly return to his post, a situational compromise representing an effort to do everything. However, when the interviewer tells him that "other people were supposed to look after his family," he says:

> In that case, he should stay at his post, because he can't help it if they get bombed. He can't help it if himself gets bombed. He should put himself in the place of the other people who his squad was supposed to take care of them. If he wastes time like that, other people might die because of his carelessness and his family was probably safe by the other squad.

This response, which would be classed Type 3, shows a deeper sense of duty than do most Type 3 answers. Thus in saying that "It doesn't matter if himself gets bombed," he seems to be saying that the orientation to the task is not a matter of unconcern about the family. Duty would be the same even if it involved his own death so he can't be blamed if it involves his family's. At the same time duty is not a matter to which personal feeling is irrelevant. This is implied in his putting himself in the

place of the people for whom he is responsible. It may possibly be implied by the notion that "other people might die and his family was safe"
if this implies a retrospective reaction in his own conscience such as
was mentioned by case 65.

11. Internalization of Parental Values by Type 5 Leads to a Concern for the Individual Situation

Both psychoanalytic and learning theories, as well as Piaget,
would lead us to expect that strong internalization of parental values
would lead to moral "rigidity." Internalization in such theories implies
some definite content or behavior disposition, e.g., "obedience" which is
very "fixed" or "strong." Such strength would lead us to expect an over-
generalization of such norms to "inappropriate" situations.

On the other hand, if some general attitude were internalized
rather than a specific taboo or habit, internalization would not be expected to lead to "rigidity." If what is internalized is a general set
"to do right" or "to do one's true duty," such a set would be a vague
orientation requiring filling in, in terms of the particular situation.
This is what is implied in the notion that one should always follow one's
conscience. Conscientious action implies that the motive to do right is
independent of reward and punishment and other such situational factors,
but that the action felt to be right is based on the individual's judgment
of the particular situation. Such a concept of conscientious action also
implies autonomy with regard to external expectations of parents and the
like. This concept is a looser one than that of a moral principle. A
principle implies some content of judgment which is consistent across situations but involves adaptation to each situation. A boy like Case 18 is
not yet really oriented to principles, yet he is oriented to flexible but

firm and autonomous conscientious action, and he can discriminate "true" duties from false ones.

12. Situational Role-taking as an Ejection of the Internalized Parent Rather Than as Sympathy and Sensitivity to Peer Approval

We have perhaps vaguely attributed this flexibility to a concept of conformity as "task." However, in addition, it appears likely that conscience is not as "internalized" as is sometimes believed. Case 18, like Case 65, is oriented to the expectations and judgments of others through situational role-taking. While situational role-taking is done by children from Level 1 onwards, such role-taking involved a projection of the natural self into the natural self of the other, the "you wouldn't like it either" or "you'd do it too." This role-taking becomes increasingly structured into a sense of rights at succeeding levels of development.

In the case of Type 5, role-taking seems to be based rather on a projection of conscience or the ideal self into others. The Type 5 boy seems to be concerned only with the reaction which someone oriented to the same general right would have toward the act.

We quoted earlier Case 65's interpretation of family expectancies in this way (Sec. D-3, this chapter).

Case 18 gives us a more graphic example of these interrelations. He is responding to pressure being put on him by the interviewer to change his mind about whether it is worse to cheat or steal on question VII:

(The law makes it worse to steal. They give a worse sentence.)
Well, the man who loaned the money was planning on getting the money back and if he didn't, he'd have to turn down some other people. And to himself he would probably think it was pretty bad, worse than stealing.

(The country could get along without loans better than with stealing—that's one reason the law might make it worse to steal.)

To the country it would be worse to rob a store but the <u>man in Joe's conscience,</u> your own conscience, you should go by it because you know when you lie to a man you feel bad and when you feel bad and you want to go back and tell the truth and otherwise you get sicker and sicker and you get so sick you go crazy.

(How do you know about that? Has you conscience ever bothered you like that?)
No, but I read in the paper a couple of times about life stories and they end up in the nuthouse because of their consciences. On that program "Medic" they were able to help this woman, but she was almost crazy before they helped her.

The unselfishly oriented judgment of the victim is equated with "the man in Joe's conscience."[1]

13. The Wish to be Respected as a Sanction

The preceding suggests the importance of one outer "sanction" to the moral judgment of a conscience-oriented person. This sanction is a legitimate judgment of a partner, usually called "having their respect."

"Respect" as opposed to "approval" implies an evaluation by another which is made by that other and cherished by the person respected independently of the relationship of the respecter and the respected. Our concern for approval is based on how much we prize him as a person, so that we cherish the approval of someone close to us more than someone distant and someone of higher status more than someone of lower status than ourselves. The more a given judgment of approval reflects the natural feeling of the other toward us, the more meaningful it tends to be.

---

[1] Sometimes this equation of the inner judge with an ideal outer in the role of the partner in the situation leads to some rather "quaint" thinking as in this response of Case 18:
(If it isn't all right to mercy kill a person, why should it be all right to mercy kill an animal, like a dog that's been run over?)
"The dog wouldn't know what's being done to it. That it isn't being helped by a doctor that is supposed to be helped by it."
The implication is that wrongness depends on a possible moral judgment by the partner, the dog, that the doctor is deviating from his role.

We saw in Type 4 a universalization of concern for approval along the lines of natural peer admiration of achievement and of reputation. As opposed to this gradual generalization of concern for external approval, we saw Type 5 as projecting its own best basis for self-judgment into others regardless of factual considerations of their reactions. This, of course, might be a primitive reaction, but its absence among our primitive types makes this seem unlikely. Such a projection is a mutual or reciprocal process of thought. One is oriented to the judgment of the other, but only insofar as one thinks the other's judgment is correct. In terms of seeking respect, the Type 5 boy seems to want to be what he respects, not just what is respected. Case 65 expressed this almost ostentatiously in his verbalizations of what he wants to be:

> I'd respect the judge more but I'd rather be the head of a company because I think they have more freedom and meet more people and you'd be running the business.

14. Obligation to Another in an Inegalitarian Relationship as Base on the Other's Respecting the Self

In fact, this concern for respect may go beyond the "mutuality" of maintaining the respect of those the self respects. It is perhaps apparent that in many relations it is less obligatory to maintain the respect of someone on whom the self depends than it is to maintain the respect of someone dependent on the self.

This is, perhaps, evident in the question: "Which is worse, a father breaking a promise to his son or a son breaking his promise to his father?" The Type 4 and Type 5 response is that it is worse for the father, since the son respects the father.

Piaget speaks of "mutual" respect or the respect between equals as the highest development of respect. Our discussion of mutual respect in

Type 4 suggested some limitations of it as a ground for a strong sense of responsibility and concern for others.

In Type 5, we might see the beginnings of a sense of obligation based on the awareness of the dependence of others on the self and a concern for maintaining the respect of these others.

Thus, Type 2 in a conflict between maintaining the approval of the father and that of the younger brother in Question II chose the father. A Type 5 concern for maintaining the respect and trust of the brother at the cost of parental disapproval is indicated in the response of Case 65, Appendix D to Question II. Relations of inegalitarian trust of dependence need not only be such as exist for the parent a unilateral concern for the welfare of the child in terms of identification by blood and convention. Rather, it may exist in a form in which the trust, dependency and respect of one person is a reciprocal stimulus to activate the duty of the other.

In this sense, a "mutual respect" orientation is not merely the seeking or maintaining of respect as a prized commodity. It is rather that being awarded respect is in itself a value which demands that it be lived up to in return. This is expressed in Case 65's response to Question II, in the conflict between seeking the respect of the father and living up to that of the brother.

15. The Value of Trust

As Case 65's response to Question II indicates, the concepts of respect and trust tend to be related. We saw Type 4 as limiting duty to contractually agreed upon responsibility beyond the letter of some agreement. Accordingly, we would expect Type 5 to see the act of delegation in terms of a rather personalized act of trust rather than a verbal agreement.

"Trust" like "respect" is a loose word and from Stage 1 on, children talk about the advantages of acting so that people will trust them. However, up until Stage 4, this is expressed merely as a desire to maintain the trust of others whose love or good will is important to the self. In Type 4, trust takes on some importance, but on a contractual basis. It represents maintenance of a specific overt agreement, which is important regardless of the status of the person having confidence in the self. A Type 5 concept of trust implies in addition an orientation to a more diffuse attitude. Here trust implies "act of faith" in the trusted persons. Such faith means an attitude that the trusted person is worthwhile so that guaranties of performance are dispensed with.

The response, classified as Type 5, to Question VII as expressed by Case 49, is:

> The one did worse who borrowed the money with no intention of paying it back. He took advantage of a person's trust. The man put his faith in him but the storekeeper just left his money there, he had no faith in the boy.

Such a response, of course, may reflect only a knowledge of cliches, but such cliches tend to be carried too far or not far enough if they are not really meaningful.[1]

A concern about violating a trust may also imply nothing more "ideal" than a sense of "fair play," of a taking advantage of another person, of a deviation from equality. However, it may also express a high evaluation of

---

[1] An example, rated Type 3 with Type 1 undertones, is the following: "Both of them boil down to the same fact. But the one who gained the confidence of the man committed the worse part. People in town trusted him and he in turn trusted them. This would probably destroy that trust and some couldn't get help they would need."

(Who would feel worse, the storeowner or the lender?)

"I imagine they would both have about the same feeling toward the other person. It would be up to the individual to be able to tell which would be madder."

conscience, of a "being good" for its own sake. Thus it symbolizes "the open society," a world without locks and policemen.

The Christian conception of mercy in its many manifestations can be seen as an expression of trust by someone in a quasi-parental role. It is not due to utility or pity alone that mercy is felt to be more important than rules and impartial justice. It is because to make men good, we believe we must first show that we feel they are capable of good.

The passage from Kierkegaard expressed the feeling of the necessity of parental trust for the development of conscience. This is true not only in the sense that the parent must trust the child to conform out of his sight. More deeply it is true in the sense that the parent, oriented to conscience, can only stimulate a generalized sense of vocation and responsibility and leave it to the maturing judgment of the child, to fill this in for himself.

On the side of the child, it may be that the parent's trust constitutes the strongest bond of obligation to maintain the parent's respect. While trust implies a mutual or reciprocal relation, it also implies an exposure, a dependence of the trustee on the trusted. So parental trust in a sense reverses the direction of dependency in the parental relations.[1]

---

[1]This does not mean that we have evidence that the parents of the boys who are high in Type 5 thinking are "trusting." Rather, two of these boys express the rare reaction that their fathers ought to be more trusting.

CHAPTER VIII

THE DEVELOPMENT OF CONCEPTS OF JUSTICE IN OUR TYPES

A. Introduction—the Area of Justice

In the present chapter we shall describe and interpret our types
in terms of some of their concepts and attitudes relevant to justice. By
focussing on each type's handling of a few concepts, we may get a clearer
picture of how each type differs from the other when confronted with the
same concepts or content.

To some extent, the concepts employed are the same as those used
in the previous chapters, since justice cannot be sharply seprated from
morality in general. Thus, we have already treated the child's orientation to punishment as a sanction for his own behavior; here we shall treat
his ideas as to how punishment ought to be administered.

The switch of emphasis is suggested by the popular attribution of
a "sense of justice" to persons as a complement to their "conscience."
Conscience guides and evaluates and motivates the actor's own conformity,
the "sense of justice" guides and motivates his desires to have others
conform.

We shall not consider the degree to which there is a unitary concept of justice for the child such as that outlined in Chapter I, Sec. A-5.
For purposes of comparison of the various developmental levels we may treat
as the field of justice, questions as to the fittingness of the hurtful or
helpful actions (or expectations) of one person to those of another.

312

Such fittingness involves some norms concerning the exchange of values between persons, whether these values are rewards and punishments or whether they are services. Exchange implies some sort of equalizing of the two or more values involved, though whether equality is itself a central concept in justice, we shall leave open. In any case, strict inequality of exchange, such as returning good for evil, is not a matter of justice, however moral it may be.

Thus, we have focussed on two chief areas of justice: the exchange of services and contract (reciprocity) on the one hand, and the administration of punishment on the other.

In the case of punishment orientations, our coding sheet for punishment in Appendix C offers a readily available summary of actual statements about punishment. A summary of the orientations of the types to reciprocity is provided by Table 17.

B. Exchange and Punishment at Level I

1. Type 0

Exchange and contract.—Concepts of exchange tend to be little used in this type. However, we have classified as type 0, a concept of exchange as necessary in a quasi-physical way and as based on sameness of the acts exchanged rather than on an equality of value. The necessity of exchange seems to be a special case of what Baldwin calls "objective necessity," it is simply an expression of fixity in the world, a restoration of order. One act must be paid back or undone by another. Such paying back is not based on the need of an individual to be grateful or vengeful, nor on mutual regard. It is not what one individual demands of another; it is not what the self demands of the world, it is what the world demands of the self (Obs. 1).[1]

The lack of role-taking or the projective value basis of this concept of exchange is shown also in the notion of payment in kind. The same thing must be returned, rather than something of equal value. Both in punitive and non-punitive exchange, there is a mechanistic equation, "an eye for an eye and a tooth for a tooth" (Obs. 1, 2, 3, 4). Exchange has a primarily negative character. Where it is used by Type 0 in our stories, it is used to justify deviance from rules and authority, not conformity. Obligations to work and to parents are not put in terms of repayment.

Exchange is not subsumed under a concept of contract, e.g., of agreement and the maintenance of expectations. Whether an individual expected to be paid back is ignored (Obs. 1).

Punishment.—Our remarks here are largely a repetition of what was stated under "exchange."

At this stage, punishment is a more or less unquestioned fact. Some definite act of punishment follows on some definite deviant act, without much concern for who does the labelling or the punishing. Punishment does not follow from a judgment by an individual or group that the specific act is wrong. Accordingly, when questioned about performing an act, the child may say it should be performed but when he is questioned about punishing, the considerations in the actor's perspective are ignored and the child will say he should be punished (Obs. 6).

In general, it may be said that there is very little relating of the punishment to any sentiment about the wrongness of the act. This is expressed in the quantitative aspects of punishment. There is no perceptible

[1]Observations are at the end of the chapter.

adjustment of the severity of the punishment to the badness of the crime. Quantitative standards tend to be in terms of the more severe, the more effectual (Obs. 9) or in terms of talion—the same for the same (Obs. 4). But basically or usually the badness of the crime is simply a reflection of the badness of the anticipated punishment.

Thus it is clear that the severity of punishment often advocated by the type has nothing to do with indignation. Were these boys to grow up unchanged we might expect them to be arbitrarily severe with regard to anyone under their discipline, e.g., their children, rather than to be indignant at unpunished crimes.

However, we might not even expect many of these boys to be severe, they simply may expect it in others. These boys anticipate severe and invariant punishment, they think it is inevitable rather than saying it should be.

The impersonality of punishment expectations may, indeed, be extreme for Type 0. We may cite 10 of 12 first-graders interviewed. They said that the wife or children of a man escaped from prison should report him to the police, even though he had done various noble deeds and had just saved their lives in a fire. Their responses seemed fairly equivalent to those of our Typ 0 10-year-olds to Question V. The basic idea was simply that punishment was immutable and had superior force behind it, not that the convict had done something for which he should be punished.

Such an orientation is not incompatible with ideas that the purpose of punishment is to prevent classes of bad acts, but such a purpose is not defined in terms of the character or welfare of the individuals involved.

Property-oriented children, who are "mixtures" or Type 0 and 1, tend to see punishment vaguely in terms of vengeance by the victim. There is a primitive standard of equality between crime and punishment, and there is a possibility of warding off legal punishment by restoring stolen goods, etc. But the "measurement" of the severity of the crime is based on the physical or economic "objective" value of the damaging consequences of the crime rather than being based on role-taking of the victim's suffering or of the actor's intentions.

3. Type 1

Exchange and contract.—We have classified as Type 1, purely prudential concepts of exchange. In Type 1 responses, there is no sense of actual obligation by the self or actor to repay favors or injuries. However, others are expected to make such repayment on the basis of natural emotions, so it is prudent for the self to build a positive balance and avoid vengeance by others (Obs. 10, 13). Thus, exchange is oriented to the self's future welfare and may involve an element of bargaining and threat.

Exchange is used in a more general sense to create motives and personal relationships where none are explicitly defined in our stories. "Duty" to parents and authority may be put on the basis of the expectation of exchange, without any sense of indebtedness (Obs. 11). The equivalence of exchanged values is indefinite, i.e., favor for favor, but not simply in terms of good will (Obs. 10a).

Punishment.—In this type, punishment has lost its necessity or inevitability and is seen as a function of the habits of judges or the whim of the individual judge. If a personal or normative judgment is made, it tends to be lenient if the boy has any sympathy with the actor. Where the high status of the actor and the non-impulsive character of the act prevents such sympathy, a punitive, perhaps Type 0, attitude is shown as was mentioned in Chapter VI, Sec. F-2 (Obs. 18 and 19).

In spite of this influence of sympathy, punishment is not seen as symbolizing disapproval of the intentions or character of the actor. Rather reasoning about punishment implies that punishment has a purely instrumental or functional value, rather than a symbolic value. Punishment should be given so the actor won't do it again or it shouldn't because he might not do it again (Obs. 16, 18). Such predictions are not based on a judgment of motive or moral worth, however. Additional reasons for leniency are the family or social need for the services of the culprit (Obs. 15).

Restoration of property is an additional alternative to punishment. Punishment may be seen as to be decided by the owner of the property involved.

Type 1 tends to see a judge as not being socially respected because of the anger of the persons he sentences, and to not wish to be a judge for fear of vengeance.

C. Exchange and Punishment at Level II

1. Type 2

Exchange.—Exchange is interpreted in terms of general attitudes of role-conformity and a positive orientation to the role partner (Obs. 20). It is accepted as a natural motive that people like and help those who like and help them (Obs. 21, 22). Thus, exchange or reciprocity is seen as the positive core of a relationship rather than in terms of definite individual "ideals" or egoistic exchanges. This element is stressed more toward parents than to peers. This type is the first to show a concept of "gratitude" (Obs. 21, 23).

In terms of the general set of this type toward positive conformity, it is positive reciprocity which is stressed and vengeance may be disavowed (Obs. 20, 22). In general, then, it is the goodness of performing a service and of relations in which services are performed which is important rather than a concept of equal exchange. Put slightly differently, the fact that alter performs a service for ego shows that ego is good and good people should have services done for them.

Punishment.—At this stage, punishment is seen as based on or symbolizing a judgment of disapproval of the individual act as of the self of the culprit, expressed by the act. This implies a judgment by intentions (cf. Chap. II, Sec. D-4). It also implies a consistency between judging an act right from the actor's perspective and judging it as not to be punished. There may be "inconsistency" only in the sense of not punishing an actor said to be wrong in the first place.

In stage 0, punishment did not involve a definite evaluation by a judge, it was automatic. In stage 1, it was at the discretion of the judge or victim, but was more or less determined by the interests of the persons involved rather than by a judgment of the badness of the act itself.

In stage 2, punishment may be determined by the judge's role-taking the culprit (Obs. 26). In older Type 2 children, it may involve a vague role-taking of the evaluations of everyone concerned (Obs. 24). In any case it involves a judgment of the actor as a bad self.

Type 2 tends to be the first to relate quantitatively severity of the punishment to severity of the individual crime (Obs. 26). The typical response to uncertainty as to whether or not to punish is to give a short sentence, rather than to make a clear decision of "guilty" or "innocent." There tends to be an awareness of the reform function of punishment, i.e., its function as leading to a general disposition to conform, not merely to repress the act committed (Obs. 35).

2. Type 3

Exchange.—Exchange is seen within a fixed social order centering around work and payment. The central idea is of a dysphoric or at least effortful performance of a required task which earns a reward. The exchange relations are obligatory. The fact of task performance obligates the authority or moral order to pay the actor, while the fact of payment obligates the actor to work. These relations are past oriented, not future oriented like Type 1's prudential approach to payment. An actor must perform the task because others expect to pay him, not because he may not get paid in the future if he doesn't perform.

As with Type 2, exchange is used to justify conformity to authority and the social order in general, not to justify deviations from it as in Type 0 and 1. Even more than in Type 2, contract and exchange are likely to be overridden if they involve deviance with regard to authority. This tends to take the familiar form of "two wrongs don't make a right."

There is a general tendency in Type 3 to equate all duty with payment relations, which we discussed in Chapter VII, Sec. C-3 (cf. Obs. 29). With many of the children of this type, such relations are not seen in terms of contract as such, though they do involve mutual expectations. Thus the services of others may be obligating independent of agreement, e.g., the services of parents (cf. Obs. 27). Such an attitude as that of Case 54 involves taking the role of the father or authority as someone who, in performing his role duties, has a legitimate expectation of getting something in return. Expectation of return may not only ignore agreement, but the good in the situation. Both Observation 27 and Observation 28 involve the acceptance of such claims even when they are outrageous in terms of their ignoral of the situation. However, such payment claims come closer to justice than simple ownership claims.

In Type 3, obligations to exchange may not only exist without contract, but may ignore purely contractual obligations. By this we mean that the focus is on the exchange of actual goods or rewards for services rendered rather than on the maintenance of an agreement or commitment lying behind such exchange (Obs. 29). Case 54 and others, in stressing the father's right to a return in Question I, neglect or subordinate the contractual element of the father's breaking of a promise. We have already quoted in Chapter VII the response that a doctor should mercy-kill on request "because the patient is paying him for his services."

Punishment.—We see as characteristic of this stage, the orientation usually thought of as that of "punitive morality," though the actual strength of tendency to demand punishment may vary, as was mentioned in Chapter VII, Sec. B-2. For our purposes, more important than willingness to punish are the concepts underlying it. We have classed as Type 3, concepts of punishment as a required payment in suffering make up for an act of wrong-doing, the concept of expiation.

In spite of Piaget's use of the term, expiation for Type 0 concepts of punishment, neither his observations nor ours seem to really warrant such usage of the concept. We say this because there is no evidence that stage 0 children have any sense that suffering undoes a crime. There is indeed a sense that bad act will and perhaps should lead to bad events or unhappiness, e.g., punishment. But such punishment is not payment of a debt, a making up for the crime, a restoration.

Type 3, on the other hand, tends to see both "retributive" and "restorative" justice as alternate forms of restoration (Obs. 31). As

Piaget himself indicates, Type 0 children tend to think the severer the punishment the better, or else to expect simple talion. Type 3 feels a definite immutable balance or equality is required, e.g., someone has "suffered enough" for a given crime (Obs. 31).

In addition, the concept of expiation involves some notion of repentance and remorse. Repentance requires not only physical pain but some re-evaluation of past action. Thus, it may be that punishment is only effective for good boys who take the role of the authority (Obs. 34).

The concept of expiatory punishment involves to some extent a denial of punishment simply as talion and vengeance. In connection with exchange, we already saw a tendency to deny that "two wrongs make a right." We have mentioned the restorative aspect of punishment. Thus, in Type 0 and 1, a culprit has merely "laid himself open" for punishment, in Type 3 he has an active obligation to be punished, to make up for his crime. Thus expiatory punishment may be seen as "for his own good," not for the good of the victim or the authority (Obs. 32). However, there is not a general denial of retaliation such as Type 2 might espouse, rather a restriction of it in terms of the legitimate moral and social order.

The boys who present the concept of expiation as repentance clearly are those with most clearly appreciable Type 2 attitudes in addition to Type 3 ones.

A more "pure" Type 3 rests retributive payment more on identification with the victim and with others who deprive themselves by conforming, as Nietzsche suggested (Chap. I, p. 6, and Chap. VI, pp. 217 f.). Some of these children actually rest punishment on the legitimate demand of the victim for punishment felt as shared and earned (Obs. 32).

For them, this concept of punishment tends to focus on consequences,

on some harm actually being done. This is not a matter of "projective badness" as in Type 0, but of the fact that if no harm is done, no harm should
be returned. Good intentions or the naturalness of the act do not count for
much if something "wrong" was done. However, the attitude is not legalistic,
e.g., if something was the "best thing that could happen in the situation,"
doing it should not be punished even if illegal.

There is a concern for regularity, for making no exceptions which
we described in Chapter VI. The exceptions are defined with regard to actual wrong done, not by classification in terms of rule. The concern for
regularity is justified by the possibility that the making of exceptions
might become generalized. With this goes the culprit's generalization that
"he can always get away with it" and the example to others that they can get
away with it too.

On the side of the judge's role, Type 3 sees the judge as oriented
to maintaining order and sees giving punishment as his duty, so that hostile
feelings are not legitimate toward him.

D. Exchange and Punishment at Level III

1. Type 4

Exchange and contract orientations.—We saw Type 3 as basing duty
on legitimate expectations of return, but said the Type 3 orientation tended
to be "pre-contractual." In Type 4, such duties, dependent on agreement or
"giving your word," are independent of actual payment relations. Such independence aids in generalizing of contractual relations to equals as well as
to authorities (Obs. 37), and to strangers as well as to kin and friends.
If offers a generalized basis for performing roles according to defined
rules independent of attitude to partners, stressed in Chapter VI. While

contractualization of exchange may add to the number of obligating relations, it may also eliminate the obligation to repay services which were
not asked for or agreed to (Obs. 38). In general, Type 4 ignores the
general functions of the other in defining duty in order to focus on specific situational agreements. Thus liberty or freedom of decision and
foreknowledge of what one was agreeing to become prerequisite to obligation. In its lowest form this may be merely "If you didn't want to do it,
you shouldn't have said it in the first place." In a more generalized form,
it may base obligation to country on the voluntary decision to stay within
its bounds and accept its benefits (Obs. 39).

Type 3 tended to base rights and duty on legitimate demands for
"payment." A prime duty is to pay for what you do or get. A prime duty
for Type 4 is to "keep your word," to fulfill legitimate demands that one
be reliable. Of course, as our discussion in Chapter VI made clear, there
may be a wide range of actual concern for "duty," and there is a tendency
to see one's primary duty as to the self's own welfare.

In any case, a contractual orientation tends to integrate the concept of truthfulness into a generalized relational basis.

Punishment orientation.—Considering first the exchange or payment
element of punishment, we may say that this too acquires a contractual basis
in Type 4. While in Type 3, the need for regular punishment was identified
with a morally demanded payment, it is accepted by Type 4 as resting on a
somewhat arbitrary basis required for agreement and maintenance of legal
functioning.

On the side of the judge, Type 4 tends to see him as contractually
obligated to carry out the law with regard to the situation. Whether he
can make an exception is a question of procedural rules, not of the boys

own insistence on regularity (Obs. 40). Here again we see the operation of fixed rule and contract in defining role obligation.

On the side of the culprit, he too must accept punishment on a quasi-contractual basis, since he freely chose to perform the act knowing the legal consequences (Obs. 42).

Related to the sense of culpability as based on free choice, and "knowing what you're doing" is an understanding of why the premeditated crim is worse than the crime of passion (Obs. 41). Perhaps also associated with the notion of rational culpability is the idea that serious criminals may be a class for whom punishment is not effectual in the sense it is for "normal" people in normal life (Obs. 44). A "disease" orientation is also associated with the respect for the "expert" of Type 4, as well as with a concern for impersonal or scientific rationality. In any case, setting the criminal up as abnormal clearly may serve a function of eliminating the Type 3 envy and indignation elements in punishment.

In general, this type—rather cold-bloodedly legalistic toward an individual culprit—is oriented to a non-punitive utilitarian view of punishment. Type 4's response to the return of the benevolent escaped convict is based on the social utility of his achievements as well as on anticipated community opinion in favor of his release. Case 63's economic orientation is perhaps an extreme of this type of "rationability" (Obs. 41).

2. Type 5

Exchange and contract orientations.—We have characterized and illustrated the more diffuse and personalized attitudes of Type 5 toward contract and exchange in terms of reciprocity, of trust, and of respect in Chapter VI. On a more conceptual level, Type 5 has little to add to Type 4 ideas about contract.

Punishment orientations.—We were not able to find any general
conceptions of punishment defining Type 5 as different from Type 4. However, the set of Type 5 was toward what kind of a decision a good judge
would make in the situation, and we rated as Type 5, various indicators
of concern for individual justice within a framework of law.

Particularly, we were concerned about sensitivity to unjust punishment under certain conditions. A Type 5 response to Question V was one
which expressed a definite sentiment of the injustice of punishing the
philanthropic ex-convict (cf. Code Sheet, Appendix B). This was differentiated from a Type 2 response advocating leniency in terms of the general
goodness and usefulness of the ex-convict. While the latter implied a
sentiment that good people shouldn't be punished, the former in addition
saw the ex-convict as definitely making up for any crime by positive service.

Thus, the Type 5 response would involve a concept of positive expiation, of positive service to society as compensating for guilt. It also
indicates a sense of the injustice of returning punishment or evil for the
doing of good. This may perhaps be interpreted as a violation of the convict's trust in society implied in his performance of philanthropic acts.
In any case it seems to reflect a concern for the conditions under which
acts of punishment and reward may be those of a good person.

E. Examples of Orientation to Exchange and to Administrating Punishment

1. Type 0—Exchange Orientations

Case 0—10 LL 90 Is
Obs. 1: Objective necessity of exchanging similar acts.
    (Question III—Why is it all right to steal if your wife is dying?)
    If you were dying, and she broke into that store and she got that
drug and you almost died and she came just in time and you drink the

326

TABLE 17

CONCEPTIONS OF EXCHANGE AND RECIPROCITY
HELD BY OUR TYPES

Type 0 a) <u>Use and limits</u>. Little use.

b) <u>Expectation reference</u>. Impersonal necessity of exchange, regardless of desirability to self or other and independent of antecedent expectations.

c) <u>Equivalencies</u>. Emphasis on sameness of acts rather than equality of subjective value.

Type 1 a) <u>Use and limits</u>. Used much. Used to define unusual or indefinite "obligations" of a role as son, friend, etc. Used where more permanent emotional and ethical orientations to partners might be expected.

b) <u>Expectation reference</u>. Exchange is described in prudential future terms, in terms of the hope or fear of repayment by the partner.

c) <u>Equivalencies</u>. Equivalence is in terms of indefinite subjective values of favor for favor.

Type 2 a) <u>Use and limits</u>. Exchange used to rationalize conventional role obligations and is limited by them, i.e., it must be seen within a context of "doing good." Tendency to disavow vengeance.

b) <u>Expectation reference</u>. Exchange is seen as part of the self's natural positive attitude toward partner. Exchange is seen as expressing gratitude for past help and liking.

c) <u>Equivalencies</u>. Intentions oriented. The expression of gratitude, positive attitudes more important than any equivalency of acts. Indefinite delay and future fantasies of return to parents, etc.

Type 3 a) <u>Use and limits</u>. Much usage of exchange to justify conformity to rule and obligation to authority. Used to identify with authority and victim. Exchange by deviating from rule or the social order is ruled out, e.g., "Two wrongs don't make a right." No general denial of retaliation, however. A claim to payment within the rules holds regardless of goodness elements of the situation.

b) <u>Expectation reference</u>. Basic concept of exchange is in terms of legitimate expectation of payment for work and for deprivation. Both the obligation of the self to work and the obligation of the authority or social order to pay are seen as strict reciprocal obligations, and are fixed and past or "debt" oriented. While mutual expectations are involved, exchange is not contingent on contractual agreement, and exchange is limited to the sphere of actual payment for services.

c) <u>Equivalencies</u>. Fairly strict demand that a given bit of toil or

TABLE 17—Continued

service be repaid. Equality of exchanged values is less important than maintenance of a given expectation, claim or right of
the "creditor." However, it may take priority over actual contractual arrangement.

Type 4 a) Use and limits. Usage of contractual maintenance to justify conformity to the expectations of any individual, in the form of
being a reliable person, being truthful, and keeping your word.
A contractual obligation may have validity even if it involves
some violation of the social order. However, valid contracts on
the whole imply being set up within a legalistic framework.

b) Expectation reference. Basic concept of exchange is contractual,
i.e., the fulfillment of an agreement or of an expectation at
which the partner could legitimately arrive. Stress on the freedom of the self in entering into the agreement, and on foreknowledge. .Actual exchange of goods and services need not be involved
in creating obligation.

c) Equivalencies. Definition by contract rather than the vaguer
necessities of paying "debts" or equalizing effort and reward.
An acceptance of the arbitrary element in the equivalencies of
an exchange.

Type 5 a) Use and limits. Uses concepts of reciprocity and contract with
regard to anyone, including inferiors who are not themselves
strictly able to make contracts. Accepts more diffuse and implicit "contracts."

b) Expectation reference. Orientation to maintaining the respect
and trust of the partner re the partner's expectations. These
expectations are general, e.g., that the self is good and that
the self is generally oriented to the personal rightful expectations of the partner. Partner's expectations and trust may be
with regard to matters unrelated to partners' actual egoistic
interests.

c) Equivalencies. Exchange is subordinated to mutuality on a symbolic attitudinal level.

drug. That's the same way you have to repay your wife.

Case 19—10 UM 103 Is.
Obs. 2: Reciprocity as talion.
      (Would "Do unto others as you would like them to do to you" be a
good rule?)
      Yes. If somebody shot you, you could shoot them back. And if
someone punches you, you could punch him back. And if a cop called
you over, you could call him over. If a teacher slapped a kid, the
kid goes to the teacher and "pow!"

Case 57—17 UL Is.
Obs. 3: Impersonal necessity of talion.
    It's a crazy thing, but I know if I take someone's life I expect someone to come after mine so that's how matters stand.

2. Type C—Punishment Orientations

Case 22—10 UL 105 Is.
Obs. A: Punishment as talion, i.e., the fit punishment is determined by doing the same thing back. Inconsistency between judgment of "wrongness" of act and decision to punish.

    (Which is worse, killing or robbing?)
    Robbing, killing you just have one less person in the world.
    (Which is really worse?)
    Killing. You'd be wanted for murder.
    (Would it be right to send someone to the electric chair for robbing?)
    It wouldn't be right unless he killed somebody. If the thing he stole isn't alive it couldn't be sent to the electric chair because it couldn't be killed, it would still be there. But a man gets killed.

Obs. 5: Punishment as determined by ownership.

    (Should he be punished for stealing the drug for his wife?)
    Send him to jail for about ten years.
    ("If the druggist asks the judge to let Heintz go, should the judge?)
    I think so because the druggist has a right because it's his own drug.

Case 12—10-1/2 UL 97 Is. (Mixed Type C and 1—cf. Obs. 66, Chap. VI.)
Obs. 6: Inconsistency of punishment judgment with previous judgment of act. Ignoral of intentions. Talion.

    (Responding to Question IV in which he previously said the doctor should mercy-kill. "What punishment should the doctor be given?")
    Well isn't that a law in the law books that for murder you get so many years? Oh you mean if I was the judge? Well if I didn't know all this, that she wanted him to, for losing somebody else's life he should lose his own life.

Obs. 7: Punishment is itself an aggressive act which may itself be punished or justify further talion. "Objective responsibility."

    (Question IV—Statement made after saying would condemn doctor to death in Obs. 6.)
    If I (as the judge) didn't know all this (that the woman wanted it) and then if I did and found out it was like that, I should be put in jail. It was my fault that he died by the electric chair.

Case 9—11 UL 125 Is.
Obs. 6: Punishment based on objective responsibility and projective value of consequences. Necessity of punishment given that damage has been done (See Appendix D, Question III for Observation).

Obs. 9 (Mixed 0 and 1): Punishment as preventive but amount determined by
the severer, the more effective. Ignoral of culprit's judgment of
his own act.

(Question I—Would the father's punishing the son for lying do any
good when his father broke his promise in the first place?)
Well, it might if he was strict. But if he just said "You have to
stay in bed an hour," he might do it again.

3. Type 1—Exchange Orientation

Case 10—LL 97 Is.
Obs. 10: Performance based on anticipating a future favor in exchange.

(Question I—What gives his father the right to tell Joe to give
him the money he had saved for camp?)
Would it be that sometime in Joe's life, he might need that much
money to go some place and he'd have to maybe come to his father for it?

Obs. 10a: Anticipation of return. Uses exchange to reach a "bargain." Role-
takes natural wish of other. (Is the Golden Rule a good rule?)

Yeah. Well if I wanted you to play baseball with me, would you
play? Well then, if you asked me to do something with you, then I'd pay
you back by doing it with you.

(Would it tell you not to steal?)
Well, like the Food Shop there, they give us leftovers and if you
robbed them, they wouldn't give them to you anymore.

Case 12—UL 109 Is.
Obs. 11: Anticipation of exchange.

(Why would you want to be a good son?)
Be good to your father and he'll be good to you.

Case 15—10 UL 113 Int.
Obs. 13: Deviance from authority motivated by anticipation of personal
vengeful reactions.

(Question V—Should the tailor report Heintz to the police?)
If he wasn't a good friend at all, he should tell. If he was a good
friend, he shouldn't; he'd be against him if he sentenced him and he'd
revenge after he got out again.

Case 76—17 LL Dolin.
Obs. 14: Deviance from authority motivated by anticipation of exchange of
favors. Role-takes natural wish of other.

I think he should keep quiet. He might want to go some place like
that and if he squeals on Joe, Joe might squeal on him. He wouldn't
want Joe to tell on him if his father brought the same situation up
with him.

4. Type 1—Punishment Orientations

Case 10—LL 97 Is.
Obs. 15: Punishment determined by need consequences.

(Question III—Should Heintz be put in jail for stealing the drug? He should go on probation. If they've got any kids, he's got to take care of them, he has to work and feed them.

Obs. 16: Punishment as preventing recurrence of the same act. Ignoral of intent or character.

(Question V—Should the tailor report Heintz to the police?) Yes, so he won't break in any more places and steal.

Obs. 17: Punishment determined by habit or custom of judge.

(Question IV—What punishment should the doctor get for mercy killing?)
If its more than first degree, he should get from one to ten years, maybe life. I watch "Dragnet" all the time.

(Should he be put in the electric chair?)
No. They should just put him in a cell for a while and let him cool off and maybe he won't do it no more. One of these days they might need him if they can't get any other doctors.

Case 76—16 UL Delinq. (Mixed Type 0 and 1).
Obs. 18: Punishment determined by habit or whim of judge. Punishment as preventing recurrence of same act. Ignoral of intent or character in predicting recurrence.

(Question III—Should Heintz be sent to jail for stealing the drug?) Depends on the judge I guess.

(If you?)
I'd give him a chance. Just because he broke the law once, no sign he'll do it again.

Obs. 19: Punishment as determined by label and talion, where no impulsive sympathy.

(Question IV—What punishment should the doctor get for mercy-killing?)
I'd give him life or the chair. He killed her just like some guy going out in the street and just shooting somebody. He took her life and he had no right to.

5. Type 2—Exchange Orientations

Case 25—13 LL 107 Int.
Obs. 20: Interpretation of exchange within a general set to be good. Subordination of exchange when it conflicts with such a set, and disavowal of vengeance.

(Would the Golden Rule be a good rule?)
I think so because that would take in about everything that way too.

(How about obeying your parents?)

Well your parents probably treat you nice, most of them do. I think mine do, and so I treat them nice too. But if they treat you cruel and you should get revenge against them, just take it as it comes. Try to be nice to them and they may change their attitude toward you.

Obs. 21: Exchange as part of a general positive set of giving to parents and as based on a return for the past, i.e., doing favors as expressing gratitude. Exchange as involving distant role reversal, i.e., of the partner less able to nurture becoming the one more capable to nurture.

(Why do you want to be a good son?)

I like to be a good son because my parents are good to me and I figure I should be good to them also. Take care of them when they're too old like if they lost their house and I had my own house, I would let them come and stay with me, give them shelter.

Case 4—10 UL 95 Int.

Obs. 22: Exchange as based on a positive disposition, e.g., gratitude. Exchange as subordinated to being good.

(Would the Golden Rule be a good rule?)
You like to treat people the way they treat you.

(How about if someone comes up and hits you, what should you do if you follow the Golden Rule, should you hit him back?)
That's only for good things.

Case 30—13 LM 115 Int.

Obs. 23: Conforming to parents as justified by a general "giving to others" unselfishness set as well as return of past services. Being good is invoked though it is not exactly a categorical duty in the situation.

(Question I—Should Joe give his father the money he has saved for camp?)
I think he should have given it to him to give somebody else the opportunity. His Dad has probably given up a lot of things for him. I'd give up something for my Dad too.

(Does his father have the right to tell him to give up the money?)
No. If he earned it, it's his money.

3. Type 2—Punishment Orientation

Case 25—13 LM 107 Int.

Obs. 24: Punishment determined by judge's role-taking the culprit and by role-taking wishes of others in situation. Sees choice as between role-taking culprit and "victim" without any principle of conflict-resolution. Judgment in terms of culprit's intentions and the situation faced by culprit. Victim has no special authority in deciding sentence.

(Question III—Should the judge send Heintz to jail for stealing the drug?)

I think he should let him go free on probation because he was stealing the drug for his wife to save her and the judge looked at all sides of it, that the druggist was charging too much. I think the judge should look at all sides of it and decide whether to send him to jail.

(Should he drop the case of the owner asks?)

Yes, the druggist sees it was his fault and now he's pleading with the judge. The judge doesn't have to, maybe he doesn't feel sorrty for Heintz.

Case 30—13 LM 115 Int.

Obs. 25: Punishment has the function of making people be good (e.g., help)
in   in general. People who are being generally good shouldn't be pun-
           ished. Punishment based on role-taking convict who role-takes
           others. Friendship means "understanding," not exchange of favors.

(Question V—Should the tailor report Heintz to the police?)

Well, I wouldn't because he's doing more help than he was in prison. Helping other people like he'd like to have helped his wife so that they wouldn't go out and steal.

(If the police ask and he is a good friend?)

He shouldn't tell, because Heintz is doing a lot of good and he probably understood why Heintz stole the money at the time he did.

Case 4—10 UL 95 Int.

Obs. 26: Quantitative compromise or minimizing sentence. Punishment deci-
           sion based on role-taking the culprit.

(Question IV—What sentence should the doctor get for mercy killing?)

I don't think they should kill him. I think they should just put him in prison. She wanted to die. I wonder if the jury was thinking that if their wives were sick and in pain and then they'd have to make the decision.

7.   Type 3—Exchange Orientation

Case 54—15-1/2 LM 104 Int.

Obs. 27a: A father has a definite legitimate expectation of a return, of
            repayment for his efforts for his children.

(Question I—Does the father have the right to tell his son to give him the money he earned for camp?)

Yes. His father has done a lot for his son and he should be able to get something in return.

Obs. 28: Expectation of reward for labor in the face of all claims of wel-
           fare in the situation.

(Question III—Does the druggist have a right to charge so much for the drug?)

He had to go through all the pains of developing it and if it worked, I think he should have the right to charge as much as he wants.

Case 14—10 UM 117 Int.
Obs. 29: Dependence of contractual obligation on actual payment and a general job role.

Question IX—If the man was a volunteer, could he leave his post?)
If he was a volunteer he could go because he only volunteered. He didn't have a commission and he didn't get pay.
The law shouldn't punish men to force them to stay though their family might be in danger. They should give them pay and a regular contract and it would be a regular job.

Case 61—16 UM 109 Int.
Obs. 30: Exchange subordinated to the order of authority.

(Question II—Should Alex keep quiet for Joe if Joe did for Alex, or should Alex tell his father on Joe?)
I think I'd still tell. Two wrongs don't make a right. The favor his brother did in the first place was wrong.

C. Type 3—Punishment Orientations

Case 54—15-1/2 LM 104 Int.
Obs.: 31 Expiatory concepts. Punishment somehow makes an act right or removes sin. Interchangeability of retributive and restitutive measures. Pain as punishment as removing sin, however the pain comes, rather than punishment as talion.

(Question III—Was it right for Heintz to steal the drug for his wife?)
Well if he saved his family's life and then was punished for it or paid back what was taken, it might not be wrong.

(Should the judge punish him for stealing?)
I think he should let him go on parole. I think there would be enough grief as it was without having to stick him in jail.

Case 50—16 LM 121 Int.
Obs. 32: Punishment as resting on role-taking the victim's legitimate demand for punishment. Rigid sense that victim and authorities claims define "duty" may legitimately demand punishment regardless of culprit's good deeds. Falling back on consequences.

(Question V—Should the tailor report Heintz as the escaped convict?)
He's still done wrong, and he's done two things wrong, escape from jail and steal the drug to begin with. I think he should report him because it's sort of like his duty. If somebody would steal something from the tailor, I would imagine he would want the person to be reported.

(Would a good person report him?)
If he knew he had done good, built the hospital, I imagine they wouldn't because they'd feel stealing the drug couldn't have been too bad a crime, since it hadn't worked anyway.

Case 26—13 LM 120 Int.
Obs. 33: Punishment as payment of "a debt" as involving the culprit's duty

to make up for his crime. Danger of making exceptions.

(Question V—Should the tailor report Heintz, as the escaped convict?)
Yes. He has to pay his debt and he escaped and that's not right. He should have waited till he got out.

(Would a good person report him?)
Maybe if they think he's gone straight and they shouldn't tell because he's making up for what he did.

(Would it be better for the country to send him to jail or not?)
Yeah. He has to pay for what he did or everyone else would be able to. Somebody might break out and if no one told on him he still might steal.

Case 29—13 LM Int.
Obs. 34: Punishment depends on its being accepted by the culprit.

(Question I—Should the father punish the boy for lying?)
Not too big a punishment, because that also might affect him and it might be wrong to give him a hard punishment. It would just ruin him, like he'd be bad.

(Would it do any good when the father broke his promise in the first place?)
I think so. If he was a good son he'd understand it.

9. Type 4—Exchange and Contract Orientation

Case 63—16 UM 114 Int.
Obs. 35: Focus on legal-contractual relations with authority rather than services rendered. Greater services by the parents do not warrant one-sided deviance.

(Question I—Should Joe refuse to give his father the money he saved for camp?)
Well I know the law says you have to, that parents have a right to take any of your earning. But I don't think it would be fair in this case. Joe was promised. He had earned the money for his trip and not for his father's sake.

(Would a loyal son loan his father the money anyway?)
It's hard to figure out. I think a loyal father wouldn't take the money, he would stick with his word in a thing like that.

Case 27—13 LM 91 Int.
Obs. 36: Role duty defined by contract and keeping one's word. Focus on contractual relations in the face of diffuse relational priorities

(Question IX—Was it wrong to leave his post to look after his family?)
They put trust in him to take care of that station and it would be better for him, he could save the whole city instead of just one family his family usually comes first, but he promised if he'd taken the thing to stay on the station.

Case 66—16 UM 112 Int.
Obs. 37: Contractual obligation to a peer justifies deviance to authority.
          Bounding of obligation by tacit agreement.

(Question II—Should Alex tell his father Joe had lied?)
I don't think he should tell. If his older brother just found out that he lied, maybe he should tell. If his older brother trusted him and wanted to get it off his chest, I don't think he should tell.

Obs. 38: Independence of contractual obligation from actual exchange of
          services.

(Question II—Should Alex refuse to reply to his father if Joe had kept quiet for him?)
That was just a gift of the brother not to tell on him and I don't think if someone gives a gift, you shouldn't have to give back the gift.

Case 49—16 UL 106 Int.
Obs. 39: Duty to country as based on voluntary acceptance of country's
          services.

(Free discussion re Jehovah's Witnesses.)
My uncle was in that religion, he tried to get me in it but after I heard about it, I didn't believe it. They don't believe in the flag and they don't believe in fighting for your country, but they're willing to live here and work in the war plants. That's what I don't see.

        10. Type 4—Punishment Orientations

Case 63—16 UM 114 Int.
Obs. 40: Judge's role, duty based on contract is to follow or carry out
          the laws. Exceptions are questions of procedure.

(Question III—Should the judge send Heintz to jail for stealing the drug?)
It's the judge's duty to the law to send Heintz to jail, no matter what the circumstances. He still robbed. The laws are made by the government or the people or somebody. The judge is elected on the basis that he is going to carry out the law. Of course he can probably make an exception but. . . .

Obs. 41: Utilitarian-economic view of justice.

(Would it do any good to send him to jail?)
He was doing it to protect his wife. It would just cost them money really, but they have no way of knowing that.

Obs. 42: Liability to punishment based on the fact that the act was com-
          mitted by free choice.

(Question IV—What punishment should the doctor get for mercy-killing?)
I suppose the judge would have to give the sentence required by law. If death, he'd have to give him death; if life, he'd have to give him life. The doctor knew what he was facing and he had every chance in the world to say "No, I won't do it."

Obs. 43:   Premeditation.

(Why is a planned or premeditated murder worse than killing someone in a fight?)

It's all planned out and you know you're going to kill someone.
This guy might have just been in a barroom fight and he didn't even
realize what he did. He might not be a real murderer at heart at all.

Obs. 44:   "Therapeutic" or disease orientation to crime.

I talked with the chaplain of Cook County and he doesn't believe
in execution because he feels so much could be done if they could
study the minds of these people and see what makes them normal and
unnormal. He says most of them aren't scared of that (execution).
The average guy doesn't think he's going to use a gun, but he gets
panicky and doesn't even think of what he's doing. And people who
commit premeditated murder, well something is the matter with them.

CHAPTER IX

SUMMARY AND IMPLICATIONS OF THE STUDY

A. A Cross-situational Development Dimension of Morality

1. A Concept of Morality

In Chapter I, we stated that we wanted to sketch out and define the moral as a fundamental dimension of social development. On the basis of philosophical conceptualizations of morality, we discussed some very general ways of thinking and feeling about action which constituted a moral orientation. We recognized that an attitude of conformity, or even of "conformity to rule" did not in itself differentiate a moral orientation from other social attitudes. The storekeeper maximizing profit, the carpenter using his saw, the S.S. man executing prisoners, are all conforming to social rule, but they are not acting in terms of a moral orientation. If conformity in general does not define morality, neither does any particular content of action or any specific rules. A Zulu and a Frenchman might do very different things and yet their choices be equally moral in terms of our criteria, criteria of internality, universality, etc. For the sake of labelling we said our criteria were those of form as opposed to those of content.

2. Findings Supporting the Concept of Morality as a Dimension of Social Development

Our a priori concept of morality was rather empty and abstract. Our actual procedure for studying moral development was an ideal-typologi-

337

cal one. On the basis of close study of our cases, six types of moral orientation were arrived at. Each type was seen as focussed on a distant set of interrelated concepts of good and bad or right and wrong expressed in typical patterns of thinking about our rather complex moral conflict situations.

These types were arranged by us as increasingly approximating our initial concept of a moral orientation. Such an arrangement appeared to represent the developmental relationships between these types. Each type appeared to be a stage or level in social development.

The evidence for believing these types to stand in a developmental hierarchy consists of the following:

1. The correlations between these types when so arranged form a quasi-simplex (Table 6).

2. This arrangement of the types provides a dimension sharply differentiating age groups (Table 7).

3. The arrangement provides a dimension significantly differentiating groups expected to be environmentally favored for social development. These were groups higher in sociometric and socioeconomic status (Tables 7 and 16).

4. The arrangement provides a dimension correlating to a moderate degree with intelligence, a variable favorable to social development (Chap. IV, Sec. D).

5. The arrangement provides a dimension correlating to a moderate degree with teacher's ratings of internalized conformity and fairmindedness (Table 15).

6. The arrangement provides a dimension differentiating delinquent from non-delinquent boys similar in age, socioeconomic status and intelligence (Table 7).

3. Negative Findings Indicating That No Other Dimension Than Morality Will Account for Social Development in Material Such as Ours

Given the arrangement of our stages as value types, is there some more specific dimension on which they show some cumulative increase than the vague one of morality itself?

Initially we set up simple quantitatively cumulative dimensions derived from the thinking of Baldwin, Mead and Piaget. These included such facets as "number of roles taken," "frequency of usage of exchange as a rationale," "ignoral of egoistic motives," etc.

Such dimensions proved to be unpromising for characterizing development for reasons elaborated in the description of the types. They also seemed unrelated to hypothetical determinants, e.g., class status for generalized perspective, peer group status for reciprocity, and delinquent and absent father status for internalization.

We found such groups differing in over-all development, and to some extent could relate specific type orientations to these groups. However, we felt in terms of the informal, and statistical analyses, we carried out, that we could not in a general way narrow down our interpretation beyond saying that greater social participation and responsibility in general is related to greater moral development in general.

The very fact that our developmental schema contains such varied elements of orientation as roles, rules, self-image, punishment, approval, sympathy, exchange, authority, indicates that we have not been able to isolate any of these elements as central in our account of the vague unity to which they all seem related.

Thus our summary in Table 17 of the development of exchange or reciprocity, so central to Piaget's theory, suggests rather the way in which general moral development transforms concepts of reciprocity, rather than the way in which some concept of reciprocity transforms moral judgment in general.

We considered also the dimensions of increased conformity and

increased situational flexibility as possibly characterizing social development. Age differences in alternatives chosen in our conflict situations
failed to support such dimensions as characterizing development in our age
range.

4. A Considerable Independence of Moral Set and Develop-
ment from Verbal Situation, the Values in It and
the Desire and Ability to Get the Right Answer

We failed to find any more precise and determinant social development dimension to order our data. Perhaps, however, the consistencies in
our data are mere artifacts of other variables, consistencies which do not
require any dimension such as "morality" for their description.

Rather than looking for general formal dimensions at all, we might
expect that our type-orientations are merely reactions to specific situations. Perhaps our types are artifacts of the situations we used rather
than representing some trend as independent of role and situation as that
suggested by the term "morality."

However, we were able to show that moral level, orientation or set,
was abstractable from the very diverse social situational roles or value
content in our verbal materials. A high degree of consistency regardless
of situations involved, was shown by our finding only one important factor
evenly loaded on all of our nine situations, when moral level of these
situations was intercorrelated (Table 9).

We considered whether this consistency could be due to varying degrees of adherence to general value systems relevant to our material. For
this purpose we examined the associations between dichotomous choices of
action in our nine situations (Table 10). We found very few significant
associations indicating that general value dimensions did not seem to be
contained in our conflict situations. Furthermore, when social group

differences in choice were analyzed, these did not reveal any subcultural value patterns but seemed rather to represent the differential sophistication or "maturity" of the groups (Table 13).

We then considered a modified view that the consistency was due to a mixture of values and intelligence. This would say that there was a general American value system which everyone tried to verbally espouse, with differences in response primarily due to intellectual ability in learning and expressiong this value system plus differential exposure to it. This hypothesis was judged not entirely adequate, both in terms of the low correlation of intelligence with our moral judgment score and in terms of analyses of the dichotomous choices.

We endeavored to analyze the meaning of the differences between such hypotheses and our own in terms of the qualitative differences between a moral set, a test-taking set, and a value-expressing set to verbal choice items.

The issue involved was whether differences in verbal morality reflected a process of integrally joined emotional and cognitive social development or a process of learning cultural habits and cliches. If the former were true, the theories of J. M. Baldwin, J. Piaget, G. H. Mead, and others, should be brought to bear on our materials. These theories describe stages of moral development as functions of development in modes of role-taking. If, however, our data on moral development could be described in terms of "learning the cultural maze" the more elaborate problems and theories of the above writers could be ignored. Our findings in favor of the former are not meant to imply anything about the comparative validity of various theories of socialization in general. Rather, they are meant to reassure the reader and the author that the problems of moral

development and the complex interpretations of material raised by them
are really problems raised by our data.

B. The Six Developmental Types and Their Implications for Theories of Moral Development

The chapters describing our types involve both description and
theoretically relevant interpretation. A summary characterization of the
types is offered in Appendix B; an even briefer one in Table 18. A summary
of the way in which these types handle one set of concepts, those of exchange and contract, is presented in Table 17 (p. 326). Typical cases are
presented in the body of the chapter and complete records of a case of each
type is presented in Appendix D. Short extracts from some newspaper interviews on desegregation in Little Rock are presented and typed in Appendix
E to indicate the wide range of persons and value areas subsumable under
our scheme.

We considered also the dimensions of increased conformity and increased situational flexibility as possibly characterizing social development. Age differences in alternatives chosen in our conflict situations
failed to support such dimensions as characterizing development in our
age range.

1. The Implications of the First Two Stages for Piaget's Theory of Moral Development

The three abstract developmental stages of J. M. Baldwin provided
a partial framework for interpreting our levels or types. Baldwin's stages
are summarized in Table 19, while Table 20 presents the two related stages
of Piaget together with our own re-interpretation of the data subsumed
under them, a re-interpretation in large part within Baldwin's less definite
concepts.

TABLE 12

SCHEMA OF DEVELOPMENTAL TYPES

Level I — Value resides in external quasi-physical happenings in bad acts, or in quasi-physical needs rather than in persons and standards.

Type 0: Obedience and punishment orientation. Egocentric deference to superior power or prestige, or a trouble-avoiding set. Objective responsibility.

Type 1: Naively egoistic orientation. Right action is that instrumentally satisfying the self's needs and occasionally other's. Relativism of value which is unshared. Naive egalitarianism and orientation to barter and exchange.

Level II — Moral value resides in performing good or right roles, in maintaining the conventional order and the expectancies of others.

Type 2: Good boy orientation. Orientation to approval and to pleasing and helping others. Conformity to stereotypical images of majority or natural role behavior, and judgment by intentions. Duty and true self-interest always coincide. Assumes authorities are always good.

Type 3: Authority and social order maintaining orientation. Orientation to "doing duty" and to showing respect for authority and maintaining the given social order for its own sake. Regard for earned expectations of others.

Level III — Moral value resides in conformity by the self to shared or shareable standards, rights or duties.

Type 4: Contractual legalistic orientation. Recognition of an arbitrary element or starting point in rules or expectations for the sake of agreement. Duty defined in terms of contract, general avoidance of violation of the will or rights of others, and majority will and welfare.

Type 5: Conscience or principle orientation. Orientation not only to actually ordained social rules but to principles of coice involving appeal to logical universality and consistency. Orientation to conscience as a directing agent and to mutual respect and trust.

We accepted the more general characterizations of Baldwin while rejecting some of Piaget's more specific elaboration and causal explanations. Our justification is based on identifying our first two types with the first two theoretical types of Baldwin and Piaget. We felt

TABLE 19

J. M. BALDWIN'S STAGES OF MORAL DEVELOPMENT[a]

I. Objective or Adualistic Stage (our Type 0)

1. Value is syntelic.

   Failure to localize or distinguish for whom a bad event is bad. The value of an event to another person is shared by the self without basis; or the evaluation of the event by the self is believed to be held by others without basis.

2. Value is projective.

   Failure to see the value of an event as a means to an end, on which its value is strictly contingent, or as an expression of a purpose which defines its value. Value of an act is dependent on its consequences and on irrelevant perceptual similarities to other valued acts. There is a general failure to differentiate good and right from other meanings of good and right.

3. Duty is perceived as based on objective or external necessity.

   "Duty" or right action is identified with that which the self "has to do" or is compelled to do by external forces, authority and sanctions.

II. Dualistic, Prudential or Intellectual Stage (our Type 1)

1. Value is relativistic.

   Judgments of right and good are relative to self-interest and judgments may be seen as conflicting where interests conflict.

2. Value is instrumental and based on need.

   The value of an object or act is based on its relation to an actual need or end involved in the particular situation.

3. "Duty" is perceived as a hypothetical imperative.

   Direction of action is not by compelling prescription or external pressure but is advisory and contingent on needs or motives of the actor.

III. Ethical or Ideal Stage (our Type 5)

1. Value is public or synomic.

   The moral value accorded by the self to the event is that which it is believed could be accorded to it by anyone. At the same time this value which the public could hold is a value based on the self's own legitimate perspective in the situation. The value is not the opinion poll value but the value which the self perceives when taking the role of "any rational man" in the society, or which we think society ought to take.

2. Value is ideal or objective.

   Events are valued not in terms of ideal desires which the self

TABLE 19—Continued

does have, but in terms of ideal desires which the self should have. It is felt that objects or events should be valued in certain ways, that value requires an effort of judgment and appreciation.

3. Duty is perceived as based on inner compulsion, or moral necessity, on conscience.

Action takes the form of a moral categorical imperative derived from the right in general, e.g., "I ought to or must do this because it is right, because I know or feel it to be right.

Exposition of the Stages contained in Chap. II, Sec. E.

TABLE 20

PIAGET'S STAGES OF MORAL DEVELOPMENT COMPARED WITH BALDWIN'S
FIRST TWO STAGES, AND AS MODIFIED BY OUR
INTERPRETATIONS OF TYPE 0 AND TYPE 1

I. Heteronomous Stage (Relative to Our Type 0)

1. Value and Conformity are "Egocentric."

2. Conformity is "Realistic," leading to a sense of "Objective Responsibility."

Piaget: There is a confusion of rules and things. Rules are oriented to as fixed sacred things. Deviance is always wrong. Acts are evaluated in terms of the "letter of law," and in terms of consequences instead of intentions.

Our interpretation: "Objective Responsibility" is merely an expression of "projective" modes of value and a failure to differentiate moral good from other kinds of good. It does not imply an orientation to rules in the usual sense of a concept of a rule-orientation. We find Type 0 are not oriented to rules as entities, but are oriented to projectively bad acts and to obedience to persons, not rules.

3. Conformity is "Heteronomous" or based on Unilateral Respect.

Piaget: "Duty" is based on a sense of heteronomous respect for adults transferred to their commands and rules. This respect, compounded of love and fear leads to an overevaluation and sense of sacredness of authority and rules.

Our interpretation: Adults must be seen representing something beyond themselves before they are "respected." While we find children of Type 0 oriented to obedience, we find little evidence that they respect authorities in any sense beyond recognizing that they are more powerful. Various kinds of response used by Piaget as indicating a sense of the "sacredness" of adults are

346

TABLE 20—Continued

interpreted as indicating cognitive naivete, independent of emotional overevaluation. Often they indicate a lack of respect for rule, against which the adult is measured rather than an idealization of the adult.

II. **Autonomous Stage** (Relative to Our Type 1)

1. Value and Conformity are Relativistic.

2. Conformity is flexible and oriented to intentions.

    Piaget: Rules are seen as the expression of human understandable purposes and as means to those purposes. Deviance may be justifiable in terms of an intent to conform to the "spirit" or purpose of the rule or in terms of a particular unusual situation. Acts are evaluated in terms of their intent.

    Our interpretation: Rules may be seen as merely instrumental acts, as commands based on the individual needs of authority. Deviance may be justified on the basis of an act being a means to a natural end. The end is not itself evaluated in terms of its worthiness for a moral self: intended consequences. Rules are seen as a basis for shared action but not as a basis of shared evaluation or judgment.

3. Conformity is Autonomous or based on Mutual Respect.

    Piaget: Conformity is based on empathic identification with the needs of others, shared goals, maintenance of agreement and a concern for approval by those approved of by the self. Conformity is to the attitudes of other equals.

    Our interpretation: These attitudes may be invoked as a basis of conformity without any really internalized conformity, shared goals or concern for others. There may be no differentiation between "legitimate" and other needs of self and all may be hedonistically oriented. Whose needs are empathized with is based on the degree to which the other comes within the boundaries of the self. Equality is not a norm but a fact. "I and my needs are as good as anyone else's." A seeking to maximize quantity of approval by direct instrumental techniques.

we found enough similarity to Piaget's types to justify this equation, together with enough differences to necessitate our reinterpretations.

The issue in its most vital aspect is as to whether the orientation of the young child to fixed labels and habits, to obedience and avoidance of punishment, implies a sense of respect or sacredness of authority and rules and a sense of guilt and indignation somewhat homologous to that of the adult authoritarian moralist.

354

If, as Piaget believes, there is such a homology, then it would be plausible to see the lines of moral development as one of increased instrumental flexibility and egalitarianism in these attitudes. Our interpretation of Type 0 was not such as to support Piaget's homology concerning the young child's respect for the rules. We felt our interpretation was strengthened by finding fairly pure Type 1 children. The egalitarian relativism of their thought was rather narrowly egoist and involved little respect for a contractual ethos which Piaget sees as naturally developing out of the earlier stage. At the same time they showed many traces of Stage 0 thinking seen by Piaget as indicative of heteronomous respect.

In general we agreed with Piaget and Baldwin in seeing young children, represented by our Stage 0, as verbally "over-conforming" because of logical defects in evaluation describable as adualisms of the subjective and the objective, and of value and fact. However, we did not see these adualisms as indicating or being facilitated by an attitude of "respect." A child who wants something just because another child wants it is illogically adualistic, but he is not displaying an attitude of respect, as the resulting combat may demonstrate.

The "adualistic" child's attitude in conforming is not fundamentally different from his attitude in deviating. When he conforms to adult rule, he is not aware that he is renouncing something (especially in theoretical and verbal situations). While conforming, he is motivated by the same mixture of impulse, fear and suggestibility which may in another occasion lead him to deviate. The need to win a prize which motivates him to cheat is as much a function of suggestibility as is the need to obey the adult which motivates him not to cheat.

The young and "adualistic" child may indeed want to be "good" or conforming, but such being good morally is confused with, and is a mere part of, his wish to have every type of good, e.g., to win. There is little reason to assume that he has any desire to do the will of the adult other than for its own sake or in the face of his own desire. His experience, we think, does not contain what Baldwin calls an "ideal self," even of an obedience-oriented variety.

We said that the adualisms of value described by Baldwin and Piaget could be seen as failures to differentiate the moral from other modes of acting and valuing. This implies that the differentiation is learned through the establishing of a more moral or ideal orientation or "self." However, a dualistic orientation may also be learned through the further development of the egoistic self.

This development may be seen in the effort of Type 1 to reduce value to desired consequences. Type 1 displays a great propensity to ask, "valuable for whom, valuable for what," and to give a narrowly egoistic answer. "Being good" is pretty well reduced to "being smart" and being smart is a matter of anticipating need consequences and adjusting means to ends.

Usually associated with Type 1's conscious subordination of action to the self's needs and desires is an equivalent though weaker recognition of the needs of others, together with more concern for distributive equality. Type 1's instrumental dualistic orientation and sense of the equality of selves Piaget sees as characteristic of his autonomous stage of development.

We can see in retrospect that learning that others have needs and that it is easier for all to take turns in itself is no guarantee of much in the way of moral development. Our delinquent boys as well as many 10-year-olds were quite sure that others, including authorities, had the same impulsive egoistic needs as they did and were aware of the value of bargaining and sharing to attain their ends. In the thinking of Type 1, the learning of the human needs of others did not form the basis of any further development or any general motive to do right and value the values of others.

The thinking of Type 0 did not seem to indicate the primitive but pervasive motivation which Piaget called "heteronomous respect" linked to the adualisms. The development of Type 0 into Type 1 accordingly would not necessarily be expected to show a pervasive moral attitude of egalitarian or "mutual respect" linked to the dissolution of the adualisms.

Thus neither of these two stages was seen as containing the basis for the development of Baldwin's ideal or ethical stage. We followed Baldwin in interposing a prudential egoistic stage between primitive conformity and moral conformity. In doing this we raise again the classical problem as to how the "egoistic" child becomes moral and "altruistic." By raising the problem in terms of the "lacks" in the thinking and feeling of our first two types, we eliminate the two traditionally popular solutions: fear, habit and obedience (Type 0), and sympathy with the needs of others (Type 1), in rather sharp and difficult terms.

Most of us are so used to seeing conformity as based on early dependency and identification necessarily modified by the growing independence of the child. Therefore, it is difficult to cope with problems as to how deep forms of conformity to "conscience" could arise from anything but this primitive early dependence.

2. Types 2 through 5 as Providing a Context for Assessing
Moral Development and Its problems

The characteristics of Baldwin's third stage and the characteristics of a moral orientation outlined in Chapter I seem embodied in our
Type 5.[1]

What does this type and the types we see as more or less succeeding the adualistic and egoistic stages contribute to our understanding of
the problem we have posed?

First, the types provide a preliminary map of the complexities of
experience and thought requisite for what we would take as moral competence. In the case of any individual person in any given cultural setting
this map would require considerable modification and elaboration. However,
without such an over-all map, we are unable to achieve any balance in our
assessment, because we do not know what may be taken fro granted in development and what needs to be stressed.

As we discussed in Chapter III, we felt that typological and developmental study may provide perspective in evaluation, though it is not
in itself any full evaluation of any particular trait.

If we assume that all children internalize the basic rules of his
society at an early age into a superego, then the stress in development
will be on giving the child a sense of his rights, of flexibility in the

---

[1]Baldwin's types and the criteria in Chapter I are the products
of a sheer logical analysis of cultural and philosophical documents and
usage; they are part of a conceptual typology. Our Type 5 is a Weberian
"ideal type," in which empirical clusters of ideas which seem to involve
these formal characteristics have been embodied in the type. From a
purely logical or philosophical point of view, it is not necessary that
a conscience-oriented person value relations of personal trust or that
he be oriented to some form of public duty. Yet a logical pattern of
thought is involved which makes it fully understandable why a person
oriented to conscience as an arbiter would, for instance, value both
personal trust and public duty.

rules, of pursuing his natural self and its interests. If we assume that it is rather rare and difficult for the child to really internalize society's rules because of his natural egoism, we may stress the need that the child learn the meaning of duty.

The implication of our developmental schema is that the dilemmas of self and the social order of situation and rule, of freedom and constraint, of inner individuality and outer reality must be faced again and again at successively higher levels of development.

At each of our three levels, our two subtypes represent opposite poles of the perpetual dilemmas of vagueness of obligation as against narrowness of obligation, of rights versus duties. However, at each of the levels the dilemma appears on a higher level in which the advances of previous levels have been more or less included.

Thus, at the level of Type 5, the firmness of conscientious decision and personal choice is consistent with an effort to consider all the values in a situation. It is just the awareness of having considered as well as one could the values in the situation which leads to firm and uncompromising choice and action.

As the Type Summary in Appendix A suggests, Types o, 3 and 5 all stress responsibility for the consequences of action as they are valued by "authority," or some objective standard, stress firm "duty" and negative sanctions. Types 1, 2, and 4 all stress the maintenance or enhancement of the purposes of a self. However, at each level the authority or self is more internalized and generalized.

In Type 0, the authority is an outer sanctioning force. In Type 3, it is a respected person whose legitimate expectations are identified with. In Type 5, it is an inner "conscience." In Type 0, obedience is to command; in Type 3, to fixed and general rule; in Type 5, to principle.

In Type 1, the self is a bundle of impulses and quasi-biological or physical needs. In Type 2, the self is a seeker of approval and positive status who wants to conform. In Type 4, it is a free voluntary agent or reasonable will.

Our schema then is to some extent dialectical. At each level, even a view strongly favoring of one polarity as opposed to the other will be less unbalanced and more inclusive and adequate. The course of development is one in which increased internalization of controls and increased individuality seem inseparable.

The three major levels may be looked at as levels of abstraction or generalization of moral regard. At the lowest level, there is basic regard only for the actual sanctions which others are believed or imagined to have at their disposal. At the second level, there is a regard for authority, the social order, and significant others for their own sake and a generalized valuing of conformity. At the third level, this is generalized to a belief in a certain regard for every individual as a basis of conformity.

3. Implications for the Explanation of Moral Development

The foregoing section leaves the impression of a rather Hegelian cognitive and intrinsic dialectic as the core of moral development. This is an almost inevitable aura of a generalized description of sequences of development in conceptualizing norms.

What more basic modes of social experience are requisite for moral development? We said the fact that we found differences of level at all stages of development for all of our social groups prevented us from specifying the kind of group or social participation which was important for various aspects of moral development.

We concluded section B-1 by saying that our Level I types did not seem to present the features of primitive but "genuine" and generalized morality which Piaget and the psychoanalysts attribute to the young child. We did not see these features as clearly present at Level II, in which conformity was felt to involve some renunciation of the self's felt interests for the sake of being a conforming being. At this level also, there was clearly present a sense of respect for and identification with parents and others who were felt to merit such respect and identification.

The conditions and experience necessary for such a development remain a question for further investigation and theorizing, and do not appear to us to be subsumable under any simple concept such as "identification with authority." Rather, given the degree of acceptance of authority shown by Type 0, further development would seem to rest on the child's learning to perceive the adult authority as himself effortfully conforming to and taking the role of some mass of patterns and purposes beyond himself. This was the process stressed by Baldwin, and it is one dependent on various kinds of cognitive development in evaluation.

Level III involves in addition to Level II's internalization of family and societal norms into an "ideal self," the sense that such norms may be the result of an individual self's thought processes. As our discussion of Type 4 indicated, this in itself does not guarantee "autonomy"; it may rather lead the individual to give up the standards he has internalized for the sake of conforming to majority will. But it does provide some criteria for examining and controlling the existing system of right and wrong. Our locating these developments in Level III suggests the

importance of both adolescent logical development and potential secondary
institutional participation as described by Mead in such a development.
As our discussion of Type 5 indicated, however, the projection of a personalized "ideal self" as described by Baldwin also may play a role in such
development. The individual may acquire a sense of personal moral judgment
by learning to place personal authorities within a more generalized and
possibly conflicting social order, or one may be able to do such placing
through an awareness of a full internalization of the basic rules of one's
authorities.

4. Over-all Consideration of the Relations between Cognitive and Moral Development

The analyses of Chapters IV and V, summarized in Section A of
this chapter, attempted to indicate the meaningfulness of morality as a
dimension of development. In part, this involved showing that such a
dimension could not be reduced to growing cognitive skill in manipulating
value cliches and in anticipating consequences. It also involved showing
that it could not be reduced to learning of "internalizing" the "right"
values as a ready-made set of preferences.

Authors, such as Mead and Baldwin, saw moral development as an
outgrowth of role-taking, a concept of sociality which cannot be classified either as purely cognitive or purely affective. Such a view is in
sharp opposition to tendencies in learning theory and psychoanalytic theory
to see the internalization of norms into a "superego" as a process independent of, and perhaps even in opposition to, cognitive or "ego" development.

Piaget's position was actually a mixture of the "optimistic" beliefs in the harmony of cognitive development and moral internalization,

helped by Mead and Baldwin, and the "pessimism" of psychoanalytic and learning theory. For Piaget, the strength of the heteronomous morality is based on various primitive forms of cognition and causes further cognitive primitiveness in the moral sphere.

Our own conclusion with regard to Piaget's theory was that the cognitive primitiveness and the punishment orientation of the "heteronomous morality" did not rest on a strong respect and identification. Correspndingly, the cognitive development of the heteronomous morality might lead to rather amoral instrumental egoism.

We did not conclude from these difficulties in the theories of Piaget and the utilitarians that moral internalization and cognitive development proceed independently of each other. But we did decide that there did not seem to be two types of "respect" or "identification" of a moral nature, one dependent on primitive cognitive mechanisms and one dependent on advanced social conceptions.

Accordingly, we feel our types reflect, on the whole, both an order of increasing internalization and an order of increased cognitive adequacy or "rationality" in the moral area. It seemed impossible to find an "internal standard" without a high degree of cognitive development. The course of moral development in our data does not seem to be describable in separable cognitive and affective areas. However, this does not imply that the growth of morality is the growth of intelligence; our correlations with intelligence contradict this.

While the most plain facts force us to recognize that children develop cognitively in a direction of greater logicality or rationality, any normative trend in the development of values is much more controversial, both on a priori and empirical grounds. However, to the extent that such trends may exist empirically, it is of great importance that they may be recognized. The adequacy of all detailed analyses of causation in the area of the learning of values seems to us to rest largely on a correct perspective in this regard. We hope our study is one step toward gaining such a perspective, the implications of which will be explored in the next section. Such implications require some explicit consideration because the criteria of usefulness we have invoked in defining and attempting to solve our problems have not been those of prediction for prediction's sake, nor prediction for the sake of control in the Utopian future.

C. General and Practical Implications of Findings Such as Ours Might Have

1. Usefulness and Implications of a Moral Dimension of Social Development for Theories of Socialization

Our findings have supported those social theorists who have seen the form and content of morality as in large part a "natural" outgrowth of social participation and development in general. To the extent to which this is true, our general conceptions of socialization must be such as to account for its moral outcomes.

Contemporary social psychology in reducing morality to conformity to given group norms has given us a view of man's psychological participation in society as the sum of his participation in small groups. Morality introduces a dimension of conformity common to all groups and transcending all. The trends of moral development we have sketched may provide a key to the developmental integration in the individual of the multiple groups to which he belongs.

If social psychology has reduced morality to all the customs and values of all the groups to which the individual currently belongs, personality psychology has tended to reduce it to the taboos the child learns before he can participate in the family group, the result is that morality is treated as largely an unconscious phenomena. From such a point of view, everyone's unconscious moral taboos are much the same, focussing on sex, aggression, incontinence, etc. As a result, it is difficult to account for conscious values.

The area of delinquency provides an example of the conflicts which arise when the developmental character of morality is ignored. In Chapter I, section C-2, we mentioned the conflict between viewing the delinquent as a normal social human in a delinquent subculture versus viewing him as a sick personality.

The sociologist sees the delinquent as holding the same formal attitude of group conformity as that held by the "moral" citizen, but directing it to different cultural content.

The psychologist or psychiatrist tends to see the delinquent as differing in general inhibition or conformity strength. He may see the delinquent as a psychopathic personality with no superego or as a punishment-seeking neurotic with too much superego.

The integrative task is to see the delinquent both as someone who does have positively definable values rather than simply as an unchecked primitive id, yet whose values do not have many of the characteristics implied by the concept of morality. Such a task implies a more gradated and developmental concept of morality than that provided by either the superego or "group conformity." Our findings on the delinquents suggest that their morality is an extension of modes of thinking common to many 10-year-olds. This indicates the importance of detailed longitudinal study of the years from 11 to 14 when most so-called "pre-delinquents" become delinquent.

Our study has indicated the feasibility of looking at individual differences in morality as representing a sequence of stages in conceptualizing the social order and the self's relation to it. There is a wide field for further development of such an approach.

2. Implications for Moral Training

Most of the theorists who have tried to explain moral development have not held the belief that the value of their work lay in its usefulness for social engineering, prediction and control. Implicitly or explicitly, they felt that the usefulness of their work lay in providing enlightened common opinion with a more adequate conception of the empirical nature of morality.

We believe such a conception is fairly essential in a scientific age for any individual who wishes to take an intelligent stance toward his own morality and that of others. While some logical positivists and intuitionists have denied the relevance of empirical study for ethics, they have also denied the possibility of taking an intelligent stance toward ethics.

Such a stance would seem to be of considerable importance in the moral training of children.

The conventional final step after the establishment of a descriptive scale of moral development might seem to be the ascertaining of techniques of child-rearing which facilitate a high score on such a scale. Then the parent who wanted his child to "be moral," could adopt these techniques as being most instrumentally effective.

Such a conception ignores the fact that moral training is based on specific moral attitudes of the parent. A parent refuses to punish a child "who doesn't know better," not because such punishment is ineffec-

tive as a habit training, but because it seems unjust. At a much later
stage, a parent refuses to punish a child because he does "know better,"
because it is unjust to deny that he is a full moral agent, and treat him
as someone still to be trained.

While there is a good deal of coincidence between a moral set
toward a child and a set to intelligently or efficiently train his character, they are not identical. Parents do not reject physical punishment or
"bribery" because they are ineffective but because they violate their moral
sense. Frequently they punish a child, not because they calculate its
effect on his future adaptation, nor simply because they are angry, but
because they are somewhat morally indignant about the action.

Such decisions are not of a sort for which advice can be given by
a psychologist in terms of efficient techniques or healthy feelings.
While such advice may allow psychologists to avoid making unscientific
moral decisions and imposing them on others, it does not really allow the
parent to avoid making them. To make them intelligently or morally, the
parent must have an understanding of his child as a moral evaluator. The
psychological information and understanding which is useful for the parent
or moral educator is of the kind which allows him to have attitudes appropriate to the child as an increasingly moral agent. It is the sort of
understanding which goes beyond instrumental prediction and control to
produce the genuine tolerance which understanding may give. Yet the understanding of the moral educator is not that of the permissive therapist; it
is an understanding which leads to higher demands as well as to forgiveness.
In part, the parent's understanding rests on some conclusions to the general
problems we have attacked. Can a general moral orientation be developed or
can the educator only help in forming specific habits and situational

adaptations? Do moral principles "naturally" grow out of basic aspects of the child's social experience in general or are they products of special training? Is an appeal to intelligence the basic sanction for moral development or should an appeal be made to categorical rights and wrongs?

In part, this understanding involves "sympathetic introspection" of typical stages of the child's moral development. Such understanding may enable the parent to see where the child is and where he has yet to go in terms of a broader frame of values than that involved in appraising conformity to home and school routines.

Such understanding is demanded if the parent is to define and communicate his and society's values in terms of their meaning for the child's development. It is required if the parent is to respond to that which is developmentally highest in the child while presenting something higher yet to be obtained.

APPENDIX A

COMPLETE INTERVIEW SCHEDULE

Situation I

Joe was a 14-year-old boy who wanted to go to camp very much. His father promised him he could go if he saved up the money for it himself. So Joe worked hard at his paper route and saved up the $40 it cost to go, and a little more besides. But just before camp was going to start, his father changed his mind about letting him go. His father's friends had decided to go on a special fishing trip and Joe's father was short the money it would cost him to go with them. So he told Joe to give him the money he had saved from the paper route. Joe didn't want to give up going to camp, so he thought of refusing to give his father the money.

Q. Should Joe refuse to give his father the money or should he give it to him? Why?

Probing Questions

A. If should give

1. Would a loyal son have to loan his father the money or is it up to Joe? (Does Joe have a right to refuse?)

2. Does his father have the right to tell Joe to give him the money? (a) Would a good father have asked for the money like that?

3. What would be the best reason for Joe to refuse?

B. If should refuse

1. Would a loyal son loan his father the money?

2. Does his father have a right to ask Joe for the money? (would a good father)

3. What would be the best reason for Joe to give his father the money?

361

4. Joe wanted to go to camp but he was afraid to outright refuse to give his father the money. So he gave his father $10 and told him that was all he had made. He took the other $40 he had made and paid for the camp with it. He told his father that the head of the camp said he could go then and pay for it later. So he went off to camp, but his father didn't have enough money to go on the fishing trip with only the $10.

Did Joe do wrong in doing that or was he justified in doing that under the circumstances?

C. Both

    5. Joe's father broke his promise about letting Joe go to camp. Was that wrong or was it all right under the circumstances?

    6. Which is worse: a son breaking a promise to his father or a father breaking a promise to his son? Why?
    (a) Why shouldn't someone break a promise anyhow?

    7. Later Joe's father found out that Joe had lied to him about the money. What should his father do when Joe gets back from camp? (If not mentioned) Should he punish Joe for lying?
    (If merely predicts) What would you do if you were Joe's father?

    8. Would the punishment do Joe good when his father had broken his promise in the first place?

Situation II

Before Joe went to camp, he told his older brother Alexander how he really made $50 and that he had lied about it to their father. Alexander wonders if he should tell his father or not. If he does tell, his father will be angry and will punish Joe. If Alexander doesn't tell, his father may never know about it.

10. Should Alexander tell his father that Joe lied about the money or should he keep it quiet what Joe has told him?

Probing Questions

A. If he should tell

    11. Would it be wrong for Alexander to keep quiet or is it up to him, how he felt about it?

    12. Why would a boy think he shouldn't tell on a friend or a brother?

    13. What would Joe think of Alex if Alex told on him?
    (a) Would he be a loyal brother if he told?
    (b) Would it be Alex' fault that Joe got punished?

14. Would he be a loyal son if he kept quiet?

15. Which is more important, being a loyal son or a loyal brother?

16. Joe also told a good friend, Sam, about how much money he had really made. Sam is no relative of Joe or Joe's father. If Joe and his brother weren't going to tell their father, should Sam tell him?

17. A few months before Joe went to camp; Alexander had taken something of their father's (to play with) and had broken it. Joe knew about it but he didn't tell on Alexander because Alexander asked him to keep quiet. Should Alexander do the same thing now for Joe and keep quiet about what Joe did or should he be loyal to his father and tell on Joe?

18. (if says should tell on 16) Suppose Alex had promised Joe he wouldn't tell, should he still tell their father?

B. **If should not tell**

11. Would it be wrong for Alex to tell or is it up to how he feels?

12. Why would he think he should tell?

13. What would Joe think of Alex if he told?
    (a) Would Joe be a bad or disloyal brother for telling?
    (b) Would it be Alex's fault if Joe got punished?

14. Would he be a loyal son if he kept quiet?

15. Which is more important, being a loyal son or a loyal brother?

16. Suppose their father actually asked Alex whether Joe had lied about how much money he had earned. Should Alex tell his father the truth or should he get out of answering?

17. (If tell on 16) A few months before Joe went to camp, Alexander had taken something of their father's (to play with) and had broken it. Joe knew about it but he didn't tell on Alexander (because Alexander asked him to keep quiet). Should Alexander do the same thing for Joe now and get out of answering, or should he tell the truth to their father about what Joe had done?

Situation III

In Europe, a woman was near death from a special kind of cancer. There was one drug that the doctors thought might save her. It was a form of radium that a druggist in the same town had recently discovered. The drug was expensive to make, but the druggist was charging 5 times what it cost him to make the drug. He paid $400 for the radium, and charged $2,000 for a small dose of the drug. The sick woman's husband, Heintz, went to everyone he knew to borrow the money, but he could only get together about

$1,000, half of what it cost. He told the druggist that his wife was dying, and asked him to sell it cheaper or let him pay later. But the druggist said, "No, I discovered the drug and I'm going to make money from it, so I won't let you have it unless you give me $2,000 now." So Heintz got desperate and broke into the man's store to steal the drug for his wife.

20. Should Heintz have done that? Why?

Probing Questions

A. **If should steal**

21. Was he right to do it or does he have a right to do it?

22. If not right, would a really good person do it?

23. Is it a husband's duty to steal the drug (or does it depend on how much he likes his wife)?

24. Suppose it wasn't Heintz's wife who was dying but it was Heintz's best friend who had cancer and who needed the drug. His friend's family didn't have enough money and wouldn't steal the drug for Heintz's friend.

    Should Heintz steal the drug to save his friend's life?

25. Suppose the drug was really worth $2,000 that the druggist wanted to charge Heintz? Would it still be all right for Heintz to steal it?

B. **If should not steal**

21. Was it wrong to do or was it up to how he felt about it?

22. Would a good person do it?
    (a) Can something be wrong which everyone would do?

23. Is it a husband's duty to steal the drug?

24. Suppose it wasn't Heintz's wife but Heintz himself? In that case, should he steal the drug so as not to die himself?

C. **Both**

25. Did the druggist have the right to charge that much?
    (a) if mention a law). There was no law saying how much he could charge.
    (b) Was Heintz going against the druggist's rights in stealing the drug?

27. Heintz decided to steal the drug and broke into the store. The druggist heard the noise and went into the store with a gun. He couldn't see clearly who Heintz was, but he started shooting at him. Would it have been wrong of the druggist if he happened to kill Heintz while he was robbing the store?

28. Is it worse to kill someone or rob someone?

    What makes it worse?

29. Suppose Heintz yelled that he would give up but the storeowner didn't trust him so he kept on shooting. If Heintz couldn't escape, would it be all right for him to shoot back at the owner and wound or kill him if that was the only way to save his own life?

30. Actually Heintz didn't shoot back but he escaped with the drug, but it didn't work on his wife. The druggist recognized him so the police arrested him for robbing. Should the judge send Heintz to jail for stealing the drug or should he let him go free?

31. Would the judge think that Heintz should have stolen the drug in that situation?

32. The judge was strict and decided he would give Heintz 10 years in jail. When the druggist heard about the sentence, he went to the judge and asked him to drop the case and let Heintz go free.

    Should the judge let Heintz go free in that case?
    (a) Should it be up to the owner whether the stealer goes to jail?

D. Pressure against those thinking husband should steal

33. (low level pressure) A lot of people don't really think Heintz should steal the drug though maybe some people would. He might end up being killed and losing a life instead of saving a life.

    (if no response) What would your opinion be on that?

    (if still unclear) Would you agree Heintz shouldn't have stolen it?

34. (if unconvinced) (high level pressure) A lot of people think that Heintz shouldn't do it because the drug was scarce and other sick people probably needed it as much as Heintz's wife. So Heintz was taking the drug from someone who could honestly buy it.

    (if no response) What would your opinion be on that point of view?

    (if still unclear) Would you agree that Heintz shouldn't have stolen it?

E. **Pressure against those thinking husband shouldn't steal**

33. (lower level pressure) A lot of people think that Heintz would be
right to steal the drug. He was doing less harm stealing the drug
than he would do harm letting his wife die. So he was doing the
best thing in choosing the lesser of the two evils.

(if no response) What would your opinion be on that?

(if still unclear) Would you agree Heintz shouldn't have stolen it?

34. (if unconvinced) (high level pressure) Some people say Heintz
has the right to break the law and steal in a case like this. They
say the idea behind the law against stealing is so that each man
can keep himself and his family alive by making a living. If the
druggist and the rest of society don't respect Heintz's right to
keep his wife alive, Heintz doesn't have to respect their right to
property if he can't keep her alive without stealing.

(if no response) What would be your opinion about that?

(if still unclear) Would you agree Heintz has the right to steal
the drug?

Situation IV

The drug didn't work, and there was no other treatment known to
medicine which could save Heintz's wife. So the Dr. knew that she had only
about 6 months to live. She was in terrible pain, but she was so weak that
a good dose of a pain-killer like ether or morphine would make her die
sooner. She was almost crazy with pain, but in her calm periods, she would
ask the Dr. to give her enough ether to kill her. She said she couldn't
stand the pain and she was going to die in a few months anyway.

40. Should the Dr. do what she asks and give her the drug that will
make her die?

Probing Questions

A. **If should not mercy-kill**

41. Would you blame the Dr. for doing it?

42. What would be best for the woman, to let her live for the 6 months
in pain or let her die?

43. Suppose the woman's husband, Heintz, felt it was best to put her
out of her pain? Would that make a difference?

44. (if law mentioned) Some countries have a law that doctors could put away a suffering person if they ask and if they will die soon anyway.

Does the Dr. have a right to do it in those countries?

(Is it wrong to have a law like that?)

45. When a pet dog is badly wounded, it is killed to end its pain. If a Dr. (is right) has the right to do that why doesn't he have the right to take this woman's life?

B. If should mercy-kill

41. Would you blame the Dr. if he didn't do it?

43. Should it be up to the woman's husband to decide?

Should there be a law giving the Dr. the right to put away a suffering person in a case like that?

45. When a pet dog is badly wounded, the Dr. is supposed to put it away to end its pain. Does the same thing apply here?

C. All respondents

46. Would it be better for the woman to ask the Dr. to make her die or to ask her husband to make her die (if she were going to ask someone to do it)?
(a) Why would the Dr. (husband) have more of a right to do it?

47. The Dr. finally decided to kill the woman, to put her out of her pain, so he did it without consulting the law. The police found out and the Dr. was brought up on trial since the court decided it was against the murder law. The jury decided he had done it so they found the Dr. guilty of murder, even though they knew the woman had asked him. What punishment or sentence should the judge give the Dr.?

48. Would it be right (wrong) to sentence him to death?

49. (if not) Why should the judge punish him at all?

Situation V

In Korea, a company of Marines was way outnumbered and was retreating before the enemy. The company had crossed a bridge over a river, but the enemy were mostly still on the other side. If someone went back to the bridge and blew it up as the enemy were coming over it, it would weaken the enemy. With the head start the rest of the company would have, they could probably then escape. But the man who stayed back to blow up the bridge would probably not be able to escape alive, there would be about 4 to 1 chance he would be killed. The captain of the company has to decide who should go back and do the job. The captain himself is the man who knows best how to lead the retreat to safety. He asks for volunteers, but no one will volunteer.

50. Should the captain order a man to stay behind at the bridge, or stay behind himself, or leave nobody behind? Why would that be best?

Probing Questions

A. **If go himself**

51. What would be the best thing for the survival of all the men, to go himself or send someone?

52. Would the captain have the right to send another man?
     (a) (if no) Would army rules give him the right?

B. **If order a man**

52. Would the captain have the right to send another man?

Situation VI

The captain finally decided to order one of the men to stay behind. One of the men he thought of was one who had a lot of strength and courage but who was a bad troublemaker. He was always stealing things from the other men, beating them up and wouldn't do his work. The second man he thought of had gotten a bad disease in Korea and was likely to die in a few months anyway, though he was strong enough to blow up the bridge.

60. If the captain was going to send one of the two men, should he send the troublemaker or the sick man? Why?

Probing Questions

A. **For all respondents**

61. (if not clear) Which man would it be fairer to send?

62. Whose life would be worth more to the company?

63. (if not clear) Would it be fair to send the troublemaker as a punishment?

64. In England a few hundred years ago the law punished a robber by hanging him to death. Was that right or wrong?

B. Pressure against sending sick man

    65. (low level) Wouldn't it be better to send the troublemaker since his life isn't worth much to anyone?

    66. (if unconvinced) (higher level) Besides he deserves some punishment and the sick man doesn't. Why should the sick man have to give up his life to save the troublemaker?

C. Pressure against sending troublemaker

    65. (lower level) Wouldn't it be better to send the sick man? He was going to die anyway, but the troublemaker might stop stealing and fighting.

    66. (if unconvinced) (high level) Besides it's using a situation like that to give a troublemaker a death punishment, and that's not fair.

D. For all respondents

    67. (if unmentioned spontaneously in V) The captain also had the idea of drawing straws to see who would go. Would that be better than sending the sick man (or troublemaker, which ever favors sending)?
        (a) (if not) Would that be the fairest thing?
        (b) (if so and think captain should go) Would that be better than going himself?

    68. The captain decided not to gamble and gave orders for the (man judged shouldn't go) to go. The man went to the captain and said he wouldn't go, because he hadn't been picked in a fair way. He said he'd go if they drew straws and he got picked, but otherwise he wouldn't go.

    Was he right or wrong to refuse to obey the captain's orders?

    (if wrong) Is it always wrong not to obey an order in the army?

Situation VII (administered after II)

    Several years later, the two grown up brothers had gotten into serious trouble. They were secretly leaving town in a hurry and needed money. Alexander, the older one, broke into a store and stole $500. Joe, the younger one, went to a retired old man who was known to help people in town. Joe told the man that he was very sick and he needed $500 to pay for the operation. Really he wasn't sick at all, and he had no intention of paying the man back. Although the man didn't know Joe very well, he loaned him the money. So Joe and Alexander skipped town, each with $500.

    70. Who did worse. Alexander who broke into the store and stole the $500, or Joe who borrowed the $500 with no intention of paying it back? Why?

Probing Questions

A. For all respondents

71. Why shouldn't someone steal from a store anyway?

72. Would Alexander have done worse according to the law or would Joe have done worse?

    Why is that? Is there a law against lying? Why not?

73. Which is worse for the country, a lot of people stealing or a lot of people lying and not paying back loans?

74. Who was probably a worse or meaner person to do what he did, Joe or Alexander?

    If Alexander - Who would you like less?

75. Who would feel worse, the storeowner who was robbed or the man who was cheated out of the loan? Why?

76. Suppose this man Joe borrowed the money from was a very good friend. Would it be worse for Joe to cheat him or would it be worse to cheat the stranger?

77. Al knew of two stores he could rob. One was owned by just one person; the other was owned by a company made up of a lot of people who had put money into the store. If he was going to rob the $500 from one of the stores, which store would it be worse for him to rob?

B. Pressure against those saying stealing is worse

78. (low level) A lot of people think that Joe did worse not paying the loan. Both of them really stole $500 but Joe lost a friend and got a bad name besides. He lied too.

    What would your opinion be about that point of view?

    Would you agree Joe did worse in cheating?

    (if unconvinced) (high level) Besides, John was breaking a trust as well as taking the money. He hurt the other person's feelings besides taking the money.

    Would you agree that Joe did worse because of that?

C. Pressure against those saying cheating is worse

78. (low level) A lot of people think Alex did worse in stealing. The law considers it worse since it puts you in jail for stealing. If you borrow money from a person the law can take it out of your wages, but you can't be put in jail for not paying it back.

What would your opinion be about that point of view?

Would you agree Alex did worse in stealing?

(if unconvinced) (higher level) Besides, in a way it's the fellow's own responsibility if he loans John the money; he doesn't have to. He should have had better judgment. The storekeeper has to keep his store open and the country has to have stores, but people could get along without loans.

Would you agree Alex did worse in stealing?

D. For all respondents

79. Why shouldn't kids copy off someone else's test in school?

Situation VIII (administered after situation IV)

While all this was happening, Heintz was in jail for breaking in and stealing the medicine. He had been sentenced for 10 years. But after a couple of years, he escaped from prison and went to live in another part of the country under a new name. He saved money and slowly built up a big factory. He gave his workers the highest wages and used most of his profits to build a hospital for work in curing cancer. Twenty years had passed when a tailor came from Heintz's home town and recognized the factory owner as being Heintz the escaped convict whom the police had been looking for back in his home town.

80. Should the tailor report Heintz to the police? Why should (n't) he?

Probing Questions

A. If should tell

81. Would it be wrong if the tailor didn't report Heintz or is it up to him?

82. Should Heintz be sent back to jail or not? Why?

83. Would it be better for the country if he were sent back to jail?

84. Suppose the tailor had been a very good friend of Heintz. Should the tailor still report him?

85. Heintz also had been going to see a Dr., a psychiatrist to help him with different worries he had. Heintz told the psychiatrist about his escaping from jail and his feeling worried and guilty about it.

Should the psychiatrist report Heintz to the police?

B. **If should not tell**

81. Would a good citizen report him?

84. Suppose the police were suspicious of Heintz and came around to the tailor and actually asked him whether Heintz was an escaped convict. The tailor had been a very good and close friend of Heintz in their home town. Should the tailor tell the police or should he get out of it or refuse to tell them?

85. Suppose the police also came around to a Dr. psychiatrist, Heintz had been going to and asked him if Heintz was the escaped convict. Heintz had told the psychiatrist about escaping from jail and all his worries and guilt about it. Should the psychiatrist tell the police or should he refuse to or get out of telling them?

Would he tell if he were just thinking about being a good psychiatrist?

C. **All respondents**

86. If someone knows evidence about a crime, the law says in court he has to tell the truth, the whole truth and nothing but the truth. But the law says a wife doesn't have to tell what she knows about her husband's crime and what the wife says doesn't count as legal evidence.

Is that a good law to have?
(a) What reasons might the lawmakers have for making that law?

87. Should the law go for psychiatrists too, so the psychiatrist wouldn't be supposed to tell on Heintz?

Why would the lawmakers make a law that doctors don't have to tell?

Situation IX

During the war in Europe, a city was often being bombed by the enemy. So each man was given a post he was to go to right after the bombing, to help put out the fires the bombs started and to rescue people in the burning buildings. A man named Diesing was made the chief in charge of one fire engine post. The post was near where he worked so he could get there quickly during the day but it was a long way from his home. One day there was a very heavy bombing and Diesing left the shelter in the place he worked and went toward his fire station. But when he saw how much of the city was burning, he got worried about his family. So he decided he had to go home first to see if his family was safe, even though his home was a long way off and the station was nearby, and there was somebody assigned to protect the area where his family was.

90. Was it right or wrong for him to leave his station to protect his family? Why?

Probing Questions

A. **If right to leave**

91. What would Diesing do if he were just thinking about being a good citizen?

92. Which is it more important to be?

93. Suppose there was actually a law that each man must go to his station right after a bombing. Would it still be right for Diesing to go to his family first?
   (a) Why does its being against the law make it wrong when it wasn't before?

B. **If wrong to leave**

91. What would Diesing do if he were just thinking of being a good husband or a good father?

92. Which is it more important to be?

93. Suppose Diesing were just a volunteer at his fire station and wasn't paid,(and there was no actual law which said he had to go to his station right after a bombing). Would it still be wrong to go to his family first?

94. (if wrong still on 93) Suppose none of the other men came to the fire station and Diesing saw men from all parts of the city going to their homes instead of to their stations. Diesing could see he couldn't do much with the engine without the other men. He could see that maybe nobody would be at their stations where Diesing's home was. Would it be wrong for him to leave his station in that case when everyone else was?

Really everyone stayed at his post except Diesing.

C. **All respondents**

95. Diesing left his post and he was later brought into court for desertion.

Should he be punished?

96. (if shouldn't) What would happen in the city if he wasn't punished?

Topic X (administered after III)

100. Are there any laws that are bad?

101. Should someone obey a law even if he thinks it is a bad law?
(Would it be wrong to break a bad law?)

102. Before the Civil War, we had laws which allowed slavery. According to the law, if a slave escaped, he had to be returned to his
owner like a runaway horse. Some people who didn't believe in
slavery disobeyed the law and hid runaway slaves and helped them
to escape. Were they doing right or wrong?

103. How about in a country like Russia where a dictator makes the
laws and we might think the laws were bad. Would it be wrong for
someone to disobey a law in Russia that he thought was a bad law?

104. Everyone always has to follow a lot of rules which tell everyone
what they should do and what they shouldn't do. There are the
laws of the country, the religious commandments, and the rules of
the family and a lot of other rules. Suppose there was a country
where the people didn't have any rules and didn't know any rules.
If you could just teach them one rule to follow, what would be
the one best rule for them to learn?

Why would that be the best rule or the most important one?

105. Are there some rules that aren't important?

106. How about the Golden Rule that says, "Do unto others as you would
like them to do unto you?" Would that be the one best rule or
most important rule if there were just going to be one or
wouldn't it? Why?

107. What should you do if someone hits you? What would the Golden
Rule say to do?

108. Suppose in this country that had no laws, there was nobody but good
people. Would they need any laws in that country?

109. Could someone be a good person if he hadn't been brought up with
any laws to follow (and just followed his natural feelings)?

Topic XI (administered at the end of interview)

110. Were any of the questions particularly hard? Why?

111. Do you think most people get the right answers to these questions,
or is there a right answer?

112. Who would know the right answer (if there was one)?

113. Do you ever have disagreements about what's right?

114. When you disagree with your parents and you can't convince them you are right, do you go along with them, or do you go your own way, or do you try to convince them?

115. On some of these questions I gave you another opinion and why I thought so. But (sometimes) you didn't change your mind at all. Suppose I had offered you $1.00 if you would change your mind and agree with me. What would you do?

APPENDIX B

SUMMARY OF CHARACTERISTICS OF OUR SIX MORAL TYPES

Summary and the Rating Forms are presented under the following headings:

1. **Value**
   Modes of attributing moral value to acts and persons. Differentiating and relating means and ends, intentions and consequences, one person's evaluation and others, etc. Modes of assessing value-consequences in the situation.

2. **Choice**
   The kind of identification with the actor in conflict and methods of resolving the conflict. The social process of moral argumentation and the capacity for making and maintaining an independent choice. The outcome chosen in the particular situation.

3. **Sanction**
   The dominant rewards, punishments or goals to which conformity is oriented.

4. **Negative Standard or Rules**
   The type of concept against which an act is assessed, on which guides conformity, e.g., taboo, rule, law. The concept of duty or moral compulsion.

5. **Self-image and Role**
   Modes of defining concepts of good person and good role. (Combined with Heading 4 in Appendix B.)

6. **Authority**
   The kind of respect accorded to authority and status and the reasons for which such respect is accorded.

7. **Content**
   The particular rules or virtues stressed by the type.

8. **Justice**
   Concern for and concepts of rights and the legitimate relation of one act, as deserved, to another. Standards of exchange, reciprocity, contract, punishment and reward. Not included in this summary because outlined in Table 17.

376

Level I - Premoral Level

No real differentiation of moral values and conformities from self-
serving and conventional conformities. Value resides in need-relevant
happenings rather than is persons or rules. No sense of an ideal self, of
a self conforming to standards or guiding action. Self-esteem is not based
on conforming to others or to standards.

Type 0 - Heteronomous Type

1. Value. Value is "Syntelic" and "projective." Both acts and consequences have a quasi-intrinsic, quasi-physical badness which is not reducible to needs, intentions, rules, etc. "Good" and "bad" are not
   judgments of merit but events appended to the self. A person is
   "morally bad" because undesirable, painful (bad) labels and sanctions
   are inflicted on him. The worse person is the one who has performed
   the act for which he will more likely be caught and sent to jail. A
   person's value tends to be perceived in terms of what he can do (power)
   and what he has (possessions) regardless of the value of these attributes to others.

2. Choice. Decisions are efforts to predict the external order. Believe
   the interviewer has the right answer without seeing him as possessing
   any special wisdom. See nothing wrong with being bribed to change their
   minds. Suggestible. Makes up facts as to the power of authority, and
   the likelihood of sanctions.

3. Sanction. The major sanction is avoidance of external punishment. The
   conforming part of the self acts only as a predicator of punishment,
   not as a judge. Punishment involves both hedonic and projective value,
   so that being punished means becoming a bad person. That which is
   "internalized" or identified with the self is the willingness to accept
   or believe in the superior power of other persons. It is not the wish
   to realize the will or aims of such persons.

4. Standard. Orientation to the avoidance of bad events, of bad acts and
   bad consequences. The badness of these events is not seen as established by rule, e.g. "a good rule is, 'Don't do bad things.'" Persons
   in authority, not rules, are obeyed. There is nothing abstractable
   from events to which persons are oriented in acting and evaluating.
   Unity of evaluation or decision is based only on everyone anticipating
   the action of the police as defining the value of the act. The police
   are not seen as part of a system to maintain some general state of
   affairs, e.g. social order and welfare, but as punishing bad acts and
   persons.
       "Duty" is what one has to do because of external force or to avoid a
   bad consequence, rather than corresponding to some real or ideal person's expectation or claim.

6. Authority. "Respect" is seen as overt obedience rather than an attitude of positively valuing the other. "Respect" is based on compulsion. Authority may also be assigned respect "projectively," in terms of the activities they overtly perform rather than heading an institution as a whole. No signs that authorities merit authority or possess personal virtues. While authorities may have special "privileges" to violate the rules, these are based not on merit but on the mere fact that they have the power to. Authority also based on possessing people and things. Some differentiation of obeying stable and legitimate power from obeying an accidental possessor of force.

7. Content. Avoiding performing punishable acts, and avoiding harm to the self, avoiding causing punishable harm to others, doing what one is told.

Type 1 - Hedonistic Egoism

1. Value. Value is relativistic, instrumental and contingent on need. Ends are individual and private, not shared except through bargaining or exchange. Some awareness of the needs of others as justifying the self's act, but no concept of giving another's welfare privacy over the self's.

2. Choice. Each individual in a conflict-situation is seen as having his own interest-determined evaluation of it. There is no basis on which to take one person's perspective as opposed to another's except one's own natural identification of the self or its interests with one person or another. Choice is made impulsively, and pressure to change one's mind is resisted on an arbitrary basis. Agreement might be voiced if to one's concrete interest in the situation, e.g. if bribed. Makes up facts about the situation to support the self's choice, and perhaps the possibility of avoiding sanctions.

3. Sanction. Tends to reduce rewards and punishments to their role in gratifying or frustrating egoistic needs.

4. Standard. The "standard" is the need or end served by the act or means. No basis for judging the value of the need or end, i.e. no image of a meritorious or good self expressed by intentions. Some concept of a "smart" predictive self who optimally adjusts means to ends and achieves whatever wishes the self has.
   Rules and laws are seen as conventions or directives of action held by a group of people, e.g. the police. Different groups may have different conventions with no overall or moral basis for coordination. Rules are not oriented to some general "right," but are either simply customary or instrumental to the ends of the individuals making them.
   "Duty" does not exist. Nobody has to obey if he is willing to take the consequences, so that there is no imperative. One can only advise means, not prescribe ends. People can ultimately do what they please. Resentment of interference, benevolent or not. "Individual rights" means that the self and its property are the self's own possessions to dispose of as it pleases.

6. **Authority.** A basically egalitarian attitude to others. "Respect" is a function of instrumental need for the other's function for the self. Expects people to dislike authorities who impose punishment or restrictions on one. All people are seen as having the same basic selves or needs. Differential role behavior is simply a function of habit and different self interests.

7. **Content.** Least advocates conforming to the social authority and rules of any of the types. The only "virtue" or "rules" strongly held or "internalized" aside from being smart is that of exchange of services and of vengeance, and distributive equality.

Level II - Generalized Conformity Level

Value resides in good and bad roles, in maintaining the conventional order and the expectancies of others. Self esteem based on general conformity to the external social order.

Type 2 - "Good Boy" Orientation

1. **Value.** Value is based on positive personal feeling for and empathy with persons. Rewards and punishments are not simply things of value to be instrumentally sought or avoided, but are expressions of positive or negative attitudes in others. Persons are recognized as having a different kind of value than things, based on a somewhat particularistic empathy with them and the concern of others for them. On a much higher level than Type 0, evaluation is "syntelic" in that there is an assumption that the evaluation of others are based on a common empathic evaluation of the situation and a common appreciation of virtue.

2. **Choice.** There is a need to be good or nice in all ways. Considerable indecision in conflict situation due to desire to conform to all labels and the natural wishes of all the others in the situation. Efforts to compromise of a naive sort. Responsive to adult and group pressure as long as it has some show of thought to it. Sees self as basically good, but not as a judge of right and wrong, nor as attempting to get others to do right or accept his judgment. Distorts or makes up facts to indicate the goodness of authority and rules.

3. **Sanction.** Seeks approval and thinks that it is good and virtuous to seek approval and status. Approval is a mixture of personal and objective factors. Disapproving reactions are seen as "hurting" the parent because of parents' liking for the child, and they hurt the child because of his liking for the parent. At the same time they are seen as oriented to a general perception of the good in a situation. Little concepts of completely objective or ideal evaluation and approval.

   Believes in sacrificing hedonic interests to be good and to gain approval, but usually equates maximizing the self's long range interests with conforming.

.. Standard. Oriented to good-role stereotypes. These are both what most
people in the role do or want to do, and what they should do. Action
is evaluated as expressing desireable dispositions of a self or role,
e.g. good motives or abilities, even though the individual act itself
falls under a bad label, violates a rule, or has bad preventable consequences.

6. Authority. Conformity to authorities is based on do-gooding personal
attributes ascribed to them, e.g. their desire to be helpful, and their
superior abilities or knowledge as to the self's welfare. Respect is
awarded for helping other people even if the self is not helped, and
for past help as well as anticipation of future help. Status roles are
seen as awarded to occupants on the basis of an evaluation of their general personal merit.

7. Content. Being good is basically liking, helping, pleasing and thinking
of the welfare of other people or of the role partner. In some upper
middle class "other-directed" children, the content is ability to "get
along with other people." These children are more peer and competitive
achievement oriented but virtue is still identified with approval and
generalized conformity to the wishes of others.

Type 3

1. Value. A clear differentiation of "right and wrong" from other modes of
value. A sense that some conformities and values are "important" and
others are not. An orientation to actual harmful consequences, and
avoiding causing harm. Some association of virtue with effort, deprivation and pain. A separation of the right from the aims and tendencies
of the natural self.

2. Choice. Rather rigid and definite in choice. Verbally tend to stick
to the rules "regardless." Not legalistic however, and a situation
can be set up where a demand for conformity to the rule and authority
is carried too far in terms of bad consequences.

3. Sanction. Considerable reliance on punishment to define and maintain
right action in others and in the self, but as symbolic of the firmness
of authority, not as hedonistic deterrent. While guilt is invoked, it
is an auxiliary rather than substitute for punishment. Primarily negatively oriented to avoiding blame or wrong rather than to winning approval.
Punishment represents the social order and may be used as indicating the
degree of wrongness of act.

.. Standard. An orientation to maintain the existing moral order as they
have understood and accepted it. Oriented to right and wrong as a unity,
rather than being oriented to avoiding particular bad acts as in Type 0.
Right corresponds to fixed and unitary claims of the general order which
any individual may claim or represent.
A concept of duty, i.e.,of a definite set of consequences or tasks
for which the self has been assigned responsibility. While obligation

is oriented to right and wrong, its focus is more in terms of role than in terms of a set of general rules. Duties correspond to definite claims which other individuals can make. These claims are based on a generally accepted social order and rules. Rules are seen as a system for guiding righteous behavior. The claims of others are not that their welfare be considered, but are fixed expectations which they have earned or are entitled to.

6. **Authority.** Authorities are seen as having a legitimate claim to be respected. Respect is due to an authority because he represents and maintains the social order. It is also due because authorities themselves conform to this order and must work hard and deprive themselves to be authorities.

7. **Content.** Some emphasis on work, task, discipline, control, for its own sake. Highest concern for property of any of our types, but no confusion of physical value with human and moral values as such.

Level III - Autonomous Level

Value resides in the conformity of the self to some shared or shareable standards of judgment. Duties are defined by general rights of others.

Type 4 - Democratic Legalists

1. **Value.** Value is seen as defined by a social perspective. Relativism of value means more than judgment being dependent on interest (Type 1). It means varying group or role-perspectives or shareable lines of thought which a given individual may take toward an issue. A strong emphasis on majority opinion or agreed upon rule as the ultimate perspective. A set to community utility and to a logic of maximizing results or minimizing cost.

2. **Choice.** A tendency to clearly separate actions which can be subsumed under agreed-upon clear rules and those which are seen as matters of individual preference or motives. Resolution of conflicts with no agreed-upon solution tends to be on prudential situational grounds. No real hierarchy of personal loyalties, but a sense of some loyalty as required in any personal relation.

3. **Sanction.** A considerable preoccupation with community or group reputation and peer approval. Parents, peers, outside authorities are all seen as basing their evaluation in terms of the evaluations of the others. Some tendency to see moral conformity in terms simply of a necessary framework of rules which are accepted and within which one maneuvers to gain status. "Guilt" is irrelevant good boy talk.

4. Standard. Duty or role obligation is defined in terms of a set of agreed upon defining rules, i.e. a code which need not have the sacredness of "right." Law itself is oriented to as the ultimate judgment of right, though its evaluative impact is limited by other considerations felt in earlier types. Some separation of the value of consensus and stability from the actual value of the concrete rule and some sense of necessary arbitrariness to rules. However, there is a general set to law as for the majority welfare, and a consideration of social utility.

Duty is also defined contractually and in terms of the violation of the will of individual others. There is some sense of general unearned rights which limit the rights and duties of any given status.

The self-image conformed to tends to be that of an intelligent or reasonable person without much distinction between prudential intelligent and achievement on one hand and moral rightness on the other. The goal is that defined as appropriate by the group and is taken for granted rather than being expressed or displayed as "being good." The self is differentiated from others by rational achievement or intelligent means in reaching these goals.

6. Authority. Roles are seen as freely chosen by the occupant, and the occupant as selected from a field of competing applicants in terms of ability. A role personality and its value is defined less by the role-activities and more by how it got there. Admiration is accorded to others for superior abilities indicated by status and reputation, and involves a shade of envy. A respect for the judgment of the "expert" within his sphere of competence. This "field" is a delimited science or art, not a general virtue and wisdom about life or about the right as in Type 2.

7. Content. A stress on maintaining contract and "reasonable" expectations of others. Stress on getting along with others. Sense of not imposing on the will of another.

Type 6 - Conscience or Principle Orientation

1. Value. Moral value is to a large extent objective, ideal and public. Thus the value of a given human life is independent of the actual functional value of the individual or of the self's particular relation to him. It is based on the fact that everyone ought to give an absolute moral value or respect to an individual human life. Action ought to be based on a correct appreciation of the values in the given situation, rather than on habitual good motives. There is an expectation that everyone in a situation ought to be oriented to the common value situation in making any claim. A claim on an actor which ignores a greater claim made by a third person upon the actor is not completely legitimate or binding. A logic more of inclusiveness and consistency of valuing than of economy and efficiency of valuing (Type 4).

2. Choice. Thoughtful but consistent in choice. "Takes a position."

3. Sanction. Invocation of guilt or self-judgment for actions which violate belief, even if they would involve no external disapproval or punishment. Concern about the respect of others rather than their approval. Such respect implies an objective evaluation by the partner in some moral transaction. It implies living up to the partner's trust in the self's worthiness.

4. Standard. Some orientation to principle. A principle is a rule of choice and judgment, with some appeal to logical generality and consistency for its support. It is not an actual socially agreed upon and enforced rule. In general, a responsibility for the value consequences in a situation beyond rule and delegated task. The limits of responsibility are not simply given but are set in terms only of more primary responsibilities in the situation, or by the limits which must be put on human beings in general. Some sense of a higher law than human law. Conformity to law and majority will are generally right or best but they do not in themselves make an individual act right regardless of all else. Moral right is differentiated from legal right.

6. Authority. Authority is no longer equated with formal authority roles but with elements potentially belonging to any human. A belief that the right judgment in a given case may be embodied in anyone. A sense of obligation to those who respect the self.

7. Content. Concern for public welfare. Some sense of personal task. Concern about avoiding deception, and maintaining personal trust.

APPENDIX C

CODING AND RATING FORMS FOR MORAL SITUATIONS

Situation I - Global Rating Guide

Type 0 - oriented to passive obedience and compliance

1. Value. No orientation to assessing the purposes involved. Going to camp is not a purpose but a permitted gratification, e.g., "he can go another year instead." Saving money is not an identified-with purpose. No evaluation of father.

2. Choice. Should give the money to father.

3. Sanction. Possibility of trouble with father.

4. Property rules and rights. Little sense of ownership rights.

5. Son role. Should give to obey, comply.

6. Authority. Simply a fact that father has power to demand money, may invoke ownership of son.

8. Justice. Little sense of the injustice of the broken promise, though knows its wrong to break promises. Some sense that if the father told the boy he could go, he should let him.

Type 1 - oriented to keeping and using what you get.

1. Value. Orientation to purpose of going to camp and to holding onto own money. No evaluation of father.

2. Choice. May be uncertain, but favors refusing the father.

3. Sanction. Assumes father can't force the issue.

4. Property rules. Simple fact that boy earned, it's his money.

5. Son role. No concern to be nice in son role.

384

6. Authority. If father wants money, he can earn it.

8. Justice. Promise is seen as bad in disappointing expectation of grati-fication.

Type 2 - Nice boy with some sense of rights

1. Value. May invoke belief that father is oriented to boy's own best wel-fare, or to family's in the situation, has an unselfish goald and knows best.

2. Choice. Conflict between benig nice boy and maintaining purpose and rights. Tends to say that "boy doesn't have to give the money but I would." Efforts at compromise by giving some money, insuring it will be paid back, etc.

3. Sanction. Assumes no negative sanctions by father.

4. Property rules. Has a right to the money. Some sense that worked hard for the money, deserves a reward.

5. Son role. Some idea of being nice, unselfish, sacrificing, grateful for past care.

6. Authority. Cf. 1, 2, 5. Doesn't invoke authority of father but being nice.

8. Justice. Some assimilation of breaking promises to not being a good son or father, not caring about other, etc.

Type 3 - Oriented to an internalized sense of the father's authority

1. Value. Accepts that boy should sacrifice his interests. May be some case that to boy's long range interests to do so, or that will even out in the end.

2. Choice. Give the money to the father. No uncertainty.

3. Sanction. A sense of the potential power of the father without actually invoking sanctions.

4. Property rules. See 6.

5. Son role. To show respect or not detract from, go against father's authority.

6. Authority. Some invocation of authority of the father on a categorical basis apart from justifying compliance in this situation as nice. Sub-sumes father under a class of persons deserving respect and reward. Tends to distinguish father's authority to determine whether boy goes to camp (or what does with money) and his right to take boy's money.

6. Justice. Promise assimilated to maintenance of parent-child authority system. Boy would lose respect for father if broke promise, etc. Not a categorical contractual attitude.

Type 4 - Oriented to a sense of contractual rights in the situation in terms of which the diffuse father-son relationship is irrelevant

1. Value. Some sense of the value of planning, maintaining purpose.

2. Choice. Refuse the money. Little uncertainty.

3. Sanction. None invoked, may have some practical sense of the father causing difficulty with no punitive symbolic value.

4. Property rules. Sense of the boy's right to the money.

5. Son role. Maybe some sense that a good son might compromise in some ways.

6. Authority. Father has no right to ask in this situation, though may also mention the legal definition of a father having rights over minor's property, e.g., "he could but shouldn't in this case."

7. Injustice. Not an actual focus on the injustice of the father, the fact that being a bad father. More focus on the promise, etc. as giving the son rights in the situation, than as "unfair."

Type 5 - Oriented to the father's injustice but in an evaluative rather than retaliative way. Otherwise like Type 4.

Situation II - Global Rating Guide

Type 0 - Unlimited tendency to tell authority

1. Value. No localization of responsibility for confessing. Punishment not modified by father's judgment of culprit as "good" for confessing. May be some illogical sense of participation in badness by sharing secret.

2. Choice. Tell.

3. Sanction. Concern to avoid punishment and trouble by the father. May unrealistically expect inevitable punishment.

4. Rule re lying. Lying concern is in terms of punishment and of keeping secrets.

5. Brother role. On probe, mentions brother's anger but this is unimportant because of mutual subordination to parents. May say even a friend should tell, so telling is not part of a "good" family role.

SITUATION I - CODING FORM

Type	1. Value and Utilities 2. Choice	4. Standard Property Rights	5. Standard Son Role 3. Sanction
0	011. Substitute - Can go next year.	041. Permitted - Father permitted paper route as giving some claim to the money.	051. Obedience - Should give to obey, comply. 031. Punishment - Father will make trouble.
1	111. Substitute - If can go on fishing trip, too, etc. 121. Exchange - Father will pay back, giving help in future.	141. Earned - He earned money, his; he should keep it.	
2	221. Compromise - Give father some of the money. 211. Reason - Father may have a reason for it re welfare of son or family.	241. Earned - The boy worked hard for money, implied should get reward	251. Help - Implies good for son to help, give to parents. 252. Sacrifice - Speaks of sacrificing, being unselfish, etc.
3	311. Even - even out in the end.		351. Respect - Give to show respect, not to go against, etc.
4	411. Plan - was an agreed upon plan, saved for the purpose, should be maintained. 421. Discuss - should discuss, point out the situation to father.		451. Irrelevant - Being good son is irrelevant re the contractual situation. 452. Right - Has a right to go to camp.
5			

SITUATION 1 - CODING FORM--Continued

Type	6. Authority - Father Role	8. Injustice in Situation, Father's Roel and Promise	9. Why Not Break Promise?
0	061. Role - It's his father, can order him to give. 062. Possess - Father owns son, etc.	081. Worse for son than father to break promise.	091. Inequal - Worse for a son to break promise, because father older, etc.
1	161. Equal - Father can earn himself, get it elsewhere if wants. 162. Need - Son needs father for food, etc. 163. Rights - Father has no right to ask, not his money.	181. Equity - Easier for father to get money. 182. Equity - Son younger, needs vacation more. 183. Copy - Boy will copy father when he grows up. 184. Disappoint - Worse for father to break promise, more independent.	191. Disappointment - Badness of breaking promise is that boy is sad, can't do what he hoped to. 192. Like - Son won't like father re breaking promise. 193. Believe - Won't believe you anymore.
2	261. Given - Father has given much in past. 262. Knowledge - Knows what is best for him. 263. Ask - Father can't command money, but cna ask.		291. Care - Shows father doesn't care about son. 292. Usual - Usually good parents don't break promise. 293. Rule - You should always keep your promise.
3	361. Age - Father has a right to demand because he is older. 362. Earn - Has right because works hard, earns money. 363. Authority - Father has authority to keep son from camp, to tell you what to do, not to take money.	381. Desert - Son earned money; don't think father should getit. 384. Equal - Equally bad for father or son to break promise.	391. Expectation - Son will feel let down by broken promise. 392. Respect - lose respect. 393. Important - If something especially unforeseen, all right to break promise.
4	462. Legal - Invokes legal definition of father's rights, tho not in this case. 463. Rights - Father has no right to ask.	481. Consist - Father should earn it as told son to. 482. Example - Father is supposed to be an example, so deviating from his role re promise breaking (on probe).	491. Confidence - Lose confidence; can't plan for future. 492. Expect - Can't expect son to do any different.
5	562. Moral - No moral right even if legal one	581. Want - A father shouldn't want to take it in the situation for his own pleasure. 582. Definitely unfair, unjust for him to ask for it.	

6. **Authority.** No invocation of a basis for father's authority. Father seen as trying to find out what's going on rather than to correct lying.

8. **Justice (Reciprocity).** No concern for the justice of brother's punishment. No concern for reciprocity or contract with brother. May say to tell even if promised not to.

Type 1 - oriented to own interests. The basic fact is that the brother will be angry because he was told on, while the father won't know actor kept the secret

1. **Value.** Thinks it is brother's own business to tell but not because of the goodness of confessing oneself.

2. **Choice. Keep quiet.**

3. **Sanctions.** Avoid punishment for everyone by keeping quiet.

4. **Lying rule.** Little concern about lying.

5. **Brother role.** May be some sympathy with brother's wish to get to camp. Some wish to avoid brother's anger, as well as labels of squealer, etc.

6. **Father's authority.** Conformity is limited to concern about his selfish anger. Father and brother are equivalent in this regard.

8. **Justice.** Reciprocity is on a future exchange basis.

Type 2 - oriented to helping both father and brother and keeping approval of both, but the superior attachment to the father and the lying element determine choice.

2. **Choice.** May be reluctant, **but says to tell** if brother won't.

3. **Sanction.** A basic concern is disapproval by the father.

4. **Lying.** Concerned that concealment is a form of lying and will lead to lying himself. Lying is a form of not being good, which arouses disappointment and disapproval by father, upsets the relationship.

5. **Brother role.** Some feeling that brothers do "stick together," that brother will be disappointed, disapprove, feel unloved. Some idea also that actor should be concerned about the character and conformity of the brother and represent or intercede for the father with him.

6. **Authority.** Some idea that father ought to know to handle the situation well, in a non-punitive sense. He should know for brother's welfare at camp, etc.

8. **Justice.** It's good, nice, fair to pay back a favor to brother. Remaining quiet not originally seen contractually, but is only involved if brother actually kept quiet for actor previously.

Type 3 - May not be very different from Types 0 and 2, but more categorical and punitive rather than punishment-avoiding

1. Value. Some concept that it's the brother's responsibility to tell and only then the actor's.

2. Choice. Tell.

3. Sanction. Some concern that the lying should be punished or corrected; whereas the orientation of Type 0 was to avoid punishment for both.

4. Lying. Lying is categorically seen as "doing wrong."

5. Brother. Thinks brother will know he deserved punishment, did wrong, and hence will not feel retaliative.

6. Authority. Father's job to maintain the rules.

7. Justice. Reciprocity elements recognized but overweighed by maintaining the order, by "2 wrongs don't make a right."

Type 4 - May not be very different from Type 1 except in containing more intermediate type elements

2. Choice. Perceives situation as partial obligations to persons partially in the wrong, and hence as a conflict of personal feelings of loyalties. Ambivalently tends to resolve it by not telling.

3. Sanction. Some concern about either partner feeling the actor is not siding with him.

4. Rule. Feelings about lying enter in only if directly asked by the father. Lying may be seen as not so bad "in brother's situation."

5. Role. A fairly impersonal orientation in terms of respecting the situational rights of the brother.

6. Authority. The father's rights are limited by his antecedent behavior in the situation.

8. Justice. Formalistic concern for contract.

Type 5. - The only, warmly felt and non-prudential belief that the brother should not be told on.

2. Choice. Definitely don't tell.

5. Role. A sense of relationally maintaining the trust of the brother, perhaps in terms of playing the "good authority" to the brother.

6. Authority. A good father would not expect confidences to be violated.

t. Justice. As in 5.

Situation III - Global Rating Guide

Type 0 - Oriented to (fearful) avoidance of stealing and punishment

1. Value. Syntelic and projective value comparison—the wife is valuable more valuable than the drug—qua more important. The badness of stealing may focus on the value of the drug.

2. Choice. May not go beyond labeling to identify with actor's dilemma. If does, may see him as unable to change outcome of situation. Says shouldn't steal.

3. Sanction. Strong concern about punishment. May see it as inevitable. May see punishment as leading to further harm to wife or making drug useless.

4. Stealing rule. Stealing is a bad,punishable act, breaking the law (as activating police).

5. Husband role. No sense of husband's role obligation in this context.

6. Injustice. May think druggist will be punished for withholding the drug or for shooting the husband. In anh case, does not see druggist's action withholding as justifying the husband's action, or as relevant to it.

Type 1 - oriented to instrumental necessity of stealing

1. Value. "The ends justify the means." Says has to, is best to, or is right to steal, to prevent wife from dying. (Without an implication that saving the wife is a good deed.)

2. Choice. Little conflict in decision to steal. Implies decision is based on instrumental reasoning or impulse.

3. Sanction. Little concern about punishment, or punishment may be avoided by repayment, etc.

4. Rule. Little concern about stealing in this situation. May see stealing in this situation as not hurting the druggist.

SITUATION II - CODING FORM

Type	1. Value and 2. Choice	3. Sanctions	4. Rule - Lying Concern and Concepts
0	021. Anyway - Father will find out anyway, so tell. 0.. Worse - will get worse punishment if not told on.	031. Trouble - Avoid later punishment for self or trouble with the father. 032. Vengeance - Brother be mad; won't play with him; beat him up.	011. Secret$_1$ - Keeping a bad secret. 012. Secret$_2$ - If someone does something wrong, you should tell the authority.
1	111. Neutral - I don't do anything can't get self in trouble. 112. Culprit - The culprit should tell himself; it's up to him; he did it. 113. Trouble - Avoid trouble for brother, so don't tell. 114. Enjoy - Let brother have, enjoy his camp.	131. Trouble - Telling father may just get him mad at actor, stir up trouble, may not achieve. 132. Exchange - Don't tell because maybe he didn't or won't tell on you; need a favor from him (spontaneously) 133. Lose - Lose a friend.	141. Ask - Don't tell even if asked (out of indifference to lying). 142. Lying - Lying wasn't bad for brother, had to get to camp.
2	221. Promise - Didn't promise not to tell. 222. Persuade - Persuade brother to tell. 223. Best - Telling father will help clear up the situation between father and son in non-punitive way; father will be understanding. 224. Wait - Don't tell until brother has had his camp.	231. Interest - "Concerned about brother's welfare, that he should grow up not to lie,etc. 232. Disapproval - Concern about disapproval of father if don't tell truth. 233. Trust - Will lose brother's trust. 234. Approval - Lose approval of friend.	241. Good - Be honest, tell the truth, not be lying to himself. 242. Brought up - Father brings you up not to lie; he doesn't lie. 243. Bad Conscience - Brother will feel bad in conscience if don't tell; hence tell.
3	321. Easier - The father will be easier on brother if he tells himself. 311. Get over - Brother would get over being mad, see he was in the wrong. 321. Promise - Could tell father if didn't actually promise or agree not to tell; implying contract.	331. Punish - The brother should be punished, corrected.	341. Rule - You should always tell the truth about what you do. 342. Wrong - The brother was wrong to lie. 441. Expediency - Brother's so bad because forced to, or by a response to father's behavior.

SITUATION II - CODING FORM—Continued

Type	1. Value and 2. Choice	3. Sanctions	4. Rule - Lying Concern and Concepts
4	422. Up to him. - Actor must choose between brother and father, no real right; it's taking sides; Antecedents - Father wasn't really right in first place. 423.		

Type	5. Role of Brother (and Friend)	6. Father's Authority (Good Brother Or Son More Important)	8. Justice - Exchange and Contract Concern
	521.		
0	051. Brother = son (on prob.), good brother is one who obeys father. 052. Friend - A friend should tell too. 053. Tattle - Be a tattletale if tells.	061. Authority's wish - Father wants to know a sufficient reason.	
1	151. Business - Not the friend's business. 152. Confide - Brother won't tell him any more secrets.	161. Need - It is more important to be good son because father can give more. 162. Harm - Won't do father harm if he doesn't know. 163. Father's wish - Father's wish to know just due to desire to go fishing.	181. Exchange - If tell, the brother will tell on the self.
	251. Ability1 - An older brother knows better, what best for his brother. 252. Ability2 - Friend doesn't know situation. 253. Expect - Father expects self to look out for brother.	261. Trust - Lost father's trust. 262. Father - His father should know about the brother re his welfare. 263. Older - His father knows what is best. 264. Care - It is more important to be loyal son because parents have cared fro you.	281. G.R. - Golden rule. 272. Fair - It wouldn't be fair to tell if brother didn't. 283. Expect - Brother expects him to do the same. 284. Usual - Most brothers will pay back favor. 285. Favor - If brother was nice to him, he should be nice and pay back favor.

SITUATION II - CODING FORM—Continued

Type	2. Value of Brother (and Friend)	5. Father's Authority (Good Brother or Son More Important)	8. Justice - Exchange and Contract Concern
2	254. Loyal - Brother will think the self isn't loyal, doesn't like him. 255. Fair - Brother would think it wasn't fair or it isn't fair to tell. 256. Usual - Usually brothers don't tell, stick together. 257. Expectations - If don't tell, brother will think actor will always support him when he lies.		
3			381. Owe - Brother's silence is seen as a debt to be paid back. 382. Important - But this situation is more important than a matter of favors. 383. 2 wrongs - Tell because 2 wrongs don't make a right.
4	451. Brother - Telling would involve some disloyalty to brother, a lack of concern for his welfare. 452. Father - it is a matter between the brother and the father only.	461. Situation - Whether more important to be good son or father depends on the situation, individuals. 462. Case - In extreme cases, should tell, not here.	461. Contract - A limited concern about contract and confidence. 482. Agree - Would be going back on his word; they agree. 483. 1st place - Brother told shouldn't have in first place if wanted it secret, unless secured promise. 464. Exchange - is not obligated as contract is.
5		561. Good father - a good father wouldn't demand a brother tell.	561. Trust - Brother trusted self not to tell; a concern about maintaining a trusting relation.

5. Husband role. Orientation to a family member or a relative whom one needs and are identified with. May be an act of exchange, but not of sacrifice or duty.

6. Injustice. Druggist's "cheating" makes it natural to steal. However, not actually indignant at the druggist, who may be seen as within his rights to charge whatever he wants.

Type 2 - Oriented to being a good family person in context where stealing would not be too disapproved.

1. Value. Intentions concern. Act justified because of the great and natural concern of the husband and his desperateness in the situation.

2. Choice. Indecisive as to right and wrong, but a natural action the self and most people would do. Focus is on the not disapproving, not on a categorical decision about the act.

3. Sanction. Says that other people wouldn't disapprove, or that the self wouldn't - that court may be lenient.

4. Stealing rule. More concern than Type 1 that stealing is bad in the situation. Husband is "willing to do anything," "really desperate."

5. Husband role. Most or any husband would love his wife enough to do it. Shouldn't steal for a friend.because don't like a friend that much (to risk jail)

6. Justice. Orientation to druggist as a mean or selfish person.

Type 3 - A categorical attitude toward stealing in conflict with some sense of responsibility for life and some indignation at druggist.

1. Value. Acknowledgment of the importance of the end, of the extremeness of the situation, e.g., a life is at stake. (In Type 0, there was an actual comparison of the importance of a life vs. of the drug, not a reaction to the urgency of the situation.) Makes a demand for certainty before stealing.

2. Choice. To some extent, sees act of stealing as one of desperation, loss of control. Some distrust of the emotional reaction of the natural self. Says no at first but may waiver, decide should steal.

3. Sanction. No mention of punishment as a sanction. May be a concern for restoring gestures to undo the wrong of stealing.

4. Rule. Some categorization of stealing as always wrong. A resistance to making exceptions to rules. A possible invocation of harming the druggist or his property rights. It is as if a decision had been made in the past that "stealing is wrong" and the decision cannot be changed for this case.

5. Husband role. A sense of obligation to the wife independent of affection, being good, etc. May be defined as delegated duty to protect, as unlimited responsibility for the safety of someone or something in one's care.

6. Justice. Some indignation against the druggist, but this does not legitimize stealing. May believe druggist is within his rights to gain the rewards of his labor.

Type 4 - Oriented to the law itself to some extent an "arbitrary" discounting of the individual situation

1. Value. The ends, situation, does not justify the means.

2. Choice. The conflict is between the legal judgment and what anyone, the rational individual would do, or is justified in doing. Expects that the legal social system could not allow such a dilemma to arise. Though "wrong," legally, tendency to say should steal.

3. Sanction. Orientation to law beyond the punishment it would involve. From the point of view of rational prudence, should risk jail.

4. Rule. Oriented to the legal judgment in this particular case, rather than the weight of the concept of stealing.

5. Role. Duty to wife is within and limited by the general legal framework. A wife should not expect a husband to steal. However, a rational and natural person would prefer stealing and jail to the loss of his wife, in a case like that.

6. Justice. Druggist still has his legal rights, regardless of his unfairness. The unfairness of the druggist is irrelevant to the legal and rational decision, though it is perceived.

Type 4 - 5 - Perceive all Type 4 features but more willingness to see action as actually right on the side of the values of the situation and justice.

1. Value. Emphasis on value of a life.

2. Choice process. Though the act is legally wrong, it is justified, right to the rational and good actor under these narrow conditions.

5. Role. If absolutely necessary, would do it for a friend, etc.

6. Justice. No justice on the druggist's side in a case of life, a sense that druggist is violating rights of life.

SITUATION 111 - CODING FORM

Type	1. Value Modes	2. Choice and 3. Sanctions, Motives	4. Rule of Stealing
·	011. Better - Better for self to let wife die than go to jail. 012. Importance - Life is more important than a drug.	031. Punished - Has to go to jail.	041. Alternate means - Could buy it, work for it, instead of stealing it.
1	111. Has - Has to or else wife will die. 112. Need - He needs it badly (is main justification). 113. Reason - Wants it for a reason.	131. Restorability - Maybe can get out of punishment bt paying later.	141. Harm - Not really harming the druggist.
2		231. Blame - I, no one, would blame him, disapprove. 232. Punishment - His punishment will be modified. 221. R&W - Act is right and wrong. Not right but would do it.	
3	311. Necessary - Only if absolutely necessary. 312. Knowledge - Must be certain drug will work.	321. Desperate - Sees stealing as act of desperation, loss of control. 322. No choice - Had no choice. 331. Restorability - If steels he must have the intention of paying later.	341. Categorical - It's still stealing and stealing is always wrong; even here.
·	411. Ends - Says ends do not justify means. 412. Not responsible - If society provides no legitimate means to drug, it is out of his hands.	431. Prudence - Would prefer stealing, years in jail, to having wife die.	441. Legalism - The law would judge him wrong or guilty.
·			511. Case - Only under these narrow conditions is it all right.

SITUATION III - CODING FORM--Continued

Type	5. Husband Role (and Friend Role)	6. Druggist's Rights and His Injustice	9. Rights re Shooting
	051. Good - Says good husband wouldn't steal (on probe)		091. Label - All right to shoot someone stealing. 092. Punished - Storekeeper will be punished for murder. 093. Importance - Can shoot because has an important drug.
1	151. If likes - if he likes his wife, he will steal. 152. Exchange - only steal as an exchange deal. 153. Relative - only steal for a relative.	181. Afford it - Shouldn't charge because people can't afford it. 182. Cheating - Druggist is cheating, charging too much, as mitigating stealing.	191. Self defense - All right to shoot, self-defense. 192. Role-take - You wouldn't want to die; it's him or you.
2	251. Love - Mentions that husband would love her enough to do it. 252. Good friend - would only steal if a very good friend. 253. Concern - wouldn't be that concerned about a friend.	281. Profit - Druggist trying to support family, entitled to some profit, etc. 282. Help - Druggist supposed to help people with the drug. 283. Mean - The druggist is mean, greedy, etc. 284. Fault - Really the druggist's fault.	293. Intentions - All right to shoot because protecting self, property, didn't know the situation.
3	351. Duty - a fixed duty to protect wife, based on marriage oath, etc. 352. Friend - A responsibility to a friend doesn't go that far, help in other ways.	381. 2 wrongs - Druggist is wrong but so is Heintz. 382. 2 wrongs - Not Heintz's responsibility if wife dies, but druggist's. 383. Earned - Druggist worked to get drug, deserves some profit. 384. Knows - He knows the druggist is wrong.	391. Right - Druggist has a right to shoot to protect his property.
4	451. Anyone - Anyone would do it. 452. Expectation - wife shouldn't expect him to steal.	481. Imprudent - Druggist being imprudent, unreasonable, even if he has right to charge. 482. Regulate - Government should regulate a scarce drug.	491. Warn - Druggist should warn before shoots (with implication of giving him a fair chance. 492. Legal - Shouldn't shoot back, be more guilty; shouldn't have entered in first place. 493. Anyone - Anyone would, however.
		561. Druggist is wrong, has no moral rights in the situation.	

Situation IV - Global Rating Guide

Type 0 - A "don't touch" attitude to life based on external authority.

1. **Value.** May imply some projective value to the woman's life, or body as a "thing."

2. **Choice.** Doesn't identify with Dr. or woman. Says not to mercy kill.

3. **Sanction.** Thinks Dr. should be punished on probe. Doesn't seem to identify with Dr. enough to stress he should avoid punishment.

4. **Rule.** If killing labels are applied, their force is unmodified by the situation.

5. **Role.** Sees the right to take the life of the woman as belonging to some external force whether husband, government, or father whose prerogatives are being interefered with.

Type 1 - Hedonistic and "private-property" view of life.

1. **Value.** Instrumental hedonistic view of life. Painful life no good. Humans different from animals only in being less dependent on others to put them away or in being less instrumentally useful to another individual.

2. **Choice.** Decision is to mercy-kill. Little conflict. Identifies with patient, e.g., "I'd want it."

3. **Sanction.** Doesn't understand that an act is punishable or suggests Dr. could avoid punishment by making it look natural, etc.

4. **Killing rule.** Act of killing isn't bad because has no effects, e.g., die anyway, she wanted it. May recommend suicide to avoid murder label.

5. **Role.** Sees the prerogative as the woman's, since it's her life.

Type 2 - Empathic and familial view of life.

1. **Value.** Value of life rests on ego's affection for family and family's affection for ego. Expectation of both sympathy for pain by all concerned and of empathic revulsion for killing.

2. **Choice.** Indecision. Tends to identify with Dr. Responds to lack of certainty, may advise that Dr. wait and see. Favors mercy-killing, but reluctant.

3. **Sanction.** Law and punishment not stressed.

5. **Role.** Sees family wishes as to be consulted, but not as authoritative. Doctor role primarily determined by conformity and help to patient.

Type 3

1. **Value.** Some sense of the lesser of the two evils. A sense of life as having a value beyond its pleasure, but not absolutistic about life being of value regardless of its uses.

2. **Choice.** A demand for certainty before acting. If law allowed, might do it in this case.

3. **Sanction.** Some concern about possible punishment but not the determining consideration.

4. **Killing rule.** Some sense of act being wrong as killing but doesn't really see it as killing in the bad sense; e.g., hurting someone else. Sees it more as suicide, which is bad. Labels retain some force in the situation, but are attenuated.

5. **Role.** Family is rather irrelevant. Doctor has some responsibility for dealing with woman's pain. Basically it is the woman'd decision to make, her responsibility to decide what is best; her pain.

Type 4 - Conflict between legal-professional code and utilitarian logic.

1. **Value.** A utilitarian view. Concerned about making a legitimate practice of euthanasia, but can't really object in this particular case. Few expressions of feeling, empathizing.

2. **Choice.** A conflict between the rules, perceived as social codes, and rational utility. "May not be right" but tends to identify with Dr. as deciding to mercy-kill.

3. **Sanction.** The legal wrong is mentioned but not punishment.

4. **Killing rule.** Sees it as an agreed upon law or professional code, not as categorical wrong action of killing. It is not really murder, killing, except in terms of the code.

5. **Role.** Same as Type 3, with additional professional code definition of role.

Type 5 - In some sense the most concerned of all about "killing," but completely non-punitive toward the doctor. Concern about a generalized respect for life. (It is sometimes difficult to distinguish this type from Type 2 or 3 in Catholics.)

SITUATION IV - Coding Form

Type	1. Value	2. Choice and Certainty	3. Sanction
0	011. Longer - Better to live longer; simply implying a bigger life is better. 012. Let her live - until she dies; implying leave it to fate.	021. Certainty - She might get over it. 022. Certainty - They might find a cure.	031. Punish - Get punished.
1	111. Hedonism - No use for her to live. 112. Role-take - I wouldn't want the pain.	121. Certainty - will die anyway.	131. Avoid punishment - Dr. could do it so it looked natural; was less punishable.
2	211. Favor - Doing her a favor in a way. 212. Empathize - Hard on Dr.; feels sorry for her, etc.	222. Wait - Should wait before deciding. 223. Leave to Dr. - Dr. would know what to do best; boy. wouldn't.	
3	311. Suffer - Can't let her suffer. 312. Lesser evil - Better than letting her suffer, etc.	321. Certainty - They can't be certain she will die. Miracles 322. Certainty - She didn't know what she was saying; didn't really mean it. 323. Certain - If they're absolutely certain; if they've done all they can.	331. Conscience - His conscience would bother him afterward.
4		421. Consult - Dr. must consult a group of specialists etc. One man shouldn't make decision. 422. Utilitarian - Not really right, but if I were he, etc. Up to the Dr., etc.	
5		521. Decision - No human can make the decision.	

SITUATION IV - CODIGN FORM--Continued

Type	4. Killing Rule	5. Husband, Dr. Role Rights and Duties	9. Why Put Away Animals, Not People?
0	041. Murder - It would be murder. 042. Law - Breaking the law. 043. Alternative - Could give something else to help the pain.	051. Ownership - Husband has authority to make decision; it's his wife. 052. Husband want - Husband wouldn't want it. 053. No right - Dr. has no right to do it; meaning "not allowed."	091. Undifferentiated - Either says mercy-kill people like animals or says don't mercy-kill animals. 092. People - Are more important with no definite meaning to important. 093. Rabies - Animals spread disease.
1	141. Murder - Wouldn't be murder because would have died anyway. 142. Suicide - She should commit suicide.	151. Ownership - It's her life, her decision re jurisdiction of law, Dr. 152. Asked - Do it because she asked.	191. Suicide - If people want to die, can commit suicide. 192. Live longer - People live longer.
2	241. Murder - Not murder unless want to kill him.	251. See Family - Seh wants to see family, they her. 252. Consult - Consult husband, family. 253. Job - A Dr. is supposed to save lives.	291. Family - Not like someone in your family; don't love them the same. 292. Identify - Don't want to kill your own species.
3	341. Taking a life - 342. Still - Still it's killing, etc. 343. Suicide - isn't right to commit suicide.	351. Contract - Dr. being paid to do what patient wants; is his duty. 352. Consult - Consult authorities as to whether he can do it. 354. Irrelevant - Husband's wishes irrelevant; doesn't really know how she's feeling. 355. Her decision - Meaning she has the hard decision.	391. Important - People are more important to society. 392. Intelligent - People are more intelligent. 393. Higher class - People are a different, higher class.
4	441. Murder - Really is murder in the eyes of the law, etc.	451. Code - Violates Dr.'s code.	
5	541. Killing - No one should be killed. 542. No right - No human being has the right to take a life.	551. Husband altruistic - If really best, if she's in terrible pain, husband would want what was best for her.	591. Feelings - Animal has feelings too, but humans have more, different feelings. 592. Shouldn't treat people in the same way as animals.

Situation V - Global Rating Guide

Type 0 - An orientation to the power and vague value of the captain.

1. Value. Some vague sense of the projective importance of the captain; that he shouldn't be the one to be killed; that he is needed. If oriented to group survival, it is as avoiding a bad happening; not an orientation to the logic of the one for the many.

2. Choice. May be some identification with captain's point of view is one of mixed preference for saving himself and feeling of usefulness to the army. The captain should send another.

4. Rule. Usually doesn't really see sending another as violating a killing rule (thought it is possible for Type 0 to apply a killing label).

5. Captain role. No sense that it is part of the captain's code to go himself.

6. Authority. Ordering a man is simply part of the captain's boss role, part of his recognized activity of ordering.

8. Distributive justice. Not concerned about inequality aspect.

Type 1 - An "every man for himself" attitude.

1. Value. Not much concern about the survival of all. Essentially that each person should look out for himself. The value of blowing up the bridge is essentially not shared; it is the captain's project.

2. Choice. The captain should go. May maintain it is not necessary for anyone to go or be sacrificed.

3. Sanctions. Doesn't mentione sanctions in the situation.

4. Rule. Usually doesn't say sending someone is "killing," but may.

5. Captain role. Captain may be considered a coward not to go, but not as undutiful or cruel. "Being brave" for an egoistic or for a dutiful purpose are not discriminated.

6. Captain's authority. Has no authority over someone else's life; viewed as the owner's property. Not clear that sees captain as having a necessary function.

8. Distributive justice. Sense that ordering a man is both imposing on his authority and is unequal.

Type 2 - Orientation to a "good and brave captain" stereotype.

1. Value. A recognition that someone must die to save the rest. Some set that the person dying is doing good, will be a hero, etc.

2. Choice. An effort to justify the captain's going as the best solution from a utilitarian point of view. The captain should go.

4. Rule. Does not actually invoke a rule that it is killing to order someone.

5. Role. Some sense that it is a good captain's job to go himself, to perform the risky tasks.

6. Authority. Captain has the authority to order though shouldn't. Has various relevant abilities.

8. Justice. Drawing lots recognized as "fairer."

Type 3 - An orientation to the authority as obligated to conform to rules about killing. (Some children classified here probably have more like a Type 0 orientation to killing taboos.)

1. Value. Primarily oriented to the life the captain is responsible for if he orders someone.

2. Choice. Tends to accept the advantage of ordering someone as per instructions. But not too much conflict. Decision not to order someone.

3. Sanction. May believe the captain would be court martialed for ordering someone.

4. Rule. A fairly categorical attitude about "ordering someone to his death." A responsibility for someone's death rather than a labelling as killing. Would be legitimate to ask for volunteers.

5. Role. May be some disclaiming of heroism aspects.

6. Authority. A sense of strong but limited authority of the captain though the bounds of authority may be or may not include ordering someone. (Where mixed with Type 2 elements, feels that ordering someone would make the men lose respect.)

8. Justice. May suggest drawing lots as a solution.

Type 4 - A conflict between utilitarian rationality and the right of the individual to retain control of his life.

1. **Value.** Sees the utilitarian solution of ordering from an economic logic or "no use" point of view. Sees it as justified from the point of view of group welfare which is the legitimate goal of the leader.

2. **Choice.** Quite indecisive. Starts fairly categorically but may move to the utilitarian view without fully accepting it.

3. **Sanction.** May wonder about having the courage to sacrifice self in that situation.

4. **Rule.** Emphasis on the individual's right to refuse to volunteer; right not to give up his life.

5. **Role.** As in topics 1 and 6.

6. **Authority.** The question of the captain's authority to order someone, is a question of what army regulations are and what the limits of the armh's power to make regulations is.

8. **Justice.** Focus on everyone's equal right to life, even if misused, rather than questions of partiality.

Type 5 - A concern about the absolute value of lives, per se, leads to an overcoming of formalistic concern about the right to life in this situation. If fully intellectualized, the line of thought would be: Sending a man is not killing if everyone will really die without it. The captain is in a sense responsible for the lives of the men who would be lost because he decided to perform the mission himself. He does not have to act so as to demonstrate his own willingness to sacrifice himself; this is a factor he may know from within. No man has the right to refuse to draw lots and sacrifice the group's lives for his own right to live. The only obstacle in ordering in this situation lies in singling someone out and so implying that his life is not of equal value with the others. This can be obviated by drawing lots.

Situation VI - Global Rating Guide

Type 0 - Orientation to getting rid of bad people and to success of mission.

1. **Value.** May see troublemaker (or even sick man) as a vague danger to get rid of. In general, oriented to predicting and avoiding bad happenings to which lives are instrumental, rather than to the lives themselves.

2. **Choice.** Tends to favor sending the troublemaker.

SITUATION V - CODING FORM

Type	1. Value	2. Choice	3. Rule
0	011. Need - Men because need the men to win war, etc. 012. Important - Better to save the life of the captain because he is more important.		031. Murder - It's murder to order; e.g., simply labelling. 032. Alternate means - Shouldn't send because can destroy bridge in another way.
1			
2	211. Sacrifice - Has to die to save all the rest; sense of heroism. 212. Family - Someone should go who has no family, etc.	221. Unwilling - If orders someone unwilling, won't do good job.	
3			330. Kills - Ordering someone to his death; like killing. 332. Regs. - Army regs. wouldn't allow it.
4	411. Wasteful - Can't lose whole company for the sake of one man. 412. Group perspective - Best from standpoint of group.		431. Right - Captain can't violate the right of the man to decide whether or not to go.
5			

SITUATION V - CODING FORM.--Continued

Type	4. Captain's Role Obligation	5. Captain's Authority - Does He Have Right to Order? Does Man Have Right to Refuse?	6. Injustice, Inequality Aspect (Drawing Straws Responses)
0		051. Right - He's the chief, he can do what he wants, give the orders. 052. Refuse - Shouldn't, can't refuse; capt. wants it--he ordered.	061. Don't draw - Sees no advantage to drawing straws, waste time, etc.
1	141. Coward - He's just a coward if he doesn't go.		161. His idea - Others don't want to, his flee. Let him go. 162. Draw straws - Everyone would have the same chance. 163. Favoritism - Eliminates picking on someone.
2	241. Job - His job to go. 242. Good₁ - A good captain would go, risk his life for his men. 243. Good₂ - Wouldn't want to order, send someone.	251. Ability - Capt. could perform mission, escape better than a subordinate. 252. Refuse₁ - Should obey cause captain knows best. 253. Refuse₃ - Shouldn't refuse because doing something for good of country.	
3	341. Respect - If orders, will lose the respect of his men.	351. Refuse₁ - It's man's duty to go, has no right in the situation to refuse. 352. Refuse₂ - Should go because captain earned his rank, his authority. 353. Army rights - Army can't authorize captain to violate man's rights.	361. Suggests draw straws - Not ordering someone.
4		451. Army Regs.- May give him right to order. 452. Refusal₁- May have right to refuse as human, not as ... 453. Refusal₂- Captain had no right to order so has right to refuse.	461. Drawing conditional₁ - Drawing straws a solution only if everyone agrees; then the chance one took in drawing. 462. Drawing conditional₂- Not too good if leads to not sending the best man not maximizing utility.
5			

8. Justice. No orientation to fairness. Some of the older children of this type may invoke retaliation against troublemaker.

Type 1 - Oriented to the objective equality of lives because of indifference to other factors.

1. Value. More oriented to the value of the life to its owner himself, and hence a concern shading over into distributive equality.

2. Choice. Send sick man.

8. Justice. Orientation to sending the one with the least to live for. No punitive orientation to troublemaker.

Type 2 - A concern about which person it is nicer to send and which person is being good go go.

1. Value. An effort to show a concern for the interests of the two men. Invokes "extraneous" values to the man, getting a medal, seeing his family, etc.

2. Choide. Either.

8. Justice. Tends to orient to the sick man's interests. Sympathy may lead to "doing the favor" of sending him, or to a concern not to take advantage of the weak.

Type 3 - Group utility with some punitiveness to which limits are set.

1. Utility. A tendency to value the men in terms of their long range value to the company.

2. Choice. Send the sick man. (Some favor sending the troublemaker, however.)

3. Justice. Some punitive orientation to troublemaker but doesn(t accept such an extreme punishment, and modifies punishment by group utility considerations. Distributive justice is in terms of the one more likely to escape.

Type 4 - Not very distinct from Type 3 except more abstracted from the situation.

1. Value. Less oriented to group utility and more oriented to the logic of losing an extra life.

2. Choice. Send sick man.

3. Justice. A set that this is not an occasion for punitive justice, a sort of "taking the law into one's own hands." A set continued from Situation V not to violate the rights of the man sent.

Type 5 - Oriented to the injustice of using the situation to punish the troublemaker. Otherwise, like Type 4.

416

SITUATION VI - CODING FORM

Type	1. Values and Utility	8. Distributive Justice	8. Punitive Justice
0	011. 2 men - Send both men to make sure job done. 012. Riddance - Sick man might infect others; get rid of him. 013. Avoid disaster - Send one who will not desert or die on way, or otherwise cause trouble.	081. Certainty - Sick man might get over it. 082. Relativism - If captain doesn't like one of men, would send him. 083. Fairness - Means one who will do the job better.	083. Riddance - Troublemaker may kill someone, so get rid of him. 084. Similarity - Troublemaker didn't kill anyone so shouldn't be killed (on probe). 085. Trial - Didn't have a trial. 086. Deserves - Troublemaker did something; sick man did nothing.
1	111. Willing - Sick man less likely to desert because he has nothing to lose.	181. Die now - Sick man will die anyway; might or will die now.	182. Restore - Can restore what he stolo. 183. Relativism - Captain would think it a fair punishment; the man wouldn't.
2	211. Family - Sick man's family wants to see him; he them. 212. Favor - It's doing the sick man a favor to send him; in pain. 213. Favor, Allow sick man to get a medal since must die anyway, do something for his country.	281. Sympathy for weak - Concern for the sick man being less able to escape, or of taking advantage of the weak	282. Bad - Troublemaker wasn't t@ bad.
3	311. Function - Troublemaker still can be made to perform his tasks; the sick man can't, relative to group survival.	381. Escape - The fairer one to send is the man more likely to escape.	382. Punishment - Mission isn't, shouldn't be looked at as punishment. 383. Reform - Troublemaker can reform, learn his lesson later. 384. Function - A guy like that is just no good in a group; in a way they're better off without him.
4	411. Economy - Captain has no business losing two lives instead of one.	481. Will - Less violating the will of the sick man to send him.	482. Crime - Isn't really a criminal; can't use that as a punishment.
5	511. Utility - Shouldn't judge life and death by usefulness to group.		

Situation VIII - Global Rating Guide

Type 0 - Oriented to punishment, anger, and objective physical damage.

1. Value. Some concern for the intrinsic value of the property and the ob-jective physical damage done; i.e., some value set on restorability apart from escaping punishment. Worse one is the one less willing or able to restore damage. May think one who stole not so bad because may pay back, i.e., "intentions" is not judged except in terms of consequences may lead to, and in terms of explicit mention in the story.

2. Choice. Either may be worse. "Both worse." Tends to think stealing worse.

3. Sanction. Concern about punishment. Thinks worse punishment for lying if lying is mentioned as worse.

4. Rules of stealing, cheating. A primitive orientation to the "form" of the act beyond its consequences in terms of the bolder act, the one which is a direct flaunting of the victim or which would surprise or shock him more.
Either "no one knew it" "not asking" makes it worse, or "going right up and lying."

5. Role. The worse person is the more punished. Friendship irrelevant except in terms of implication for restoration.

8. Justice. Reaction of victims based on objective damage and possibility of restoration or on boldness of culprit, not on disappointed expecta-tions.

Type 1 - Reduction of both acts to need consequences for self (and other).

1. Value. Possible concern form, or denial that, cash is needed by the vic-time for a concrete purpose.

2. Choice. Unhesitant or unqualified choice that stealing is worse.

3. Sanction. Consideration of which can escape punishment more easily a dominant concern in comparison.

4. Rules of stealing and cheating. No concern about the lying element. Realistic view of cheating in terms of elements making it safer, and a positive view of it as cleverer.

5. Role. No concept of worse person. Worse to cheat a friend because lose a friend, get bad reputation, etc.

8. <u>Justice</u>. Reactions of victims as self-interested more than punitive, not oriented to disappointed expectations.

Type 2 - Orientation to informal disapproval value of the two acts.

1. <u>Value</u>. Adds up disapproved actions and intentions, eg., lying plus stealing is worse than just stealing.

2. <u>Choice</u>. Says cheating is worse.

3. <u>Sanction</u>. Wishes to think both equally punishable.

4. <u>Rules of stealing, cheating</u>. Focus on lying or on cheating. Conceive of lying as deceiving another person.

5. <u>Role</u>. Oriented to a concept of the worse person, sees act as worse if directed against a person who is good or likes you, e.g., a friend or a philanthropic person.

8. <u>Justice</u>. Some sense of victim's disapproval, at the lying, but not a stressing of the victim's disapporited expectations as a final criteria.

Type 3 - More internalized orientation to rule and to harmful consequences than Type 0.

1. <u>Value</u>. More set to economic consequences than Type 2, use of money for public services, existence of insurance, etc.

2. <u>Choice</u>. An effort to discount approval aspects and get down to hard categories and consequences. "Both the same, neither intended to pay back," "both are stealing." <u>If forced to say, cheating is worse.</u>

3. <u>Sanction</u>. Some concern about the law, but punishment not the dominant motive. But own judgment not usually differentiated from law aspect.

4. <u>Stealing</u>. A categorical attitude toward stealing, and a sense of identification with the victim and his rights.

5. <u>Role</u>. A set to ignore the niceness of the actor or the victim.

6. <u>Justice</u>. Victim's concern based on objective loss, disappointment at hard-earned expectations, or disturbance of public function.

Type 4 - A fairly hardheaded but contractual orientation.

2. <u>Choice</u>. Some indecision as a Type 3 categoricalness, but definitely decides cheating is worse.

3. <u>Sanction</u>. Clearly aware law is worse in stealing, but does not determine the decision.

4. **Stealing rule, cheating rule.** Emphasis on cheating as "giveng your word," as contract, rather than as not "being nice."

5. **Role.** Some sense of cheating as greater deviation from a reliable self.

6. **Justice.** Loaner seen as trusting, but a rather impersonal concept of trust, e.g., disappointed trust is disappointed expectation of payment, sense of cheating as taking unfair advantage. Victim would be angry both at himself and culprit.

Type 5 - Type 4 with additional elements.

2. **Choice.** Cheating worse clearly.

4. **Stealing** and cheating rule. Act of stealing is not as bad because impersonal. Legal view is irrelevant in comparison.

5. **Role.** Some sense of cheating as building a false self-image.

8. **Justice.** Emphasis on victim's reaction of disappointment in image of the borrower as worthy and of himself as doing something good, e.g., losing faith in trustability of human nature. Some sense of the unusual nature of loaner's trust.

Situation VIII - Global Rating Guide

Type 0 - Compliance with authority, often with a sense of the inevitability of punishment.

1. **Value and utility.** Little concern for convict's philanthropic activities.
   i) Concern displayed is in terms of future consequences, of not having H. there to run things.
   ii) Or focus on H's factory, importance, instead of on worthiness.

2. **Choice - report convict.** (May be indecisive.)

3. **Sanction.** Some concern that might be punished if didn't report convict. Tends to believe convict will get worse punishment if not reported.

4. **Standard.** Primary concern is obedience to police. Definition of telling as reporting a bad act or person as well as obedience.

5. **Role.** Friendship and family roles do not change "duty," but this is not because of a general set to ignore circumstances.

8. **Punitive justice.** No concept of personal merit. Punishment as given and unchangeable; e.g., H. has to complete his sentence. No expectation of mercy.

SITUATION VII - CODING FORM

Type	1. Value	2. Choice and 3. Sanctions	4. Stealing Rule
3	011. Intention - Cheater had no intention of returning so worse. 012. Restorability re the victim's interest, or authority. 013. Damage - Amount of physicl damage done.	031. Punishment - The worse is the one with the worse fixed punishment. 032. Punishment - Punishment or trouble with some sense of affect, severity later regret, etc. 033. Punishment - One is worse because he is able to escape punishment.	041. Labelling - "breaking the law," "10 commandments," "taking someone else's property." 042. Equivalence - Doesn't see cheating as stealing, taking. 043. Boldness - Stealing as more overt deviation.
1	111. Need - one may not have as much private need as another	131. Restorability - Better means can get out of punishment easier, can pay back. 132. Expect - Leader wouldn't send cops.	
2		221. Add - Addition of labels; lied and stole. 231. Sanctions - Wants to believe there is some punishment for cheating as bad as for stealing.	241. Good - It isn't ever good, to steal, etc. 242. Worked - They work real hard in the store, for the money; said persuasively, i.e., "be nice and think of them, sympathize with them."
3	311. Insurance 312. Service - Worse is taking it from the one performing a community service. 313. Need - May force the store to close, may not be recoverable.	321. Both - Both reduce to the same.	341. Earned - He earned it; it shouldn't be taken from him. 342. Role-taking - You don't want what you earn stolen. 343. Categorical - Just shouldn't steal, have no right to.
4		431. Respect - Partner would lose respect.	441. Unequal - Victim worked hard for money, thief if didn't.
5	511. Feel worse - worse act is that which makes other feel worse in the situation.		

SITUATION VII - CODING FORM--Continued

Type	7. Cheating and Good Self	8. Justice - Victim Reaction and Expectations	9. Law Making Perspective Worse for Country, Etc.
0	051. Criminal - Become a criminal, get habit, etc., i.e., stealing. 052. Worse person means punishment likelihood. 053. Boldness - Lying as face-to-face deviation.	081. Expect - Store-owner will feel worse cause knows he won't get it back. 082. Angry - Angry because cheated, lied to.	Harmful consequences re the individual act: 091. Restorability. 092. Habit - Go on to worse things, could led to killing, etc.
1	151. Lie - Suggests culprit can lie to get out of punishment. 152. Friend - Lose your friends if cheat a friend. 153. Friend - A friend might not call in the cops.	181. Others' responsibility - Not so bad to cheat because it was his own free will. 182. Role-taking - If you had a store, wouldn't like being stolen from.	
2	251. Friend - Worse to cheat and violate a friendship. 252. Other - Other person was doing a favor, was nice.		
3		381. Work - Worse is taking from one who had to work harder. 382. Work - Feel worse as above. 383. Equal - Both out the same money.	391. Stealing worse - Worse for country is harmful consequences, is if everyone started doing it, getting away with it. 392. Revenge - Everyone would revenge by stealing, etc.
4	451. Deceived - A deception rather than explicit lying. 452. Taking advantage - of other's sympathy, charity, trust.	481. Blame self - Will blame himself for foolish trust, as making it worse to cheat.	491. Cheating worse - Because undermines social relation more, couldn't trust anyone.
5	551. Violating trust.	581. Disappointed motive - Thought he was doing good, could help others. 582. Impersonality - Storekeeper expects such a loss, is oriented impersonally.	

422

Type 1 - Indifferent permissive attitude or a conflict between immediate semi-egoistic needs vs Type 0 concerns.

1. Value. Some concept of convict doing good, but pretty much reduced to actual need consequences and to staying out of trouble rather than personal goodness.

2. Decision. Don't report, especially if friend or other interests involved. Sees it as a personal decision.

3. Sanction. May invent egoistic interests, rewards, bribes, fear of revenge, dependence on hospital.

4. Standard. On probe, says good citizen should report, but this is rather irrelevant.

5. Role. Friendship or family determine not telling on need grounds.

6. Punitive justice. Sees punishment as preventive and hence unnecessary in this case, since H. is not stealing now and probably won't in future (if only because doesn't need to). Punishment is not seen as unjust, however, and there is no reference to H.'s intentions and general goodness. No anticipation of mercy by authorities.

Type 2 - "Doing good" oriented.

1. Value and utility. He's activities seen as doing good, as expressing his reform, altruistic sympathies, self-sacrifice, and helping others.

2. Choice.- Conflicted. Definitely doesn't want H. to be punished but does not wish to incur disapproval of authorities. May compromise and tell, counting on authorities to be merciful. However, tendency is not to tell.

4. Standard. Wants to be helpful to the authorities. A more general orientation to the good citizen role than specific acts of obedience, reporting bad acts, or clearing oneself.

5. Role. Sentiment of loyalty to family or good friend.

6. Punitive justice. Punishment's purpose is to make people be or do good." "H. is doing more good out of jail than in." Expectation that authorities will consider merits of the case.

Type 3 - Rigid rule-maintaining orientation.

1. Value and utility. Utility is rather irrelevant. The fact that H's new life started with a deviant act tends to invalidate it. Punitive justice takes priority over utility.

2. __Choice__. In favor of reporting convict.

3. __Sanction__. If any mention of punishment for actor, it is to define re-porting as the citizen's duty.

4. __Standard__. Reporting convict is part of a tendency to actively maintain the rules and punitive justice.

5. __Role__. Friendship role does not change duty.

6. __Punitive justice__. Some acceptance of or demand for regularity, in-variability, about punishment; e.g., can't make exceptions." B. must go back and do it the right way."

Type 4 - Conflict between legal duty and utility.

1. __Value and utility__. Some sense of the citizen role as also involving concern for utility or community welfare. May be oriented to public opinion, e.g., mentions H's good community reputation, so that imprisoning is seen as a decision the community would not approve. Tends to trans-late convict's being good into social utility.

2. __Choice__. Conflict is between a legally defined citizen role and a more sympathetic and utilitarian view. Tends to see the choice as a personal decision, which a friend role would determine. First impulse may be to comply but turns to a __decision not to report__.

3. __Sanctions__. Prudent enough not to be concerned about sanctions for not reporting unless actually asked by the police.

4. __Standard__. Some sense of a citizen role as obedience to law regardless of personal judgment about the situation. Tendency to report is not because H. should be punished.

5. __Role__. Oriented to friend and family role in terms of confidentially and to the understanding view one takes (of acts) in friend role.

6. __Punitive justice__. Understands the demand for regularity as well as leniency. Sees the functions of punishment as having been unofficially carried out in this case.

Type 5 - Type 4 with much stronger concern about abetting an act of injustice.

1. __Value__. Utility, but subordinated to a more personal sense of injustice.

2. __Choice__. Opposes reporting convict.

3. __Sanction__. Least sanction oriented.

4. **Standard.** Accepts that authority is unjust in the situation but may question the implication that obedience to law be based on the individual's personal judgment as to the justice of the law.

8. **Punitive justice.** Turning H. in is letting a good person down, or invalidates the concept of trust and mutual aid on which H's philanthorpic action has been based.

Situation X - Global Rating Guide

Type 0 - Compliance with authority.

1. **Value.** No real comparison of value of the lives involved.

2. **Choice.** "Choice" made on grounds of inability to successfully deviate, e.g., family too far away, etc., but may waver. Stay at post.

3. **Sanction.** May mention possible punishment for desertion. Stay if against the law, or possible punishment. Or stay to get paid.

4. **Rule (Post-duty).** Sees "duty" as the performance of prescribed actions "going to your post, putting out fires;" not as responsibility for lives.

5. **Family role.** No rule, affect or role definition of an obligation to the family in the situation. Replaceable at home by other means.

6. **Justice.** No response to the division of labor as obligating. Enters only as probability of family being saved.

Type 1 - Pursuit of semi-selfish interests in the immediate situation.

1. **Value.** Prefers the survival of own family to that of others. (Lacks additional "goodness" elements of such a prizing shown by Type 2.) Alternately the ends justify the means; e.g., "if he didn't, they might die," "he wanted to look after his family."

2. **Choice.** Choice may rest on impulsive identification; "I'd do it," or "wouldn't you?" Choice is unconflicted. To to family.

3. **Sanction.** May imply ignoring law and punishment.

4. **Rule.** May respond in terms of actual neededness or replaceability at post.

5. **Role.** A more or less egoistic ownership or identification-based preference for the lives of family.

8. **Justice** - Same as Type 0.

SITUATION VIII - CODING FORM

Type	1. Value or Utility Situation	2. Choice and Use of Friend Role	3. Sanctions
	011. Important - Heintz has factory, is important person. 012. Worse - H. will only get worse sentence if not reported.		031. Pun. He may get in trouble, be punished himself.
1	111. Needed - He is needed to run the hospital.	121. Up to him.	131. Bribe - Get bribe from H. 132. Reward - Get reward. 133. Revenge - H. would avenge himself if reported. 134. Use - May need to use H's hospital.
2	211. Good - He is trying to help people, doing charity, doing good for his country.	221. Lenient - Authorities would be lenient, so not so bad to turn him in. 222. Persuade - Persuade judge to be lenient, tell his deeds. 223. H. friend - If good friend, don't tell on H.	
3	311. Good - He is doing more good out than in jail.	321. Friend irrelevant - Friendship irrelevant re duty to report.	331. Punish - is guilty legally for not reporting, used to define citizen role.
4	411. Reputation - H. has a good reputation in community, has proved self worthy.	421. Persuade - Might try to persuade H. to give self up, but not tell. 422. Understand - A friend would understand H's actions.	
5		521. Trust - Trusted friend and community.	531. Couldn't - I couldn't get myself to turn culprit in, in such a case. Some sense of remorse about it.

Type	4. Law and Citizen Role	8. Punitive Justice	9. Privileged Communication to Wife and Psychiatrist
6	611. Cops - Police are looking for him; should obey, help police.	081. Escaped - He escaped, broke out of jail.	091. Has to - wife has to report husband, can't understand doesn't have to.

426

Type	4. Law and Citizen Role	8. Punitive Justice	9. Privileged Communication to Wife and Psychiatrist
0	042. Law - Against law not to tell.	082. Has to - Has to finish his term. Impersonal necessity.	092. Again - Might do it again.
1	141. Business - Not tailor's business to report; or doesn't have to; can do what he wants.	181. Trouble - Staying out of trouble now. 182. Chance - Give him another chance. 183. Again - He won't steal again because doesn't need to, or hasn't been stealing.	191. Revenge - Wife's immunity is to prevent revenge, killing her. 192. Interests - Dr. would lose business, wife support, etc.
2	241. If cops want - If cops really are looking, tell so as not to frustrate.	281. Bad - Wasn't too bad in first place. 282. Role-take - If sent back, H. would only get mad.	291. Feel - Law allows because knows wife; psychiatrist would find it hard to tell. 292. Help - Because Dr. is helping cure him. 293. Break up - Break up marriage.
3	341. Duty - It is a citizen's duty to tell. 342. Deserve - Good citizen would probably think he deserved it.	381. Suffer - H. has suffered enough. 382. Correct - Did wrong in escaping, must make it up. 383. Role-take - T. should take role of the vengeful victim. 384. Exceptions - Can't make exceptions.	391. Shouldn't - Wife or Dr. should tell if doing something wrong, serious. 392. Bad law - A bad law cause go free though committed crime. 393. Code - Because Dr. has code not to tell.
4	441. Up to citizen - In this case it is the individual citizen's decision in situation, if considers. 442. If me - Not saying I'm real good citizen, but I wouldn't. 443. Tell but - Tailor's legal duty to tell--independent of whether he should be jld.	481. 20 years - After 20 years, can't expect recurrence of crime, etc. 482. 1st place - H. shouldn't have been sent to jail in 1st place. 483. Qua - Qua convict, return qua person no.	491. Confidence - Law should allow a sphere of confidence, privacy. 492. Protect client - To protect client from possible abuse, of confidence by Dr.
5	541. Always. Can't always oppose law on basis of own judgment. 542. Unjust. The court authorities were being unjust.	561. Restoration - H. has paid any debt to community for stealing.	591. Trust - Relationships based on trust or loyalty.

Type 2 - A family-oriented being good.

1. **Value.** A set to maximize "being good," not to maximize lives saved. The good is saving lives and it is as good or bettrr to save your family's lives as anyone else's. The orientation is to "thinking of one's family" vs. "thinking of other people."

2. **Choice.** Some conflict. Deserting is right and wrong. Efforts to deny he is choosing because he is helping whichever he does. **Favors leaving post.**

3. **Sanction.** Law will change decision, but pay is irrelevant. May be concerned about family disapproval.

4. **Rule.** Tends to see post duty as a matter of "helping other people."

5. **Family role.** Defined in terms of a concern for the family and duty to them not entirely oriented to the probability that they will be safe or be helped well by others.

6. **Justice.** Same as Type 0.

Type 3.- Orientation to assigned responsibility, vital consequences, and regularity.

1. **Value.** A concern for lives lost or a smaller number of lives saved because of the actor's deviance--a sense of what the actor might feel or be responsible for. The conflict is between "what most people would do," and "what's right," as a fixed categorical rule. Maybe an orientation to the destruction of the city as more than an issue of the indivudual lives involved.

2. **Choice.** **Says to stay.**

3. **Sanctions.** Staying is somewhat contingent on pay, law, etc., rather than on abstract agreement and utility.

4. **Rule.** A statement that this contingency was ruled out in advance when the role was assigned. This may be associated with the idea that if he didn't want to commit himself, he shouldn't have done so in advance. Some sense that everyone else is doing the same thing.

5. **Family role.** Tends to limit duty in the situation. Not his responsibility in the situation, someone else's.

6. **Justice.** Some concern for unfairness to others who are conforming and who are protecting others when he protects his own family.

Type 4 - Oriented to making a rational, logical choice.

1. Value. May be some appeal to the logic or rationality of the greater god. The emphasis is not on the actual damage but on the unreasonableness of sacrificing the many for the few. Some awareness of conflicting roles as conflict between the private and public; what the actor would think and the point of view of the public, the country, etdc.

2. Choice. Some conflict. Aware of the validity of the other point of view. Recognized a certain justification or legitimacy in the individual's preferring the welfare of one's family over the welfare of the community. In a sense, choice involves standards of value or points of view which cannot be compared, subjective vs. objective or public rationality. However, the solution in this situation is in favor of objective value.

3. Sanction. Says to stay even though no pay and no law.

4. Post duty. An orientation to contractual responsibility, but this does not in itself settle the decision. More of a set of the actual expectations of government and public than Type 3.

5. Family role. Not too different from Type 2, but less oriented to love and niceness.

6. Justice. Less oriented to the reciprocity and unfairness aspect than Type 3, because of a more public-oriented and rationalistic attitude that in such an extreme situation, such personal expectancies don't count.

Type 5 - Like Type 4 but with some feeling on the public side which does not ignore the feelings of commitment to family.

1. Value. Saving the many lives is more a matter of justice than of logic. Each individual has the right to have his life protected equally.

2. Choice. A more unconditional choice to remain at the post. At the same time an effort to genuinely feel or verbalize the situation.

3. Sanction. Duty does not depend on sanctions or law. More expression of feelings of concern for the vital values, possible remorse, etc., than the other types.

4. Post-duty. Same as Type 4, but more conception of it in terms of public welfare.

5. Family role. An expectation that they should expect actor to do the right even at their cost.

6. Justice - As in 1.

SITUATION IX - CODING FORM

Type	1. Value	2. Choice and 3. Sanction	4. Post duty
		021. Both - Should do both, protect family and do assigned task. 022. Both - Could take fire engine to own house, etc. 031. Punishment - Would get punished for leaving. 032. Pay - Stay to get paid.	041. Act - Prescribed activity supposed to put out fire, not supposed to leave, mention activity didn't do. 042. Job - His job. 043. Law - Breaking the law. 044. Label - Desertion.
1	111. Relativism - He values family more as a primary basis of choice, implying not concerned about others.	121. I would - Egocentric or impulsive identification with actor. 122. Wouldn't you?	141. Substitute - Maybe someone else would replace him. 142. Need - They need him at the post. 143. Need - Don't need him, 144. Law - Right even if against the law.
2	211. Intent - You're saving, helping people when you help family. 212. Intent - You're protecting family by being at post. 213. Intent - He was intending to do both tasks, so shouldn't be punished for going to family first.	221. Both right and wrong - In a way. 222. Most - What most would do provides the answer. 223. Natural - Only natural, etc.	241. Help - Support to help, protect save other people. 242. Law unnatural - Law shouldn't force men to stay apart from their families.
3	311. Quantity - Save more lives. 312. Responsible - Someone dies because of him, probably. 313. City - Whole city might be destroyed because of him. 314. City - Helping his country more by staying at post.	321. Most - Most men would but it's not right.	341. Rule - Assigned in advance to perform duties at all times. 342. Contract - Knew what he was getting in to. 343. Payment - Payment increases obligation. 344. Responsible - Delegated responsibility for lives. 345. Permission - Might ask authorities, men, for permission to go.
4		421. Usually - Usually one's first duty is to the family but-- 422. Stay even though no pay and no law, because of contractual responsibility.	

SITUATION IX - CODING FORM--Continued

Type	1. Value	2. Choice and 3. Sanction	4. Post Duty
5	511. Equal value - Others whom he must look after are someone's loved ones, family. 512. Many over the few - if used as a principle.	521. Feelings - His natural feelings themselves shouldn't decide the issue. 522. Retrospective - Must act so that his own later judgment would approve.	
Type	8. Family Role and Rule; and Citizen vs. Family	8. Division of Labor Aspect	9. Expectations, what Others Men, Public and Family Would Think 091. Fam. think - (On probe) fam. would think he had to stay at post. 092. Coward - Other men would be mad, think a coward.
3			191. D.K. - Wouldn't know, would think him dead, etc.
1	151. Owner - Protect his own family; based on ownership or investment in them. 152. Worry - You're worried about your family, not about other people. 153. Substitute - Can get along without him at home, get to shelter.	181. D.L. as utility - Others protecting his family (means only) it is unnecessary to desert.	
2	251. Love - You love your family, etc. 252. Worry - You're naturally very worried about your family. 253. Protect - You're supposed to protect, care for your family at all times. 254. First duty - is to your family. 255. Citizen - A good citizen thinks about others as well as his family.		291. Family think - Family would think he didn't care about them. 292. Expect - Family look to him for protection. 293. Role-take - Would understand because they have family too, etc., think him a good family man.

SITUATION IX - CODING FORM--Continued

Type	7. Family Role and Rule; and Citizen vs. Family	8. Division of Labor Aspect	9. Expectations, what Other Men, Public and Family Would Think
3	351. Responsibility - Isn't his fault if something happens to his family--re Div. Labor.	381. D.L. as obligating - Others were looking after his family; he should look after others'. 382. Example - Others will follow his example. 383. Everyone - If everyone deserted, chaos.	391. Lose respect - Man would lose respect. 392. Resent - They stayed; why couldn't he? Think he wasn't fair. 393. Deserter - Would consider him a deserter.
4	451. Citizen - Can't say which role comes first in general, depends on situation.		591. Family altruistic - Family would, should expect him to do what is right in situation. 592. Role-take public - Should consider expectancies of public, of people responsible for.

ALL SITUATIONS - PUNISHMENT CODING SHEET

Type	1. Situational Values, Intentions, Consequences Role-Taking Culprit	2. Choice Processes Compromise Identification with Judge Role (Including Ideal Sort)	3. Interest, Functions of Punishment
3	011. Consequences - Be punished because **well**-intentioned criminal turned out not to do any good.	021. Impersonal has to - Inevitability of being punished which involves no decision by anyone, nor a rule of quotation. 022. Ideal - Be a judge, like the power.	031. Prevention1 - Punish to prevent culprit from doing again (with disregard of motives) or because might do it again. 032. Prevention2 - Punish to prevent recurrence which is bad for culprit.
1	111. Relativism - (on probe) says whether punishment is judged, fair depends on judges' interests. 112. Role-taking - Whether judge thinks culprit had depends on whether he had been in the same situation and did the same. 113. Needed - Shouldn't punish because culprit needed object. 114. Consequences - Would have happened anyway, so don't punish.	121. Predicts - What judge would actually do, with no identification. 122. I would - Says what would do with no sense of the demands of the judge role. 123. Ideal1 - Don't want to be judge, don't like punishing, ordering. 124. Ideal2 - Don't want to be a judge, culprit dislikes, revenges.	131. Prevention - Punish to teach culprit not to 132. Example - Punishment shows not to act, rule should be obeyed. 133. Another chance - Give him another chance. (Used somewhat inappropriately.). 134. Dependents - Modify punishment because of needs for culprit's services.
2	211. Person - Culprit wasn't (being) a bad person or wasn't in past. 212. Role-taking - Role takes intentions; response of culprit as natural, appropriate; recreates demand of situation. 213. Role-taking2 - Whether judge thinks culprit acted right depends on such role-taking.	221. Predicts - Predicts how judge would think, decide, assuming that judge is good. Says what he could do, etc. 222. Modify1 - Don't give too much punishment, not the extreme, etc. 223. Modify2 - Culprit wasn't that bad to get extreme punishment.	

ALL SITUATIONS - PUNISHMENT CODING SHEET--Continued

Type	1. Situational Values, Intentions, Consequences Role-Taking Culprit	2. Choice Processes Compromise Identification with Judge Role (including Ideal Sort)	3. Interest, Functions of Punishment
	311. Purpose - Culprit didn't do act arbitrarily or for no reason.	321. Should - (Definitely verbalizes that) culprit should get a certain punishment.	331. Example - If didn't punish in this case, others (everyone) might think they could.
	312. Desperate - Act was necessary, culprit desperate, etc.	322. If me - If I were the judge . . . (and then gives impulsive reaction.)	332. $Unfair_1$ - Unfair to others who get punished for similar offenses.
3	313. Role-taking - Should role-take vengeful victim.	323. Modify - Must give some sentence because was guilty, but minimal.	333. $Unfair_2$ - Unfair to those who conform.
	314. Role-taking - Doesn't matter what judge would do, should only think of "justice."	324. Ideal - Don't want to be judge because too much responsibility, might convict innocents, difficult decisions.	334. $Prevent_1$ - To commit severe crime, must be born bad or abnormal; therefore, punishment not a deterrent.
	315. Choice - Culprit's choice was the best in that situation.		335. $Prevent_2$ - Culprit must respect punisher, authority for punishment to deter.
	411. Antecedents - Father shouldn't punish (in 1) because not right in first place.	421. D.K. - I don't know some of the relevant features of law, but given my knowledge, would say . . .	431. $Prevent_1$ - Need special techniques to rehabilitate criminals.
	412. Role-taking - Judge should role-take community opinion.	422. $Ideal_1$ - Want to be because admire his intelligence, etc.	432. $Prevent_2$ - Punishment doesn't deter unless culprit judges he did wrong.
	413. Intent - Had no criminal intent.	423. $Ideal_2$ - Want to be judge because like responsibility, knowledge decision making involved.	433. Utility - Remarks as to a need to minimize the economic costs of imprisonment.
	414. $Role-taking_2$ - Anyone would do it (implying punishment only if can expect people not to do it.		
	415. Knew - Punish because culprit knew the punishment; that was the chance he took.		
	416. $Role-taking_3$ - I understand how culprit felt, but . . .		

ALL SITUATIONS - PUNISHMENT CODING SHEET--Continued

Type	4. Breaking a Rule as Basis for Punishment	5. Judge's Role Obligation / 6. His Authority (Including Respect Sort)	8. Justice - Non-instrumental Aspects: Retaliation and Restoration
0	041. Law - Punish because he broke the law, committed a crime. 042. Label - Punish because he was wrong stealing, etc. 043. Wrong - Did something he wasn't supposed to, something wrong. 044. Alternate means - punish because could take alternate means, didn't have to. 045. First offense - Leniency because first offence (uses inappropriately).	051. Job - Judge's job is to punish, not to judge action, situation, etc. 061. Respect$_1$ - Respect, because can't be a criminal in that job. 062. Respect$_2$ - Respect because prevents crime (projective value). 063. Respect$_3$ - Respect him because has power (projective value). 065. Respect$_4$ - Have to or else.	081. Mechanical equivalence - He didn't kill anyone so do(n't) kill him. 082. Talion - Let him suffer the same thing, see what it's like. 083. Physical - Suggests physical punishment.
1		151. Victim determined - The victim or owner or family should determine the punishment. 152. Habit determined - Judge's response determined by role habit and indifference to values of others. 161. Respect$_1$ - Victim respects judge for restoring property, etc. 162. Respect$_2$ - People (criminal) resent him, don't like.	181. Deprivation - Suggests deprivation as a punishment. 182. Restorability - Don't punish because culprit can give or pay back the object to the victim.
	241. Label - The label doesn't apply really to the situation; not really stealing, murdering.	251. Please - Judge should consult wishes of victim and everyone else including jury.	281. Restore - Judge, punisher should help restore the situation in various non-punitive or unofficial ways.

ALL SITUATIONS - PUNISHMENT CODING SHEET--Continued

Type	4. Breaking a Rule as Basis for Punishment	5. Judge's Role Obligation / 6. His Authority (Including Respect Sort)	8. Justice - Non-Instrumental Aspects: Retaliation and Restoration		
2	242. Good - Punish because it isn't good to--because you should always . . .	252. Both sides - Judge should look at both sides (implying a judgment by situational sympthy). 261. Respect$_1$ - Judge knows a lot 262. Respect$_2$ - Respect judge for helping criminal do right, helping town, etc.			
3	341. Still - Still the act, still wrong. 342. Knew - Culprit knew he was "wrong." 343. Exceptions - Law can't make exceptions. 344. Kill - Death sentence, punishment still sees as killing.		381. Explation$_1$ - Culprit should pay for what did. 382. Explation$_2$ - Has suffered enough. 383. Remorse - Punish to teach him he did wrong, make him feel remorse, etc. 384. Work - Suggests hard work as a punishment in I.		
4	441. Ignorance of the Law - Is no excuse; should have ascertained the law.	451. Role-determined - Judge's job is to realize the law in the given case. 452. Circumstances - Judge should consider the circumstances, situation, within the limits set gv the law.	481. Denial of Talion - Punishment not a matter of getting even. 482. No capital punishment - Against capital punishment, not a deterrent.		
4		461. Respect. Respect for ability to make fair, impartial decisions.			
5					

RESPONSES OF SAMPLE CASES

Characteristics of Subjects Used to Illustrate Levels of
Response to Moral Conflict Situations

Case Number	Modal Level	Age	IQ	Class	Sociometric	Delinquency
9	0	9-1/2	125	U.L.	Isolate	
77	0	16	?	L.L.	?	Delinq.
19	1	10-1/2	103	U.M.-L.M.	Isolate	
76	1	16-1/2	?	U.L.	?	Delinq.
15	2	10-1/2	118	U.M.	Integrate	
25	2	13	109	L.M.	Integrate	
54	3	15-1/2	104	U.L.	Integrate	
29	3 (4)	13	107	U.L.	Integrate	
66	4	16	112	U.M.	Integrate	
63	5	16	115	U.M.	Integrate	

_29

Situation 1 - Sample Responses for Each Type

Type 0 (2)

Case 9: (Should Joe refuse to give his father the money?). Well, if he wanted to go to camp bad and his father said that he couldn't go; well, he promised him in the first place and that if he saved up enough money he could go. I think that his father should have saved his own money. His father should have saved up enough money and then they both would have had enough money to go.

(Should he give or refuse?) Give it to him. Well, you should be nice to your parents and do what they say.

(Would it be wrong for him to refuse?) Yes (wrong). Well, he wanted to go to camp and his father said he couldn't and he wanted to go on a fishing trip and if he refused to give his father the money, he could have taken away most of his privileges, and stuff too.

(Have right to refuse?) Yeah, he has the right. Well, his father said that he could go to camp if he saved up enough money and his father changed his mind and wants to go on a fishing trip; while Joe will be sad because he wanted to go and his father wouldn't let him.

(Does his father have the right to tell him to give him the money?) Yes, he has the right. Well, his father—he does stuff for Joe and Joe should do something for his father.

(Was it wrong for the father to break his promise to his son?) Yes.

(What harm would it do?) Well, he promised Joe that he would let him go, and he said—he changed his mind.

(Worse for father to break promise or son to?) I think a father to break his promise to his son. Well, his father is older than his son and if he broke the promise, well, he'd be excused the first time but he could do it over and over and then he wouldn't be excused. But the boy, he might do it a lot of times and then they'd excuse him. But his father's older than him and he should know better than the boy.

(Joe lied, what should his father do when he gets back?) Well, he should talk to him and ask him why he lied and if Joe said why he lied his father might take away his privileges or something.

Type 1

<u>Case 77</u>: (Should Joe refuse to give his father the money? Why?) He should
refuse to give it to him because he made it by himself and his
father told him that he could go if he saved up the money.

(Does his father have the right to tell him to give him the money?)
No, I think Joe should have refused him because he saved the
money up and he worked for it himself.

(Was it wrong for the father to break his promise to his son?) Yes.

(What harm would it do?) Well, if his father makes him another
promise, Joe won't know whether to believe him or not.

(Worse for father to break promise or son to?) Father to break a
promise to his son. Just like I said, he promised him he could
go somewhere and something like that, and then when the time came
and he had the money all saved up and his father breaks his
promise and says no; and he wouldn't know whether to believe him
the next time.

(Joe lied, what should his father do when he gets back?) I don't
know. He should punish him because Joe didn't have permission or
anything like that to go. He told him in the beginning that he
could go but he didn't tell him when the time came that he could
go.

Type 1 (2)

<u>Case 19</u>: (Should Joe refuse to give his father the money? Why?) I think
that Joe should give his father the money, then they both should
enjoy the fishing trip.

(Father wouldn't take Joe.) Well then I think Joe should keep the
money because Joe worked hard for that money.

(if he has right) (Does his father have the right to tell him to
give him the money?) No, he doesn't. Because Joe's father--well,
he didn't pitch in any money and Joe worked for it and his father
didn't help Joe.

(Was it wrong for the father to break his promise to his son?)
I think it would be wrong for Joe's father.

(What makes it wrong?) That's a difficult one, too. Well, . . .
I forgot what I was going to say. Well, Joe had his heart on
going to camp and then when his father told him he couldn't it
just broke Joe's heart.

(Worse for father to break promise or son to?) Well, I think it
would be a father breaking a promise to his son; well, uh (little
laugh.) Well, Joe . . . I don't know what to say to that one.
Well, I think a father should be more loyal to his son than the
son to his father. Because the father is more grown up than the
boy and the boy is younger, and when it comes to camp the son just
says, "Oh boy, now I'm going to have a good time and everything"
and he asks his father and when his father says no, he's just
disappointed.

(Joe lied, what should his father do when he gets back?) Well, I
think the father would be mad at him because Joe lied to him and
there the son was not loyal to his father; he was not honest to
his father, and his father took what he had made and then he . . .
Wasn't the father going to pay the son back? (yes.)

Type 1 (4)

Case 76: (Should Joe refuse to give his father the money? Why?) I think
he should refuse. Well, after all he worked for the money and he
saved it up, and his father promised him he could go to camp.
So I think he should have a right to it.

(if he has right) (Does his father have the right to tell him to
give him the money?) No, he shouldn't; he's got the right to
tell him, his parents. But I don't think he should give it up if
it's his.

(Father has spent money. Doesn't that give him the right?) Well,
I don't know; parents are supposed to bring their kids up. I
still don't think he should ask for the money.

(Was it wrong for the father to break his promise to his son?)
Yes, I think so.

(What harm?) Sort of breaks the kid's heart that he can't go to
camp, and working for the money and asking his Dad to give it to
him when it's practically his.

(Worse for father to break promise or son to?) I don't know.

(Joe lied, what should his father do when he gets back?) I don't
know what he'll do. Probably give him a licking or bawling out for
lying to him.

Type 2

Case 15: (Should Joe refuse to give his father the money? Why?) I'd say to
give it to him. Well, that would be pretty selfish for this little
boy--well, I think his father would pay him back.

(Have right to refuse?) Well, it would be up to him; it's his
money--he earned it.

(if has right) (Does his father have the right to tell him to
give him the money?)

(What gives him the right?) Well, he wanted to go to camp so bad--
well, if his father's trip was more important, if I was Joe, I'd
give it to him.

Type 2

Case 25: I think that Joe worked very hard to get to that camp, and since
his father's short of money for maybe other purposes--I don't
think it said why he was short of money, did it? If he was short
of money and he needed to put a payment on his house, that Joe
should sacrifice a little for his father and give Joe the money.
And his father will most likely repay him in some other respect.

(if should give) (Would it be wrong for him to refuse? Does he
have the right to?) I don't think it would, after all he worked
for the money. He made it himself. Now if his father gave it to
him, he shouldn't refuse, because it's his father's money anyway.
If his father needs that money very desperately to make a payment
on his house or car, he should sacrifice it. And then again since
he worked for it, maybe he should want that money to go to camp
with it. If I was him, I would sacrifice it, and give it to my
father.

(For fishing trip) Then I don't think he should give it to him.
Because his father didn't work for it and he did; he should use
it for his own cause, for his camping and have some fun.

(if has right) (Does his father have the right to tell him to
give him the money?) I don't think he does. Because he wanted
to go on this fishing trip and the son wanted to go to camp, and
the son made the money, and I think the son has that opportunity
to go to camp because it's his money.

(Father has spent money. Doesn't that give him the right?) Yeah,
I think that Joe should think on both sides. Of his fun, and of
what his father has done for him, and then maybe he could decide
which one he would want--to give his money to his father first or
for himself.

(Was it wrong for the father to break his promise to his son?)
I think it was.

(What harm would it do?) The son doesn't trust him as much; he
doesn't have as much respect for him. As if he would keep his
promise, he would have more respect for him, and when he grows up
he thinks his father's an Indian giver or something.

(Worse for father to break promise or son to?) Son breaking promise
to his father. Because his father probably respects his son, too,
to a certain respect. He brought him up and--so that he would keep
his promises and do whatever he said, not when he broke it, his
father doesn't have as much respect for him, because he broke his
promise, and he brought him up the way that he should keep his
promises and brought him up good.

(Joe lied, what should his father do when he gets back?) Give him
a little scolding, for a ming to him. And since Joe said the camp
master said he could pay $10, and the rest later, I think he should
have done that and given the $40 to his father instead of the other
way.

(Punish or just talk?) Talk to him. Because the father, again,
didn't tell him that he was going on a fishing trip. Bod dis, so
that's why I think the father should only talk to him about lying.

Type 3

Case 54: (Should Joe refuse to give his father the money? Why?) I think
he should give him the money. He can go to camp next year, and
if his father needed it more than he did, well, his father has
done a lot of things for him and he's asking for something in return.

(if should give) (Would it be wrong for him to refuse?) Wrong for
him to refuse.

(if he has right) (Does his father have the right to tell him to
give him the money?) Yes. He's done a lot of things for his son
probably, and I think he should be able to get something back from
him.

(Father has spent money. Doesn't that give him the right?)

(Was it wrong for the father to break his promise to his son?)
I think if you promise something, you ought to try and keep your
promise, but if it isn't possible, no.

(What harm would it do?) Well, I think he wouldn't trust him so
much next time. He wouldn't work hard as much, or wouldn't get
his money, or wouldn't want to go.

(Worse for father to break promise or son to?) Worse for father;
I think he'd have more influence on the development of the son.

(Joe lied, what should his father do when he gets back?) I think
he should punish him for lying by not letting him go to camp the
next year, or give him some kind of punishment.

(Why?) Teach him not to lie.

(Do any good?) I don't know—I think if the son really liked his father, it would. Well, if he liked this person that punished him, he probably wouldn't do it the next time but if he didn't like his father and his father beat him, next time he'd go do the same thing.

Type 3

Case 29: (Should Joe refuse to give his father the money?) Why? I think he should give it to him. Because I think his father should know best what he should do with his money.

(if should give) (Would it be wrong for him to refuse? Does he have the right to?) Well, it could be wrong, but in another way—well, I think it would be wrong to go against the father.

(What way might not?) Well, he might want to go so bad that he can hardly give it up.

(Have right to refuse?) I think so unless there's a real reason why he should give it up.

(if has right) (Does his father have the right to tell him to give him the money?) Yes, he does. Because he is his elder and he should be able to tell him.

(Was it wrong for the father to break his promise to his son?) In a way it would be wrong, but if he needed the money badly, he would have a right to want it, if he had to have it. You shouldn't really break your promises, because if you tell someone you'll do it, you should do it. What they want you to do.

(What harm would it do?) Might let the person down. Like in this case, it might of let the son down.

(Worse for father to break promise or son to?) Father breaking promise to son, because the son is younger and it might take effect on him. Might give him in later life a—well, he might make promises and then never keep them.

(Joe lied, what should his father do when he gets back?) I think he should tell him that he shouldn't have lied; he could have come to him and asked him about the money, if he could please go to camp. He probably could have got the money some way.

(Punished?) Not too big a punishment, but yes, somehow.

(Why not too big?) Like before, that also might affect him and he may—well, it might be wrong to give him a hard punishment like that. It would just ruin him—like he'd be bad or something.

Type 4 (1)

Case 66: (Should Joe refuse?) I think that since he earned the money, he has a right to use it himself.

(Father have right to ask?) I don't think he has right to tell him to give him the $, but Joe might be nice son, and he could say that Dad wants $ more than he does, and he might give it to him.

(Father broke promise. Wrong?) Think wrong, but maybe if something different came up, but under condition, don't think he should have changed mind just because he wanted to go some place.

(Which worse, son breaking promise or father?) Father breaking promise--head of family setting example.

(What should father do when Joe gets back from camp?) Talk to him about lying. Don't think if good father would try to punish, because son earned money himself, but should talk about lying to people.

(Punishment about lying have anything to do with fact that son earned money himself?) Yeah, father had something to do with lying--only way Joe could get to camp and father wanted to take money away, so that's all he could do.

Type 4 - 5

Case 65: (Should Joe refuse to give his father the money? Why?) Don't think it's a question of actually refusing; his father could take it away from him anyway. But I don't think his father should want to take it away; the boy wanted to go to camp. And he worked hard. I don't think the father should say, "you give me the money; I want to go somewhere."

(Wouldn't be being disloyal, son or not?) If his father asked him if he would be kind enough to give him the money, if I was the boy-- gee, I don't know what I'd do. I think I'd probably give it to him. But if the boy has his heart set on it, I don't think the father has right to ask. I don't think he has a moral right to ask him, because the boy worked for it.

(Why not have moral right? Been taking care of boy all years.) Well, I know that's all true; he's been taking care of the boy but the boy's gotta have some sense of being able to do what he wants to do. He worked for that and if his parents okayed it, I certainly think he should go. You can't always use that argument, "I brought you up all these years"; parents kind of have an obligation to do that.

(You mean without expecting anything in return?) (excited voice) Oh, no, they certainly deserve a lot in return. But something like this when the boy did it on his own; he was the one who went out and earned it, he should certainly be allowed to go. Father shouldn't ask him.

Situation II - Sample Responses for Each Type

Type O

Case 9: (Should Alex tell his father about Joe?) Tell him. Tell his father. Because if you keep it a secret and he finds out a little while after, he might be harder on him. (Would he be wrong not to?) Alexander is supposed to tell and it would be wrong if he didn't because his father wanted him to.

(Should he tell if he's just a friend?) Yes.

(Why would he think he shouldn't?) If he should tell they might not play with each other and they'd get mean for telling.

(Would Joe think he wasn't a good brother?) He'd be mad at him but he wouldn't be a bad brother. Joe might do it on Alexander sometime and Alexander wouldn't say that.

(If Joe had protected him before?) It would be bad not to tell. They might find out anyway. If you want to keep friends, he shouldn't tell.

(If he promised?) I think he should; he might tell his father.

Type O

Case 77: (Should Alex tell his father about Joe?) He could tell him and be on the safe side on his own.

(Would it be wrong if he didn't?) Yeah. If he told, then his father wouldn't have anything against him.

(Why would someone think he shouldn't tell on a friend or brother?) I don't know.

(Should he tell if his brother had kept quiet for him?) He could and then he might not. It all depends on Alexander whether he should or he shouldn't.

(What would be best or right?) To tell his father what Joe had done.

Type 1 (0)

Case 19: (Should Alex tell his father about Joe?) It's yes and no. If Alex were honest, he might tell. If Joe had told him to keep it a secret, he wouldn't be keeping a secret very good, and you might call him a tattle tale.

(Which should he do?) Well, I wish I were Alex. Then I would know. If you say, "I'm not going to tell," and then you tell, you're lying. If he doesn't, he's helping something he shouldn't because the son had lied and he could have gone to camp next year.

(Would Joe think he wasn't a good brother?) Yes.

(Should he tell if a friend?) No, then it's none of his business.

(If he was actually asked?) Then he'd have to tell or it would be a lie and he'd be making a sin.

(If Joe had told him before?) Keep quiet or Joe might get carried away and blab.

Type 1

Case 76: (Should Alex tell his father about Joe?) I think he should keep quiet. He might want to go someplace like that, and if he squeals on Joe, Joe might squeal on him.

(Would it be wrong for him to tell?) It wouldn't be wrong.

(Why wouldn't it be wrong?) It wouldn't be wrong; after all his father made a promise and he should keep it.

(What would Joe think about Alex?) I don't think he'd think very much of his brother.

(Would he think he wasn't a good brother?) He'd think he was a squealer or a rat. He didn't want his brother to tell on him.

(Should Bob tell if asked by his father?) Tell him he didn't know nothing about it. As I said before, he might want to go someplace, and he wouldn't want Joe to tell on him if his father brought the same situation up.

Type 0

Case 15: (Should Alex tell his father about Joe?) I think he should tell his father. Well, you shouldn't keep anything away from your father so long, because he'll find out anyway.

(Why would someone think he shouldn't tell on a friend or a brother?) Well, if his father wants him to tell, anything, he should tell his father everything because it's not very nice to keep a lie away from your father or your mother.

(What would Joe think if Alex told?) Well, he'd be pretty sore at him, but after a while he'd tell him the reason that he had to.

(Would he think Alex was not being a loyal brother?) Well, I think a loyal brother should not tattle on him; but if his father says to him, You have to tell me whatever happens--I mean not a little argument--like something really bad happens, I think he should.

(Wouldn't that be disloyal?) No. Like my sister, she told on me. My mother she wants to tell anything that happens, see --so . . . I think so.

(Should Sam tell?) You mean Sam's the friend? I'd say so, yeah. Well, like his father--see, he wants to find out what's the matter because he found out he was right about something, so he wants to know about it and he probably told Sam about it and he wants Sam to tell him anything he can find out.

Type 2

Case 25: (Should Alex tell his father about Joe?) In all respect I think that he should have told his father, since he didn't make no promise to Joe that he wouldn't tell. Otherwise his father would know he was lying too.

(Why would someone think he shouldn't?) Because of their respect. If they should tell, they probably wouldn't respect them as much.

(If Joe protected him before?) I think so. He did a favor for him and I think Joe should do a favor for his brother.

(Even if his father asked him directly?) I think he should tell. If you just say, "No," you're going to blush right in front of him because you're lying and he'd know something was wrong right there.

(Even if he promised?) He would maybe say, "No," but he'd probably blush and give himself away anyway. In all respect for his father, he should tell.

Type 3 (0)

Case 34: (Should Alex tell his father about Joe?) I think it would be up to Joe to tell. He was the one who did it and he should have the responsibility to tell himself.

(If he wouldn't?) Then I think Alex should tell, because it's uncorrected.

(Why would someone think he shouldn't?) Some people think if they're squealing on another guy, they're doing more harm.

(Would Joe think he wasn't a good brother?) I don't think he'd like it too much for a while, but I think he'd get over it after about it.

(If Joe had protected him before?) I think that he would to get it corrected. On the whole, I think that it wouldn't make too much difference.

Type 2 (3)

Case 29: (Should Alex tell his father about Joe?) I think he should tell. Then his father would know ahead of time, and then he could probably get the money for him instead of not knowing about it.

(Why would someone think he shouldn't tell on a friend or a brother?) Because they might be close to him, and they might think it will hurt him.

(How would it hurt him?) Well, if you let him down as a friend, he wouldn't think you'd be a good friend if you'd tell on him. He'd think his friend wasn't loyal to him.

(If Joe protected him before?) No, I don't think so--well, it would be right in the way they think; it's being loyal to each other, but to be right they should tell their father. You should tell the truth to your father. Let him know everything almost. Well, it's better than being loyal, doing something for the other person, if he did something for you. Your father is older than you and he would know better than your brother would, and he probably could give you better advice if you were in trouble or something.

Type 4

Case 66: (Should Alex tell his father?) I don't think he should tell, because Joe didn't have to tell his father he had done that. If his older brother just found out he had lied, maybe he should tell his father. But if his brother just trusted him and wanted to get it off his chest, I don't think he should tell. He should let Joe tell himself.

(Would it be wrong?) Just a choice of what he wants to do. If he likes his brother a lot, he shouldn't tell.

(If his father asked?) Should probably tell so he wouldn't be
lying. But it depends. If it was this kind of a father and they
didn't like him and he likes his brother real well, he'd probably
lie about it.

(Would Joe have a right to expect him to keep quiet?) No. If
he didn't want anyone to tell on him, he shouldn't have told anyone in the first place.

(How about if Joe had protected him?) That doesn't have too much
to do with it. It's still up to his brother, what he wants. But
he might be afraid Joe would tell on him so that would be another
reason why he wouldn't want to. That was just a gift of the
brother not to tell and I don't think you should have to give back
such a gift.

(Why shouldn't a friend tell then?) A family has a close relationship and they know each other and the father's head of the
family. The two brothers would have to have some sense of loyalty
to the father and a neighbor wouldn't.

Type 5

Case 65:   (Should Alex tell his father?) If I was in that position, I
wouldn't tell my father. I suppose the truth should, may, come
out, but I know I wouldn't tell the father in that case.

(Wrong for Alex to tell, or right?) Well, he would gain respect
from his father if he told but then again, he would be deceiving
his brother because his brother confided in him, and I don't
think that confidence should be broken--even though the father
would be happy to know.

(Father have a right to expect Alex to tell on brother?) No, I
don't think so. Around our house--if somebody does something
and the other children know about it, my father will, if the information is told him that one of the other brothers has done
something, he'll be grateful for the information, but at the same
time, his respect will go down in the eyes of that tattle tale,
because he did tattle in a way.

If the father had brought him up right, I think the son wouldn't
tell on his brother; he would have that much respect for his
brother. I think the son would just let the two work it out for
themselves.

(Should Bob tell the truth if his father asked him?) If the
father would ask Al, I would think that he should tell--if asked,
but I certainly wouldn't go out of my way to approach the father
about it. If asked, he shouldn't lie about it.

(If Joe had protected him before?) If Joe had stuck up for Alex
earlier, I would do the same thing. I would stick up for Joe if
father asked--yes. If my brother had kept quiet about what I
had done, and then my brother did something, I would keep quiet
about it too. If your brother had that much respect for you not
to tell on you, I'd do the same thing for him--even though it
would be lying.

Situation III - Sample Responses for Each Type

Type O

Case 9:   (Should he have stolen the drug to save his wife?) No, well he
could have, he should have raised some money and when he got
enough money, he should buy the drug instead of stealing it.

(But it would be too late then. Would it still be wrong?) Yeah,
because if he stole the drug, he might get caught and then he'd
have to put it back and he'd be in jail and then he wouldn't be
able to raise the money.

(Would his wife want him to?) No, because she'd think that was
wrong.

(Should judge send him to jail?) Send him to jail. He'd learn a
lesson not to steal again.

(Interviewer applies pressure that all right to steal.) Yes, he
could have stole the drug and after his wife got better, he could
pay for it.

(Would Heintz have the right to then?) No because his wife was
practically dead and he couldn't pay for it, well he didn't have
no right to steal it.

One year later: (R.G. had been pressured to change his mind and complied
on the first interview)

(Should he have stolen the drug to save his wife?) I think he had
kind of a right. He could pay him later. Like if he had two or
three jobs then he could pay for it. His wife was sick and if she
didn't get the drug pretty quick she would die. Maybe his wife
is an important person, maybe she runs a store and that store has
only that one kind of thing and if the lady dies, the man will
give up the store.

You're not supposed to kill anybody and if he didn't give her any
drug, that would be just like killing her. Like Hart's drugstore
downtown, if they didn't give any medicine like to a lady, then
she'd probably die and then they'd pin it on that man that he
didn't sell that drug.

(Would it be all right to send the druggist to the electric chair?)
Well if they knew she couldn't be cured it wouldn't. But if she
could be, I think they should because she could be an important
lady like Betsy Ross, she made the flag. Like if it was President
Eisenhower they'd put the man in the electric chair, because it
wouldn't be fair.

(Should they be more punished if someone important dies?) Like if
someone important is up in a plane and he is allergic to heights
and the hostess doesn't want to give it to him because she's only
got enough for one and she has a sick friend in the back. Well
if he's an important person they'd probably put the hostess in
the ladies' jail because she didn't help him.

(Why should they give it to the important person?) Well like if
a man was guarding a dam and he caught sick and he's an important
man, and if the dam broke the water would go over all the houses.
They should give it to him instead of a poor lady.

(Which is more important, saving the life of one important person
or a lot of unimportant people?) All the people who aren't important because one man just has one house; maybe an awful lot of
furniture, but a whole bunch of people have a lot of furniture
and some of these poor people might have a lot of money and it
doesn't look it. Maybe they've got some little children and
they're saving it for their college education.

Type O

Case 77: (Should he have stolen the drug to save his wife?) No because
he could have went to some bank and borrowed some if he hadn't
already went to the bank.

(He had tried everything and couldn't get anymore money. Would
you still say it was wrong or was it all right?) Wrong. Breaking
a law. Breaking into the place and stealing it.

(Would a good husband do it?) Yes.

(Would it be his duty?) No. Because if she knew that he stole it
that might have made her sicker.

(Would it be wrong if he left the money he had?) No, because he
could have went and reported what he done and the police might
not have been so bad--they might have saw it his way and knew that
his wife was dying and gone to the owner and made it all right for
him to pay the rest later.

(Should he be sent to jail?) I don't know.

444

Type 1

Case 19: (Should he have stolen the drug to save his wife?) Yes sir.
Well he needed it for a reason. This man, it just cost him $100
and he shouldn't have charged more than 5 times more than he
payed for it. It wouldn't be right.

(Would the druggist have a right to charge that much if there
was no law against it?) No sir.

(Would it be all right for Heintz to steal it if it really was
worth $2000?) No sir. Because if it costz $2000 then it's worth
$2000.

(Is it his duty as a good husband, does he have to steal it?)
You might say "Yes" in a way.

(In what way?) Why did I say 'way'? Well, it depends on him. If
he loves his wife a lot, it would.

(If he doesn't?) Then it wouldn't be a very happy house, they'd
always be fighting.

(Suppose it was just a good friend?) I don't think so. Well, he
loves his wife more than a friend. A friend is just a friend.

(Would it be right for the owner to shoot Heintz?) It would be
right. (Why?) I don't know.

(All right to shoot back?) Do unto others as you have them do
unto you. (What does that mean here?) Do what they do to you.

(Should the judge send him to jail?) I would let him go free.
(Would the judge think it was right?) If I were the judge, I
would say yes. But it would be up to the jury.

(Should the judge drop the punishment if the owner asked him to?)
Yes sir. The owner calls the punishment.

(It's against the law. Doesn't that make it wrong?) In a way.
If he's using it for a reason, it isn't wrong. And if he paid it
back after he stole it, it wouldn't be wrong.

Type 1

Case 70: (Should he have stolen the drug to save his wife?) I think so.
After all, if your wife was going to die and you didn't have the
money, would you steal it?

(Would a good person?) I don't know.

452

(Was he right to do it?) It wasn't right to steal but I wouldn't
let my wife die. After all, the guy who invented it shouldn't be
selling it for that much anyway.

(Would it be a good husband's duty?) Is it what? Yeah, I guess
so.

(If it were just a good friend, should he?) I don't know. I
don't think so. You're not as closely related to your friend as
to your wife. After all, your wife is in your family.

(Did the druggist have a right to charge that much?) Yeah, he has
every right if there's no law against it. He could probably
charge a million dollars if he wanted to.

(Would it be wrong?) No, but he wouldn't sell it.

(Would the druggist be right to shoot him?) He should have called
the police. It would be first or second degree murder on him.

(Should storeowners have the right to shoot?) Not unless it's
self defense.

(Why should the police?) The cops are paid for it.

(Right for Heintz to shoot back?) Yes, self defense.

(Should the judge send Heintz to jail?) What happened to his wife?
If his wife wasn't dead and just any excitement over something
like that might kill her, then the judge ought to let her off.

(Would the judge think that what Heintz did was right?) I don't
know.

(Should judge drop punishment if owner asks?) If the guy drops
the charges, there ain't no charges, so the judge can't send him.

(Interviewer applies pressure that Heintz was wrong because drug
needed.) Well, the druggist has more of the drug hasn't he?

(No, he only had that small amount. Wouldn't you agree that in
that case it was wrong?) No, I don't agree.

(Did Heintz have a right to break the law and steal the drugs in
that case?) If he didn't need it, he wouldn't.

Type 2 (1)

Case 15: (Should he have stolen the drug to save his wife?) Well, if he
couldn't get the money somewhere else-- He shouldn't have done
that really, but if he couldn't get the money any where else, and
his wife was dying, I think he'd do anything for her.

(Is it his duty to?) No. It's against the law to steal because it's not right to take something that isn't yours.

(Would most husbands? Would you?) Yeah, if there wasn't any other way to do it.

(Suppose he were just a good friend? Should he still do it?) Real good friend? Well, if he was a real good friend, I think so.

(Is it more wrong to steal it for a friend than for a wife?) Yes, because he married her and he loves her more than he does his friend.

(But does that make it more wrong?) I'd say so, because he wouldn't feel so bad because of his friend but he'd still feel real bad. But not as bad as if his wife had cancer.

(Does the druggist have the right to charge that much for the drug?) He should sell it cheaper if his wife was dying. I think it would be up to the druggist. He made the drug after all, and he wanted to make it himself and he wouldn't want to have a law against how much he wanted to charge--how much he had to.

(Is it wrong to kill Heintz if necessary to protect your property?) No, it wouldn't be because after all that cost a lot of money, $400, to get it made.

(Is it all right for Heintz to shoot back in self defense?) No, I don't think so. Tell him to stop and he'd give him back the gun.

(Heintz said he'd stop but the owner didn't believe him so he kept on shooting.) In that case, I'd say it would be self defense.

(Then would it be all right?) Yes, because Heintz said he'd give up but the man kept on shooting; he couldn't just stand there.

(What punishment for Heintz? Why?) I'd say, keep him in jail. Well, after all, he didn't get shot and he stole something.

(Would the judge think he'd do the same in Heintz's place?) I'd say so.

(Then would the judge be willing to punish Heintz?) Well, it's up to him, because he did it against the law. After all, he doesn't let him go free just because he'd stole. You're not supposed to.

(What good would it do to punish?) Punishment wouldn't do any good.

Type 2 (3)

Case 25: (Should he have stolen the drug to save his wife?) I don't think so. But then a in, I don't think they could put him in jail for that because it's the druggist's fault. It only cost $400 and he's charging $2000 plus maybe taking a life. The man could only raise $1000 so I think in order to save his wife, I think it would be all right to break in the store and take that drug.

(According to the law, the druggist could charge what he wanted.) That puts a different light on it. If he discovered it and its with the law, the other man shouldn't have no right to break in. It's stealing the drug what doesn't belong to him. Well, I think the druggist was unfair not to let him pay later.

(Would a good husband do it?) I think so.

(Would Heintz be wrong then?) No, because he loved his wife and he wanted to save her. I think anyone would.

(Was it right for the druggist to shoot?) No, because the druggist didn't know who it was. It was dark and he couldn't see. To protect your property and yourself too. In many cases when people steal and they see someone else they would kill them for fear they would tell.

(Was it right to shoot back?) I think so. He had no way out so I think for his life too, he should.

(Should he be punished?) I think he should let him go free on probation because he was stealing the drug for his wife to save her and the judge looked at all sides that the druggist was charging too much. I think the judge should look at all sides of it and decide whether or not he should send him to jail for burglarizing the store.

(Should he drop the case if the owner asks?) Yes, the druggist sees it was his fault and now he's pleading with the judge. He doesn't have to. Maybe he didn't feel sorry for Heintz and he didn't care.

Type 3

Case 54: (Should he have stolen the drug to save his wife?) Yes, I think he should have. If he got it, he could pay him back later when he got the extra $1000. But if it wouldn't have helped her, I don't think he should have done it.

(Was he wrong or right to do it?) No, I don't think it was right for him to do it.)

(Suppose it were just a good friend?) Then it wouldn't be right. If he needed the money or something, maybe they could arrange to get it, but if they couldn't, I think it was up to that family to get the drug.

(Does the druggist have the right to charge that much?) He had to go through all the pains of developing it and if it worked, I think he should have the right to charge as much as he wants to.

(Is it wrong for him to shoot at Heintz?) No, I think in any store or bank, if someone breaks in they'd naturally shoot at him.

(Isn't killing someone worse than robbing?) I don't think so, if it's in protection.

(All right to shoot back?) Yes. The objective of the owner was to kill the guy even if he would surrender.

(Should the judge send Heintz to jail?) No. There would be enough grief as it was, without having to stick him in jail. He should attempt to pay him back.

(Would the judge think Heintz was in the right?) No. He might not put himself in that position, what he'd do.

(Examiner pressures that he was right to steal.) Well, in that case, I think it would be natural for him to steal. But just because he wanted to steal, I don't think it was right.

(Further pressure.) If he saved his family's life and then was punished for it or paid it back, I don't think it would be wrong.

Type 3

Case 29: (Should he have stolen the drug to save his wife?) No, he shouldn't, because the druggist was partly at fault. He could have let him pay later instead of going all the way of stealing it.

(Was he wrong to steal then?) Yes, he was wrong, but he was very desperate to get it, because his wife was dying.

(Even if there was no other way?) It's never good to steal anything. If he was that desperate, there might have been a way to get help from charity or some payment plan.

(Was it a husband's duty?) I guess in a way it is. It could be. But you shouldn't steal even in a situation like that.

(Would a good person?) I think even a good person in that situation might just get mad enough to do a thing like that.

(Does the druggist have a right to charge that much?) Well, if

there's a law against it. There isn't? Then there would be
nothing wrong with his way. He could charge as much as he wants
to if there's no limit.

(Is it wrong for him to shoot Heintz?) No, it would have been like
self defense. Defense of his property. He was trying to protect
his property and the only way he could do it was to shoot.

(Is it right for Heintz to shoot back?) No, but in a moment like
that I think a person probably would. He'd been robbing the
store and the man had been chasing after him to protect his own
rights. He would have been charged with murder besides robbery.

(Should H. be punished?) I think they should let him go free on
probation. He wanted his wife to live and the druggist wouldn't
sell it to him even on his word that he would pay later. And that
made him so he had to get it, to steal it.

(Should the judge drop the case if asked by the owner?) He should,
but he wouldn't have to. He might think this man was a common
thief.

Type 4

Case 66: (Should he have stolen the drug to save his wife?) I don't think
he should have broken in. I think the druggist should have let
him have it for less money, because he wouldn't lose anything by
selling it for $1000. The druggist should have realized that if
someone was dying, he must not be a very nice guy to do that.

(Was he wrong to steal?) He shouldn't have broken in. I don't
know what else he could have done though, since the druggist was
that kind of man.

(Is it a husband's duty?) I don't know if it's a husband's duty
to steal but I think most husbands would do everything they could
to save their wife's life. If he did all he could to get it and
the only way he could get it was to do something wrong, he wouldn't
be responsible. According to the law it would be wrong to steal
from that man but I think it's up to what Heintz wanted to do. If
it happened to me, I think I'd probably steal if that was the only
way. It's his conscience. He might know that it's wrong, but it's
up to him to decide whether he'd rather go to jail than have his
wife die.

(Does the druggist have the right to charge that much for the drug?)
I think he had the right to, but I don't think he should. It
would be all right, but nobody except rich people could afford it.

(Was he wrong to shoot at Heintz?) I don't think so because there's
a law against breaking in and he didn't know who it was, so there's
nothing wrong according to the law.

(Wrong to shoot back?) If someone was desperate, they would, but I don't think it's right.

(What punishment?) I don't know if the judge can do anything about it. There's a law that says they put him in jail for robbing, but I don't know if they make an exception for him or not.

(What would you do if you were the judge?) I'd consider he was trying to get the drug to save another person's life and let him go free.

(Drop case if owner asks?) I'm not sure about what the law says, whether if you drop charges whether you can convict him or not.

Type 5 (4)

Case 66:   (Should he have stolen the drug to save his wife?) I imagine if you took it to court, they would say no because I imagine no matter how bad it is, the worst way out is to steal. Even though it did cost a lot of money, I think in a law court, he would be charged guilty. However, in case like that, if it was that bad, if the druggist was that low, I wouldn't blame him if his wife got that drug and was saved. I think that's a case of necessity. However, the druggist was pretty low in not lowering the price.

(Right to do it?) Just in that particular situation. In the eyes of the law he wouldn't be doing the right thing, but in the eyes of the moral law he would. If he had exhausted every possible way, I think to save a life would be worth it.

(Would everyone probably do it?) Lot of things involved--if really loved wife, and had tried every way, I think most people would steal. It's better to go to prison for a while than have your wife die in a case like that. However, I think if he did let his story known through paper, the town would clamp down on that person--rather than his fighting whole war by himself.

(Good husband supposed to? Duty as a husband?) Under the conditions that he tried every means, I would say that--and if he knew that this drug would probably cure her, I would say that anyone who had a loved one would do it. Not necessarily a husband, but maybe a brother or sister.

(Suppose he were just a good friend. Should he still do it?) If best friend, as far as stealing is concerned, I would leave it up to some closer person. Like maybe he had wife or brother. I wouldn't leave the stealing up to me if just friend. I'd really have to be close to that person.

(If Heintz not good friend but knew him and felt sorry?) Gee . . . well, if nobody else was doing anything. If family had tried every means and if the man was just laying there getting worse and worse,

I would say--it would still be all right, I think. If a man's life is involved, I think it would be all right to do something like that.

(Heintz's responsibility if wife died and he didn't steal drug?) I would say yes, if he was sure that drug could cure her because in a way, it was just--which worse stealing or letting wife die--if he knew that drug could save her, I think he should feel guilty. I think he should feel guilty for not stealing--yes. If it would have saved her.

(Wrong if drug worth $2000?) I don't think it really matters that much--how much drug is worth. Even if it is worth $2000, I think the same would hold.

(Does the druggist have the right to charge that much for the drug?) If it wasn't worth it, I would say that it somebody had no other way of getting the money, I would say definitely to give it away. But if druggist did have business sense, would charge what they could afford, but in case where they couldn't get the money, he should feel guiltiest if she dies. Even if it cost a million, it's still a life of somebody.

(Heintz going against druggist's rights?) I think that good druggist would have the welfare of sick people over his personal pocket and . . . he . . . the rights of the druggist should take in his feeling for the welfare of the people, but . . . kinda tricky questions.

(What punishment for Heintz?) (Why?) You mean if I was the judge? (O.K.) If I was the judge, taking these circumstances into consideration, I would compromise and give him a short penalty. But I think if I was a good judge, I would try to join with Heintz and raise money..

(Do right to send Heintz to jail--do any good?) You have to protect the welfare of the citizens too. You can't let a store breaker just go scot free. Maybe most of the people in that town didn't give a darn about his wife. Since the majority rules, you have to have the welfare of them.

(Why care more about welfare of storekeeper than of Heintz's wife?) The storekeeper is an example, there are laws set up to protect people and a good judge would simply realize those laws and give some sort of sentence even though it may be under horrible conditions. Maybe his wife as you say is dying; I think even though, the people should be protected in some way--some small sentence.

Situation IV - Sample Responses for Each Type

Type O (1)

Case 9:   (Should the Dr. do it?) Yes.

(Is it his duty to?) No, I don't think so. Well, if she wanted him to do it, he could do it; but if she had a husband, well he wouldn't stand for it and he'd say not to do it and then he wouldn't have no right to do it.

(But if husband wanted him to, then he'd have right?) Yeah, I suppose so.

(Why not put person away like an animal?) No, because an animal-- you can have plenty animals but you can't have that of people. I mean you couldn't have a lot of animals. Like if you have a pet, and he dies, like a dog, he dies and you could always get another one but if your--say this man married a woman, and she died, and he married another woman, he wouldn't have a wife just the same as the one he had.

(Should there be a law that Dr. can take life?) Yes.

(Why would it be wrong then?). Because he didn't have no right to do it; I mean he did it without anybody saying he could do it.

(What punishment?) Either he could be put in jail for a few years, or--for a few years--or about thirty years--or something . . .

(If Dr. right--Why should he be punished at all?) Because he shouldn't have done it. I mean--she asked him to. Well, he shouldn't have done it anyway.

Type O

Case 77: (Should the Dr. do it?) No. They could do something to take the pain away besides giving her gas or ether or something like that to put her out of her misery. Something that would ease the pain.

(Wrong of her to ask Dr?) No.

(Why not put person away like an animal?) I don't know. I don't know that.

(Better for husband to do it?) Better to ask the Dr. cause the Dr. would know how to do it better than her husband because he has the right things to do it with.

453

(What punishment?) Sentence him somewhere, somehow--I don't know.

(Death sentence right?) I don't know.

Type 0 (1)

Case 19: (Should the Dr. do it?) He shouldn't give it to her because he
should let her live until she dies. Well, she might be cured,
of her cancer. Someone could pop up with that kind of medicine
just about 2 or 3 months before.

(What would Dr. think best for woman?) Let her live. Her husband
could enjoy his wife if she was alive. I had my eye on those two
kids who live on top of me. I keep on looking over there while
you're talking to me and I never listen. Jean and Joey.

(Why don't you listen?) I'm just sitting here like that and you're
blabbing away and I just keep watching them.

(Why not put person away like an animal?) Not all the times they
put an animal out of pain. Sometimes they take it to a vet and
it's cured.

(Should people have right to kill animal if it's going to die?)
No sir.

(Wrong to have law that can do it?) No, sir because the wife might
want to live until she dies, and they say they give the Dr. permission to do it; well, it's up to the woman.

(Better for husband to do it?) I would have asked the Dr. if I
was her because the Dr. could be accused of murder and he could be
put to death too.

(Then why ask the Dr.?) Well, if she asked the husband to kill
her, then he would be accused of murder, and if there was a law
that the Dr. could do it, well . . .

(What punishment?) If I was the judge, I'd set him free. (Why?)
Well, on second thought I wouldn't because the wife could have
killed herself. She could have found a knife and killed herself
and the Dr. wouldn't have to do it.

Type 0

Case 76: (Should the Dr. do it?) No, the Dr. hasn't got a right to take
anybody's life. (Why?) Ten commandments to the Bible says thou
shall not kill--or life for life.

(Why not put person away like an animal?) Well, that is not a
human being.

461

(Differenc ?) After all, if the woman wants to kill herself, she
can go out and take some poison or something. If a dog wants to
kill itself, they don't know what to say.

(All right for her to kill self?) No, I don't think she would wait.
It says thou shalt not take thou own life. It's against the law.

(Better for husband to do it?) Ask the Dr. to do it. Well, the
husband would get put in jail for it, for killing his wife. Yeah,
after all the Dr. could say she got into it herself and took it.

(What punishement?) Well, if he was stupid enough to do it, they
ought to give him life in prison or the electric chair. (Why?)
That's the punishment by the law. Well, if he killed another
person, . . .? a . . . life for life.

Type 2 (1)

Case 15: (Should t' Dr. do it?) Well, if she asked him to, I think he
should. Because she's in great pain and asked him to do it.

(Good Dr. have to or have right to refuse?) He has the right to
refuse. Because in 6 months they might find a cure in 6 months.

(What Dr. think best for woman?) Stay in pain or just die? Well,
I'd say I'd rather live longer than just die right off like that.

(Does Dr. have right?) If she asked him, he would.

(Depend on whether husband agreed?) I think it would be up to
husband too. If he just killed the wife right off, he'd think
the Dr. was trying to kill her or something; he'd drive him crazy.
If he didn't want to wait, and she died, well, they'd have to
bury her. He wants to look at her a little more, wouldn't you say?

(Why not put person away like an animal? Same thing apply here?)
I don't know; I never heard of it any place. A pet dog, I've
heard of it--a cow, but not of people.

(Same thing with people as with pet dogs?) I don't think so. A
pet dog, you don't love as much as you love your own wife.

(Should be law--either way?) Well, if she was going to die anyway, I think he could.

(Better for husband to do it?) Better to ask the Dr. The Dr.
would know better than her husband. I think Dr. has more right
because if the husband did it to her, he might feel guilty about it
sometime.

(What punishment?) Well, I don't think it should be murder; after
all, she was going to die anyway.

(Still taking a life.) Well, I think you'd give him about 30 years, at the most.

(What would you do if judge?) At the most, I'd give him about 30 years, but after all, she asked him to, and she was going to die anyway.

Type 3 (2)

Case 25: (Should the Dr. do it?) I think it would be suicide like, because she'd be taking her own live, which would be a sin. I mean, if somebody would murder you, it wouldn't be a sin--I mean, the other person would have the sin. I think the Dr. should let her live.

(Why sin to take own life?) As it says in the Bible, it's suicide; you're not supposed to.

(Why bad?) She'll be sinning--a great sin, and I think it says in the Bible if you take your own life, you won't go to heaven. I think that maybe she didn't read the Bible, and didn't know anything, not know any better, and she could have ordered the Dr. to do it. But I think if she knew better, I don't think she should do it.

(What punishment?) I don't think the judge should give him the electric chair or the gas chamber or anything like that. I think he should be put in jail maybe, but then again he should have told the judge that it was on her own request to have her be killed. I think that she should have had a witness when the judge asked this so that witness could have told the judge his part of the story also, because maybe the judge wouldn't believe him. I think he should only get about a year--just so he'd never do it again.

(Death sentence right?) Wrong.

(Why?) Because he didn't murder her for no reason at all. It was her own idea to have her killed to put her out of her pain. So he did it because she wanted it to be done but I think the judge would take that into consideration and not give him the death penalty.

Type 3 (1)

Case 54: (Should the Dr. do it?) Well, if they don't have any cure for her, I think that would be best. There's no reason to torture a person if they're going to die anyway.

(Why not put person away like an animal?) They would think they got a better chance of recuperating than some of the other animals-- they're higher.

(What way?) Mental.

(Better for husband do it?) Better for her to ask the Dr. to do it . . . conscience . . . kill his own wife.

(What punishment?) I don't think he should give him any. She was better off by having him kill her, and she wanted it anyway.

Type 3

Case 29: (Should the Dr. do it?) I don't think so; he shouldn't because he could get into trouble for doing a thing like that. Unless he had permission from one of the other drs. or officials.

(OK then?) Well, I think if she wanted it--it would be her decision then.

(Person have right to kill self if she's in that pain, and her family agree?) Yes, I think. Well, in a way she has a right to if the pain hurts her that much and she knows she's going to die.

(What way doesn't she?) Not right to take your own life, neither.

(Why?) Could be called murdering yourself. Wouldn't be right to take away your life that way. Unless you absolutely had to-- it hurt that much.

(Wrong if legal?) Yes, if she wanted it that way, he probably should do it.

(Why not put person away like an animal?) The human life--it would be different. They have more brains--have a better brain, and they'd feel it, and they might be able to live through it if they didn't have too serious an injury. Not in this case, but in another. You wouldn't kill them, I mean, like an animal. Because they could live through it.

(Better for husband to do it?) The Dr. It would be too much shock on the husband to let him do it.

(What punishment?) Well, if he has to be a sentence, I think it should be a small sentence because, he was doing it for the woman herself. He wasn't doing it for himself to kill her in cold blood like--. He was doing it for her; she wanted it done.

(Death sentence wrong?) Yes. I think so. He'd be doing this as a Dr. not as a person. He'd be doing this for the woman.

(If husband did it?) Not entirely, if she wanted it and he thought it would be better for her.

Type 3 (1)

Case 66: (Should the Dr. do it?) I don't think so; I think the Dr. is supposed to try to save a life rather than take a life.

(Would he be bad Dr?) No, I think he should try and continue to do something. Even if in pain. Might possibly be something that would come up that she would be saved.

(Isn't Dr. supposed to relieve pain, and do things patient wants?) Sort of hard situation. I don't know what he'd do.

(Dr. have right?) I don't know whether there's any law or not, or if that man's husband would want Dr. to kill her. I don't know what he should do.

(Why not put person away like an animal?) An animal's an entirely different thing than a human being; it's just--I don't know. An animal just isn't classified like a person, I can't explain it that way, but that's just the way it is.

(Better for husband to do it?) If she asked Dr. better because if she asked husband, then it might look like he was trying to murder her. But with Dr. everybody takes it for granted that he knows what he's doing, but if she dies then they wouldn't think he was trying to kill her.

(What punishment?) Even though they knew that he did do it intentionally, I don't think they should try to get him a sentence because if she was going to diefor sure anyway, I don't think-- sort of tough choice. Maybe the woman should have committed suicide herself and then not get Dr. and husband involved. Her own responsibility.

Type 3 (5)

Case 65: (Should the Dr. do it?) No, I don't think so because that's the same as suicide. I know it would put her out of her pain, but I don't think Dr. has any right to kill her because that would be essentially what it would do.

(Why doesn't he have the right?) It's the same as murder even though she wants it, it would still be murder.

(Would it be murder?) I think so, even if she asked because--if she took it herself it would be suicide which is also against one of God's laws, and I think it would be murder--yes.

(Worse for him to do it than to let her commit suicide?) Well, it's the question of suicide over murder. If you had to choose one, suicide would probably be it.

(Why suicide so bad?) You should let nature take its course. If the Lord wants to take you, he should take you and you shouldn't kill yourself.

(Why not put person away like an animal?) Animals are dumb, they're ignorant and the lowest things probably on earth. And killing an animal isn't the same as killing a human being. Because a human life is much more important than an animal.

(Why? Still a life.) (exasperated laugh.) Animals--I suppose have feelings like everybody else, but they're just beasts of burden. It wouldn't actually be against any laws to shoot a dog in pain, whereas a human being is much more important; it would be worse to kill a human being.

(Better for husband to do it?) I think probably the husband. If it is against the Dr.'s. oath I wouldn't ask him. I'd probably ask the husband.

(Who has more of a right?) I don't think you can talk about who more of right, but I think the husband who is closer to her, has more of a right.

(What punishment?) If I were the judge, I would give varying lengths. I certainly wouldn't give him the death penalty. From 10 to 20 years or something, whereas after he served his 10 to 20 years, if he had been good, put him on probation or something. I would suppose that not less than 10 years or more than 25.

(Wrong to give death sentence?) Yes, because if there are degrees of murder, as I think there are, this certainly wouldn't be the worse.

Situation V - Sample Responses for Each Type

Type 0

Case 9: (Should captain order a man, stay behind himself, or leave nobody behind?) I think he should order a man to stay behind. If he ordered someone else to stay in charge of the whole company, then-- the person might do wrong, and then go someplace else, and then he wouldn't be there to see what happens. And then if he didn't want anybody there, the enemy would get close on their trail. And then if he ordered somebody to stay there--he'd blow up the bridge; he'd probably get killed too, but they wouldn't care.

(Have right to order another?) Yes, I think he would. He's a general isn't he? Well, he's head of it and he can do whatever he wants.

Type 0

Case 77: (Should captain order a man, stay behind himself, or leave nobody behind?) Order one.

(Right to order somebody to go?) Yeah.

(Which would be best for the whole army?) Yeah, if nobody would volunteer.

(Better than him going himself?) I don't know. a) Him to go himself, I guess.

Type 1 (2)

Case 19: (Should captain order a man, stay behind himself, or leave nobody?) A-a-ah. I'm afraid I don't have one of those answers for this problem.

(Have to.) Well, you know he couldn't have gave them directions on how to go and he could have volunteered his life.

(Why better?) O, well, all the men probably had families, and some children; and the captain didn't--you know his parents probably died, and he probably didn't have a girl-friend and all that. And you know, he probably just alone in the world, so . . .

(Wouldn't the man he ordered be alone too?) Well, he could or he could not be alone.

(Which would be best for the whole army?) Right there, if they had grenades, he could probably tie some grenades together, put a cord on them and just throw the grenades on the bridge and that could blow up them.

(Have right to order someone else?) No sir, he would not have the right to order someone else. He does not have the authority to take someone else's life.

Type 1 (3)

Case 76: (Should captain order a man, stay behind himself, or leave nobody behind?) If nobody wants to volunteer, I don't think he should order anyone. I think he should stay behind himself if he wants to do that or nobody should stay behind.

(Have right to order man to go?) Nope. He's got the right to order him around but he hasn't the right to order them to take their own life.

(Which would be best for the whole army?) If they want to blow up the bridge, they should all stay there and cover up the one that was gonna blow up the bridge.

Type O (2)

Case 15: (Should captain order a man, stay behind himself, or leave nobody behind?) In order to try and save most of their lives--all of them would probably get killed, I'd say the captain should stay himself.

(Better if sent another?) Yeah, he could order another, but he'd just be a coward.

(Captain have right to order someone else?) Yes, because Rin-tin-tin; he's a lieutenant, and he couldn't go back himself because--he would have if he could have, but there were too many Indians and he couldn't travel fast enough, so he sent Rusty because he was littler and could go fast on horse, and less chance of his being seen.

(What best for company?) He should send another man back and they should wait under shelter wherever they were till after blew up. Because if he went himself the men would probably wander around and get under enemy line and get captured.

Type 2

Case 2: (Should captain order a man, stay behind himself, or leave nobody behind?) I think since nobody volunteered, and he's--if one person doesn't sacrifice his life, everybody will have to die. Since nobody would sacrifice, and if he should pick somebody, probably nobody would do it. So I think maybe he should sacrifice his own life and save the other men.

(Which would be best for the whole army?) Since nobody would want to go, I think he should go himself, and get the job done right. Probably are some in that whole company who could find the way out. There should be somebody in that whole company, usually is, I guess.

(Why worse to send someone than self?) It wouldn't matter if he would send somebody--he would do it against his will, and he maybe wouldn't do it at all and disobey completely.

Type 3

Case 29: (Should captain order a man, stay behind himself, or leave nobody behind?) I don't think he should stay behind because as it said in the story, he could lead the retreat the best and I don't think he should order a man to do it because it would be going against his will. And I don't think they should leave him alone. (laughs) So that leaves me pretty . . . well, if somebody had to do it, then I think he should do it himself. Because if no one wanted to do it, someone had to volunteer and if no one would volunteer, I guess he'd be the one in line for it.

(Why not order?) That would be going it against their will. No one should boss a person around on their life like that.

(Which would be best for the whole army?) That they wouldn't leave anything to blow it up and they'd retreat fast.

(Then all get killed.) Then it has to be a volunteer.

Type 4

Case 66: (Should captain order a man, stay behind himself, or leave nobody behind?) I don't think that he should have anybody stay behind. If nobody wanted to volunteer, I don't know what the rules are in the army, whether it's his right to make somebody stay behind or not, I'm not sure. I don't think that he--it's almost sure death probably. I don't think he should make a man stay behind if he doesn't want to.

(If army regs. give him a right?) Well, I think that--probably have to decide what he'd think he should do. If he thinks that's the best thing that he could save a lot of his own men, or get the war over faster by doing that, then he'd probably want to send someone back, if that would save so many other lives.

Type 5 (4)

Case 6?: (Should captain order a man, stay behind himself, or leave nobody behind?) You say that the captain could best lead them to safety from then on? Well, if there was danger from then on--heavy danger, I would send somebody . . . well, it's a question of which is more dangerous, the enemy from behind or the enemy ahead.

(Behind more dangerous.) Then if enemy behind more dangerous, if I was the captain I would go back myself. Of course, I'm saying that now, and thinking maybe on the field of battle I wouldn't, but if there was more danger from behind, he should go back and blow it up himself if there are no volunteers. Rather than appoint someone.

(Captain have right?) If there was danger ahead where only the captain could lead them through, I would say, even though it would mean his death, I would appoint somebody. But if the danger ahead isn't too important I would go back myself.

Situation VI - Sample Responses for Each Type

Type O (1)

Case 9: (Should the captain send the sick man or the trouble-maker?) Troublemaker. Because if he sent the sick man, when the sick man got half way there he might die without blowing it up. And then if he sends the troublemaker, he might not do his job or something, but he might.

(Which man would it be fairer to send?) Troublemaker. Because he's stronger. And the other one might die before he got there.

(Disease wouldn't kill him for months. Still be fair to send troublemaker?) Yeah, because he's a strong man; he could do the job. But the person who has the disease, he might not die right then, but he wouldn't be strong enough to go back.

(Be fair punishment to send troublemaker?) Yeah, I think so.

(Better to draw straws?) Draw straws would be okay. They could send another man, and keep the --- If the troublemaker did something else, they could keep the troublemaker locked up or something. Chained up--or they couldn't go on. They'd have a camp there and then when they come back from the journey, they'd let him go. But the sick man--they could order somebody else from the group.

Type O (1)

Case 77: (Should the captain send the sick man or the troublemaker?) I don't know.

(Which man would it be fairer to send?) Troublemaker, I guess.

(Why? Any special reason?) No.

(Better to draw straws?) Might be. I don't know.

(Have a right to refuse?) It don't matter by now. Because by that time, while they've been over there talking about it and by now and by the time they're over there talking about it, they're all over there. All the enemies are over there. They would have been dead by now. Thought you were going to get me on that one, didn't you?

Type 1

Case 76: (Should the captain send the sick man or the troublemaker?) Sick man. The sick man's going to die anyway. He might as well die now--die in action.

(His duty to volunteer?) Might be. Well, everybody else would probably live for about 40-50 years. If he's going to die, he might as well die in action, and get a medal--his wife get a medal or something for it. Medal of honor.

(Have a right to refuse?) He has right. Why should they just pick him. It would be fairer if they draw straws or pick a name out of a hat.

Type 1 (0)

Case 15: (Should the captain send the sick man or the troublemaker?) Troublemaker--let's see now. Would he have enough strength to get back too? He wouldn't have as much chance--sick man--if sick, he wouldn't have enough fighting strength. And the man, he wouldn't want to be saved himself, so he'd blow up the bridge.

(Troublemaker?) Yes. He'd want to get himself saved too so if he had enough courage he'd just blow up the bridge and they'd all be saved.

(4 to 1 chance.) I'd say troublemaker, because other man would have worse chance. Oh, you mean he'd probably get caught anyway, and he was going to die anyway? Well, I think the sick man--was going to die anyway.

(Would it be fair punishment?) Yes. After all, he stole from the men and everything and he still had a chance.

(Better to draw straws?) Yeah, probably would.

(Right for troublemaker to refuse?) I'd say it would be right-- after all, his life is at stake.

(Army reg. say he has to?) Yes, if he was a lower, like if he was a lieutenant and he was private. He couldn't have all of the authority to refuse.

Type 2

Case 25: (Should the captain send the sick man or the troublemaker?) Hard decision. I think he should send the sick man because the sick man would not be committing suicide. He'd be doing it for his country.

I don't think it would be counted as suicide. Taking his own
life; he'd be doing it to try and save others--save his country.
And try to escape at the same time so he could live a little
longer. But then again the troublemaker; he has strength and
courage.

(Which man would it be fairer to send?) Sick man, because he still
has enough strength, and he's been ordered by the captain to do his
duty for his country.

(Duty to volunteer?) No. Because really he isn't very good. If
anybody should volunteer it would be the troublemaker. Because
he isn't as sick as the other; he can do his job probably lots
better. I think he should volunteer.

(Better to draw straws?) I think so; much better. Because it's
only fair whoever gets the straw. It's much better than sending
the troublemaker and the sick man--either one.

(Better than going himself?) Yes. It would be fair.

(Be right to refuse?) Wrong, because the captain chose him for
that duty. He should obey the captain's orders.

(Have right to refuse?) I don't think so in the army. If you're
told to do something, you're supposed to do it.

Type 3 (2)

Case 29: (Should the captain send the sick man or the troublemaker?) In my
opinion, I think he should send the sick man. Because if he was
going to die he could be helping his country at the same time as--
he'd be dying a slow death anyway. Even without his being killed
by going back to blow up the bridge.

(Would it be fairer?) Yes, because he had a chance to live, and
the other had a bad wound and wasn't going to live--I think they
could sacrifice the guy who was not going to live.

(Better to draw straws?) It would be more fair to the sick man
because anybody would have a chance to stay behind by picking a
name and so I think it would be more fair to pick straws.

(Fairer than his going himself?) Yes, cause he didn't have any
choice.

(Have a right to refuse?) Wrong because--he was picked because they
thought he could do it and he was a troublemaker also, and he deserves something like that because he was making trouble for everyone else and so they chose him. So he didn't have any right to do
anything against it. I still think though it would be better to

save the able-bodied man. Because he's still as strong. And by that, he might learn a lesson for that other guy having to go. He might learn a lesson not to do bad things.

Type 4 (1)

Case 66: (Should the captain send the sick man or the troublemaker?) The sick man if he was going to die for sure. If that man knew that he was going to die, I don't think he'd mind going back there.

(Better to draw straws?) If they all agreed on it, I think it would be better than just picking one man.

(If they didn't agree--just ordered?) They'd have to do it, but I don't . . .

(Troublemaker right to refuse?) According to the rules of the army, I guess he'd be wrong but as a person in the world I think he may have a right to not want to go maybe. But of course, I don't know--usually in war, I don't know if they think about that now.

Type 5

Case 65: (Should the captain send the sick man or the troublemaker?) Oh, brother, gee. There's one question that you could not say. One man's going to die, and I don't think you should send a man, even though he's a bad egg, to meet his death. Sure he's been a bad guy, and hitting people, and stealing and stuff, but you shouldn't take advantage of a war situation like that and say, "Okay, you go out there and get killed." I don't think--I couldn't answer that.

(Then wouldn't it be better to send the sick man? Life over anyway?) But maybe it isn't; maybe some Dr. in the states could fix him up. That's a question I couldn't answer.

(Troublemaker right or wrong to refuse?) I can see his point of view, but I would say he was wrong. Because the captain should know better than anybody. And I could see his point of view, and maybe I'd do the same thing if I were him, but I think if the captain chose him, he should go. Unless he feels strongly that the captain's prejudiced--that the captain really wanted to get rid of him.

(If he felt that way, would he have the right to refuse?) Yes, the captain, just for personal reasons, I would certainly complain. But if he chose him because he thought he could do the best job I don't think he has any right to complain.

Situation VII - Sample Responses for Each Type

Type O

Case 9: (Who did worse, Al who broke into the store or John who borrowed the money?) I think Joe, that man that went up to the man and told him that he had a--couldn't pay for his operation. I think that man. Well, because he didn't have no intent to pay him back--the man that gave him the money but the man that stole from the store, he might pay it back.

(He didn't intend either.) I still think the man that walked up to the man and asked him for the money. Because when he walked up to him he lied and the other guy, he just went and stole it.

(Why shouldn't someone ever steal from a store?) Because they might get caught by the police and they'll be spending their time in jail and wish they'd never done it.

(What harm?) Well, the people at the store--they don't have enough money then, when they steal. And the people that stole the money, he sort of went, if you steal something, you always get sorry that you stole it and you want to take it back but you don't take it back.

(Why?) Well, you want to have it and still you know it's wrong to take it and you feel sorry that you took it but you just took it on account of you needed some money.

(What makes you feel sorry?) Well, if he might feel bad in one thing but he might go and do another thing. And if he took the thing, he might feel sorry that he took it because it isn't nice to steal and if he stole it then he thinks about it and thinks about it and never does anything about it.

(Which is worse, for the country, stealing or cheating?) Stealing from stores. Because he'd be stealing from a store, and the other man, he'd get paid back. Suppose the man that stole from the store, I mean the man that got cheated out of the money, the other man that cheated him, well he'd go to him and if he saw that he was related--relatives, he could ask them for the money.

(If everybody started stealing?) War probably. Well, because everybody's stealing from each other; probably when he'd try stopping him, he'd try stopping him and there'd be a fight.

(Who would feel worse, storeowner or lender?) The man with the store. Becuase the guy who was cheated out of it, he was the man that gave, he gave away money and they'd get the money back any other time but the storekeeper didn't have no idea that he was going to be robbed--that his store's going to be robbed.

(You mean guy who was cheated expected not to get back?) He was expecting that the person was going to give it back to him, but the storekeeper didn't even know that what happened--didn't even know that he was going to be robbed.

Type 0

Case 77: (Who did worse, Al who broke into the store or John who borrowed the money?) The one that broke in the store and stole the $500. Well, because the one that broke in the store, that was more worse than asking somebody for the $500. And he broke in the store instead of asking for it.

(Why shouldn't someone ever steal from a store?) If somebody stole from a store and everybody thought it was all right, then everybody else would start stealing from the store and they'd think they could get away with it.

(Then what?) There would be a lot of trouble and they wouldn't leave a good time or anything like that.

(Which would you feel worse about, cheating or stealing?) Stealing from a store. Because you know that the police would be looking for you if you stole it from a store. And then the guy that you borrowed it from; he wouldn't bother sending the police out looking for you because he'd think that the guy would bring it back sooner or later.

(Suppose the lender was a good friend. Is cheating him still not as bad as stealing? Worse. (Why?) Cause if he was a very good friend of John's then he wouldn't have very many friends when he got out. Cause if he got sent to prison, well then that guy was bound to tell somebody and then that would go all over. Wouldn't be able to get many friends.

(Which is worse for the country, stealing or cheating?) Cheating from a store.

(Who would feel worse, storeowner or lender?) Man who was cheated out of the loan. Because the store, they most likely got insurance on the store or something like that.

Type 1

Case 19: (Who did worse, Al who broke into the store or John who borrowed the money?) John who borrowed the $500 and said he would pay it back, and not pay it back. That's a toughie. That man had expected that $500 back because maybe he needed it. Some coming day.

Joe, he went right up to the man and lied to him, and just--you
know, as soon as the man--he put it in his pocket, and then the
two boys fled town, and the man didn't even know what happened.

(Why shouldn't someone ever steal from a store?) Well, thou
shalt not steal; one of the ten commandments.

(What harm?) The grocer might have to pay the bills and he might
have to use some of the $500. He might have to pay the food bill
that comes in.

(Who would feel worse, storeowner or lender?) I think the man who
was cheated out of a loan. Because the boy just took it right
under his nose.

(Be madder?) Yes sir.

Type 1

Case 76: (Who did worse, Al who broke into the store or John who borrowed
the money?) I think the other one did, that broke into the store.
Well, breaking a law--stealing. After all, the guy might need it
in his store, and this other guy that loaned the money out--he's
probably got millions anyway. He won't miss it.

(Why shouldn't someone ever steal from a store?) Like somebody
going out and stealing a car or something. (So?) Somebody else's
property--you're breaking the law.

(What harm?) Might get put in prison for it. On the other hand,
this guy he could say his buddy died anyway; the operation was a
failure.

(Which would you feel worse doing?) I think borrowing money from
a guy and not paying it back. It would be the better. Nine times
out of ten, the guy ain't going to go out looking for you, and he'd
only report it missing.

(Suppose the lender was a good friend. Is cheating him still not
as bad as stealing?) Yeah, I think so, because you never can
trust your best friend anyway.

(Which is worse for the country, stealing or cheating?) People
stealing from stores. After all, if everybody went around stealing
from stores, there wouldn't be any use of having stores. Everybody'd go around stealing.

(If everybody cheated?) I don't know; I don't think very many do
that because the guy wouldn't put it in the paper and they wouldn't
find out about it.

(Who would feel worse, storeowner or lender?) Storeowner was
robbed. After all, the guy that works in the store; he might not
have good business or something and he might need the money.

(How about the guy who loaned it?) Well, if someone's going to
loan money, they got a lot of money. He wouldn't miss it.

Type 2

Case 15: (Who did worse, Al who broke into the store or John who borrowed
the money?) I'd say Joe, because Joe went to this man who loaned
and loaned and wouldn't pay him back. I don't think that would
be very nice. And he had no intentions of paying it back; he
skipped town. Well, the other one just stole it. I think Joe's
brother, Alex, would have the worst of it.

(Why shouldn't someone steal from a store?) Stealing isn't very
good business because the money doesn't belong to you.

(What harm does it do?) The people that buy their money, they
work real hard for it; then if they steal, then they can't get
anything, if they work for it.

(Which is worse according to the law?) Stealing from the store.
Borrowing it without any intentions. He could pay it back; he
just didn't have any intentions. But that man, if he stole it,
he just run--he wouldn't. The guy that took the $500, he couldn't
be blamed for anything if he paid him back.

(Which is worse for the country, stealing or cheating?) I'd say
cheating people out of loans. Sometimes, you wouldn't have so
many murders; if they got cheated out of a loan, they could get
it paid back without even getting any charge on him. Just pay the
money back; it's not like stealing.

(Which is worse for the country?) People stealing from stores.

(Who would feel worse, storeowner or lender?) I'd say the man in
the store. Because, the man that loaned money, he's got more
money, and he can always get more money than that and the man that
has the store, he just has that money there, and $500 is a lot to
him.

(Then why is it worse to cheat?) I said that at the loan company
he could get more money back and at the store, that money is a
real lot to him.

(This is not a loan company.) Well, in that case, I think the man.
Just intentions, a kind hearted man would feel pretty bad, but that
man in the store, he can earn that money faster because he's got a
store. But that thing that I'm telling you--I want to know if that
man that gave him the $500, was in business or retired. Did he have
a lot of money?

Type 2

Case 25: (Who did worse, Al who broke into the store or John who borrowed the money?) I think John did worse, that borrowed the money. He lied to the man and said he was going to pay it back. There must be some thing for that, if you're going to pay for it, that you have to sign it. I think he did worse because he lied and also took the money. In Al's case, he just broke into the store and took the money and did not lie to anybody.

(Why shouldn't someone ever steal from a store?) Because the money doesn't rightfully belong to them; they didn't work for it.

(Which is worse for the country, stealing or cheating?) Cheating other people out of loans, because as I said before, you're telling a lie and then get the money also, but in breaking stores, you're just taking money. But then in the loan situation, it may be that man signed a paper where he would be or something . . . Well, I think the loan would be worse for the country.

(What would happen if everybody stole?) Everything would go to pieces, crime would be outnumbering the good people and they'd just be stealing and everything would go to pieces--just be a bad country.

(And if everybody cheated?) Same thing there--bad country, everybody'd be cheating everybody.

(Who would feel worse, storeowner or lender?) Storeowner, because he works so hard for that money, doing the business and then somebody breaks into the store and there it goes, so his work is done for nothing.

(Law couldn't jail you.) But they could do something to you; they could sue you--they must do something.

(So what effect on you?) I thought the store was then, because I thought that if you cheated somebody, you're sure to get put in jail too. And if you skip town, that would be even worse.

Type 2 (0)

Case 54: (Who did worse, Al who broke into the store or John who borrowed the money?) I think Joe did. He took the money and lied besides. Al only stole the money, he didn't make any promise to pay it back.

(Why shouldn't someone ever steal from a store?) If they all just stole like that for no reason, just to get out of town, everybody's life would be in danger. Just hit people over the head and take their money.

(Which is worse for the country?) Stealing because they could always get their loans back in some other way. Of course they might not be able to find Joe again and you can always catch someone in the act of stealing.

(Who would feel worse?) The storeowner. He would have it invested and he would know it wasn't coming back but the lender would always have hopes.

Type 4

Case 29: (Who did worse, Al who broke into the store or John who borrowed the money?) John, I think. Well, in that way he was deceiving a person and in sort of a way telling him he needed the money for an operation. I think it's worse to lie to a person to get the $500 than steal it outright. That's worse than stealing; you can hurt a person by taking it like that. People would feel bad if they were cheated and think they were played for a sucker, if you say it that way.

(Why shouldn't someone ever steal from a store?) It isn't right to steal, and this man could start an outbreak of different things like that and it could affect some younger person to thinking stealing is easier than working for money.

(Then what?) They'd think that's the easiest way and there'd be more robbers and there'd probably be more getting away with it.

(Why does the law make stealing worse?) In stealing it, you're taking it without the person knowing. In cheating you're telling them at least, you're giving them a chance to say yes or no.

(Which is worse for the country, stealing or cheating?) I think it's bad both ways, but the one that I think is worse is mostly cheating. Even good friends would cheat each other and it would become so universal and even maybe the president would start cheating in different ways.

(What if everybody stole?) There wouldn't be any order and everything would be just mixed up and everybody'd be stealing from everybody else and nobody'd be getting anywhere.

(Who would feel worse, storeowner or lender?) Man who was cheated, I think. (Why?) He'd feel let down; he wouldn't think that he could trust people anymore.

Type 4

Case 66: (Who did worse, Al who broke into the store or John who borrowed the money?) I think Joe did worse because he gave his word because he told he needed $, made pretty big line out of that. Alex just

took the money, didn't try to lie--just went in and took it, but
didn't give his word, just went in and took it.

(Why giving his word make it worse?) Everybody, when they give
their word that they're going to do something--that's the way life
is. When you're going to give your word, you should do what you
say and not just lie because other people have to put trust in you
and if you do lie, then you're not too well respected.

(Why shouldn't someone steal from store?) Not his money--has no
right to it. Just the way it's been for long time. Shouldn't
just take other people's money--not your property. Shouldn't break
into other people's places and take things that don't belong to
you and try to get something for nothing.

(Who worse according to law?) Breaking into store--probably be
punished most for that but when he said he was just going to borrow
the $ from that other man with no intention of paying back, I don't
think there's too much of a law to do with that.

(Why does law treat stealing more severely?) I think both pretty
bad. Seems funny they don't have law about borrowing. Think there
should be laws about both.

(Which worse for country to have going on?) Probably lot of people
lying because if there are a lot of them you can never tell--
they're not honest about anything. Might be honest people but
something might go wrong with their life and they just have to have
that $ or they're sunk. People who lie might go around for rest of
life like that, but somebody that robs, might just do that for one
time.

(Who feel worse?) Man who cheated. Because he trusted, and thought
he'd get money back and thought he'd been taken by that man, and
thought he could trust him.

(Who have more right to be mad?) The guy that loaned because he
had been cheated, but the guy who was robbed didn't know it was
going to happen because he couldn't have done much about it anyway.

Type 5 (4)

Case 65: (Who did worse, Al who broke into the store or John who borrowed
the money?) I think they're both pretty bad. It kind of depends
on if the old man was poor or if he wouldn't miss the money. I
think tho, if he's going to steal it--I think the one who lied to
the old man is doing worse because I think that it's better to just
break into the store and steal money than to deceive somebody. Because maybe that old man respected the boy--and then he skipped
town with his money. I think that was a worse thing to do.

(Why shouldn't someone ever steal from a store?) Stealing is wrong.
It's as simple as that. Well, I've just always accepted it as
being wrong. It says in the Bible too that you shouldn't steal.
What harm? Takes away money from somebody who worked for it hard.
Say this storekeeper worked hard for money--it's his. Nobody
should steal it from him.

(Which is worse according to the law?) I think according to law,
Alexander.

(Why law make that a worse crime?) Technically the law feels that a
person should have enough sense to look into the matter before
giving someone money as the storekeeper. The law would say that
the storekeeper should have looked into the matter and seen if he
really was sick--called his home. The boy was breaking the respect
and trust by lying to him but the law would say that he should have
looked into it. I imagine they'd have to. Actually that's more
of a personal matter--the law doesn't provide for every person
who's deceived by a boy--they have to provide for welfare of everybody like just plain stealing from store.

(Stealing do more harm to welfare of everybody?) Yes, as I say before Joe who deceived the old man; it was more of a personal matter.
The man should have checked into it more. Al robbed from store;
violating federal law. Why don't they make the other thing a law?
Cause human nature wouldn't allow that. People I suppose have tendencies to believe in somebody and you can't write that down in the
law books.

(Which worse--lots of people stealing or not paying back loans?)
Probably be stealing from stores worse. I don't think there are as
many people in the world who would be taken in by story like that.
The law can't protect every individual; they can't have people on
the spot like that all the time. They just have to protect the best
they can. They'd probably have to have psychiatrists standing on
every street corner, if they wanted to protect the old man in a
case like that.

(Who worse or meaner?) I'd say Joe, the one who deceived the old man.

(Who had more right to be mad?) Storekeeper because his money was
taken from him without him being able to resist at all; whereas the
old man--he should be mad at himself for being taken in for something without checking. I mean, just to hand somebody some money
because he said he's sick--that's dumb.

(Who would feel worse?) Old man, definitely.

Situation VIII - Sample Responses for Each Type

Type C

Case A: (Should tailor report Heintz? Why?) Yes, cause he could still--in

20 years he should have two men that he could trust to leave them in charge and then he could go back to jail for a few years, because if he doesn't serve his time he might have to go back for a longer term.

(Should Heintz be sent back to jail?) No, but . . . he doesn't have to be sent back, but if the man did, he should tell him because if he didn't tell, Heintz might go away and they might never have a chance to find him again.

(Why shouldn't he be sent back?) Because he started a factory and he might not be able to finish it, and it might be ruined. If a storm comes up--it might ruin it.

Type 0 (1)

Case 77: (Should tailor report Heintz? Why?) I don't know. I don't see why he should; he's doing good there and everything like that--keeping out of trouble--And then in a way he should.

(What way?) He was sentenced to prison for so many years and then he escaped. The tailor you say knew him as an escaped; well then he should report him.

(What would a good citizen do? Would it be his duty to report him?) Yeah.

(Should Heintz be sent back to jail?) No.

(Would it be better for the country if he were sent back?) I don't see why; he hasn't been doing anything. He's been raising enough money and running a factory and things like that--building a hospital, and keeping himself out of trouble and stuff like that.

(If the tailor is a good friend should he tell?) He should tell the police I guess.

Type 1

Case 19: (Should tailor report Heintz? Why?) I think not I don't think he should, but . . . I don't think he should.

(Why do you think he shouldn't?) He was doing a lot for certain cancer and the money that he had saved, he was putting up for cancer.

(What would a good citizen do?) I'm afraid I don't have an answer.

(Should Heintz be sent back to jail?) No. No, sir. Extremely not. If he went back to jail, he might get life in prison and they won't be able to finish the factory.

(If the tailor is a good friend should he tell if he is asked?)
Remember when you told me about Joe and Alex. Remember I said
if--maybe Joe would get a good thing for Alexander and he won't
tell? Well, it's the same way right here. Maybe Heintz did a
very good thing for the tailor and the tailor wanted to pay him
back.

Type 1

Case 76: (Should tailor report Heintz? Why?) No, I don't think so. After
all, he got out and he went straight. And he's doing a good cause.

(What would a good citizen do?) Yes, I think he would. Well, a
good citizen would probably think that if he got outside he might
do it again; he did it once and he did it again.

(Is it his duty to?) Yeah.

(Would it be better for the country if he were sent back?) No, I
think it would be better for the country if he weren't because
he's trying to invent some medicine or something for a hospital
and they might not have it if they put him back in jail.

(If the tailor is a go   friend should he tell if he is asked by
the police?) I should think he'd say he didn't know nothing
about it. Well, he wouldn't want to tell on his best friend.

Type 1 (2)

Case 15: (Should tailor report Heintz? Why?) Well, if he was a good friend,
I don't thin' so because he was doing good now.

(If he wasn' good friend?) Well, if he wasn't a good friend at
all, I think he should. If he was a good friend he should because
if he's a good friend, he'd be against him if he sentenced him and
he's revenge after he got out again. But if he wasn't his friend,
and he didn't know him at all, he should.

(Would good citizen have to report?) Yes, I think so.

(Good friend have to keep quiet?) He wouldn't have to, but if I
was friend of his I would.

(Why good citizen have to report him?) He wouldn't be loyal to
his country if he didn't tell--Well, after 20 years I don't think
they should sentence him again because he was going on the right
path--track.

Type 2

Case 25: (Should tailor report Heintz? Why?) Now the druggist pleaded for
him to be let out--to drop the case, and evidently the judge didn't
do it. So I think that the tailor should tell the judge about it--
to where he was, and I think his case should be brought up in
court again. And all the good things that he has done for his
country would be enough that he wouldn't be sentenced back to jail
gain. I mean, building the hospital for the people who are sick,
and giving his employees the highest wages he couud afford, I think
that he shouldn't be sentenced back to jail again. I think the
judge would take a look at that and how he helped. But I think in
all fairness the tailor should tell the judge about it, because
after all if he was still escaping and they would probably still
be looking for him, and if he would bring him back and see what he
has done, I think they would let him go. I mean, to fairness to
him, and everybody.

(Probably be sent back.) Well, if this tailor knows that the judge
was awful strict, and he sees what Heintz has done for the community and the state of the country, I don't think the tailor would
tell the judge. And I also don't think that the workers under
Heintz would want it either, because he's given them the best pay
and . . . this hospital.

(What would a good citizen do? Report?) I don't think so.

(Does he have right not to tell?) Yes. Because he sees that what
he has done, and maybe some day he might be in that same hospital,
where if he might send Heintz to jail--tell the judge--maybe the
hospital will be torn down or something.

(If he is asked directly if he is a friend of Heintz?) Since the
judge isn't very nice, and he knows that Heintz has built this
factory and hospital I don't think he should tell.

Type 3 (0)

Case 54: (Should the tailor report Heintz? Why?) Yes, I think he should.
He shouldn't have tried to escape from jail in the first place;
I think he should be sent back to jail or have a parole.

(Should he tell if he is a good friend?) I think he should.

(Would it be better for the country to send him back?) No, but it
would be better for him. He should have waited until he got out
to start his factory. Now he's got to go back and do it the right
way.

Type 3

Case 29: (Should tailor report Heintz? Why?) Yes, I think so. It's his duty as a citizen.

(Might a good citizen decide not to tell?) Yes, it might be that way, because he's doing much good in the way he was using his money after he escaped.

(Should it be a citizen's duty always?) Not always. If the man has become a good man and doesn't steal or anything like that, and there's the clean living and that, I--well, they should tell, and they should also recommend to the jury that would be trying him, that he has been leading a good life.

(If the tailor is a good friend, should he tell?) Yes, it's still his duty, even if he was a good friend of this man.

(Should Heintz be sent back to jail?) I don't think so--after he's been doing all these good deeds, but probably he would have to. Because court had sentenced him to those ten years, and he had escaped so he probably would have to finish his term.

(If you were judge would you send him back to jail?) Well, yes, but not for a long sentence.

(Would it be better for the country if he were sent back?) It might and it might not. He might get the urge to steal again--he had once, but then again he might keep doing good things and he might help the country a lot.

Type 4

Case 66: (Should tailor report Heintz? Why?) I think it might possibly be his duty to tell them, since--in the first place, I don't think he should have been sentenced, but I think maybe it was that other man's responsibility to turn him into the police. But he might have been a good friend of Heintz and he might have seen that he was doing good work there and doing a lot of good so he might just not have reported.

(Wrong if didn't?) No, wouldn't think it would be wrong.

(What would a good citizen do?) I think it's up to the individual person whether he does or not.

(Should Heintz be sent back to jail?) I don't think he should for what he did. I don't think they should have put him in jail at all.

478

Type II

Case 65: (Should tailor report Heintz? Why?) He should because it would
be against the law to harbor an ex-convict. However, I think that
he could possibly with a good lawyer and understanding people involved, and the fact that he had built up good reputation for himself where he was living now, I think those things considered, I
think maybe he could get free of the charge. But if I were the
tailor, I would tell on him, tell the police because the law says
so--yes.

(Shouldn't be sent back to jail?) I think the tailor should report
him but if I were the judge I wouldn't send him back to jail, because of the fact that he had made amends for what he did, and he
had good reputation in the town. I wouldn't send him back.

(Judge not too merciful.) Oh brother. You mean the tailor knowing
that he wouldn't get a good break, should he report him? Oh man,
well, if it were a democratic country and the people loved it and
the rules were lawfully made by the majority, I would say yes.
But you didn't denote which European country it was. If it were
dictatorial country, I would say no, because in a dictorial country
the laws aren't made by the people.

(If democracy, but stiff punishment still.) Well, I would say if
it's a democracy, he should report him.

(Any value to it besides just being lawful--guy be sent back to
jail.) I would say yes--well, I don't know if there'd actually
be any sense to it, but if the law provides for it, I would say
yes. However, I can see the other point of view and wouldn't hold
it against the man if he wouldn't turn him in.

(If the tailor is a good friend should he still tell?) Oh, brother,
I would say yes. Well, if I would say it would change the situation, I'd be contradicting myself, but I wouldn't know how to
answer that. All I could say is either way in a case like that.

(Not right or wrong?) No, not a right or wrong. Course if the
authorities found out, they'd probably deem it wrong not to report
him.

Situation IX - Sample Responses for Each Type

Type 1 (0)

Case 9: (Was it right or wrong to leave station?) He was right. Because
other times he saved somebody else's lives, but this time if he went
and saved someone else's life, even his family might die. And he
might want to save them first.

486

(What would the other men think if Diesing left his station?)
They wouldn't like it. He's the chief, and they need his help,
and they wouldn't know what to do. Say a house was on fire, but
they couldn't get em out unless they chopped half the building
that wasn't on fire.

(Suppose it was actually forbidden by law?) He should stay. Cause
if he wanted to go to his family, he might as well just stay with
his family and not have the job, because if he was going to go to
his family every time the bombs fell . . . they wouldn't need him,
because he wasn't doing anything on the post.

(What punishment?) Yes. Cause he shouldn't have left his post.
He should have remembered that there was somebody else near his
house--another post, and that he should look after the people that
he was supposed to, and when he was done with that, then go home.
Cause his family might get out of their home and get to a shelter
place.

Type 0

Case 77: (Was it right or wrong to leave the station?) Wrong. Cause he
should have gave the warning before he left.

(Gave warning.) Wrong, cause he should have--if he was on that
one particular spot, he could have saw that his folks were, or his
family was all right or not.

(They on other end of town.) Well, I don't know.

(What would you do?) If I had a responsibility like that, I would
have went to the fire station first. He could have had some contact to see whether his folks were all right or not--whether his
family was all right or not.

Type 1

Case 19: (Was it right or wrong to leave station?) Yes, he would be wrong--
it would be right to leave his post then to protect his family.

(Why?) Well, maybe his family--maybe the radar from the bombs hit
near his family's house and anyone has warned them about it.

(What would happen if he did leave his station?) Well, maybe they
wouldn't have anybody to put out the fire or maybe the fire would
spread because of his leaving the station.

(What would the other men think if Diesing left his station?) The
other men would probably think, "Well, if he's leaving, why can't
I," so they would probably leave and no one might be saved. Except
their families.

(Suppose it was actually forbidden by law?) Yes sir. (Still right?) Well, he loves his family in one place, and he doesn't want to see them get hurt.

(What punishment?) No sir. Well, he wanted to protect his family--in one place.

(Was it right or wrong to leave station?) I think it was right for him to leave his station to protect his family. Wouldn't you?

(Yeah, I might do it, but why would that make it right?) After all, he is only a volunteer.

(But could save more lives at station.) Well, there's other men there; they don't need him--all he does is boss them around.

(What would the other men think if Diesing left his station?) I don't think they'd like very much of him any more.

(Wouldn't they take off?) Yeah, I think they should station every man near to his home.

(Suppose it was actually forbidden by law?) No, he'd be breaking the law.

(What punishment?) Yeah.

(What good?) Well, if there was a law about it, he shouldn't leave.

Type 2 (3)

Case 15: (Was it right or wrong to leave station?) I think most men would do that but it's wrong. Because after all, more people's life ais at stake. His wife and child might be saved but all those other people were down there that they might need.

(Can something be wrong if everybody would do it?) I don't say everybody--most people, but if he was a fire chief, I think he should keep to duty.

(What would the other men think if Diesing left his station?) I don't think they would respect him very much. A fire station in area where he lived. The wife wouldn't worry because she knew he had to stay where he was supposed to be.

(More important to be good citizen or good family man?) What mean?

(Good family man go home, good citizen stay.) Good citizen. Just worrying about your family and nobody else wouldn't be very good.

(If D. volunteer--no pay?) He would be better off if he was just a volunteer.

(Why make a difference if paid?) Should stay if paid, cause he's getting paid; wouldn't get paid if he left when fire in his area.

(What punishment?) Just a volunteer you mean? Well, it just a little law or you <u>had</u> to do it? Like jaywalking, you just don't have to . . .

Type 2

Case 25: (Was it right or wrong to leave station?) Doesn't say whether his house was by the fire, does it?

(All throughout the city.) Then I don't think he could do much to save the city, because the whole city's about destroyed. I think his duty is to go back home now to save his family.

(If law?) No; if there was a law, he should go to his station then.

Type 3

Case 29: (Was it right or wrong to leave station?) Wrong because they were all assigned posts and they had to stay at their posts at all times and there would have been a station for that house also, so they would have escaped anyway because there was a station probably near there.

(What would the other men think if Diesing left his station?) They'd probably think it wasn't fair, because then they could probably go to their houses too and save their own family also.

(Suppose everyone else had left?) No, because everybody else left their houses so he probably could leave for his too. Everybody else was going to their own houses, and he couldn't do nothing by himself, and there would be nobody there to help him at that fire position. So he could have went and gotten his own too.

(What punishment?) Yes, because he shouldn't leave his post. Because it wouldn't be fair to the rest of the men because they could have took off and gone to their homes too but they stayed at their posts to help fight the fires around them.

Type 3

Case 66: (Was it right or wrong to leave station?) Wrong because he was given the responsibility to be in charge of the fire station and if left to go to own family, a lot of other houses might have burned down.

(If just thinking of being good husband or good father?) Go home.

(Volunteer--no pay, no law, still wrong to go to family first?)
Still probably would be, because he it was still his responsibility.
If he left, a lot of people might die.

(What punishment?) Probably should if he was the only one that
left his post--well, was there a law for that?

(Yeah) I think he probably should be punished if there was a law
and he was the only one who deserted.

Type 5

Case 65: (Was it right or wrong to leave station?) He's putting the safety
of the few over the safety of many. He might save only 3 or 4
of own family. I think definitely you should put the safety of
many over the safety of a few.

(Why if the few happens to be your family?) Well, I don't think
it matters who it is--even if it's your father, even if it's
family, because people in these burning buildings are somebody's
loved ones too. And tho maybe he'd be miserable the rest of his
life, I still think you should put the safety of the many over the
safety of the few.

(If just thinking about being good family man?) I think he'd still
go to his fire station because I think his wife would respect him
more for trying to save many people than saving themselves. Just
think how terrible he'd feel if he went home and found his family
was perfectly all right. And without him, maybe 10 people died
in the burning building. He would feel worse and his family would
respect him less for it.

(What would the other men think if he left?) I suppose that they
wouldn't actually hold it against him but I don't think that they
would respect him highly for it. Because here the other people in
the fire station probably had families too, and they stayed on.

(Make any difference if volunteer or getting paid, or against the
law?) I think that no matter what he was, volunteer or what, even
just a passer-by, I would think that if he was able to help more
people than he could at home, then he should stay on and help them.

(If others left, so he thought his own home not protected?) I
would say in most cases even if he was a passer-by, he should help
the many rather than the few. However, if he saw anybody going
to their own home, and there's nobody at the fire station, and he
saw the people around his area, and the families were coming from
other parts . . . I mean, I think it should be all one or the other.
I think they should all worry about themselves or they should all
worry about their stations. But I'd take the safety of the many
over the safety of the few no matter what.

EXAMPLES FROM INTERVIEWS IN LITTLE ROCK

All materials quoted from Sitton, C., "Troubled Actors in the Little Rock Drama," New York Times Magazine, October 5, 1958.

Type 0 - A Militant Segregationist Housewife

Why is she opposed to school desegregation? "I think it's Biblically wrong. I don't think God intended for the races to mix. I think it would lead to race mixing and I love my children too much. In ten or fifteen years it would lead to that. You can't bring them [Negroes] into the schools and then tell your children thatit's wrong to intermarry. Intermarriage? I just know it's wrong. The cat and the dog don't mate."
The "Communists" are at the bottom of it all. "I couldn't fight so hard if it was just nine little niggers who wanted an education."

Other-Directed Type 2

A senior girl at Central High, who had planned to go to college next year.

"I am not an integrationist but I want to go back to school. Integration will have to come because they can't close the school. I love Central and I want to graduate from Central."

She made no effort to make friends with the nine Negroes who attended Central. At first she felt this might have been because it would have been unpopular with her friends. But then she says: "If nobody cared I still wouldn't be friendly. I wouldn't be rude to them. I just don't care to be friends. Her only explanation for her attitude is her Southern upbringing. She has seen Negroes and whites dancing together on television which surprises her. "I wouldn't. I just couldn't do that. I think it will be years and years before they go to dances and belong to the same clubs with us."

Type 3 - A Police Officer

There is nothing of the cynic about him, although his job, law enforcement, might cause him to lean in that direction. He has a sense of fair

403

play, and therein lies his difficulty. It is hard for him to justify his attitude toward desegregation: "I actually feel that the Negro is inferior and I hate to say it."

He was "pretty liberal" before he went into the Army. His training company was about 40 per cent Negro. His company commander was a Negro, of whom he says: "He was fine; he was all right." But the others, to him, were a sorry lot; their characteristics typified all he dislikes in the Negroes here--laziness, dirtiness, lack of initiative, immorality. "These people are like animals--a lot of them are." No longer a liberal, he calls himself a moderate segregationist.

Thus school desegregation would bring social desegregation and the opportunity for intermarriage. "Is there any logical stopping place?" he asks. He also denies that desegregation would materially aid the Negro but contends that it would depress the standards of the white schools.

Type 4 - A Lawyer

Clinton Rodman is typical of those who have sought a middle ground in the controversy--the moderates. He and his kind do not necessarily favor desegregation. But they do look upon the Supreme Court's decision as the law, distasteful perhaps, but the law just the same.

"When you are in such a small minority, you sometimes stop to wonder if you're right," he says. He confesses that at one point he did come to believe that the Supreme Court was wrong.

The young attorney favors integration "in principle" but thinks that decades will pass before it is an accomplished fact in the South.

"As an abstract proposition, when you deny a minority the rights and privileges that are granted by the state to others, that is discrimination per se."

Integration will come eventually, for economic reasons if for no others. "It's prohibitive, to have two of everything."

He does see some concrete grounds for the bitter animosity of some segregationists. Of the Negro in Little Rock, he says immorality, unclean personal habits, the squalor of many homes and poor health standards make him objectionable to whites. "These tend to negate the incentive to help him."

Type 5 - A Negro Doctor

(It is obviously easier for a Southern Negro than for a Southern white to sound Type 5 on this issue.)

"The grandchildren of Orval Faubus and Amis Guthridge and others will thank God for the N. A. A. C. P., which chose to wage the battle in the courts and not in the streets," he says.

Of the criticisms leveled at his race here because of its living standards, he says: "Christian men and women should not magnify the shortcomings of others, especially when they are in part responsible for their condition. Full expression of talents and potential should not be denied anyone in that way."

The doctor has a ready answer for the many whites and those few Negroes who say that the N. A. A. C. P.'s push for desegregated schools has hurt the good relations that existed between the two races. There was peace before, he concedes, but not good relations. "By good relations you mean that the Negro can travel freely in all aspects of community life." Besides, justice for all can't come too fast.

As our children attend school with white children, they will be able to talk over their common problems and they will be able to understand each other better." This is his hope. But the legal barriers must be lowered first so that the whites who want to promote better understanding can do so.

Q-SORT INSTRUMENTS

Items for Social Respect Q-sort - (Rated under the instruction, "How much do people all over the country respect these persons?")[1]

Directly interacts with public

	Physical Functions	Social Authority	Symbolic Functions
High Status	1. doctor	2. judge	3. psychiatrist
Medium Status	4. nurse	5. juryman	6. teacher
Low status	7. lifeguard	8. policeman	9. librarian

No direct interaction with public

High Status	10. head of large food company	11. senator	12. law professor
Medium Status	13. airline pilot	14. army captain	15. artist or painter
Low Status	16. farmer	17. army private	18. printer

19. job of boy's father

---

[1] The rating is made into the following forced distribution of item cards:

score for pile:	0	1	2	3	4
No. of cards in pile:	2	4	7	4	2

486

Items for Ideal Self Q-Sort (Rated under the instruction, "How much do you want to be this kind of person?")[1]

Personal Roles

	Relational Conformity	External Achievement
Peer Roles	1. a good leader with his friends	3. a good ball player
	2. a good friend	4. a good sport
Family Roles	5. a good father	7. someone who takes after his father
	6. a good son	8. someone who does things which make his family proud of him

Occupational Roles

Higher Status	9. judge	11. head of large food company
	10. doctor	12. someone who works to get ahead in life
Medium Status	13. teacher	15. airline pilot
	14. army private	16. printer
	17. job of boy's father	

---

[1]The rating is made on the following forced distribution of item cards:

score for pile:	0	1	2	3	4
No. of cards in pile:	2	4	5	4	2

REFERENCES

1. Abel, Theodora. "Moral Judgment in Subnormal Children," J. Abnorm. Soc. Psychol. (1941), 36.

2. Adorno, T. W., Frenkel-Brunswick, Else, Levinson, D. J., and Sanford, R. N. The Authoritarian Personality. New York: Harper, 1950.

3. Aristotle. Ethics. New York: Random House, 1952.

4. Baldwin, J. M. Social and Ethical Interpretations in Mental Development. New York: Macmillan, 1906.

5. _____. Thoughts and Things or Genetic Logic. 3 vols. New York: Macmillan, 1906-1911.

6. _____. Genetic Theory of Reality. New York: Putnam's, 1915.

7. Bell, G. B., and Hall, H. E. "The Relationship Between Leadership and Empathy," J. Abnorm. Soc. Psychol. (1954), 49, 156-157.

8. Bergson, H. The Two Sources of Morality and Religion. Garden City, New York: Doubleday Anchor, 1954.

9. Blumer, H. Movies and Conduct. New York: Macmillan, 1933.

10. Bonney, M. E., and Powell, J. "Differences in Social Behavior between Sociometrically High and Sociometrically Low Children," J. Educ. Res. (1953), 46, 481-495.

11. Caruso, I. H. "La Notion de Responsibilité et de Justice Immanente Chez L'Enfant," Arch de Psychologie (1943), 29, entire No. 114. English translation on file at U. of Chicago Psychology Department Library.

12. Cohen, A. Delinquent Boys. Glencoe, Ill.: Free Press, 1955.

13. Cronbach, L. J., and Gleser, Goldine, "Assessing Similarity between Profiles," Psychol. Bull. (1953), 50, 456-473.

14. Duncan-Jones, A. Butler's Moral Philosophy. Baltimore: Penguin Books, 1952.

14a. Durkheim, E. The Division of Labor in Society. Glencoe, Ill.: Free Press, 1947.

486

15. Dymond, Rosalind, Hughes, Anne, and Raabe, Virginia. "Measurable Changes in Empathy with Age," J. Consult. Psychol. (1952), 16, 202-206.

16. Foote, N. N., and Cottrell, L. S. Identity and Interpersonal Competence. Chicago: Univ. of Chicago Press, 1955.

17. Gessell, A., Ilg, Frances, and Ames, Louise. Youth, the Years from Ten to Sixteen. New York: Harper, 1956.

18. Guttman, L. in Lazarsfeld, P. (Ed.). "Mathematical Thinking in the Social Sciences. Glencoe, Ill.: Free Press, 1954.

19. Hare, C. "The Moral Judgment." Paper read at University of Chicago, Fall, 1957.

20. Harris, D., Clark, K., and Valasek, F. "The Measurement of Responsibility in Children," Child Develop. (1954), 25, 21-28.

21. Hartley, E., Rosenbaum, M., and Schwartz, S. "Children's Perceptions of Ethnic Group Membership," J. Psychol. (1948), 26, 399-405.

22. Hartshorne, H. and May, M. Studies in Character. New York: Macmillan, 1929. 3 vols.

23. Havighurst, R., and Taba, Hilda. Adolescent Character and Personality. New York: John Wiley, 1949.

24. Hughes, E. C. "Dilemmas and Contradictions of Status," Amer. J. Sociol. (1945), 50, 353-359.

25. Hugo, V. Les Miserables. New York: Standard Book, 1931.

26. Hume, D. An Enquiry Concerning the Principles of Morals. LaSalle, Ill.: Open Court, 1946.

27. Inhelder, Barbel and Piaget, J. The Growth of Logical Thinking from Childhood to Adolescence. New York: Basic Books, 1958.

28. Kierkegaard, S. Either/Or, vol. 2. Princeton: Princeton U. Press, 1949.

29. Lerner, E. Constraint Areas and the Moral Judgment of Children. Menosha, Wis.: Banta, 1937.

30. _____. "Perspectives in Moral Reasoning," Amer. J. Sociol. (1937), 43, 249-69.

31. Lippit, Rosemary. "Popularity Among Preschool Children," Child Developn. (1941), 12, 305-332.

32. MacRae, D., Jr. "The Development of Moral Judgment in Children." Unpublished Ph. d. dissertation, Harvard U., 1950.

33. _____. "A Test of Piaget's Theories of Moral Development," J. Abnorm. Soc. Psychol. (1954), 49, 14-18.

34. Mandelbaum, M. The Phenomenonology of Moral Experience. Glencoe, Ill.: The Free Press, 1945.

35. Mann, G. W. and Mann, H. P., "Age and Intelligence of a Group of Juvenile Delinquents," J. Abnorm. Soc. Psychol. (1939), 24, 351-360.

36. Mead, G. H. Mind, Self and Society. Chicago: U. of Chicago Press, 1934.

37. _____. "The Psychology of Punitive Justice," Amer. J. Sociol. (1918), 23, 577-602.

37a. _____. "Natural Rights and the Theory of the Political Institution," J. Philos. (1915), 12, 141-55.

37b. _____. "The Philosophical Basis of Ethics," Int. J. Ethics (1908), 18, 311-23.

38. Mill, J. S. Utilitarianism. New York: Liberal Arts Press, 1949.

39. Newcomb, T. M. Social Psychology. New York: Dryden, 1950.

40. Nietzsche, F. The Geneology of Morals. New York: Random House, Modern Library, no date.

41. Parsons, T., and Shils, E. (Ed.). Toward a General Theory of Action. Cambridge, Harvard U. Press, 1951.

42. Peck, R. F. "The Psychology of Moral Character." Unpublished doctoral dissertation. Univ. of Chicago, 1951.

43. Perry, R. B. Realms of Value. Cambridge: Harvard U. Press, 1954.

44. Piaget, J. The Moral Judgment of the Child. Glencoe, Ill.: Free Press, 1948.

45. _____. Language and Thought of the Child. New York: Harcourt Brace, 1932.

46. _____. The Psychology of Intelligence. London: Routledge & Kegan Paul, 1950.

47. Remmers, H. H., and Radler, D. H. The American Teenager. Indianapolis-New York: Bobbs-Merrill, 1957.

48. Riesman, D., Denney, R., and Glaser, N. The Lonely Crowd. New York: Doubleday Anchor, 1953.

49. Schatzman, L. and Strauss, A. "Social Class and Modes of Communication," Amer. J. Sociol. (1955), 60, 329-338.

50. Sears, R., Maccoby, E. and Levin, H. Patterns of Child-Rearing. Evanston, Ill.: Row-Peterson, 1958.

51. Sharp, F. C. Good Will and Ill Will. Chicago: U. lf Chicago Press, 1950.

52. Sidgewick, Henry. Methods of Ethics. London: Macmillan, 1901.

53. Siegel, S. "Level of Aspiration and Decision Making," Psychol. Rev. (1957), 64, 253-61.

54. Smith, A. The Theory of Moral Sentiments, in Schneider, H. (Ed.) Adam Smith's Moral and Political Philosophy. New York: Hafner, 1948.

55. Spencer, H. Data of Ethics. New York: Appleton, 1879.

56. Stendler, Celia B. Children of Brasstown. Urbana, Ill.: U. of Illinois, Bureau of Research and Service, College of Education, 1949.

57. _____. "A Study of Some Socio-moral Judgments of Junior High School Students," Child Developm. (1949), 20, 15-28.

58. Stephen, L. The Science of Ethics. London: Smith, Elder, 1882.

59. Stephenson, W. The Study of Behavior. Chicago: U. of Chicago Press, 1953.

60. Sullivan, H. S. Clinical Studies in Psychiatry. New York: Norton, 1956.

61. Thomas and Znaniecki. The Polish Peasant in Europe and America. New York: Knopf, 1927.

62. Thomson, G. H. The Factorial Analysis of Human Ability. Boston: Houghton Mifflin, 1951 (5th ed.)

63. Thurstone, L. Multiple Factor Analysis. Chicago: U. of Chicago Press, 1947.

64. Turner, E. in Kuhlen, R. G., and Thompson, G. G. (Ed.) Psychological Studies in Human Development. New York: Appleton-Century Crofts, 1952.

65. Weber, M. The Methodology of the Social Sciences. Glencoe, Ill.: Free Press, 1949.

66. _____. The Protestant Ethic and the Spirit of Capitalism. New York: Scribner's, 1930.

67. Whiting, J. W. and Child, I. Child Training and Personality. New Haven: Yale U. Press, 1953.

68. Wundt, W. Ethics. Vol. I, The Facts of the Moral Life. New York: Macmillan, 1897.

ACKNOWLEDGMENTS

Kohlberg, Lawrence. "The Development of Modes of Moral Thinking and Choice in the Years 10 to 16." (Chicago, IL: University
of Chicago, 1958): i–viii, 1–491. Reprinted with the permission of the Estate of Lawrence Kohlberg. Courtesy of the
University of Chicago Library.